Undergraduate Topics in Computer Science

Undergraduate Topics in Computer Science (UTiCS) delivers high-quality instructional content for undergraduates studying in all areas of computing and information science. From core foundational and theoretical material to final-year topics and applications, UTiCS books take fresh, concise, and modern approach and are ideal for self-study or for a one- or two-semester course. The texts are all authored by established experts in their fields, reviewed by an international advisory board, and contain numerous examples and problems. Many include fully worked solutions.

For further volumes:
http://www.springer.com/series/7592

Maurizio Gabbrielli and Simone Martini

Programming Languages: Principles and Paradigms

 Springer

Prof. Dr. Maurizio Gabbrielli
Università di Bologna
Bologna
Italy

Prof. Dr. Simone Martini
Università di Bologna
Bologna
Italy

ISSN 1863-7310
ISBN 978-1-84882-913-8   e-ISBN 978-1-84882-914-5
DOI 10.1007/978-1-84882-914-5
Springer London Dordrecht Heidelberg New York

British Library Cataloguing in Publication Data
A catalogue record for this book is available from the British Library

Library of Congress Control Number: 2010922995

Translated from the original Italian edition: "Linguaggi di programmazione: principi e paradigmi", published in 2006 by McGraw-Hill Companies, Publishing Group Italia.

Printed on acid-free paper

Springer is part of Springer Science+Business Media (www.springer.com)

To Francesca and Antonella,
who will never want to read this book
but who contributed to it being written.

To Costanza, Maria and Teresa, who will read it perhaps,
but who have done everything to stop it being written.

Foreword

With great pleasure, I accepted the invitation extended to me to write these few lines of Foreword. I accepted for at least two reasons. The first is that the request came to me from two colleagues for whom I have always had the greatest regard, starting from the time when I first knew and appreciated them as students and as young researchers.

The second reason is that the text by Gabbrielli and Martini is very near to the book that I would have liked to have written but, for various reasons, never have. In particular, the approach adopted in this book is the one which I myself have followed when organising the various courses on programming languages I have taught for almost thirty years at different levels under various titles.

The approach, summarised in 2 words, is that of introducing the general concepts (either using linguistic mechanisms or the implementation structures corresponding to them) in a manner that is independent of any specific language; once this is done, "real languages" are introduced. This is the only approach that allows one to reveal similarities between apparently quite different languages (and also between paradigms). At the same time, it makes the task of learning different languages easier. In my experience as a lecturer, ex-students recall the principles learned in the course even after many years; they still appreciate the approach which allowed them to adapt to technological developments without too much difficulty.

The book by Gabbrielli and Martini has, as central reference point, an undergraduate course in Computer Science. For this reason, it does not have complex prerequisites and tackles the subject by finding a perfect balance between rigour and simplicity. Particularly appreciated and successful is the force with which they illuminate the connections with other important "areas of theory" (such as formal languages, computability, semantics) which the book rightly includes (a further justification for their inclusion being that these topics are no longer taught in many degree courses).

Giorgio Levi, Pisa.

Introduction

Facilius per partes in cognitionem totius adducimur
(Seneca, *Epist.* 89,1)

Learning a programming language, for most students in computing, is akin to a rite of passage. It is an important transition, soon recognised as insufficient. Among the tools of the trade, there are many languages, so an important skill for the good computer professional is to know how to move from one language to another (and how to learn new ones) with naturalness and speed.

This competence is not obtained by learning many different languages from scratch. Programming languages, like natural languages, have their similarities, analogies and they inherit characteristics from each other. If it is impossible to learn tens of languages well, it is possible completely to understand the mechanisms that inspire and guide the design and implementation of hundreds of different languages. This knowledge of the "parts" facilitates the understanding of the "whole" of a new language and therefore underpins a fundamental methodological competence in the life of the computing professional, at least as far as it allows them to anticipate innovations and to outlive technologies that grow obsolete.

It is for these reasons that a course on the general aspects of programming languages is, throughout the world, a key step at advanced level for a computing professional (at university or in a profession). The fundamental competences which a computing professional must possess about programming languages are of at least four types:

- Some aspects that are properly considered linguistic.
- Knowledge of how language constructs can be implemented and the relative cost of these implementations.
- Knowledge of those architectural aspects influencing implementation.
- Compilation techniques.

It is rare that a single course deals with all four of these aspects. In particular, description of architectural aspects and compilation techniques are both topics that are sufficiently complex and elaborate to merit independent courses. The remaining 2 aspects are primarily the content of a general course on programming languages and comprise the principle subject of this book.

The literature is rich in texts dealing with these subjects. Generations of students have used them in their learning. All these texts, though, have in mind an advanced reader who already understands many different programming languages, who already has a more than superficial competence with fundamental mechanisms and who is not afraid when confronted by a fragment of code written in an unknown language (because they are able understand it by analogy using the differences between it and what they already know). These are texts, then, that we can say are on "comparative languages". These are long, deep and stimulating, but they are *too* long and deep (read: difficult) for the student who begins their career with a single programming language (or at most 2) and who still has to learn the basic concepts in detail.

This text aims to fill this gap. Experts will see that the content in large measure reflects classical themes. But these very themes are treated in an elementary fashion, assuming only the indispensable minimum of prerequisites. The book also avoids being a catalogue of the differences between different existing programming languages. The ideal (or reference) reader is one who knows one language (well) (for example, Pascal, C, C++ or Java). It is better if they have had some exposure to another language or paradigm. References to languages that are now obsolete have also been avoided and code examples are rarely written in a specific programming language. The text freely uses a sort of pseudo-language (whose concrete syntax was inspired by C and Java) and seeks, in this way, to describe the most relevant aspects of different languages.

Every so often, the boxes at the top of pages contain development of material or a note on a basic concept or something specific about common languages (C, C++, Java; ML and LISP for functional languages; PROLOG for logic-programming languages). The material in boxes can almost always be omitted on a first reading.

Every chapter contains a short sequence of exercises which should be understood as a way of demonstrating an understanding of the material. There are no truly difficult exercises or any that require more than 10 minutes for their solution.

Chapter 3 (Foundations) deals with themes that are not usually encountered in a book on programming languages. It is, however, natural, while discussing static semantics and comparing languages, to ask what are the limits to syntactic analysis of programs and whether what can be done in one language can also be done in another. Rather than send the reader to another text, given the cultural and pragmatic relevance of these questions, we decided to answer these questions directly. In an informal but rigorous manner, in the space of a few pages, we present the undecidability of the halting problem. We also show that all general purpose programming languages express the same class of functions. This helps students who do not always have complete courses on foundations understand the principal results on the limitations on computations.

As well as principles, the text also introduces the three principal *programming paradigms*: object oriented (a theme that is already obligatory in computing), functional and logic programming. The need to write an introductory text is the reason for the exclusion of important themes, such as concurrency and scripting languages, whose mastery represent important skills.

Use of the text   The text is first of all a university textbook, even if there is an almost total absence of mathematical and formal prerequisites (this lack makes the book suitable for personal study by the professional who wishes to deepen their knowledge of the mechanisms that lie behind the languages they use). The choice of themes and the presentation style were largely influenced by the experience of teaching the content as part of the degree course in Computer Science in the Faculty of Mathematical, Physical and Natural Sciences at the University of Bologna.

In our experience, a course on programming languages for 6 credits in the second year of a 3-year degree course can cover most of the fundamental aspects covered in the first ten chapters (say 4/5 of them) and, perhaps, including a brief outline of one of the remaining paradigms. With increase in student maturity, the quantity of material that can be presented will clearly increase. In a master's degree course, the material could also be completed by a treatment of compilation.

Acknowledgements   Our thanks to Giorgio Levi goes beyond the fact that he had the grace to write the Foreword. Both of us owe to him our first understanding of the mechanisms that underpin programming languages. His teaching appears in this book in a way that is anything but marginal.

Ugo Dal Lago drew the figures using METAPOST, Cinzia Di Giusto, Wilmer Ricciotti, Francesco Spegni and Paolo Tacchella read and commented attentively on the drafts of some chapters. The following people pointed out misprints and errors: Irene Borra, Ferdinanda Camporesi, Marco Comini, Michele Filannino, Matteo Friscini, Stefano Gardenghi, Guido Guizzunti, Giacomo Magisano, Flavio Marchi, Fabrizio Massei, Jacopo Mauro, Maurizio Molle, Mirko Orlandelli, Marco Pedicini, Andrea Rappini, Andrea Regoli, Fabiano Ridolfi, Giovanni Rosignoli, Giampiero Travaglini, Fabrizio Giuseppe Ventola. We gladly acknowledge the support of the Dipartimento di Scienze dell'Informazione of the Università di Bologna towards the English translation.

Maurizio Gabbrielli
Bologna

Simone Martini
Bologna

Contents

Chapter 1
Abstract Machines

Abstraction mechanisms play a crucial role in computing because they allow us to manage the complexity inherent in most computational systems by isolating the important aspects in a specific context. In the field of programming languages, these mechanisms are fundamental, both from a theoretical viewpoint (many important concepts can be appropriately formalised using abstractions) and in the practical sense, because programming languages today use common abstraction-creating constructs.

One of the most general concepts employing abstraction is the *abstract machine*. In this chapter, we will see how this concept is closely related to the programming languages. We will also see how, without requiring us to go into the specific details of any particular implementation, it allows us to describe what an implementation of a programming language is. To do this, we will describe in general terms what is meant by the *interpreter* and the *compiler* for a language. Finally, will see how abstract machines can be structured in hierarchies that describe and implement complex software systems.

1.1 The Concepts of Abstract Machine and of Interpreter

In the context of this book, the term "machine" refers clearly to a computing machine. As we know, an electronic, digital computer is a physical machine that executes algorithms which are suitably formalised so that the machine can "understand" them. Intuitively, an abstract machine is nothing more than an abstraction of the concept of a physical computer.

For actual execution, algorithms must be appropriately formalised using the constructs provided by a programming language. In other words, the algorithms we want to execute must be represented using the instructions of a programming language, $\mathscr{L}$. This language will be formally defined in terms of a specific syntax and a precise semantics—see Chap. 2. For the time being, the nature of $\mathscr{L}$ is of no concern to us. Here, it is sufficient to know that the syntax of $\mathscr{L}$ allows us to use a given finite set of constructs, called instructions, to construct programs. A *program* in $\mathscr{L}$

M. Gabbrielli, S. Martini, *Programming Languages: Principles and Paradigms,*
Undergraduate Topics in Computer Science,
DOI 10.1007/978-1-84882-914-5_1, © Springer-Verlag London Limited 2010

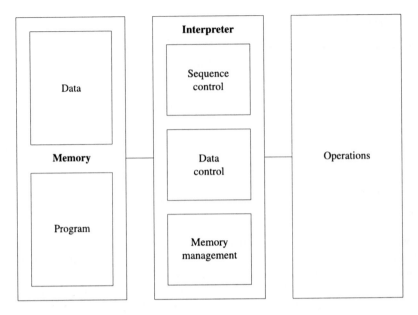

Fig. 1.1 The structure of an abstract machine

(or program written in $\mathscr{L}$) therefore is nothing more than a finite set of instructions of $\mathscr{L}$. With these preliminary remarks, we now present a definition that is central to this chapter.

Definition 1.1 (Abstract Machine) Assume that we are given a programming language, $\mathscr{L}$. An *abstract machine* for $\mathscr{L}$, denoted by $\mathscr{M}_{\mathscr{L}}$, is any set of data structures and algorithms which can perform the storage and execution of programs written in $\mathscr{L}$.

When we choose not to specify the language, $\mathscr{L}$, we will simply talk of the abstract machine, $\mathscr{M}$, omitting the subscript. We will soon see some example abstract machines and how they can actually be implemented. For the time being, let us stop and consider the structure of an abstract machine. As depicted in Fig. 1.1, a generic abstract machine $\mathscr{M}_{\mathscr{L}}$ is composed of a *store* and an *interpreter*. The store serves to store data and programs while the interpreter is the component that executes the instructions contained in programs. We will see this more clearly in the next section.

1.1.1 The Interpreter

Clearly the interpreter must perform the operations that are specific to the language it is interpreting, $\mathscr{L}$. However, even given the diversity of languages, it is possible to discern types of operation and an "execution method" common to all interpreters. The type of operation executed by the interpreter and associated data structures, fall into the following categories:

1. Operations for processing primitive data;
2. Operations and data structures for controlling the sequence of execution of operations;
3. Operations and data structures for controlling data transfers;
4. Operations and data structures for memory management.

We consider these four points in detail.

1. The need for operations such as those in point one is clear. A machine, even an abstract one, runs by executing algorithms, so it must have operations for manipulating primitive data items. These items can be directly represented by a machine. For example, for physical abstract machines, as well as for the abstract machines used by many programming languages, numbers (integer or real) are almost always primitive data. The machine directly implements the various operations required to perform arithmetic (addition, multiplication, etc.). These arithmetic operations are therefore primitive operations as far as the abstract machine is concerned[1].

2. Operations and structures for "sequence control" allow to control the execution flow of instructions in a program. The normal sequential execution of a program might have to be modified when some conditions are satisfied. The interpreter therefore makes use of data structures (for example to hold the address of the next instruction to execute) which are manipulated by specific operations that are different from those used for data manipulation (for example, operations to update the address of the next instruction to execute).

3. Operations that control data transfers are included in order to control how operands and data is to be transferred from memory to the interpreter and vice versa. These operations deal with the different store addressing modes and the order in which operands are to be retrieved from store. In some cases, auxiliary data structures might be necessary to handle data transfers. For example, some types of machine use stacks (implemented either in hardware or software) for this purpose.

4. Finally, there is memory management. This concerns the operations used to allocate data and programs in memory. In the case of abstract machines that are similar to hardware machines, storage management is relatively simple. In the limit case of a physical register-based machine that is not multiprogrammed, a program and its associated data could be allocated in a zone of memory at the start of execution and remain there until the end, without much real need for memory management. Abstract machines for common programming languages, instead, as will be seen, use more sophisticated memory management techniques. In fact, some constructs in these languages either directly or indirectly cause memory to be allocated or deallocated. Correct implementation of these operations requires suitable data

---

[1] It should, however, be noted that there exist programming languages, for example, some declarative languages, in which numeric values and their associated operations are not primitive.

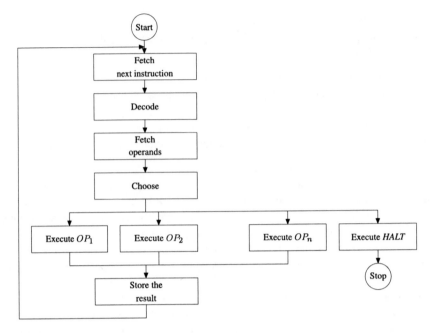

Fig. 1.2 The execution cycle of a generic interpreter

structures (for example, stacks) and dynamic operations (which are, therefore, executed at runtime).

The interpreter's execution cycle, which is substantially the same for all interpreters, is shown in Fig. 1.2. It is organised in terms of the following steps. First, it fetches the next instruction to execute from memory. The instruction is then decoded to determine the operation to be performed as well as its operands. As many operands as required by the instruction are fetched from memory using the method described above. After this, the instruction, which must be one of the machine's primitives, is executed. Once execution of the operation has completed, any results are stored. Then, unless the instruction just executed is a halt instruction, execution passes to the next instruction in sequence and the cycle repeats.

Now that we have seen the interpreter, we can define the language it interprets as follows:

Definition 1.2 (Machine language) Given an abstract machine, $\mathcal{M}_{\mathcal{L}}$, the language $\mathcal{L}$ "understood" by $\mathcal{M}_{\mathcal{L}}$'s interpreter is called the *machine language* of $\mathcal{M}_{\mathcal{L}}$.

Programs written in the machine language of $\mathcal{M}_{\mathcal{L}}$ will be stored in the abstract machine's storage structures so that they cannot be confused with other primitive data on which the interpreter operates (it should be noted that from the interpreter's viewpoint, programs are also a kind of data). Given that the internal representation of the programs executed by the machine $\mathcal{M}_{\mathcal{L}}$ is usually different from its external representation, then we should strictly talk about two different languages. In any

"Low-level" and "High-level" languages

A terminological note is useful. We will return to it in an historical perspective in Chap. 13. In the field of programming languages, the terms "low level" and "high level" are often used to refer, respectively, to distance from the human user and from the machine.

Let us therefore call *low-level*, those languages whose abstract machines are very close to, or coincide with, the physical machine. Starting at the end of the 1940s, these languages were used to program the first computers, but, they turned out to be extremely awkward to use. Because the instructions in these languages had to take into account the physical characteristics of the machine, matters that were completely irrelevant to the algorithm had to be considered while writing programs, or in coding algorithms. It must be remembered that often when we speak generically about "machine language", we mean the language (a low-level one) of a physical machine. A particular low-level language for a physical machine is its *assembly language*, which is a symbolic version of the physical machine (that is, which uses symbols such as ADD, MUL, etc., instead of their associated hardware binary codes). Programs in assembly language are translated into machine code using a program called an *assembler*.

So-called *high-level* programming languages are, on the other hand, those which support the use of constructs that use appropriate abstraction mechanisms to ensure that they are independent of the physical characteristics of the computer. High-level languages are therefore suited to expressing algorithms in ways that are relatively easy for the human user to understand. Clearly, even the constructs of a high-level language must correspond to instructions of the physical machine because it must be possible to execute programs.

case, in order not to complicate notation, for the time being we will not consider such differences and therefore we will speak of just one machine language, $\mathscr{L}$, for machine $\mathscr{M}_\mathscr{L}$.

1.1.2 An Example of an Abstract Machine: The Hardware Machine

From what has been said so far, it should be clear that the concept of abstract machine can be used to describe a variety of different systems, ranging from physical machines right up to the World Wide Web.

As a first example of an abstract machine, let us consider the concrete case of a conventional physical machine such as that in Fig. 1.3. It is physically implemented using logic circuits and electronic components. Let us call such a machine $\mathscr{M}\mathscr{H}_{\mathscr{L}H}$ and let $\mathscr{L}H$ be its machine language.

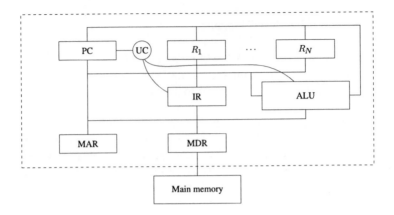

Fig. 1.3 The structure of a conventional calculator

For this specific case, we can, using what we have already said about the components of an abstract machine, identify the following parts.

Memory   The storage component of a physical computer is composed of various levels of memory. Secondary memory implemented using optical or magnetic components; primary memory, organised as a linear sequence of cells, or words, of fixed size (usually a multiple of 8 bits, for example 32 or 64 bits); cache and the *registers* which are internal to the Central Processing Unit (CPU).

Physical memory, whether primary, cache or register file, permits the storage of data and programs. As stated, this is done using the binary alphabet.

Data is divided into a few primitive "types": usually, we have integer numbers, so-called "real" numbers (in reality, a subset of the rationals), characters, and fixed-length sequences of bits. Depending upon the type of data, different physical representations, which use one or more memory words for each element of the type are used. For example, the integers can be represented by 1s or 2s complement numbers contained in a single word, while reals have to be represented as floating point numbers using one or two words depending on whether they are single or double precision. Alphanumeric characters are also implemented as sequences of binary numbers encoded in an appropriate representational code (for example, the ASCII or UNI CODE formats).

We will not here go into the details of these representations since they will be examined in more detail in Chap. 8. We must emphasise the fact that although all data is represented by sequences of bits, at the hardware level we can distinguish different categories, or more properly *types*, of primitive data that can be manipulated directly by the operations provided by the hardware. For this reason, these types are called *predefined types*.

The language of the physical machine   The language, $\mathcal{L}H$ which the physical machine executes is composed of relatively simple instructions. A typical instruction with two operands, for example, requires one word of memory and has the format:

```
OpCode Operand1 Operand2
```

where `OpCode` is a unique code which identifies one of the primitive operations defined by the machine's hardware, while `Operand1` and `Operand2` are values which allow the operands to be located by referring to the storage structures of the machine and their addressing modes. For example,

```
ADD R5, R0
```

might indicate the sum of the contents of registers R0 and R5, with the result being stored in R5, while

```
ADD (R5), (R0)
```

might mean that the sum of the contents of the memory cells whose addresses are contained in R0 and R5 is computed and the result stored in the cell whose address is in R5. It should be noted that, in these examples, for reasons of clarity, we are using symbolic codes such as ADD, R0, (R0). In the language under consideration, on the other hand, we have binary numeric values (addresses are expressed in "absolute" mode). From the viewpoint of internal representation, instructions are nothing more than data stored in a particular format.

Like the instructions and data structures used in executing programs, the set of possible instructions (with their associated operations and addressing modes) depends on the particular physical machine. It is possible to discern classes of machine with similar characteristics. For example, we can distinguish between conventional CISC (Complex Instruction Set Computer) processors which have many machine instructions (some of which are quite complex) and RISC (Reduced Instruction Set Computers) architectures in which there tend to be fewer instructions which are, in particular, simple enough to be executed in a few (possibly one) clock cycle and in pipelined fashion.

Interpreter With the general structure of an abstract machine as a model, it is possible to identify the following components of a physical (hardware) machine:

1. The operations for processing primitive data are the usual arithmetic and logical operations. They are implemented by the ALU (Arithmetic and Logic Unit). Arithmetic operations on integers, and floating-point numbers, booleans are provided, as are shifts, tests, etc.
2. For the control of instruction sequence execution, there is the Program Counter (PC) register, which contains the address of the next instruction to execute. It is the main data structure of this component. Sequence-control operations specifically use this register and typically include the increment operation (which handles the normal flow of control) and operations that modify the value stored in the PC register (jumps).

3. To handle data transfer, the CPU registers interfacing with main memory are used. They are: the data address register (the MAR or Memory Address Register) and the data register (MDR or Memory Data Register). There are, in addition, operations that modify the contents of these registers and that implement various addressing modes (direct, indirect, etc.). Finally, there are operations that access and modify the CPU's internal registers.

4. Memory processing depends fundamentally on the specific architecture. In the simplest case of a register machine that is not multi-programmed, memory management is rudimentary. The program is loaded and immediately starts executing; it remains in memory until it terminates. To increase computation speed, all modern architectures use more sophisticated memory management techniques. In the first place, there are levels of memory intermediate between registers and main memory (i.e., cache memory), whose management needs special data structures and algorithms. Second, some form of multi-programming is almost always implemented (the execution of a program can be suspended to give the CPU to other programs, so as to optimise the management of resources). As a general rule, these techniques (which are used by operating systems) usually require specialised hardware support to manage the presence of more than one program in memory at any time (for example, dynamic address relocation).

All the techniques so far described need specific memory-management data structures and operations to be provided by the hardware. In addition, there are other types of machine that correspond to less conventional architectures. In the case of a machine which uses a (hardware) stack instead of registers, there is the stack data structure together with the push and pop operations.

The interpreter for the hardware machine is implemented as a set of physical devices which comprise the Control Unit and which support execution of the so-called *fetch-decode-execute* cycle. using the sequence control operations. This cycle is analogous to that in the generic interpreter such as the one depicted in Fig. 1.2. It consists of the following phases.

In the *fetch* phase, the next instruction to be executed is retrieved from memory. This is the instruction whose address is held in the PC register (the PC register is automatically incremented after the instruction has been fetched). The instruction, which, it should be recalled, is formed of an operation code and perhaps some operands, is then stored in a special register, called the instruction register.

In the *decode* phase, the instruction stored in the instruction register is decoded using special logic circuits. This allows the correct interpretation of both the instruction's operation code and the addressing modes of its operands. The operands are then retrieved by data transfer operations using the address modes specified in the instruction .

Finally, in the *execute* phase, the primitive hardware operation is actually executed, for example using the circuits of the ALU if the operation is an arithmetic or logical one. If there is a result, it is stored in the way specified by the addressing mode and the operation code currently held in the instruction register. Storage is performed by means of data-transfer operations. At this point, the instruction's execution is complete and is followed by the next phase, in which the next instruction is fetched and the cycle continues (provided the instruction just executed is not a stop instruction).

It should be noted that, even if only conceptually, the hardware machine distinguishes data from instructions. At the physical level, there is no distinction between them, given that they are both represented internally in terms of bits. The distinction mainly derives from the state of the CPU. In the fetch state, every word fetched from memory is considered an instruction, while in the execute phase, it is considered to be data. It should be observed that, finally, an accurate description of the operation of the physical machine would require the introduction of other states in addition to fetch, decode and execute. Our description only aims to show how the general concept of an interpreter is instantiated by a physical machine.

1.2 Implementation of a Language

We have seen that an abstract machine, $\mathcal{M_L}$, is by definition a device which allows the execution of programs written in $\mathcal{L}$. An abstract machine therefore corresponds uniquely to a language, its *machine language*. Conversely, given a programming language, $\mathcal{L}$, there are many (an infinite number) of abstract machines that have $\mathcal{L}$ as their machine language. These machines differ from each other in the way in which the interpreter is implemented and in the data structures that they use; they all agree, though, on the language they interpret—$\mathcal{L}$.

To *implement* a programming language $\mathcal{L}$ means implementing an abstract machine which has $\mathcal{L}$ as its machine language. Before seeing which implementation techniques are used for current programming languages, we will first see what the various theoretical possibilities for an abstract machine are.

1.2.1 *Implementation of an Abstract Machine*

Any implementation of an abstract machine, $\mathcal{M_L}$ must sooner or later use some kind of physical device (mechanical, electronic, biological, etc.) to execute the instructions of $\mathcal{L}$. The use of such a device, nevertheless, can be explicit or implicit. In fact, in addition to the "physical" implementation (in hardware) of $\mathcal{M_L}$'s constructs, we can even think instead of an implementation (in software or firmware) at levels intermediate between $\mathcal{M_L}$ and the underlying physical device. We can therefore reduce the various options for implementing an abstract machine to the following three cases and to combinations of them:

- implementation in *hardware*;
- simulation using *software*;
- simulation (emulation) using *firmware*.

Microprogramming

Microprogramming techniques were introduced in the 1960s with the aim of providing a whole range of different computers, ranging from the slowest and most economical to those with the greatest speed and price, with the same instruction set and, therefore, the same assembly language (the IBM 360 was the most famous computer on which microprogramming was used). The machine language of microprogrammed machines is at an extremely low level and consists of *microinstructions* which specify simple operations for the transfer of data between registers, to and from main memory and perhaps also passage through the logic circuits that implement arithmetic operations. Each instruction in the language which is to be implemented (that is, in the machine language that the user of the machine sees) is simulated using a specific set of microinstructions. These microinstructions, which encode the operation, together with a particular set of microinstructions implementing the interpretation cycle, constitute a *microprogram* which is stored in special read-only memory (which requires special equipment to write). This microprogram implements the interpreter for the (assembly) language common to different computers, each of which has different hardware. The most sophisticated (and costly) physical machines are built using more powerful hardware hence they can implement an instruction by using fewer simulation steps than the less costly models, so they run at a greater speed.

Some terminology needs to be introduced: the term used for simulation using micro-programming, is *emulation*; the level at which microprogramming occurs is called *firmware*.

Let us, finally, observe that a microprogrammable machine constitutes a single, simple example of a *hierarchy* composed of two abstract machines. At the higher level, the assembly machine is constructed on top of what we have called the microprogrammed machine. The assembly language interpreter is implemented in the language of the lower level (as microinstructions), which is, in its turn, interpreted directly by the microprogrammed physical machine. We will discuss this situation in more depth in Sect. 1.3.

Implementation in Hardware

The direct implementation of $\mathcal{M}_{\mathcal{L}}$ in hardware is always possible in principle and is conceptually fairly simple. It is, in fact, a matter of using physical devices such as memory, arithmetic and logic circuits, buses, etc., to implement a physical machine whose machine language coincides with $\mathcal{L}$. To do this, it is sufficient to implement in the hardware the data structures and algorithms constituting the abstract machine.[2]

---

[2]Chapter 3 will tackle the question of why this can always be done for programming languages.

The implementation of a machine $\mathcal{M}_{\mathcal{L}}$ in hardware has the advantage that the execution of programs in $\mathcal{L}$ will be fast because they will be directly executed by the hardware. This advantage, nevertheless, is compensated for by various disadvantages which predominate when $\mathcal{L}$ is a generic high-level language. Indeed, the constructs of a high-level language, $\mathcal{L}$, are relatively complicated and very far from the elementary functions provided at the level of the electronic circuit. An implementation of $\mathcal{M}_{\mathcal{L}}$ requires, therefore, a more complicated design for the physical machine that we want to implement. Moreover, in practice, such a machine, once implemented, would be almost impossible to modify. In would not be possible to implement on it any future modifications to $\mathcal{L}$ without incurring prohibitive costs. For these reasons,in practice, when implementing $\mathcal{M}_{\mathcal{L}}$, in hardware, only low-level languages are used because their constructs are very close to the operations that can be naturally defined using just physical devices. It is possible, though, to implement "dedicated" languages developed for special applications directly in hardware where enormous execution speeds are necessary. This is the case, for example, for some special languages used in real-time systems.

The fact remains that there are many cases in which the structure of a high-level language's abstract machine has influenced the implementation of a hardware architecture, not in the sense of a direct implementation of the abstract machine in hardware, but in the choice of primitive operations and data structures which permit simpler and more efficient implementation of the high-level language's interpreter. This is the case, for example with the architecture of the B5500, a computer from the 1960s which was influenced by the structure of the Algol language.

Simulation Using Software

The second possibility for implementing an abstract machine consists of implementing the data structures and algorithms required by $\mathcal{M}_{\mathcal{L}}$ using programs written in another language, $\mathcal{L}'$, which, we can assume, has already been implemented. Using language $\mathcal{L}'$'s machine, $\mathcal{M}'_{\mathcal{L}'}$, we can, indeed, implement the machine $\mathcal{M}_{\mathcal{L}}$ using appropriate programs written in $\mathcal{L}'$ which interpret the constructs of $\mathcal{L}$ by simulating the functionality of $\mathcal{M}_{\mathcal{L}}$.

In this case, we will have the greatest flexibility because we can easily change the programs implementing the constructs of $\mathcal{M}_{\mathcal{L}}$. We will nevertheless see a performance that is lower than in the previous case because the implementation of $\mathcal{M}_{\mathcal{L}}$ uses another abstract machine $\mathcal{M}'_{\mathcal{L}'}$, which, in its turn, must be implemented in hardware, software or firmware, adding an extra level of interpretation.

Emulation Using Firmware

Finally, the third possibility is intermediate between hardware and software implementation. It consists of simulation (in this case, it is also called emulation) of the data structures and algorithms for $\mathcal{M}_{\mathcal{L}}$ in microcode (which we briefly introduced in the box on page 10).

Partial Functions

A function $f : A \rightarrow B$ is a correspondence between elements of A and elements of B such that, for every element a of A, there exists one and only one element of B. We will call it $f(a)$.

A *partial function*, $f : A \rightarrow B$, is also a correspondence between the two sets A and B, but can be undefined for some elements of A. More formally: it is a relation between A and B such that, for every $a \in A$, if there exists a corresponding element $b \in B$, it is unique and is written $f(a)$. The notion of partial function, for us, is important because, in a natural fashion, programs define partial functions. For example, the following program (written in a language with obvious syntax and semantics and whose core will however be defined in Fig. 2.11):

```
read(x);
if (x == 1) then print(x);
            else while (true) do skip
```
computes the partial function:

$$f(n) = \begin{cases} 1 & \text{if } x = 1 \\ \text{undefined} & \text{otherwise} \end{cases}$$

Conceptually, this solution is similar to simulation in software. In both cases, $\mathcal{M}_{\mathcal{L}}$ is simulated using appropriate programs that are executed by a physical machine. Nevertheless, in the case of firmware emulation, these programs are microprograms instead of programs in a high-level language.

As we saw in the box, microprograms use a special, very low-level language (with extremely simple primitive operations) which are stored in a special read-only memory instead of in main memory, so they can be executed by the physical machine at high speed. For this reason, this implementation of an abstract machine allows us to obtain an execution speed that is higher than that obtainable from software simulation, even if it is not as fast as the equivalent hardware solution. On the other hand, the flexibility of this solution is lower than that of software simulation, since, while it is easy to modify a program written in a high-level language, modification of microcode is relatively complicated and requires special hardware to re-write the memory in which the microcode is stored. The situation is anyway better than in the hardware implementation case, given that microprograms can be modified.

Clearly, for this solution to be possible, the physical machine on which it is used must be microprogrammable.

Summarising, the implementation of $\mathcal{M}_{\mathcal{L}}$ in hardware affords the greatest speed but no flexibility. Implementation in software affords the highest flexibility and least speed, while the one using firmware is intermediate between the two.

1.2.2 Implementation: The Ideal Case

Let us consider a generic language, $\mathscr{L}$, which we want to implement, or rather, for which an abstract machine, $\mathscr{M}_{\mathscr{L}}$ is required. Assuming that we can exclude, for the reasons just given, direct implementation in hardware of $\mathscr{M}_{\mathscr{L}}$, we can assume that, for our implementation of $\mathscr{M}_{\mathscr{L}}$, we have available an abstract machine, $\mathscr{M}o_{\mathscr{L}_o}$, which we will call the *host machine*, which is already implemented (we do not care how) and which therefore allows us to use the constructs of its machine language $\mathscr{L}o$ directly.

Intuitively, the implementation of $\mathscr{L}$ on the host machine $\mathscr{M}o_{\mathscr{L}_o}$ takes place using a "translation" from $\mathscr{L}$ to $\mathscr{L}o$. Nevertheless, we can distinguish two conceptually very different modes of implementation, depending on whether there is an "implicit" translation (implemented by the simulation of $\mathscr{M}_{\mathscr{L}}$'s constructs by programs written in $\mathscr{L}o$) or an explicit translation from programs in $\mathscr{L}$ to corresponding programs in $\mathscr{L}o$. We will now consider these two ways in their ideal forms. We will call these ideal forms:

1. *purely interpreted implementation*, and
2. *purely compiled implementation*.

Notation

Below, as previously mentioned, we use the subscript $\mathscr{L}$ to indicate that a particular construct (machine, interpreter, program, etc.) refers to language $\mathscr{L}$. We will use the superscript $\mathscr{L}$ to indicate that a program is written in language $\mathscr{L}$. We will use $\mathscr{P}rog^{\mathscr{L}}$ to denote the set of all possible programs that can be written in language $\mathscr{L}$, while $\mathscr{D}$ denotes the set of input and output data (and, for simplicity of treatment, we make no distinction between the two).

A program written in $\mathscr{L}$ can be seen as a partial function (see the box):

$$\mathscr{P}^{\mathscr{L}} : \mathscr{D} \to \mathscr{D}$$

such that

$$\mathscr{P}^{\mathscr{L}}(Input) = Output$$

if the execution of $\mathscr{P}^{\mathscr{L}}$ on input data *Input* terminates and produces *Output* as its result. The function is not defined if the execution of $\mathscr{P}^{\mathscr{L}}$ on its input data, *Input*, does not terminate.[3]

---

[3]It should be noted that there is no loss of generality in considering only one input datum, given that it can stand for a set of data.

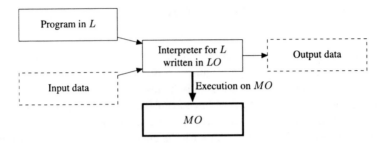

Fig. 1.4 Purely interpreted implementation

Purely interpreted implementation In a *purely interpreted implementation* (shown in Fig. 1.4), the interpreter for $\mathscr{M}_{\mathscr{L}}$ is implemented using a set of instructions in $\mathscr{L}o$. That is, a program is implemented in $\mathscr{L}o$ which interprets all of $\mathscr{L}$'s instructions; this is an interpreter. We will call it $\mathscr{I}_{\mathscr{L}}^{\mathscr{L}o}$.

Once such interpreter is implemented, executing a program $\mathscr{P}^{\mathscr{L}}$ (written in language $\mathscr{L}$) on specified input data $D \in \mathscr{D}$, we need only execute the program $\mathscr{I}_{\mathscr{L}}^{\mathscr{L}o}$ on machine $\mathscr{M}o_{\mathscr{L}o}$, with $\mathscr{P}^{\mathscr{L}}$ and D as input data. More precisely, we can give the following definition.

Definition 1.3 (Interpreter) An interpreter for language $\mathscr{L}$, written in language $\mathscr{L}o$, is a program which implements a partial function:

$$\mathscr{I}_{\mathscr{L}}^{\mathscr{L}o} : (\mathscr{P}rog^{\mathscr{L}} \times \mathscr{D}) \to \mathscr{D} \quad \text{such that } \mathscr{I}_{\mathscr{L}}^{\mathscr{L}o}(\mathscr{P}^{\mathscr{L}}, Input) = \mathscr{P}^{\mathscr{L}}(Input) \quad (1.1)$$

The fact that a program can be considered as input datum for another program should not be surprising, given that, as already stated, a program is only a set of instructions which, in the final analysis, are represented by a certain set of symbols (and therefore by bit sequences).

In the purely interpreted implementation of $\mathscr{L}$, therefore, programs in $\mathscr{L}$ are not explicitly translated. There is only a "decoding" procedure. In order to execute an instruction of $\mathscr{L}$, the interpreter $\mathscr{I}_{\mathscr{L}}^{\mathscr{L}o}$ uses a set of instructions in $\mathscr{L}o$ which corresponds to an instruction in language $\mathscr{L}$. Such decoding is not a real translation because the code corresponding to an instruction of $\mathscr{L}$ is executed, not output, by the interpreter.

It should be noted that we have deliberately not specified the nature of the machine $\mathscr{M}o_{\mathscr{L}o}$. The language $\mathscr{L}o$ can therefore be a high-level language, a low-level language or even one firmware.

Purely compiled implementation With *purely compiled implementation*, as shown in Fig. 1.5, the implementation of $\mathscr{L}$ takes place by explicitly translating programs written in $\mathscr{L}$ to programs written in $\mathscr{L}o$. The translation is performed by a special program called *compiler*; it is denoted by $\mathscr{C}_{\mathscr{L},\mathscr{L}o}$. In this case, the language $\mathscr{L}$ is usually called the *source language*, while language $\mathscr{L}o$ is called the *object language*. To execute a program $\mathscr{P}^{\mathscr{L}}$ (written in language $\mathscr{L}$) on input

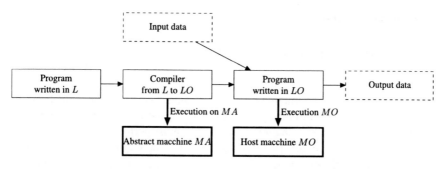

Fig. 1.5 Pure compiled implementation

data D, we must first execute $\mathcal{C}_{\mathcal{L},\mathcal{L}_0}$ and give it $\mathcal{P}^{\mathcal{L}}$ as input. This will produce a compiled program $\mathcal{P}c^{\mathcal{L}_0}$ as its output (written in $\mathcal{L}o$). At this point, we can execute $\mathcal{P}c^{\mathcal{L}_0}$ on the machine $\mathcal{M}o_{\mathcal{L}_0}$ supplying it with input data D to obtain the desired result.

Definition 1.4 (Compiler) A compiler from $\mathcal{L}$ to $\mathcal{L}o$ is a program which implements a function:

$$\mathcal{C}_{\mathcal{L},\mathcal{L}_0} : \mathcal{P}rog^{\mathcal{L}} \rightarrow \mathcal{P}rog^{\mathcal{L}_0}$$

such that, given a program $\mathcal{P}^{\mathcal{L}}$, if

$$\mathcal{C}_{\mathcal{L},\mathcal{L}_0}(\mathcal{P}^{\mathcal{L}}) = \mathcal{P}c^{\mathcal{L}_0}, \tag{1.2}$$

then, for every $Input \in \mathcal{D}^4$:

$$\mathcal{P}^{\mathcal{L}}(Input) = \mathcal{P}c^{\mathcal{L}_0}(Input) \tag{1.3}$$

Note that, unlike pure interpretation, the translation phase described in (1.2) (called *compilation*) is separate from the execution phase, which is, on the other hand, handled by (1.3). Compilation indeed produces a program as output. This program can be executed at any time we want. It should be noted that if $\mathcal{M}o_{\mathcal{L}_0}$ is the only machine available to us, and therefore if $\mathcal{L}o$ is the only language that we can use, the compiler will also be a program written in $\mathcal{L}o$. This is not necessary, however, for the compiler could in fact be executed on another abstract machine altogether and this, latter, machine could execute a different language, even though it produces executable code for $\mathcal{M}o_{\mathcal{L}_0}$.

---

[4]It should be noted that, for simplicity, we assume that the data upon which programs operate are the same for source and object languages. If were not the case, the data would also have to be translated in an appropriate manner.

Comparing the Two Techniques

Having presented the purely interpreted and purely compiled implementation techniques, we will now discuss the advantages and disadvantages of these two approaches.

As far as the purely interpreted implementation is concerned, the main disadvantage is its *low efficiency*. In fact, given that there is no translation phase, in order to execute the program $\mathscr{P}^{\mathscr{L}}$, the interpreter $\mathscr{I}_{\mathscr{L}}^{\mathscr{L}o}$ must perform a decoding of $\mathscr{L}$'s constructs while it executes. Hence, as part of the time required for the execution of $\mathscr{P}^{\mathscr{L}}$, it is also necessary to add in the time required to perform decoding. For example, if the language $\mathscr{L}$ contains the iterative construct for and if this construct is not present in language $\mathscr{L}o$, to execute a command such as:

```
P1: for (I = 1, I<=n, I=I+1) C;
```

the interpreter $\mathscr{I}_{\mathscr{L}}^{\mathscr{L}o}$ must decode this command at runtime and, in its place, execute a series of operations implementing the loop. This might look something like the following code fragment:

```
P2:
    R1 = 1
    R2 = n
L1: if R1 > R2 then goto L2
    translation of C
    ...
    R1 = R1 + 1
    goto L1
L2: ...
```

It is important to repeat that, as shown in (1.1), the interpreter does not generate code. The code shown immediately above is not explicitly produced by the interpreter but only describes the operations that the interpreter must execute at runtime once it has decoded the for command.

It can also be seen that for every occurrence of the same command in a program written in $\mathscr{L}$, the interpreter must perform a separate decoding steep; this does not improve performance. In our example, the command C inside the loop must be decoded n times, clearly with consequent inefficiency.

As often happens, the disadvantages in terms of efficiency are compensated for by advantages in terms of *flexibility*. Indeed, interpreting the constructs of the program that we want to execute at runtime allows direct interaction with whatever is running the program. This is particularly important, for example, because it makes defining program debugging tools relatively easy. In general, moreover, the development of an interpreter is simpler than the development of a compiler; for this reason, interpretative solutions are preferred when it is necessary to implement a new language within a short time. It should be noted, finally, that an interpretative implementation allows a considerable reduction in memory usage, given that the program is stored only in its source version (that is, in the language $\mathscr{L}$) and no new code is produced, even if this consideration is not particularly important today.

The advantages and disadvantages of the compilational and interpretative approaches to languages are dual to each other.

The translation of the source program, $\mathscr{P}^{\mathscr{L}}$, to an object program, $\mathscr{P}c^{\mathscr{L}o}$, occurs separately from the latter's execution. If we neglect the time taken for compilation, therefore, the execution of $\mathscr{P}c^{\mathscr{L}o}$ will turn out to be more efficient than an interpretive implementation because the former does not have the overhead of the instruction decoding phase. In our first example, the program fragment P1 will be translated into fragment P2 by the compiler. Later, when necessary, P2 will executed without having to decode the for instruction again. Furthermore, unlike in the case of an interpreter, decoding an instruction of language $\mathscr{L}$ is performed once by the compiler, independent of the number of times this instruction occurs at runtime. In our example, the command C is decoded and translated once only at compile time and the code produced by this is executed n times at runtime. In Sect. 2.4, we will describe the structure of a compiler, together with the optimisations that can be applied to the code it produces.

One of the major disadvantages of the compilation approach is that it loses all information about the structure of the source program. This loss makes runtime interaction with the program more difficult. For example, when an error occurs at runtime, it can be difficult to determine which source-program command caused it, given that the command will have been compiled into a sequence of object-language instructions. In such a case, it can be difficult, therefore, to implement debugging tools; more generally, there is less flexibility than afforded by the interpretative approach.

1.2.3 Implementation: The Real Case and The Intermediate Machine

Burly purely compiled and interpreted implementations can be considered as the two extreme cases of what happens in practice when a programming language is implemented. In fact, in real language implementations, both elements are almost always present. As far as the interpreted implementation is concerned, we immediately observe that every "real" interpreter operates on an internal representation of a program which is always different from the external one. The translation from the external notation of $\mathscr{L}$ to its internal representation is performed using real translation (compilation, in our terminology) from $\mathscr{L}$ to an intermediate language. The intermediate language is the one that is interpreted. Analogously, in every compiling implementation, some particularly complex constructs are simulated. For example, some instructions for input/output could be translated into the physical machine's language but would require a few hundred instructions, so it is preferable to translate them into calls to some appropriate program (or directly to operating system operations), which simulates at runtime (and therefore interprets) the high-level instructions.

Can interpreter and compiler always be implemented?

At this point, the reader could ask if the implementation of an interpreter or a compiler will always be possible. Or rather, given the language, $\mathscr{L}$, that we want to implement, how can we be sure that it is possible to implement a particular program $\mathscr{I}_{\mathscr{L}}^{\mathscr{L}o}$ in language $\mathscr{L}o$ which performs the interpretation of all the constructs of $\mathscr{L}$? How, furthermore, can we be sure that it is possible to translate programs of $\mathscr{L}$ into programs in $\mathscr{L}o$ using a suitable program, $\mathscr{C}_{\mathscr{L},\mathscr{L}o}$?

The precise answer to this question requires notions from computability theory which will be introduced in Chap. 3. For the time being, we can only answer that the existence of the interpreter and compiler is guaranteed, provided that the language, $\mathscr{L}o$, that we are using for the implementation is sufficiently expressive with respect to the language, $\mathscr{L}$, that we want to implement. As we will see, every language in common use, and therefore also our $\mathscr{L}o$, have the same (maximum) expressive power and this coincides with a particular abstract model of computation that we will call *Turing Machine*. This means that every possible algorithm that can be formulated can be implemented by a program written in $\mathscr{L}o$. Given that the interpreter for $\mathscr{L}$ is no more than a particular algorithm that can execute the instructions of $\mathscr{L}$, there is clearly no theoretical difficulty in implementing the interpreter $\mathscr{I}_{\mathscr{L}}^{\mathscr{L}o}$. As far as the compiler is concerned, assuming that it, too, is to be written in $\mathscr{L}o$, the argument is similar. Given that $\mathscr{L}$ is no more expressive than $\mathscr{L}o$, it must be possible to translate programs in $\mathscr{L}$ into ones in $\mathscr{L}o$ in a way that preserves their meaning. Furthermore, given that, by assumption, $\mathscr{L}o$ permits the implementation of any algorithm, it will also permit the implementation of the particular compiling program $\mathscr{C}_{\mathscr{L},\mathscr{L}o}$ that implements the translation.

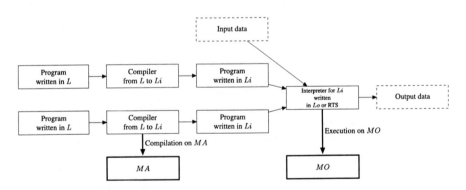

Fig. 1.6 Implementation: the real case with intermediate machine

The real situation for the implementation of a high-level language is therefore that shown in Fig. 1.6. Let us assume, as above, that we have a language $\mathscr{L}$ that has to be implemented and assume also that a host machine $\mathscr{M}o_{\mathscr{L}o}$ exists which has already been constructed. Between the machine $\mathscr{M}_{\mathscr{L}}$ that we want to implement and the host machine, there exists a further level characterised by its own language, $\mathcal{L}_i$ and by its associated abstract machine, $\mathcal{M}_{i\mathcal{L}_i}$, which we will call, the intermediate language and intermediate machine, respectively.

As shown in Fig. 1.6, we have both a compiler $\mathcal{C}_{\mathcal{L},\mathcal{L}_i}$ which translates $\mathcal{L}$ to $\mathcal{L}_i$ and an interpreter $\mathcal{I}_{\mathcal{L}_i}^{\mathcal{L}_o}$ which runs on the machine $\mathcal{M}_{o\mathcal{L}_o}$ (which simulates the machine $\mathcal{M}_{i\mathcal{L}_i}$). In order to execute a generic program, $\mathcal{P}^{\mathcal{L}}$, the program must first be translated by the compiler into an intermediate language program, $\mathcal{P}_i^{\mathcal{L}_i}$. Next, this program is executed by the interpreter $\mathcal{I}_{\mathcal{L}_i}^{\mathcal{L}_o}$. It should be noted that, in the figure, we have written "interpreter or runtime support (RTS)" because it is not always necessary to implement the entire interpreter $\mathcal{I}_{\mathcal{L}_i}^{\mathcal{L}_o}$. In the case in which the intermediate language and the host machine language are not too distant, it might be enough to use the host machine's interpreter, extended by suitable programs, which are referred to as its runtime support, to simulate the intermediate machine.

Depending on the distance between the intermediate level and the source or host level, we will have different types of implementation. Summarising this, we can identify the following cases:

1. $\mathcal{M}_{\mathcal{L}} = \mathcal{M}_{i\mathcal{L}_i}$: purely interpreted implementation.
2. $\mathcal{M}_{\mathcal{L}} \neq \mathcal{M}_{i\mathcal{L}_i} \neq \mathcal{M}_{o\mathcal{L}_o}$.
   (a) If the interpreter of the intermediate machine is substantially different from the interpreter for $\mathcal{M}_{o\mathcal{L}_o}$, we will say that we have an implementation of an interpretative type.
   (b) If the interpreter of the intermediate machine is substantially the same as the interpreter for $\mathcal{M}_{o\mathcal{L}_o}$ (of which it extends some of its functionality), we will say that we have a implementation of a compiled type.
3. $\mathcal{M}_{i\mathcal{L}_i} = \mathcal{M}_{o\mathcal{L}_o}$, we have a purely compiled implementation.

The first and last cases correspond to the limit cases already encountered in the previous section. These are the cases in which the intermediate machines coincide, respectively, with the machine for the language to be implemented and with the host machine.

On the other hand, in the case in which the intermediate machine is present, we have an interpreted type of implementation when the interpreter for the intermediate machine is substantially different from the interpreter for $\mathcal{M}_{o\mathcal{L}_o}$. In this case, therefore, the interpreter $\mathcal{I}_{\mathcal{L}_i}^{\mathcal{L}_o}$ must be implemented using language $\mathcal{L}_o$. The difference between this solution and the purely interpreted one lies in the fact that not all constructs of $\mathcal{L}$ need be simulated. For some constructs there are directly corresponding ones in the host machine's language, when they are translated from $\mathcal{L}$ to the intermediate language $\mathcal{L}_i$, so no simulation is required. Moreover the distance between $\mathcal{M}_{i\mathcal{L}_i}$ and $\mathcal{M}_{o\mathcal{L}_o}$ is such that the constructs for which this happens are few in number and therefore the interpreter for the intermediate machine must have many of its components simulated.

In the compiled implementation, on the other hand, the intermediate language is closer to the host machine and the interpreter substantially shares it. In this case, then, the intermediate machine, $\mathcal{M}_{i\mathcal{L}_i}$, will be implemented using the functionality of $\mathcal{M}_{o\mathcal{L}_o}$, suitably extended to handle those source language constructs of $\mathcal{L}$

which, when also translated into the intermediate language $\mathscr{L}i$, do not have an immediate equivalent on the host machine. This is the case, for example, in the case of some I/O operations that are, even when compiled, usually simulated by suitable programs written in $\mathscr{L}o$. The set of such programs, which extend the functionality of the host machine and which simulate at runtime some of the functionality of the language $\mathscr{L}i$, and therefore also of the language $\mathscr{L}$, constitute the so-called *run-time support* for $\mathscr{L}$.

As can be gathered from this discussion, the distinction between the intermediate cases is not clear. There exists a whole spectrum of implementation types ranging from that in which everything is simulated to the case in which everything is, instead, translated into the host machine language. What to simulate and what to translate depends a great deal on the language in question and on the available host machine. It is clear that, in principle, one would tend to interpret those language constructs which are furthest from the host machine language and to compile the rest. Furthermore, as usual, compiled solutions are preferred in cases where increased execution efficiency of programs is desired, while the interpreted approach will be increasingly preferred when greater flexibility is required.

It should also be noted that the intermediate machine, even if it is always present in principle, is not often actually present. The exceptions are cases of languages which have formally stated definitions of their intermediate machines, together with their associated languages (which is principally done for portability reasons). The compiled implementation of a language on a new hardware platform is a rather big task requiring considerable effort. The interpretive implementation is less demanding but does requires some effort and often poses efficiency problems. Often, it is desired to implement a language on many different platforms, for example when sending programs across a network so that they can be executed on remote machines (as happens with so-called *aplets*). In this case, it is extremely convenient first to compile the programs to an intermediate language and then implement (interpret) the intermediate language on the various platforms. Clearly, the implementation of the intermediate code is much easier than implementing the source code, given that compilation has already been carried out. This solution to the portability of implementations was adopted for the first time on a large scale by the Pascal language, which was defined together with an intermediate machine (with its own language, P-code) which was designed specifically for this purpose. A similar solution was used by the Java language, whose intermediate machine (called the JVM—Java Virtual Machine) has as its machine language the so-called Java Byte Code. It is now implemented on every type of computer.

As the last note, let us emphasise the fact, which should be clear from what we have said so far, that one should not talk about an "interpreted language" or a "compiled language", because each language can be implemented using either of these techniques. One should, instead, talk of interpretative or compiled implementations of a language.

Fig. 1.7 The three levels of a microprogrammed computer

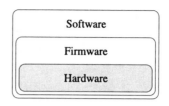

1.3 Hierarchies of Abstract Machines

On the basis of what we have seen, a microprogrammed computer, on which a high-level programming language is implemented, can be represented as shown in Fig. 1.7. Each level implements an abstract machine with its own language and its own functionality.

This schema can be extended to an arbitrary number of levels and a hierarchy is thus produced, even if it is not always explicit. This hierarchy is largely used in software design. In other words, hierarchies of abstract machines are often used in which every machine exploits the functionality of the level immediately below and adds new functionality of its own for the level immediately above. There are many examples of hierarchies of this type. For example, there is the simple activity of programming. When we write a program $\mathscr{P}$ in a language, $\mathscr{L}$, in essence, we are doing no more than defining a new language, $\mathscr{L}_{\mathscr{P}}$ (and therefore a new abstract machine) composed of the (new) functionalities that $\mathscr{P}$ provides to the user through its interface. Such a program can therefore be used by another program, which will define new functionalities and therefore a new language and so on. It can be noted that, broadly speaking, we can also speak of abstract machines when dealing with a set of commands, which, strictly speaking, do not constitute a real programming language. This is the case with a program, with the functionality of an operating system, or with the functionality of a middleware level in a computer network.

In the general case, therefore, we can imagine a hierarchy of machines $\mathscr{M_{L}}_0$, $\mathscr{M_{L}}_1, \ldots, \mathscr{M_{L}}_n$. The generic machine, $\mathscr{M_{L}}_i$ is implemented by exploiting the functionality (that is the language) of the machine immediately below ($\mathscr{M_{L}}_{i-1}$). At the same time, $\mathscr{M_{L}}_i$ provides its own language $\mathscr{L}_i$ to the machine above $\mathscr{M_{L}}_{i+1}$, which, by exploiting that language, uses the new functionality that $\mathscr{M_{L}}_i$ provides with respect to the lower levels. Often, such a hierarchy also has the task of masking lower levels. $\mathscr{M_{L}}_i$ cannot directly access the resources provided by the machines below it but can only make use of whatever language $\mathscr{L}_{i-1}$ provides.

The structuring of a software system in terms of layers of abstract machines is useful for controlling the system's complexity and, in particular, allows for a degree of independence between the various layers, in the sense that any internal modification to the functionality of a layer does not have (or should not have) any influence on the other layers. For example, if we use a high-level language, $\mathscr{L}$, which uses an operating system's file-handling mechanisms, any modification to these mechanisms (while the interface remains the same) does not have any impact on programs written in $\mathscr{L}$.

Fig. 1.8 A hierarchy of
abstract machines

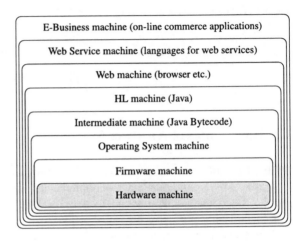

A canonical example of a hierarchy of this kind in a context that is seemingly distant from programming languages is the hierarchy[5] of communications protocols in a network of computers, such as, for example, the ISO/OSI standard.

In a context closer to the subject of this book, we can consider the example shown in Fig. 1.8.

At the lowest level, we have a hardware computer, implemented using physical electronic devices (at least, at present; in the future, the possibility of biological devices will be something that must be actively considered). Above this level, we could have the level of an abstract, microprogrammed machine. Immediately above (or directly above the hardware if the firmware level is not present), there is the abstract machine provided by the operating system which is implemented by programs written in machine language. Such a machine can be, in turn, seen as a hierarchy of many layers (kernel, memory manager, peripheral manager, file system, command-language interpreter) which implement functionalities that are progressively more remote from the physical machine: starting with the nucleus, which interacts with the hardware and manages process state changes, to the command interpreter (or shell) which allows users to interact with the operating system. In its complexity, therefore, the operating system on one hand extends the functionality of the physical machine, providing functionalities not present on the physical machine (for example, primitives that operate on files) to higher levels. On the other hand, it masks some hardware primitives (for example, primitives for handling I/O) in which the higher levels in the hierarchy have no interest in seeing directly. The abstract machine provided by the operating system forms the host machine on which a high-level programming language is implemented using the methods that we discussed in previous sections. It normally uses an intermediate machine, which, in the diagram (Fig. 1.8), is the Java Virtual machine and its bytecode language. The level provided by the abstract machine for the high-level language that we have implemented (Java

---

[5]In the literature on networks, one often speaks of a *stack* rather than, more correctly, of a hierarchy.

Program Transformation and Partial Evaluation

In addition to "translation" of programs from one language to another, as is done by a compiler, there are numerous transformation techniques involving only one language that operate upon programs. These techniques are principally defined with the aim of improving performance. Partial evaluation is one of these techniques and consists of evaluating a program against an input so as to produce a program that is specialised with respect to this input and which is more efficient than the original program. For example, assume we have a program $P(X, Y)$ which, after processing the data X, performs operations on the data in Y depending upon the result of working on X. If the data, X, input to the program are always the same, we can transform this program to $P'(Y)$, where the computations using X have already been performed (prior to runtime) and thereby obtain a faster program.

More formally, a partial evaluator for the language $\mathscr{L}$ is a program which implements the function:

$$\mathscr{P}eval_{\mathscr{L}} : (\mathscr{P}rog^{\mathscr{L}} \times \mathscr{D}) \to \mathscr{P}rog^{\mathscr{L}}$$

which has the following characteristics. Given a generic program, P, written in $\mathscr{L}$, taking two arguments, the result of partially evaluating P with respect to one of its *first input D_1* is:

$$\mathscr{P}eval_{\mathscr{L}}(P, D_1) = P'$$

where the program $\mathscr{P}'$ (the result of the partial evaluation) accepts a single argument and is such that, for any input data, Y, we have:

$$\mathscr{I}_{\mathscr{L}}(P, (D_1, Y)) = \mathscr{I}_{\mathscr{L}}(P', Y)$$

where $\mathscr{I}_{\mathscr{L}}$ is the language interpreter.

---

in this case) is not normally the last level of the hierarchy. At this point, in fact, we could have one or more applications which together provide new services. For example, we can have a "web machine" level in which the functions required to process Web communications (communications protocols, HTML code display, applet running, etc.) are implemented. Above this, we might find the "Web Service" level providing the functions required to make web services interact, both in terms of interaction protocols as well as of the behaviour of the processes involved. At this level, truly new languages can be implemented that define the behaviour of so-called "business processes" based on Web services (an example is the Business Process Execution Language). Finally, at the top level, we find a specific application, in our case electronic commerce, which, while providing highly specific and restricted functionality, can also be seen in terms of a final abstract machine.

1.4 Chapter Summary

The chapter has introduced the concepts of abstract machine and the principle methods for implementing a programming language. In particular, we have seen:

- The *abstract machine*: an abstract formalisation for a generic executor of algorithms, formalised in terms of a specific programming language.
- The *interpreter*: an essential component of the abstract machine which characterises its behaviour, relating in operational terms the language of the abstract machine to the embedding physical world.
- The *machine language*: the language of a generic abstract machine.
- *Different language typologies*: characterised by their distance from the physical machine.
- The *implementation of a language*: in its different forms, from purely interpreted to purely compiled; the concept of *compiler* is particularly important here.
- The *concept of intermediate language*: essential in the real implementation of any language; there are some famous examples (P-code machine for Pascal and the Java Virtual Machine).
- *Hierarchies of abstract machines*: abstract machines can be hierarchically composed and many software systems can be seen in such terms.

1.5 Bibliographic Notes

The concept of abstract machine is present in many different contexts, from programming languages to operating systems, even if at times it is used in a much more informal manner than in this chapter. In some cases, it is also called a virtual machine, as for example in [5], which, however, presents an approach similar to that adopted here.

The descriptions of hardware machines that we have used can be found in any textbook on computer architecture, for example [6].

The intermediate machine was introduced in the first implementations of Pascal, for example [4]. For more recent uses of intermediate machine for Java implementations, the reader should consult some of the many texts on the JVM, for example, [3].

Finally, as far as compilation is concerned, a classic text is [1], while [2] is a more recent book with a more up-to-date treatment.

1.6 Exercises

1. Give three examples, in different contexts, of abstract machines.
2. Describe the functioning of the interpreter for a generic abstract machine.

3. Describe the differences between the interpretative and compiled implementations of a programming language, emphasising the advantages and disadvantages.

4. Assume you have available an already-implemented abstract machine, C, how could you use it to implement an abstract machine for another language, L?

5. What are the advantages in using an intermediate machine for the implementation of a language?

6. The first Pascal environments included:

   - A Pascal compiler, written in Pascal, which produced P-code (code for the intermediate machine);
   - The same compiler, translated into P-code;
   - An interpreter for P-code written in Pascal.

   To implement the Pascal language in an interpretative way on a new host machine means (manually) translating the P-code interpreter into the language on the host machine. Given such an interpretative implementation, how can one obtain a compiled implementation for the same host machine, minimising the effort required? (Hint: think about a modification to the compiler for Pascal also written in Pascal.)

7. Consider an interpreter, $\mathscr{I}^{\mathscr{L}}_{\mathscr{L}1}(X, Y)$, written in language $\mathscr{L}$, for a different language, $\mathscr{L}1$, where X is the program to be interpreted and Y is its input data. Consider a program P written in $\mathscr{L}1$. What is obtained by evaluating

$$\mathscr{P}eval_{\mathscr{L}}(\mathscr{I}^{\mathscr{L}}_{\mathscr{L}1}, P)$$

i.e., from the partial evaluation of $\mathscr{I}^{\mathscr{L}}_{\mathscr{L}1}$ with respect to P? (This transformation is known as Futamura's first projection.)

References

1. A. V. Aho, R. Sethi, and J. D. Ullman. *Compilers: Principles, Techniques, and Tools.* Addison-Wesley, Reading, 1988.
2. A. W. Appel. *Modern Compiler Implementation in Java.* Cambridge University Press, Cambridge, 1998. This text exists also for C and ML.
3. T. Lindholm and F. Yellin. *The Java Virtual Machine Specification*, 2nd edition. Sun and Addison-Wesley, Cleveland, 1999.
4. S. Pemberton and M. Daniels. *Pascal Implementation: The p4 Compiler and Interpreter.* Ellis Horwood, Chichester, 1982.
5. T. Pratt and M. Zelkowitz. *Programming Languages: Design and Implementation*, 4th edition. Prentice-Hall, New York, 2001.
6. A. Tannenbaum. *Structured Computer Organization.* Prentice-Hall, New York, 1999.

Chapter 2
How to Describe a Programming Language

A programming language is an artificial formalism in which algorithms can be expressed. For all its artificiality, though, this formalism remains a *language*. Its study can make good use of the many concepts and tools developed in the last century in linguistics (which studies both natural and artificial languages). Without going into great detail, this chapter poses the problem of what it means to "give" (define or understand) a programming language and which tools can be used in this undertaking.

2.1 Levels of Description

In a study which has now become a classic in linguistics, Morris [6] studied the various levels at which a description of a language can occur. He identified three major areas: *grammar*, *semantics* and *pragmatics*.

Grammar is that part of the description of the language which answers the question: which phrases are correct? Once the alphabet of a language has been defined as a first step (in the case of natural language, for example, the Latin alphabet of 22 or 26 letters, the Cyrillic alphabet, etc.), the *lexical* component, which uses this alphabet, identifies the sequence of symbols constituting the *words* (or *tokens*) of the language defined. When alphabet and words have been defined, the *syntax* describes which sequences of words constitute legal phrases. Syntax is therefore a relation between signs. Between all possible sequences of words (over a given alphabet), the syntax chooses a subset of sequences to form phrases of the language proper.[1]

---

[1] In linguistics, obviously, things are more complicated. In addition to the lexical and the syntactic levels, there is also a morphological level which is distinct from the two previous ones. At the morphological level, the different forms assumed by words (or phrases) as a function of their grammatical function are defined. For example in the lexicon (that is, the dictionary, the thesaurus of the language in question), we find the word "bear" with the associated lexical value given by the image of the animal that everybody knows. At the morphological level, on the other hand, the word is the convertible into the root "bear" and the morpheme "-s" which signals the plural. The natural language's phonetic aspects are also present but they are of no interest to us here.

M. Gabbrielli, S. Martini, *Programming Languages: Principles and Paradigms*,
Undergraduate Topics in Computer Science,
DOI 10.1007/978-1-84882-914-5_2, © Springer-Verlag London Limited 2010

Semantics is that part of the description of the language which seeks to answer the question "what does a correct phrase mean?" Semantics, therefore, attributes a *significance* to every correct phrase. In the case of natural languages, the process of attribution of meaning can be very complex; in the case of artificial languages the situation is rather simpler. It is not difficult to assume, in this case, that semantics is a relation between signs (correct sentences) and meanings (autonomous entities existing independently of the signs that are used to describe them). For example, the meaning of a certain program could be the mathematical function computed by that program. The semantic description of that language will be constructed using techniques allowing us, when given a program, to fix the function the program computes.

It is at the third level that the principal actor makes its appearance on the scene, the person who uses a certain language. *Pragmatics* is that part of a language description which asks itself "how do we use a meaningful sentence?" Sentences with the same meaning can be used in different ways by different users. Different linguistic contexts can require the use of different sentences; some are more elegant, some are antiquated, or more dialect-based than others. Understanding these linguistic mechanisms is no less important than knowing the syntax and semantics.

In the case of programming languages, we can add a fourth level to the three classical ones: the *implementation* level. Given that the languages that interest us are procedural languages (that is, languages whose correct phrases specify actions), it remains for us to describe "how to execute a correct sentence, in such a way that we respect the semantics". A knowledge of the semantics is, in general, enough for the language user, but the software designer (and more importantly the language designer) is also interested in the process with which operative phrases implement the state under consideration. It is precisely this which is described by the language implementation.

We can give a fairly rudimentary example which we hope will serve our purposes. Let us consider the natural language used to express recipes in cooking. The syntax determines the correct sentences with which a recipe is expressed. The semantics is about explaining "what is" a recipe, independent of its (specific) execution. Pragmatics studies how a cook ("that cook") interprets the various sentences of the recipe. In the end, the implementation describes the way (where, and with what ingredients) the kitchen recipe transforms into the dish that the semantics prescribes.

In the next sections, we analyse the role performed by the four levels when they are applied to programming languages.

2.2 Grammar and Syntax

We have already said that the grammar of a language first establishes the alphabet and lexicon. Then by means of a syntax, it defines those sequences of symbols corresponding to well-formed phrases and sentences (or to "sentences" in short). Clearly, at least from the viewpoint of natural language, the definition of the (finite) alphabet is immediate. Even the lexicon can be defined, at least to a first approximation, in a simple fashion. We will be content, for the time being, with a finite vocabulary; we can simply list the words of interest to us. This is certainly what happens with natural languages, given that dictionaries are finite volumes![2]

How do we describe the syntax? In a natural language, it is the same natural language which is used, in general, to describe its own syntax (classical examples are grammar textbooks for various languages). Also a syntax for a programming language is often described using natural language, particularly for the older languages. Natural language, though, often introduces ambiguity in its syntactic description and, in particular, it is of no use in the process of translating (compiling) a program in a high-level language into another (generally, at a lower level) language.

Linguistics, on the other hand, through the work in the 1950s of the American linguist Noam Chomsky, has developed techniques to describe syntactic phenomena in a formal manner. This description uses formalisms designed specifically to limit the ambiguity that is always present in natural language. These techniques, known as generative grammar, are not of much use in describing the syntax of natural languages (which are too complex and highly sophisticated). Instead, they are a fundamental tool for describing the syntax of programming languages (and particularly their compilation, as we will briefly see in Sect. 2.4).

Example 2.1 We will describe a simple language. It is the language of palindromic strings, composed of the symbols a and b.[3] Let us therefore begin by fixing the *alphabet*, $A = \{a, b\}$. We must now select, from all strings over A (that is finite sequences of elements of A), the palindromic strings. The simplest way to do this is to observe that there is a simple recursive definition of a palindromic string. Indeed, we can say (this is the basis of the induction) that a and b are palindromic strings. If, then, s is any string that we know already to be palindromic, then so are asa and bsb (this is the induction step).

It is not difficult to convince ourselves that this definition captures all and only the palindromic strings of odd length over A. It remains to account for even-length strings, such as *abba*. To include these as well, we add the fact that the empty string (that is the string which contains no symbol from the alphabet) is also a palindromic string to the base case of the inductive definition. Now our definition categorises all and only the palindromic strings over the alphabet A. If a string really is a palindromic string, for example *aabaa*, or *abba*, there exists a sequence of applications of the inductive rule just mentioned which will construct it. On the other hand, if a string is not a palindromic string (for example *aabab*), there is no way to construct it inductively using the rules just introduced.

Context-Free Grammars, which we introduce in the next section, are a notation for the concise and precise expression of recursive definitions of strings such as

---

[2]In programming languages, the lexicon can also be formed from an infinite set of words. We will see below how this is possible.

[3]A string is palindromic if it is identical to its mirror image. That is, the string is the same when read from left to right or right to left. A famous example in Latin is, ignoring spaces, the riddle "in girum imus nocte et consumimur igni".

the one we have just seen. The inductive definition of palindromic strings can be expressed in grammatical form as:

$$P \rightarrow$$
$$P \rightarrow \mathbf{a}$$
$$P \rightarrow \mathbf{b}$$
$$P \rightarrow \mathbf{a}P\mathbf{a}$$
$$P \rightarrow \mathbf{b}P\mathbf{b}$$

In these rules, P stands for "any palindromic string", while the arrow $\rightarrow$ is read as "can be". The first three lines will be immediately recognised as the basis of the inductive definition, while the last two form the induction step.

2.2.1 Context-Free Grammars

The example just given is an example of a *context-free grammar*, a fundamental device for the description of programming languages. We begin by introducing a little notation and terminology. Having fixed a finite (or denumerable) set A, which we call the *alphabet*, we denote by A^* the set of all *finite strings over* A (that is finite length sequences of elements of A; the $*$ operator is called *Kleene's star*). Let us immediately observe that, according to the definition, the sequence of length zero also belongs to A^*—this is the empty string, denoted by ϵ.

A *formal language over the alphabet* A is nothing more than a subset of A^*. A formal grammar serves to identify a certain subset of strings from all those possible over a given alphabet.[4]

Definition 2.1 (Context-Free Grammar) A context-free grammar is a quadruple (NT, T, R, S) where:

1. NT is a finite set of symbols (non-terminal symbols, or variables, or syntactic categories).
2. T is a finite set of symbols (terminal symbols).
3. R is a finite set of *productions* (or *rules*), each of which is composed of an expression of the form:

$$V \rightarrow w$$

where V (the *head* of the production) is a single non-terminal symbol and w (the body) is a string composed of zero or more terminal or non-terminal symbols (that is w is a string over $T \cup NT$).

---

[4] In formal languages, a sequence of terminal symbols which appears in a language is usually called a "word" of the language. We do not use this terminology; instead we speak of strings, to avoid ambiguity with words and phrases of a language (natural or artificial), in the sense in which they are normally understood.

4. S is an element of NT (the *initial symbol*).

According to this definition, therefore, the grammar in the example shown in Example 2.1 is composed of the quadruple $(\{P\}, \{a, b\}, R, P)$, where R is the set of productions used in the example.

Let us observe that, according to the definition, a production can have an empty body, that is, it can be composed of the null symbol, or, more properly, can be formed from the *empty string*, ϵ. We will see in a later section how a given grammar defines a language over the alphabet formed from its terminal symbols. Let us begin however with an example.

Example 2.2 Let us see a simple grammar that describes arithmetic expressions (over the operators $+$, $*$, $-$, both unary and binary). The atomic elements of these expressions are simple identifiers formed from finite sequences of the symbols a and b.

We define the grammar $G = (\{E, I\}, \{\mathbf{a}, \mathbf{b}, +, *, -, (,)\}, R, E)$, where R is the following set of productions:

1. $E \rightarrow I$
2. $E \rightarrow E + E$
3. $E \rightarrow E * E$
4. $E \rightarrow E - E$
5. $E \rightarrow -E$
6. $E \rightarrow (E)$

7. $I \rightarrow \mathbf{a}$
8. $I \rightarrow \mathbf{b}$
9. $I \rightarrow I\mathbf{a}$
10. $I \rightarrow I\mathbf{b}$

Unlike the grammar in Example 2.1, this one has more than one non-terminal symbol corresponding, in an informal way, to an expression (E) or to an identifier (I). Note, once more, how the productions are a synthetic way to express recursive definitions. In this case, we are dealing with two definitions (which have been graphically separated), of which one (the one for E) uses in its base case the non-terminal symbol inductively defined using the other recursive definition.

BNF   In the context of programming languages, context-free grammars were used for the first time in the definition of the language Algol60. In the report that introduced Algol60, the grammar that defines the language is described using a notation that is slightly different from the one we have just introduced. This notation, (considered, among other things, to be usable with a reduced character set, that does not include arrow, cursives, upper case, etc.) goes under the name of *Backus Naur normal form* (BNF), named after two authoritative members of the Algol committee (John Backus who had previously directed the Fortran project and had written the compiler for it—the first high-level language, and Peter Naur). In BNF:

Fig. 2.1 A derivation of the
string **ab** $*$ (**a** + **b**)

$$
\begin{aligned}
E &\Rightarrow_3 E * E \\
  &\Rightarrow_1 I * E \\
  &\Rightarrow_{10} I\mathbf{b} * E \\
  &\Rightarrow_7 \mathbf{ab} * E \\
  &\Rightarrow_6 \mathbf{ab} * (E) \\
  &\Rightarrow_2 \mathbf{ab} * (E + E) \\
  &\Rightarrow_1 \mathbf{ab} * (I + E) \\
  &\Rightarrow_7 \mathbf{ab} * (\mathbf{a} + E) \\
  &\Rightarrow_1 \mathbf{ab} * (\mathbf{a} + I) \\
  &\Rightarrow_8 \mathbf{ab} * (\mathbf{a} + \mathbf{b})
\end{aligned}
$$

- The arrow "$\rightarrow$" is replaced by "::=".
- The non-terminal symbols are written between angle brackets (for example $\langle Exp \rangle$ and $\langle Ide \rangle$ could be the two non-terminal symbols of the grammar of Example 2.2).
- Productions with the same head are grouped into a single block using vertical bar ("|") to separate the productions. In Example 2.2, the productions for E could therefore be expressed as follows:

$$\langle E \rangle ::= \langle I \rangle \mid \langle E \rangle + \langle E \rangle \mid \langle E \rangle * \langle E \rangle \mid \langle E \rangle - \langle E \rangle \mid -\langle E \rangle \mid (\langle E \rangle).$$

Moreover, some notations mix symbols (for example, use of the vertical bar, the arrow and non-terminal symbols written in italic upper case).

Derivations and languages   A grammar inductively defines a set of strings. We can make explicit the operative aspect of this inductive definition using the concept of derivation.

Example 2.3 We can ensure that the string **ab** $*$ (**a** + **b**) is correct according to the grammar of Example 2.2, reading the productions as "rewriting rules", and by repeatedly applying them. We use a bigger arrow ("$\Rightarrow$") to denote the operation of string rewriting. We can then proceed as follows. We start with the initial symbol, E, and rewrite it using a production (which we are allowed to select). Let us, for example, use production (3), and we obtain the rewriting $E \Rightarrow E * E$. Now we concentrate on the right-hand side of this production. We have two E's that can be rewritten (expanded) independently of each other. Let us take the one on the left and apply production (1) to obtain $E * E \Rightarrow I * E$. We can now choose whether we expand I or E (or the other way round). Figure 2.1 shows the rewriting that we have just started, developed until the string **ab** $*$ (**a** + **b**) has been derived. The production used is represented by each $\Rightarrow$s' subscript.

We can capitalise on this example in the following definition.

Definition 2.2 (Derivation) Having fixed a grammar, $G = (NT, T, R, S)$, and assigned two strings, v and w over $NT \cup T$, we say that w is immediately derived

Fig. 2.2 A derivation tree for
the string $\mathbf{ab} * (\mathbf{a} + \mathbf{b})$

$$E \Rightarrow_3 E * E$$
$$\Rightarrow_6 E * (E)$$
$$\Rightarrow_2 E * (E + E)$$
$$\Rightarrow_1 E * (E + I)$$
$$\Rightarrow_8 E * (E + \mathbf{b})$$
$$\Rightarrow_1 E * (I + \mathbf{b})$$
$$\Rightarrow_7 E * (\mathbf{a} + \mathbf{b})$$
$$\Rightarrow_1 I * (\mathbf{a} + \mathbf{b})$$
$$\Rightarrow_{10} I\mathbf{b} * (\mathbf{a} + \mathbf{b})$$
$$\Rightarrow_7 \mathbf{ab} * (\mathbf{a} + \mathbf{b})$$

from v (or: v is rewritten in a single step into w), if w is obtained from v by substituting the body of a production of R whose head is V for a non-terminal symbol, V, in v. In this case, we will write $v \Rightarrow w$.

We say that w is derived from v (or: v is rewritten to w) and we write $v \Rightarrow^* w$, if there exists a finite (possibly empty) sequence of immediate derivations $v \Rightarrow w_0 \Rightarrow w_1 \Rightarrow \cdots \Rightarrow w$.

Using the notation just introduced, and using the grammar for expressions that we have used so far we can write, for example $E * E \Rightarrow^* \mathbf{ab} * (\mathbf{a} + I)$. Particularly interesting are those derivations where on the left of the $\Rightarrow^*$ symbol there is the grammar's initial symbol and on the right is a string solely composed of *terminal* symbols. In a certain sense, these are maximal derivations which cannot be extended (by rewriting a non-terminal) either on the left or right. Following the intuition that has led us to the introduction of grammars, these derivations are the ones that give us the correct strings as far as the grammar is concerned.

Definition 2.3 (Generated Language) The language generated by a grammar $G = (NT, T, R, S)$ is the set $\mathscr{L}(G) = \{w \in T^* \mid S \Rightarrow^* w\}$.

Note that this definition, in accordance with everything we said at the start of Sect. 2.2.1, defines precisely a language over T^*.

Derivation Trees The derivation of a string is a sequential process. In it, there are steps that must be performed in a certain order. For example, in Fig. 2.1, it is clear that the first $\Rightarrow_{10}$ must follow the first $\Rightarrow_3$ because production (10) rewrites the non-terminal symbol I which does not exist in the initial string (which is composed of only the initial symbol E) which is introduced by production (3). But there are some steps whose order could be exchanged. In the derivation in Fig. 2.1, for example, each time that it is necessary to rewrite a non-terminal symbol, the leftmost is always chosen. We could imagine, on the other hand, concentrating first on the rightmost non-terminal symbol, thereby obtaining the derivation shown in Fig. 2.2.

The two derivations that we have given for the string $\mathbf{ab} * (\mathbf{a} + \mathbf{b})$ are, in a highly intuitive way, equivalent. Both reconstruct the structure of the string in the same way (in terms of non-terminal and terminal strings), while they differ only in the

Fig. 2.3 A derivation tree for
the string **ab** ∗ (**a** + **b**)

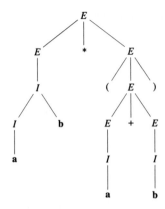

order with which the productions are applied. This fact is made explicit in Fig. 2.3
which represents the derivation of the string **ab** ∗ (**a** + **b**) in the form of a tree.

Definition 2.4 Given a grammar, $G = (NT, T, R, S)$, a derivation tree (or parse
tree) is an ordered tree in which:

1. Each node is labelled with a symbol in $NT \cup T \cup \{\epsilon\}$.
2. The root is labelled with S.
3. Each interior node is labelled with a symbol in NT.
4. If a certain node has the label $A \in NT$ and its children are $m_1, \ldots, m_k$ labelled
   respectively with $X_1, \ldots, X_k$, where $X_i \in NT \cup T$ for all $i \in [1, k]$, then $A \rightarrow$
   $X_1 \ldots X_k$ is a production of R.
5. If a node has label ϵ, then that node is the unique child. If A is its parent, $A \rightarrow \epsilon$
   is a production in R.

It is easy to see that, a derivation tree can be obtained from any derivation. It is
enough to start at the root (labelled with the initial symbol) and successively adding
a level of children corresponding to the production used during the derivation. By
applying this procedure to the derivation of Fig. 2.1, the derivation tree of Fig. 2.3
is obtained. Let us now apply this construction procedure to the derivation tree in
Fig. 2.2. Again, the tree in Fig. 2.3 is obtained. The two derivations result in the
same tree, and this fact corresponds to the intuition that the two derivations were
substantially equivalent.

Derivation trees are one of the most important techniques in the analysis of programming language syntax. The structure of the derivation tree indeed expresses,
by means of its subtrees, the logical structure that the grammar assigns to the string.

Trees

The concept of tree is of considerable importance in Computer Science and is also used a great deal in common language (think of a genealogical tree, for example). A tree is an information structure that can be defined in different ways and that exists in different "spaces". For our purposes, we are interested only in ordered, rooted trees (or simply *trees*) which we can define as follows. A (rooted, ordered) tree is a finite set of elements called *nodes*, such that if it is not empty, a particular node is called *the root* and the remaining nodes, if they exist, are partitioned between the elements of an (ordered) n-tuple $\langle S_1, S_2, \ldots, S_n \rangle$, $n \geq 0$, where each S_i, $i \in [1, N]$ is a tree.

Intuitively, therefore, a tree allows us to group nodes into levels where, at level 0, we have the root, at level 1 we have the roots of the trees $S_1, S_2, \ldots, S_n$ and so on.

Another (equivalent) definition of tree is often used. It is probably more significant for the reader who is familiar with genealogical trees, botanical classifications, taxonomies, etc. According to this definition, a tree is a particular case of a graph: a (rooted, ordered) tree is therefore a pair $T = (N, A)$, where N is a finite set of *nodes* and A is a set of ordered pairs of nodes, called *arcs*, such that:

- The number of arcs is equal to one less than the number of nodes.
- T is *connected*, that is, for each pair of nodes, $n, m \in N$, there exists a sequence of distinct nodes $n_0, n_1, \ldots, n_k$ such that $n_0 = n$ and $n_k = m$ and the pair (n_i, n_{i+1}) is an arc, for $i = 0, \ldots, k - 1$.
- A (unique) node, r, is said to be the *root* and the nodes are ordered by level according to the following inductive definition. The root is at level 0; if a node n is at level i, and there exists the arc $(n, m) \in A$ then node m is at level $i + 1$.
- Given a node, n, the nodes m such that there exists an arc $(n, m) \in A$ are said to be the *children* of n (and n is said to be their *parent*); for every node $n \in N$, a total order is established on the set of all the children of n.

Using a curious mix of botanical, mathematical and "familiar" terms, nodes with the same parent are said to be *siblings* while nodes without children are said to be *leaves*. The root is the only node without a parent.

For example, the tree in Fig. 2.4 corresponds to the following derivation:

$$
\begin{aligned}
E &\Rightarrow_2 E + E \\
&\Rightarrow_3 E * E + E \\
&\Rightarrow_1 I * E + E \\
&\Rightarrow_7 \mathbf{a} * E + E \\
&\Rightarrow_1 \mathbf{a} * I + E \\
&\Rightarrow_8 \mathbf{a} * \mathbf{b} + E \\
&\Rightarrow_1 \mathbf{a} * \mathbf{b} + I \\
&\Rightarrow_7 \mathbf{a} * \mathbf{b} + \mathbf{a}
\end{aligned}
$$

Fig. 2.4 A derivation tree for
the string **a** ∗ **b** + **a**

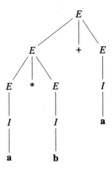

Fig. 2.5 Another derivation
tree for the string **a** ∗ **b** + **a**

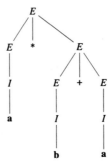

In the tree in Fig. 2.4, we can see that the subexpression **a** ∗ **b** appears as a left child
of a sum. This expresses the fact that the string **a** ∗ **b** + **a** must be interpreted as "first
multiply **a** by **b** and add the result to **a**", given that in order to compute the sum, the
operand present in the left subtree is needed.

Ambiguity Let us consider the following derivation (again using the grammar of
Example 2.2):

$$
\begin{aligned}
E &\Rightarrow_3 E * E \\
&\Rightarrow_1 I * E \\
&\Rightarrow_7 \mathbf{a} * E \\
&\Rightarrow_2 \mathbf{a} * E + E \\
&\Rightarrow_1 \mathbf{a} * I + E \\
&\Rightarrow_8 \mathbf{a} * \mathbf{b} + E \\
&\Rightarrow_1 \mathbf{a} * \mathbf{b} + I \\
&\Rightarrow_7 \mathbf{a} * \mathbf{b} + \mathbf{a}
\end{aligned}
$$

If we construct the corresponding derivation tree, we obtain the tree in Fig. 2.5.
Comparing the trees in Figs. 2.4 and 2.5, it can be seen that we have two different
trees producing the same string. Reading the leaves of the two trees from left to
right, in both cases, we obtain the string **a** ∗ **b** + **a**. Let us observe, however, that
the two trees are radically different. The second assigns a structure to the same
string that is quite different (and therefore reveals a different precedence implicit in
the arithmetic operators). If we want to use derivation trees to describe the logical

structure of a string, we are in a bad position. The grammar of Example 2.2 is incapable of assigning a unique structure to the string in question. According to how the derivation is constructed, the precedence of the two arithmetic operators differs. Let us now see a formal definition of these concepts.

First, let us be clear about what it means to read or visit the leaves of a tree "from left to right". Visiting a tree consists of following a path through the tree's nodes so that each node is visited exactly once. There are different ways to visit nodes (depth-, breadth-first and symmetric), which, when applied to the same tree, produce different sequences of nodes. If only the leaves are considered, however, each and every one of these methods produces the same result for which we can use the following definitions:

Definition 2.5 Let $T = (N, A)$, be a non-empty, ordered tree with root r. The result of the left-to-right traversal of T is the sequence of nodes (leaves) obtained by the following recursive definition:

- If r has no children, the result of the traversal is r.
- If r has k children, $m_1, \ldots, m_k$, let $T_1, \ldots, T_k$ be the subtrees of T such that T_i has m_i as its root (T_i therefore contains m_i and all of that part of T which is underneath this node). The result of the traversal is the sequence of nodes obtained by visiting T_1 to T_k in turn, from left to right.

A this point, we can say what it means for a string to admit a derivation tree.

Definition 2.6 We say that a string of characters admits a derivation tree T if it is the result of a left-to-right traversal of T.

Finally, we can give the definition that interests us.

Definition 2.7 (Ambiguity) A grammar, G, is *ambiguous* if there exists at least one string of $\mathscr{L}(G)$ which admits more than one derivation tree.

We remark that ambiguity comes not from the existence of many derivations for the same string (a common and innocuous property) but from the fact that (at least) one string has more than one derivation *tree*.

An ambiguous grammar is useless as description of a programming language because it cannot be used to translate (compile) a program in a unique fashion. Fortunately, given an ambiguous grammar it is often possible to transform it into another, unambiguous, grammar that generates the same language.[5] Techniques for grammar disambiguation are outside the scope of this book. By way of example, Fig. 2.6 shows an unambiguous grammar whose generated language coincides with the one in Example 2.2.

---

[5]There exist pathological cases of languages which are generated only by ambiguous grammars. These languages have no relevance to programming languages.

Fig. 2.6 An unambiguous grammar for the language of expressions

$$G' = (\{E, T, A, I\}, \{\mathbf{a}, \mathbf{b}, +, *, -, (,)\}, R', E)$$

$$E \rightarrow T \mid T + E \mid T - E$$
$$T \rightarrow A \mid A * T$$
$$A \rightarrow I \mid -A \mid (E)$$
$$I \rightarrow \mathbf{a} \mid \mathbf{b} \mid I\mathbf{a} \mid I\mathbf{b}$$

We have a grammar which interprets the structure of an expression according to the usual concept of arithmetic operator precedence. Unary minus ("-") has the highest precedence, followed by $*$, followed in their turn by $+$ and binary $-$ (which have the same precedence). The grammar interprets, then, a sequence of operators at the same level of precedence by association to the right. For example, the string $\mathbf{a} + \mathbf{b} + \mathbf{a}$ will be assigned the same structure as the string $\mathbf{a} + (\mathbf{b} + \mathbf{a})$. The absence of ambiguity is paid for by increased complexity. There are more non-terminals and the intuitive interpretation of the grammar is therefore more difficult.

The need to provide unambiguous grammars explains the contortions that appear in the definitions of some programming languages. For example, Fig. 2.7 shows an extract of the official grammar for Java's conditional command (its if) (the non-terminal symbols are printed in italic, while the terminal symbols in this extract are if, else and brackets).

This grammar is interesting for two reasons. First, note that what are formally considered single symbols (terminal or non-terminal) in context-free grammars are here represented by words composed of a number of characters. For example, if represents a single terminal symbol and, analogously, *IfThenElseStatement* represents a non-terminal symbol.

This happens because, in the definition of a programming language, it is preferential to use meaningful words (if, then, else) which can, up to certain limits, suggest an intuitive meaning, rather than symbols which would be harder to understand by the language user. In other words, as we will better see in the next chapters, that the use of (meaningful) symbolic names definitely makes programming easier. Analogously, for non-terminal symbols, they make the grammar easier to understand. It is definitely better to use names such as *Statement* rather than single symbols.

The second interesting aspect of the grammar is its complex nature. This complexity is necessary to resolve the ambiguity of strings (programs) such as the one exemplified by the following skeleton program:

```
if (expression1) if (expression2) command1;
    else command2;
```

Java, like a great many other programming languages allows conditional commands both with an else branch and without it. When an if command without else is combined with an if with an else branch (as in the case of the program appearing above), it is necessary to determine which of the two ifs is the owner of the single else. The grammar in Fig. 2.7 is an unambiguous one which makes

Statement ::= ... | *IfThenStatement* | *IfThenElseStatement* |
    StatementWithoutTrailingSubstatement
StatementWithoutTrailingSubstatement ::= ... | *Block* | *EmptyStatement* |
    ReturnStatement
StatementNoShortIf ::= ... | *StatementWithoutTrailingSubstatement* |
    IfThenElseStatementNoShortIf
IfThenStatement ::= `if` (*Expression*) *Statement*
IfThenElseStatement ::=
    `if` (*Expression*) *StatementNoShortIf* `else` *Statement*
IfThenElseStatementNoShortIf ::=
    `if` (*Expression*) *StatementNoShortIf* `else` *StatementNoShortIf*

Fig. 2.7 Grammar for Java conditional commands

"an `else` clause belong to the innermost `if` to which it might possibly belong" (from the Java definition [3]). In simple words, the `else` is paired with the second `if` (the one which tests `expression2`). Intuitively, this happens because, once an `if` command with an `else` is introduced by use of the non-terminal symbol *IfThenElseStatement*, the command in the *then* branch will be unable to hold an `if` command without an `else`, as can be seen by inspection of the rules which define the non-terminal symbol *StatementNoShortIf*.

2.3 Contextual Syntactic Constraints

The syntactic correctness of a phrase of a programming language sometimes depends on the *context* in which that phrase occurs. Let us consider, for example, the assignment `I = R+3;`. Assuming that the productions in the grammar that are used permit the correct derivation of this string, it might be, though, incorrect at the exact point in the program at which it occurs. For example, if the language requires the declaration of variables, it is necessary for programs to contain the declarations of `I` and `R` before the assignment. If, then, the language is typed, it would not accept the assignment if the type of the expression `R+3` is not compatible[6] with that of the variable `I`.

Strings that are correct with respect to the grammar, therefore, can be legal only *in a given context*. There are many examples of these contextual syntactic constraints:

- An identifier must be declared before use (Pascal, Java).
- The number of actual parameters to a function must be the same as the formal parameters (C, Pascal, Java, etc.).

---

[6]All these concepts will be introduced below. For now, an intuitive understanding of these concepts will suffice.

- In the case of assignment, the type of an expression must be compatible with that of the variable to which it is assigned (C, Pascal, Java, etc.).
- Assignments to the control variable of a `for` loop are not permitted (Pascal).
- Before using a variable, there must have been an assignment to it (Java).
- A method can be redefined (*overridden*) only by a method with the same signature (Java) or with a compatible signature (Java5).
- ...

These are, to be sure, syntactic constraints. However, their contextual nature makes it impossible to describe them using a context-free grammar (the name of this class of grammars was chosen purpose). A book on formal languages is required to go into detail on these issues; here, it suffices to note that there exist other types of grammar, called contextual grammars.[7] These grammars permit the description of cases such as this. These grammars are difficult to write, to process and, above all, there are no automatic techniques for efficient generation of translators, such as exist, on the other hand, for context-free grammars. This suggests, therefore, that use of grammars should be limited to the non-contextual description of syntax and then to express the additional contextual constraints using natural language or using formal techniques such as transition systems (which we will see in Sect. 2.5 when we consider semantics).

The term *static semantic constraint* is used in programming language jargon to denote the contextual constraints that appear in the syntactic aspects of a language. In the jargon, "syntax" in general means "describable using a context-free grammar", "static semantics" means "describable with verifiable contextual constraints on a static basis using the program text", while "dynamic semantics" (or simply "semantics") refers to everything that happens when a program is executed.

The distinction between context-free and context-dependent syntax (that is, static semantics) is established precisely by the expressive power of context-free grammars. The distinction between syntax and semantics is not always clear. Some cases are clear. Let us assume, for example, that we have a language whose definition establishes that should a division by 0 happen during execution, the abstract machine for the language *must* report it with an explicit error. This is clearly a dynamic semantic constraint. But let us assume, now, that the definition of another language is specified as follows:

A program is syntactically incorrect when a division by 0 *can happen*.

The program in Fig. 2.8 would be syntactically incorrect in this hypothetical language because there exists a sequence of executions (those in which the `read` command assigns the value 0 to A) which causes division by zero. Does the constraint that we have stated above (which certainly cannot be expressed in a free grammar) belong to static or dynamic semantics? It is clear that it refers to a dynamic event

---

[7]In extreme synthesis, in a contextual grammar, a production can take the form (which is more general than in a context-free grammar) $uAv \rightarrow uwv$, where u, v and w are strings over $T \cup NT$. Fundamental to this production, the non-terminal symbol A can be rewritten to w only if it appears in a certain context (the one described by u and v).

Fig. 2.8 A program that can cause a division by 0

```
int A, B;
read(A);
B = 10/A;
```

Fig. 2.9 An abstract syntax tree

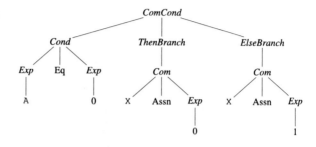

(division by zero) but the constraint, to be meaningful (that is, that it really does exclude some programs) would have to be detected statically (as we have done for the simple program given above). A person can decide that it is syntactically incorrect without executing it but only from looking at the code and reasoning about it). More important than its classification, is understanding whether we have a verifiable constraint or not. Otherwise stated, is it really possible to implement an abstract machine for such a language, or does the very nature of the constraint imply that there can exist no abstract machine which is able to check it in a static fashion for an arbitrary program?

These are questions that we cannot immediately answer, even though they are very important, because they concern what we can, and cannot, do with an abstract machine. We will concern ourselves with these questions in the next chapter (Chap. 3).

2.4 Compilers

The moment has arrived at which to see in outline how the syntactic description of a language can be used automatically to translate a program. We know from Chap. 1 that such an automatic translator is called a *compiler*, whose general logical structure is shown in Fig. 2.10. It is characterised by a cascaded series of phases. The various phases, starting with a string representing the program in the *source* language, generate various internal intermediate representations until a string in the *object* language is generated. Note that, as seen in the previous chapter, in this context, "object language" does not necessarily equate to "machine code" or to "low-level language". It is merely a language towards which the translation is directed. In what follows, we briefly describe the different phases of compilation. We do not pretend to explain how to construct a compiler (see [1]), but just to fix some ideas useful for our study of programming languages.

Lexical analysis The aim of lexical analysis is to read the symbols (characters) forming the program sequentially from the input and to group these symbols into

Fig. 2.10 Organisation of a compiler

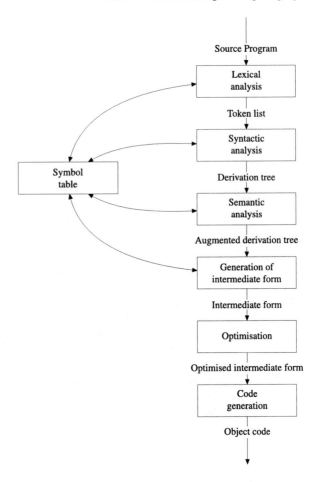

meaningful logical units, which we call *tokens*, (which are analogous, for our programming language, to the words in the dictionary of a natural language). For example, the lexical analyser of C or Java, when presented with the string x = 1 + foo++; will produce 7 tokens: the identifier x, the assignment operator =, the number 1, the addition operator +, the identifier foo, the auto increment operator ++ and finally the command termination token ; . Particularly important tokens are the reserved words of the language (such as for, if, else, etc.), operators, open and close brackets (such as { and } in C or Java, but also those such as begin and end in Pascal). Lexical analysis (or *scanning*) is a very simple operation which scans the input text of the source program from left to right, taking a single pass to recognise tokens. No check is yet made on the sequence of tokens such as, for example, checking that brackets are correctly balanced. As discussed in detail in the box, the technical tool used for lexical analysis is a particular class of generative grammars (regular grammars). The use of a grammar to describe the elements of the lexicon is due both to the necessity of efficiently recognising these elements, and to

Abstract and Concrete Syntax

The grammar of a programming language defines the language as a set of strings. This set of strings corresponds in a natural way to the set of their derivation trees. These trees are much more interesting than the strings. First, they abstract from the specific lexical characteristic of the tokens. It can also happen that lexically different structures can result in the same tree. The tree depicted in Fig. 2.9 could correspond to the Pascal string:

```
if A=0 then X:=0 else X:=1
```

or to the Java string:

```
if (A==0) X=0; else X=1;
```

As we have already repeatedly observed, derivation trees are interesting because they express the canonical structure that can be assigned to the string.

Not all derivation trees correspond to legal programs. We know that static semantic analysis has the task of selecting those trees satisfying the contextual constraints of the language. The set of trees resulting from this process constitutes the *abstract syntax* of language. This is a much more convenient way of thinking of a language if we are interested in its manipulation (and not merely in writing correct programs in it).

the fact that, unlike the case of natural language lexicons, lexicons for programming languages can be formed from an infinite set of words and therefore a simple list, so the one used in a normal dictionary is inadequate (think, for example, of the possibility of defining identifiers as sequences of characters of arbitrary length starting with a particular letter).

Syntactic analysis   Once the list of tokens has been constructed, the syntactic analyser (or *parser*) seeks to construct a derivation tree for this list. This is, clearly, a derivation tree in the grammar of the language. Each leaf of this tree must correspond to a token from the list obtained by the scanner. Moreover, these leaves, read from left to right, must form a correct phrase (or a sequence of terminal symbols) in the language. We already know that such trees represent the logical structure of the program which will be employed by the successive phases of compilation.

It can happen that the parser is unable to construct a derivation tree. This happens when the input string is not correct with reference to the language's grammar. In such a case, the parser reports the errors it has encountered and compilation is aborted. In reality, lexical and syntactic analysis are interleaved in a more direct fashion than appears from these notes (in particular, the two phases are not sequential but the scanner produces a token for each invocation of the parser); more details can be obtained from one of the many texts on compilers.

Regular Grammars

The difference between lexical and syntactic analysis can be made precise using
a formal classification of grammars. If a grammar has all productions of the form
$A \rightarrow bB$ (or in the form $A \rightarrow Bb$), where A and B are non-terminal symbols (B can
also be absent or coincide with A) and b is a single terminal symbol, the grammar
is said to be *regular*. In Example 2.2, the (sub-) grammar based on the non-terminal
symbol I is a regular grammar (while the subgrammar for E is not).

The expressive power of regular grammars is highly limited. In particular, using
a regular grammar, it is not possible to "count" an arbitrary number of characters.
As a consequence, it is not possible to express the balancing of syntactic structures
such as brackets using a regular grammar.

Technically, lexical analysis is the first phase of translation which checks that
the input string can be decomposed into tokens, each of which is described by a
regular grammar (in Example 2.2, lexical analysis would have recognised the sequences of **a** and **b** as instances of the non-terminal symbol I).

Once the sequence of tokens has been obtained, syntactic analysis takes place
using a properly context-free grammar which uses the tokens produced by the preceding lexical analysis as its terminal symbols.

Semantic analysis   The derivation tree (which represents the syntactic correctness
of the input string) is subjected to checks of the language's various context-based
constraints. As we have seen, it is at this stage that declarations, types, number of
function parameters, etc., are processed. As these checks are performed, the derivation tree is *augmented* with the information derived from them and new structures
are generated. By way of an example, every token that corresponds to a variable
identifier will be associated with its type, the place of declaration and other useful
information (for example its *scope*, see Chap. 4). To avoid the useless duplication
of this information, it is, in general, collected into structures external to the derivation tree. Among these structures, the one in which information about identifiers
is collected is called the symbol table. The symbol table plays an essential role in
successive phases.

At the cost of boring the reader, so that we do not confuse it with what we call
semantics in Sect. 2.5, let us note that the term semantic analysis is an historical
relic and that it is concerned with context-based syntactic constraints.

Generation of intermediate forms   An appropriate traversal of the augmented
derivation tree allows an initial phase of code generation. It is not yet possible to
generate code in the object language, given that there are many optimisations left to
do and they are independent of the specific object language. Moreover, a compiler
is often implemented to generate code for a whole series of object languages (for
example, machine code for different architectures), not just one. It is useful, therefore, to concentrate all choices relating to a specific language in a single phase and

to generate code to an intermediate form, which is designed to be independent of both the source and the object languages.

Code optimisation   The code obtained from the preceding phases by repeatedly traversing the derivation tree is fairly inefficient. There are many optimisations that can be made before generating object code. Typical operations that can be performed are:

- Removal of useless code (*dead code removal*). That is, removal of pieces of code that can never be executed because there is no execution sequence that can reach them.
- *In-line expansion* of function calls. Some function (procedure) calls can be substituted by the body of the associated function, making execution faster. It also makes other optimisations possible.
- Subexpression factorisation. Some programs compute the same value more than once. If, and when, this fact is discovered by the compiler, the value of the common subexpression can be calculated once only and then stored.
- Loop optimisations. Iterations are the places where the biggest optimisations can be performed. Among these, the most common consists of removing from inside a loop the computation of subexpressions whose value remains constant during different iterations.

Code generation   Starting with optimised intermediate form, the final object code is generated. There follows, in general, a last phase of optimisation which depends upon the specific characteristics of the object language. In a compiler that generates machine code, an important part of this last phase is register assignment (decisions as to which variables should be stored in which processor registers). This is a choice of enormous importance for the efficiency of the final program.

2.5 Semantics

As is intuitively to be expected, the description of the semantics of a programming language is somewhat more complex than its syntactic description. This complexity is due both to technical problems, as well to the need to mediate between two opposing issues: the need for exactness as well as for flexibility. As far as exactness is concerned, a precise and unambiguous description is required of what must be expected from every syntactically correct construct so that every user knows *a priori* (that is before program execution), and in a manner independent of the architecture, what will happen at runtime. This search for exactness, however, must not preclude different implementations of the same language, all of which are correct with respect to the semantics. The semantic specification must therefore also be flexible, that is, it must not anticipate choices that are to be made when the language is implemented (and which therefore do not play a part in the definition of the language itself).

It would not be difficult to achieve exactness at the expense of flexibility. It is enough to give the semantics of a language using a specific compiler on a specific architecture. The official meaning of a program is given by its execution on this architecture after translation using that compiler. Apart form the difficulty of speaking in general about the semantics of the language's constructs, this solution has no flexibility. Although we have constructed what we claim to be a semantics, there exists only one implementation (the official one) and all the other implementations are completely equivalent. But to what level of detail is the canonical implementation normative? Is the computation time of a particular program part of its definition? Is the reporting of errors? How can typically architecture-dependent input/output commands be ported to a different architecture? When the implementation technology of the physical machine changes, how is the semantics, which we have incautiously defined in terms of a specific machine, affected?

One of the difficulties of semantic definition is really that of finding the happy medium between exactness and flexibility, in such a way as to remove ambiguity, still leaving room for implementation. This situation suggests using formal methods to describe the semantics. Methods of this kind have existed for a long time for the artificial languages of mathematical logic and they have been adapted by computer scientists for their own ends. Yet, some semantic phenomena make formal description complex and not easily usable by anyone who does not have the appropriate skills. It is for this reason that the majority of official programming language definitions use natural language for their semantic description. This does not detract from the fact that formal methods for semantics are very often used in the preparatory phases of the design of a programming language, or to describe some of its particular characteristics, where it is paramount to avoid ambiguity at the cost of simplicity.

Formal methods for semantics divide into two main families: *denotational* and *operational* semantics.[8] Denotational semantics is the application to programming languages of techniques developed for the semantics of logico-mathematical languages. The meaning of a program is given by a function which expresses the input/output behaviour of the program itself. The domain and codomain of this function are suitable mathematical structures, such as the environment and the memory (store), that are internal to the language. Refined mathematical techniques (continuity, fixed points, etc.) allow the appropriate treatment of phenomena such as iteration and recursion (see [8]).

In the operational approach, on the other hand, there are no external entities (for example, functions) associated with language constructs. Using appropriate methods, an operational semantics specifies the behaviour of the abstract machine. That is, it formally defines the interpreter, making reference to an abstract formalism at a much lower level. The various operational techniques differ (sometimes profoundly) in their choice of formalism; some semantics use formal automata, others use systems of logico-mathematical rules, yet others prefer transition systems to specify the state transformations induced by a program.

---

[8]For completeness, we should also talk about algebraic and axiomatic semantics, but simplicity and conciseness require us to ignore them.

$$Num ::= 1 \mid 2 \mid 3 \mid \ldots$$
$$Var ::= X_1 \mid X_2 \mid X_3 \mid \ldots$$

$$AExp ::= Num \mid Var \mid (AExp + AExp) \mid (AExp - AExp)$$
$$BExp ::= \textbf{tt} \mid \textbf{ff} \mid (AExp == AExp) \mid \neg BExp \mid (BExp \wedge BExp)$$

$$Com ::= \textbf{skip} \mid Var := AExp \mid Com; Com \mid$$
$$\textbf{if } BExp \textbf{ then } Com \textbf{ else } Com \mid \textbf{ while } BExp \textbf{ do } Com$$

Fig. 2.11 Syntax of a simple imperative language

This is not a book in which an exhaustive treatment of these semantic techniques can be given. We content ourselves with a simple example of techniques based on transition systems to give a semantics for a rudimentary imperative language. This technique, called SOS (Structured Operational Semantics, [7]), is highly versatile and has been effectively used in giving the semantics to some languages including Standard ML (an influential functional language).

Figure 2.11 shows the grammar of a simple language. For reasons of readability (and so that we can obtain a concise semantics), we have a grammar with infinite productions for the *Num* and *Var* non-terminal symbols. The explicit presence of brackets around each binary operator application eliminates possible problems of ambiguity.

We need to introduce some notation. We will use n to denote an arbitrary *Num* (numeric constant); using X, we will denote an arbitrary *Var* (variable). We write a for an arbitrary *AExp* (arithmetic expression). We use b to denote an arbitrary *BExp* (boolean expression, where **tt** and **ff** denote the values *true* and *false*, respectively). We write c for arbitrary *Comm* (commands). We use, when needed, subscripts to distinguish between objects of the same syntactic category (for example, we will write a_1, a_2, etc., for *AExps*).

State The semantics of a command in our language uses a simple memory model which stores values of *Var*. In this model, a *state* is a finite sequence of pairs of the form (X, n) which we can read as "in the current state, the variable X has the value n" (in our little language, the value will always be an integer but we can easily imagine more complex situations). Given a command c (that is a derivation tree that is correct according to the grammar in Fig. 2.11), its reference state is given by a sequence of pairs which includes all *Vars* which are named in c. We denote an arbitrary state by σ or τ, with or without subscripts.

We need to define some operations on states: modification of an existing state and the retrieval of a variable's value in the current state. To this end, given a state, σ, a *Var* X and a value v, we write $\sigma[X \leftarrow v]$ to denote a new state that is the same as σ but differs from it by associating X with the value v (and thereby losing any previous association to X). Given a state, σ, and a variable, X, we write $\sigma(X)$ for the value that σ associates with X; this value is undefined if X does not appear in the domain of σ (σ is therefore a partial function).

Example 2.4 Let us fix $\sigma = [(X, 3), (Y, 5)]$, we have $\sigma[X \leftarrow 7] = [(X, 7), (Y, 5)]$. We also have $\sigma(Y) = 5$ and $\sigma[X \leftarrow 7](X) = 7$; $\sigma(W)$ is undefined.

Transitions Structured operational semantics can be seen as an elegant way of defining the functioning of an abstract machine without going into any details about its implementation.[9] This functioning is expressed in terms of the elementary computational steps of the abstract machine. The formal way in which structured operational semantics defines the meaning of a program, c, is in terms of a *transition* which expresses a step in the transformation (of the state and/or of the program itself) induced by the execution of the command. The simplest form of transition is:

$$\langle c, \sigma \rangle \rightarrow \tau,$$

where c is a command, σ the *starting state* and τ the *terminal state*. The interpretation that we give to this notation is that if we start the execution of c in the state σ, the execution terminates (in a single step) with state τ. For example, the transition which defines the **skip** command is

$$\langle \textbf{skip}, \sigma \rangle \rightarrow \sigma.$$

It can be seen that we have a command that does nothing. Starting in any state, σ, **skip** terminates leaving the state unchanged.

In more complex cases, a *terminal situation* will be reached not in a single large step, but rather in many little steps which progressively transform the state (starting with σ); the command, c, is progressively executed a part at a time until the whole has been "consumed". These little steps are expressed by transitions of the form:

$$\langle c, \sigma \rangle \rightarrow \langle c', \sigma' \rangle.$$

For example, one of the transitions which define the conditional command will be:

$$\langle \textbf{if tt then } c_1 \textbf{ else } c_2, \sigma \rangle \rightarrow \langle c_1, \sigma \rangle,$$

This means that if the boolean condition is true, the command in the **then** branch must be executed. Some transitions, finally, are *conditional*: if some command, c_1, has a transition, then the command c has another transition. Conditional transitions take the form of a *rule*, expressed as a fraction:

$$\frac{\langle c_1, \sigma_1 \rangle \rightarrow \langle c_1', \sigma_1' \rangle \qquad \langle c_2, \sigma_2 \rangle \rightarrow \langle c_2', \sigma_2' \rangle}{\langle c, \sigma \rangle \rightarrow \langle c', \sigma' \rangle}.$$

We read this rule in the following way. If the command, c_1, starting in state σ_1, can perform a computational step that transforms itself into command c_1' in state

---

[9]Using terminology which we will use again in the final chapters of this book, we can say that it is a *declarative* description of the language's abstract machine.

$$\langle X, \sigma \rangle \rightarrow \langle \sigma(X), \sigma \rangle$$

$$\langle (n + m), \sigma \rangle \rightarrow \langle p, \sigma \rangle \qquad \langle (n - m), \sigma \rangle \rightarrow \langle p, \sigma \rangle$$
$$\text{where } p = n + m \qquad\qquad \text{where } p = n - m \text{ e } n \geq m$$

$$\frac{\langle a_1, \sigma \rangle \rightarrow \langle a', \sigma \rangle}{\langle (a_1 + a_2), \sigma \rangle \rightarrow \langle (a' + a_2), \sigma \rangle} \quad \frac{\langle a_2, \sigma \rangle \rightarrow \langle a'', \sigma \rangle}{\langle (a_1 + a_2), \sigma \rangle \rightarrow \langle (a_1 + a''), \sigma \rangle}$$

$$\frac{\langle a_1, \sigma \rangle \rightarrow \langle a', \sigma \rangle}{\langle (a_1 - a_2), \sigma \rangle \rightarrow \langle (a' - a_2), \sigma \rangle} \quad \frac{\langle a_2, \sigma \rangle \rightarrow \langle a'', \sigma \rangle}{\langle (a_1 - a_2), \sigma \rangle \rightarrow \langle (a_1 - a''), \sigma \rangle}$$

Fig. 2.12 Semantics of arithmetic expressions

σ_1', and if the command c_2, starting in σ_2, can perform a computational step and transform itself into the command c_2' in state σ_2', then the command, c, starting in the state σ can perform a computational step and transform itself into the command c' in state σ'. It is clear that a specific rule will express a number of meaningful relationships between c, c_1 and c_2 (and their respective states). In general, c_1 and c_2 will be subcommands of c.[10]

Expression semantics   Figure 2.12 shows the rules for the semantics of arithmetic expressions. The first three rules are terminal rules (that is, the computation to the right of the arrow is in a form to which no more transitions can be applied). In order of presentation, they define the semantics of a variable, of addition in the case in which both of the summands are constants, of subtraction in the case in which both its arguments are constants and its result is a natural number. Note that no semantics is given for expressions such as $5 - 7$. The second group of four rules is formed of conditional rules. The first pair defines the semantics of sums and expresses the fact that to calculate the value of a sum, it is necessary first to evaluate its two arguments separately. Note how the semantics specifies *no order of evaluation* for the arguments of an addition. Subtraction is handled in a similar fashion.

Figure 2.13 shows the semantics of logical expressions and adopts the same ideas as for arithmetic expressions. Note that in this figure, *bv* denotes a boolean value (**tt** or **ff**).

Command semantics   It can be seen how the state, σ, always remains unaltered during the evaluation of an expression and how it is only used to obtain the value of a variable. This changes for the semantics of commands as shown in Fig. 2.14. Note how the rules in the Figure are essentially of two types: those which, for every command, express the actual computational step for that command (this holds for rules $(c1)$, $(c2)$, $(c4)$, $(c6)$, $(c7)$ and $(c9)$), as well as those which serve just to make

---

[10]It will not have escaped the attentive reader that what we have called conditional rules are, in reality, inductive rules forming part of the definition of transition relations.

$$\langle (n == m), \sigma \rangle \rightarrow \langle \textbf{tt}, \sigma \rangle \qquad\qquad \langle (n == m), \sigma \rangle \rightarrow \langle \textbf{ff}, \sigma \rangle$$
$$\text{if } n = m \qquad\qquad\qquad\qquad \text{if } n \neq m$$

$$\langle (bv_1 \wedge bv_2), \sigma \rangle \rightarrow \langle bv, \sigma \rangle$$
$$\text{where } bv \text{ is the } and \text{ of } bv_1 \text{ and } bv_2$$

$$\langle \neg\textbf{tt}, \sigma \rangle \rightarrow \langle \textbf{ff}, \sigma \rangle \qquad\qquad\qquad \langle \neg\textbf{ff}, \sigma \rangle \rightarrow \langle \textbf{tt}, \sigma \rangle$$

$$\frac{\langle a_1, \sigma \rangle \rightarrow \langle a', \sigma \rangle}{\langle (a_1 == a_2), \sigma \rangle \rightarrow \langle (a' == a_2), \sigma \rangle} \qquad \frac{\langle a_2, \sigma \rangle \rightarrow \langle a'', \sigma \rangle}{\langle (a_1 == a_2), \sigma \rangle \rightarrow \langle (a_1 == a''), \sigma \rangle}$$

$$\frac{\langle b_1, \sigma \rangle \rightarrow \langle b', \sigma \rangle}{\langle (b_1 \wedge b_2), \sigma \rangle \rightarrow \langle (b' \wedge b_2), \sigma \rangle} \qquad \frac{\langle b_2, \sigma \rangle \rightarrow \langle b'', \sigma \rangle}{\langle (b_1 \wedge b_2), \sigma \rangle \rightarrow \langle (b_1 \wedge b''), \sigma \rangle}$$

$$\frac{\langle b, \sigma \rangle \rightarrow \langle b', \sigma \rangle}{\langle \neg b, \sigma \rangle \rightarrow \langle \neg b', \sigma \rangle}$$

Fig. 2.13 Semantics of boolean expressions

$$\langle \textbf{skip}, \sigma \rangle \rightarrow \sigma \quad (c1)$$

$$\langle X := n, \sigma \rangle \rightarrow \sigma[X \leftarrow n] \quad (c2) \qquad \frac{\langle a, \sigma \rangle \rightarrow \langle a', \sigma \rangle}{\langle X := a, \sigma \rangle \rightarrow \langle X := a', \sigma \rangle} \quad (c3)$$

$$\frac{\langle c_1, \sigma \rangle \rightarrow \sigma'}{\langle c_1; c_2, \sigma \rangle \rightarrow \langle c_2, \sigma' \rangle} \quad (c4) \qquad \frac{\langle c_1, \sigma \rangle \rightarrow \langle c_1', \sigma' \rangle}{\langle c_1; c_2, \sigma \rangle \rightarrow \langle c_1'; c_2, \sigma' \rangle} \quad (c5)$$

$$\langle \textbf{if tt then } c_1 \textbf{ else } c_2, \sigma \rangle \rightarrow \langle c_1, \sigma \rangle \quad (c6)$$
$$\langle \textbf{if ff then } c_1 \textbf{ else } c_2, \sigma \rangle \rightarrow \langle c_2, \sigma \rangle \quad (c7)$$

$$\frac{\langle b, \sigma \rangle \rightarrow \langle b', \sigma \rangle}{\langle \textbf{if } b \textbf{ then } c_1 \textbf{ else } c_2, \sigma \rangle \rightarrow \langle \textbf{if } b' \textbf{ then } c_1 \textbf{ else } c_2, \sigma \rangle} \quad (c8)$$

$$\langle \textbf{while } b \textbf{ do } c, \sigma \rangle \rightarrow \langle \textbf{if } b \textbf{ then } c; \textbf{while } b \textbf{ do } c \textbf{ else skip}, \sigma \rangle \quad (c9)$$

Fig. 2.14 Semantics of commands

the computation of a subcommand (or of a subexpression) progress. The semantic description of our language is now complete.

Computations   A *computation* is a sequence of transitions which cannot be extended by another transition. Moreover, each transformation in a computation must be described by some rule.

Example 2.5 Let us consider the following program, c:

$$X := 1; \text{ while } \neg(X == 0) \text{ do } X := (X - 1)$$

Let us fix a state which includes all the variables mentioned in the program, for example, $\sigma = [(X, 6)]$. We can calculate the computation of c in σ as follows. To abbreviate the notation, we write c' to denote the iterative command **while** $\neg(\mathbf{X} ==$ **0) do** $X := (X - 1)$. It is not difficult to see that the computation generated by c is the following:

$$\langle c, \sigma \rangle$$
$$\rightarrow \langle c', \sigma[X \leftarrow 1] \rangle$$
$$\rightarrow \langle \text{if } \neg(X == 0) \text{ then } X := (X - 1); c' \text{ else skip}, \sigma[X \leftarrow 1] \rangle$$
$$\rightarrow \langle \text{if } \neg(1 == 0) \text{ then } X := (X - 1); c' \text{ else skip}, \sigma[X \leftarrow 1] \rangle$$
$$\rightarrow \langle \text{if } \neg\text{ff then } X := (X - 1); c' \text{ else skip}, \sigma[X \leftarrow 1] \rangle$$
$$\rightarrow \langle \text{if tt then } X := (X - 1); c' \text{ else skip}, \sigma[X \leftarrow 1] \rangle$$
$$\rightarrow \langle X := (X - 1); c', \sigma[X \leftarrow 1] \rangle$$
$$\rightarrow \langle X := (1 - 1); c', \sigma[X \leftarrow 1] \rangle$$
$$\rightarrow \langle X := 0; c', \sigma[X \leftarrow 1] \rangle$$
$$\rightarrow \langle c', \sigma[X \leftarrow 0] \rangle$$
$$\rightarrow \langle \text{if } \neg(X == 0) \text{ then } X := (X - 1); c' \text{ else skip}, \sigma[X \leftarrow 0] \rangle$$
$$\rightarrow \langle \text{if } \neg(0 == 0) \text{ then } X := (X - 1); c' \text{ else skip}, \sigma[X \leftarrow 0] \rangle$$
$$\rightarrow \langle \text{if } \neg\text{tt then } X := (X - 1); c' \text{ else skip}, \sigma[X \leftarrow 0] \rangle$$
$$\rightarrow \langle \text{if ff then } X := (X - 1); c' \text{ else skip}, \sigma[X \leftarrow 0] \rangle$$
$$\rightarrow \langle \text{skip}, \sigma[X \leftarrow 0] \rangle$$
$$\rightarrow \sigma[X \leftarrow 0]$$

The computation in the example just discussed is a *terminated* computation, in the sense that, after a certain number of transitions, a situation is reached in which no other transition is possible. It can be seen that, moreover, the definition of computation that we have given above does *not* require that a computation be finite but only that *it cannot be extended*. There is, therefore, the possibility that there are infinite computations, as the following example demonstrates:

Example 2.6 Consider the following program, d:

$$X := 1; \text{ while } (X == 1) \text{ do skip}$$

Assume we are in the state $\tau = [(X, 0)]$. Let d' be the command **while** $(X == 1)$ **do skip**. We have:

$$\langle d, \tau \rangle$$
$$\rightarrow \langle d', \tau[X \leftarrow 1] \rangle$$
$$\rightarrow \langle \text{if } (X == 1) \text{ then skip} ; d' \text{ else skip}, \tau[X \leftarrow 1] \rangle$$
$$\rightarrow \langle \text{if } (1 == 1) \text{ then skip} ; d' \text{ else skip}, \tau[X \leftarrow 1] \rangle$$

$$\rightarrow \langle \textbf{if tt then skip} ; d' \textbf{ else skip}, \tau[X \leftarrow 1] \rangle$$
$$\rightarrow \langle \textbf{ skip} ; d', \tau[X \leftarrow 1] \rangle$$
$$\rightarrow \langle d', \tau[X \leftarrow 1] \rangle$$
$$\rightarrow \ldots$$

There exist, therefore, two fundamentally different types of computations: *finite* ones (also called *terminating*) and *divergent* ones (that is, infinite ones which correspond, intuitively, to looping programs).

2.6 Pragmatics

If a precise description of the syntax and semantics of a programming language is (and must be) given, the same is not true of the pragmatics of the language. Let us recall that, for our purposes, the pragmatics of a language answers the question "what is the purpose of this construct?" or "what use is a certain command?" It is clear, therefore, that the pragmatics of a programming language is not established once and for all during its definition (that is, the definition of its syntax and semantics). On the contrary, it evolves with the use of the language. All suggestions about programming style are part of pragmatics. For example, there is the principle that jumps (gotos) should be avoided at all possible times. The choice of the most appropriate mode for passing parameters to a function is also a pragmatic question, as is the choice between bounded and unbounded iteration.

In a sense, the pragmatics of a programming language coincides with software engineering (the discipline which studies methods for the design and production of software) and is not much studied there. For many other aspects, on the other hand, clarifying the purpose and use of constructs is an essential part of the study of a programming language. It is for this that we will often refer below to pragmatics, possibly without making it explicit that we are so doing.

2.7 Implementation

The final level of programming language description will not be considered in this book in details. As we amply saw in the previous chapter, implementing a language means writing a compiler for it, as well as implementing an abstract machine for the compiler's object language; or to write an interpreter and implement the abstract machine in the language in which the interpreter is written. Alternatively, as happens in practice, a mix of both techniques is employed. Once more, this is not a book in which we can be exhaustive about these matters. But it would not be correct to present the constructions of programming languages without some reference to their implementation cost. Even without specifying the set of constructions in an interpreter, for each construct, we should always ask: "How is it to be implemented?", "At what cost?" The answer to these questions will also help us better to understand the linguistic aspect (because a certain construct is formed in a certain way), as well as the pragmatic one (how can a certain construct best be used).

2.8 Chapter Summary

The chapter introduced the fundamental techniques for the description and implementation of a programming language.

- The distinction between syntax, semantics, pragmatics and implementation. Each of these disciplines describes a crucial aspect of the language.
- Context-free grammars. A formal method essential for the definition of a language's syntax.
- Derivation trees and ambiguity. Derivation trees represent the logical structure of a string. The existence of a unique tree for every string permits a canonical interpretation to be assigned to it.
- Static semantics. Not all syntactic aspects of a language are describable using grammars: Static semantic checks are concerned with eliminating from legal programs those strings which, though correct as far as the grammar is concerned, do not respect additional contextual constraints.
- The organisation of a compiler.
- Structured operational semantics. A formal method for describing the semantics of programming languages based on transition systems.

2.9 Bibliographical Notes

The literature on the topics of this chapter is enormous, even considering only introductory material. We limit ourselves to citing [4], the latest edition of a classic text on formal languages used by generations of students. For compiler-construction methods, we refer the reader to [1] and [2]. An introduction to operational semantics is [5], which also deals with denotational semantics; at a more advanced level, see [8], which also deals with denotational semantics.

2.10 Exercises

1. Consider the grammar G'', obtained from that in Fig. 2.6 by substituting the productions for the non-terminal symbol T with the following:

$$T \rightarrow A \mid E * T.$$

   Show that G'' is ambiguous.
2. Give the obvious ambiguous grammar for the conditional command if, then, else.

3. Using the grammar fragment in Fig. 2.7 as a reference point, construct a derivation tree for the string

```
if (expression1) if (expression2) command1
    else command2
```

Assume that the following derivations exist:
Expression $\Rightarrow^*$ expression1,
Expression $\Rightarrow^*$ expression2,
StatementWithoutTrailingSubstatement $\Rightarrow^*$ command,
StatementWithoutTrailingSubstatement $\Rightarrow^*$ command.

4. Define a grammar that will generate all the pairs of balanced curly brackets (braces).
5. Define a grammar that generates the language $\{a^n b^m \mid n, m \geq 1\}$ using only productions of the form $N \rightarrow tM$ or $N \rightarrow t$, where N and M are any non-terminal symbol and t is any terminal symbol. Try to give an intuitive explanation of why there exists no grammar with these characteristics which generates the language $\{a^n b^n \mid n \geq 1\}$.
6. Modify the rule of Fig. 2.12 so as to describe a right-to-left evaluation of arithmetic expressions.
7. Calculate the computation of the command

$$X := 1; \ \textbf{while} \ \neg(X == 3) \ \textbf{do} \ X := (X + 1)$$

starting with a chosen state.
8. In Example 2.5, the last transition has as its right member only a state (and not a pair composed of a command and a state). Is this always the case in a finite computation? (Hint: consider the command $X := 0; X := (X - 1)$, starting with any state whatsoever which includes X.)
9. State what the computation corresponding to the following command is:

$$X := 1; \quad X := (X - 1); \quad X := (X - 1); \quad X := 5$$

10. Considering Exercises 8 and 9, state a criterion which allows the division of finite computations into those which are correct and those which terminate because of an error.

References

1. A. V. Aho, R. Sethi, and J. D. Ullman. *Compilers: Principles, Techniques, and Tools*. Addison-Wesley, Reading, 1988.
2. A. W. Appel. *Modern Compiler Implementation in Java*. Cambridge University Press, Cambridge, 1998.
3. J. Gosling, B. Joy, G. Steele, and G. Bracha. *The Java Language Specification, 3/E*. Addison Wesley, Reading, 2005. Available online at http://java.sun.com/docs/books/jls/index.html.

4. J. E. Hopcroft, R. Motwani, and J. Ullman. *Introduction to Automata Theory, Languages, and Computation*. Addison-Wesley, Reading, 2001.
5. C. Laneve. *La Descrizione Operazionale dei Linguaggi di Programmazione*. Franco Angeli, Milano, 1998 (in Italian).
6. C. W. Morris. Foundations of the theory of signs. In *Writings on the Theory of Signs*, pages 17–74. Mouton, The Hague, 1938.
7. G. D. Plotkin. A structural approach to operational semantics. Technical Report DAIMI FN-19, University of Aarhus, 1981.
8. G. Winskel. *The Formal Semantics of Programming Languages*. MIT Press, Cambridge, 1993.

Chapter 3
Foundations

In this chapter, we will not be concerned with programming languages but with the limits of the programs that we can write, asking whether there exist problems that no program can solve. A motivation for this research is the question that we asked at the end of Sect. 2.3: that is, is it possible to construct a static semantic analyser which can verify constraints imposed by the programming language's definition? We will soon discover, however, that the answer to the question is rather more general and is, in reality, a kind of absolute limit to what can (and cannot) be done with a computer. Although the material in this chapter can appear abstract, our treatment is wholly elementary.

3.1 The Halting Problem

In Sect. 2.3, we asked if there exists a static semantic analyser able to determine whether a program can generate a division by zero error during execution. Instead of tackling this problem, we will examine a larger problem, one that is also more interesting. We will ask whether there exists a static analyser able to discover whether a program, when provided with certain input data, will loop. There is no need to emphasise the usefulness of a check of this kind. If we know, prior to execution, that a given program will loop when presented with some input data, we will have a way of showing automatically that it definitely contains an error.

A static analyser is nothing more than a program used as a subprogram of a compiler. Let us, therefore, fix a programming language, $\mathscr{L}$, in which we will write programs. Given a program, P, and an input x, we write $P(x)$ to denote the result of the computing P on x. We should note that, in general, the program P might not terminate on x because of a loop or of an infinite recursion. Writing $P(x)$, therefore, we do not necessarily indicate a computation that terminates. Without loss of generality, we can now reformulate the question as:

Does there exist a program, H, that, having been given as input a program P (in the language $\mathscr{L}$) and its input data x, will terminate and print "yes" if $P(x)$ terminates, and terminate and print "no" if $P(x)$ loops?

M. Gabbrielli, S. Martini, *Programming Languages: Principles and Paradigms*,
Undergraduate Topics in Computer Science,
DOI 10.1007/978-1-84882-914-5_3, © Springer-Verlag London Limited 2010

We emphasise that H has two inputs. It must always terminate (we do not want a compiler that loops!) and it must function on every program, P, written in $\mathscr{L}$ and every input x. We can then assume, again without loss of generality, that H is written in the language $\mathscr{L}$, since $\mathscr{L}$, to be interesting, must be in a language in which it is possible to write all possible programs.[1]

We now show our hand. We want to show that there exists no program H with the behaviour we have just discussed. We will argue by contradiction, assuming we can have such an H, and from this we will derive a contradiction. The reasoning might seem a little contorted at first sight but requires no advanced knowledge. The argument, however, is subtle and elegant; the reader should read it more than once and be sure of understanding the critical role of self application.

1. Let us assume, by contradiction, that we have a program H with the properties stated above.
2. Using H, we can write a program K, with only one input (which will be another program), with the following specification:

   The program K, given P as input, terminates printing "yes" if $H(P, P)$ prints "no"; it goes into a loop if $H(P, P)$ prints "yes".

   Writing the program K, given that H is available, is simple. We read the input P, call H as a subprogram, passing P as first and second parameter. We wait until H terminates (this will certainly happen, given H's specification). If $H(P, P)$ terminates and prints "no" (we can assume that we can intercept this printing and stop it from appearing on the output), K prints "yes". If, on the other hand, $H(P, P)$ prints "yes", then K goes into an infinite loop programmed for the purpose.

   If we recall the specification of H, we can summarise the semantics of K as:

$$K(P) = \begin{cases} \text{"yes"} & \text{if } P(P) \text{ does not terminate,} \\ \text{does not terminate} & \text{if } P(P) \text{ does terminate.} \end{cases} \quad (3.1)$$

   At first sight the application of P to itself seems strange. There is no miracle. P will receive an input consisting of a string representing the text of P.[2]
3. Let us now execute K on its own text. That is, we focus on $K(K)$. What is its behaviour? If we substitute K for P in (3.1), we obtain:

$$K(P) = \begin{cases} \text{"yes"} & \text{if } K(K) \text{ does not terminate,} \\ \text{does not terminate} & \text{if } K(K) \text{ does terminate.} \end{cases} \quad (3.2)$$

4. Now let us observe that (3.2) is absurd! It says that $K(K)$ terminates (printing "yes") when $K(K)$ fails to terminate and that it does not terminate when $K(K)$ terminates.

---

[1] Clarifying the sense of "all possible programs" is actually one of the aims of this chapter.

[2] If we had assumed that the input to P was a number, the string comprising the text of P can read as a number: a number i, whose bits denote the individual characters in the text of P.

5. Where does this contradiction come from? Not from K itself, which, as we have seen, is a simple program which uses H. The contradiction arises from having to assume the existence of a program with the properties of H. Therefore, H cannot exist.

We have therefore proved that there exists no *decision procedure* (in the language $\mathscr{L}$) capable of determining whether any another program in $\mathscr{L}$ terminates on an arbitrary input. We use here decision procedure in the technical sense of a program that: (i) works for arbitrary arguments; (ii) always terminates and (iii) determines (by responding "yes" or "no") those arguments which are solutions to the problem and those which are not.

This result, one of fundamental importance in computing, is called the *undecidability of the halting problem*. Many other interesting problems are undecidable in the same way. We will discuss some in the next section after first having discussed the characteristics of $\mathscr{L}$ from which the result derives. We can thus tackle the problem of the expressive power of programming languages.

3.2 Expressiveness of Programming Languages

At first sight, the result we obtained in the last section can appear fairly limited. If we take a language different from $\mathscr{L}$, perhaps the program H can exist without generating a contradiction.

Upon reflection, though, we have not assumed much about $\mathscr{L}$. We have used $\mathscr{L}$ in an implicit way to define the program K, given H (that is, at Step 2 of the proof). To be able truly to write K, the following conditions must be satisfied:

1. There must be some form of conditional available in $\mathscr{L}$, so that the cases in the definition of K can be distinguished;
2. It must be possible to define functions which do not terminate in $\mathscr{L}$ (we must therefore have at our disposal some form of iteration or recursion).

At this level of detail, $\mathscr{L}$ is nothing special. What programming language does not provide these constructs? If a language provides these constructs, it can be used in place of $\mathscr{L}$ in the proof, showing that a program like H exists in *no* programming language worth its salt.

The undecidability of the halting problem is not, therefore, a contingent fact, related to any particular programming language, nor is it the expression of our inability as programmers. On the contrary, it is a limitation that is in some way absolute, indissolubly linked to the intuitive concepts of program (algorithm) and with that of programming language. It is a principle of nature, similar to the conservation of energy or to the principles of thermodynamics. In nature, there exist more problems and functions than there are programs that we can write. There are problems to which there correspond no program that is anything but insignificant; the halting problem is definitely one of them.

Rather, as argued in Sect. 3.3, the problems for which there exists a program for their solution constitute only a tiny part of the set of all possible problems.

As with the halting problem, when we say that some problem is undecidable, we mean that there exists no program such that: (i) it accepts arbitrary arguments; (ii) it always terminates and (iii) it determines which arguments are solutions to the problem and which are not. We will stray too far if we begin a proof of the undecidability of any other important problems; the interested reader can consult any good text on the theory of computability for them. We can however list some undecidable problems without attempting to explain all the terms used or to undertake any proofs.

The following problems are undecidable:

- Determine whether a program computes a constant function;
- Determine whether two programs compute the same function;
- Determine whether a program terminates for every input;
- Determine whether a program diverges for every input;
- Determine whether a program, given an input, will produce an error during its execution;
- Determine whether a program will cause a type error (see the box on page 204).

Undecidability results tell us that they do not exist general software tools which will automatically establish significant properties of programs.

3.3 Formalisms for Computability

To make the discussion of $\mathcal{L}$ more precise, we need to fix a programming language and show that the reasoning of the previous section applies to it. Historically, the first language in which the impossibility of writing program H was shown was the language of the Turing Machine. The Turing Machine language is a notation which is, at first sight, highly rudimentary. It was introduced in the 1930s by the mathematician Alan M. Turing. It is summarised in the *Turing Machines* box. It is at first sight surprising that such a rudimentary formalism (there is no predefined arithmetic; everything turns on the positioning of a finite number of symbols on a tape) could be good enough to express computations as sophisticated as those needed to write K on the basis of H. More surprising is the fact that there exists a Turing Machine which can act as an interpreter for others; that is a machine which, once an input has been written on its own tape, as well as the (appropriately coded) description of a generic machine and an input for it, executes the computation which that machine would perform on that input. This interpreter is, to all intents and purposes, a (very simple) computer like those that we know today (program and data in memory, fundamental cycle which interprets program instructions).

A function is *computable in a language* $\mathcal{L}$ if there exists a program in $\mathcal{L}$ which computes it. More precisely, the (partial—see the box on page 12) function $f : A \to B$ is computable if there exists a program P with the following properties: for each element $a \in A$, whenever P is executed on an input a, which we write $P(a)$, it terminates providing as an output $f(a)$ if $f(a)$ is defined; the computation $P(a)$ does not terminate if f is undefined at a.

Turing Machines

A Turing machine is composed of an infinite tape, divided into cells, each of which stores a single symbol from a finite alphabet. A mobile head reads from and writes to the tape. At any time, the head is positioned over a single cell. The machine is controlled by a finite-state controller. At each step in the computation, the machine reads a symbol from the tape and, according to the state of the machine and symbol that it has read, the controller decides which symbol to substitute for it on the tape and if the head is to move to the left or to the right; the controller therefore enters another state (remember, there is a finite number of states). The controller of a Turing machine can be seen as its associated program.

We might expect there to be fewer functions computed by a Turing Machine than those which can be computed by a sophisticated, modern programming language. In investigating this question, there have been many suggestions since the 1930s formalisms for expressing algorithms (programs), amongst which there are the General Recursive Functions of Church-Gödel and Kleene (which make no reference to programming languages), the Lambda Calculus (which we will examine in Chap. 11), and then all current programming languages. Indeed, all these formalisms and languages can be simulated by each other. That is, it is possible in each of these formalisms to write an interpreter for any of the others. From this, it follows that they are all equivalent in terms of the functions that they compute. They all compute exactly the same functions as the Turing Machine. In principle, therefore, every algorithm is expressible in any programming language. This is frequently expressed by saying that *all programming languages are Turing complete* (or *Turing equivalent*). The undecidability results can also be expressed by saying that there exist functions which cannot be computed (with a Turing Machine, or, by the above, in any programming language).

If all languages are equivalent with respect to the functions they compute, it is clear that they are not equivalent as far as their flexibility of use, pragmatics, abstraction principles and so on, are concerned. And often this complex of properties is referred to as the *expressiveness* of a language.

While all these computability formalisms provide a definite result about equivalence in terms of the functions that can be expressed, these same formalisms are useless when discussing the expressiveness of languages. In fact, even now, there is no agreement on how formally to tackle these aspects.

3.4 There are More Functions than Algorithms

In Sect. 3.1, we gave a specific example of a uncomputable function. We can give another proof that there exist functions which cannot be computed using a simple cardinality argument (though, unlike in Sect. 3.1, we will not produce a specific example). That is, we show that, in nature, there are more functions than algorithms.

First of all, let us consider any formal system which allows us to express algorithms and which, for simplicity we can assume to be a programming language, $\mathscr{L}$, (this could, however, be generalised to a wider definition). It is easy enough to see that the set of all possible (finite) programs that can be written in $\mathscr{L}$ is *denumerable*, that is, they can be put into one-one correspondence with the natural numbers (which we denote by $\mathbb{N}$). We can, in fact, first consider the set P_1 containing all programs of length one (which contain a single character), then the set P_2 containing all programs of length two, and so on. Every set, P_i, is finite and can be ordered, for example lexicographically (first all programs which begin with a, then all those which begin with b, and so on by succeeding characters). It is clear that by doing this, by taking into account the ordering produced by the subscript in the sets $P_1, P_2, \ldots$, and then doing the same with the internal indices in each set, we can count (or enumerate) all possible programs and therefore put them into one-one correspondence with the natural numbers. In more formal terms, when this has been done, we can say that the cardinality of the set of all programs writable in $\mathscr{L}$ is equal to the cardinality of the naturals. Let us now consider the set $\mathscr{F}$ containing all the functions $\mathbb{N} \to \{0, 1\}$. An important theorem of Cantor states that this set is not denumerable but has a cardinality which is strictly greater than that of $\mathbb{N}$. Given that every program expresses a unique function, the set $\mathbb{N}$ is too small to contain all the functions in $\mathscr{F}$ as programs in $\mathscr{L}$.

Let us see a direct proof of the fact that $\mathscr{F}$ is not denumerable. Let us assume that $\mathscr{F}$ is denumerable, that is it is possible to write $\mathscr{F} = \{f_j\}_{j \in \mathbb{N}}$. Let us observe, first of all, that we can put $\mathscr{F}$ into one-one correspondence with the set $\mathscr{B}$ of all the infinite sequences of binary numbers. To each $f_j \in \mathscr{F}$, there corresponds the sequence $b_{j,1}, b_{j,2}, b_{j,3}, \ldots$, where $b_{j,i} = f_j(i)$, for $i, j \in \mathbb{N}$. Therefore if $\mathscr{F}$ is denumerable, so too is the set $\mathscr{B}$. Since $\mathscr{B}$ is denumerable, we can enumerate its elements one after the other, listing, for each element (for every sequence), the binary digits which comprise it. We can arrange such an enumeration in an infinite square matrix:

$$b_{1,1}, \quad b_{1,2}, \quad b_{1,3}, \quad \ldots$$
$$b_{2,1}, \quad b_{2,2}, \quad b_{2,3}, \quad \ldots$$
$$b_{3,1}, \quad b_{3,2}, \quad b_{3,3}, \quad \ldots$$
$$\vdots$$

where row j contains the sequence for the jth function. Writing $\bar{b}$ for the complement of the binary number b, let us now consider the sequence of binary numbers $\bar{b}_{1,1}, \bar{b}_{2,2}, \bar{b}_{3,3}, \ldots$. This sequence (since it is an infinite sequence of binary numbers) is certainly an element of $\mathscr{B}$, however it does *not* appear in our matrix (and therefore does not appear in our enumeration) for the reason that each line is different at *at least one* point. Along the diagonal, the sequence found in the matrix has elements $b_{j,j}$, while, by construction, the new sequence has the element $\bar{b}_{j,j}$ in position j.

We have therefore a contradiction: we had assumed that $\mathscr{F} = \{f_j\}_{j \in \mathbb{N}}$ was an enumeration of *all* functions (that is, of all sequences), while we have constructed

Church's Thesis

The proofs of equivalence of the various programming languages (and between the various computability formalisms) are genuine theorems. Given the languages $\mathcal{L}$ and $\mathcal{L}'$, write first in $\mathcal{L}$ the interpreter for $\mathcal{L}'$ and then write in $\mathcal{L}'$ the interpreter for $\mathcal{L}$. At this point $\mathcal{L}$ and $\mathcal{L}'$ are known to be equivalent. A proof of this type has been effectively given for all existing languages, so they are therefore provably equivalent. This argument would, in reality, leave open the door to the possibility that sooner or later someone will be in a position to find an *intuitively computable* function which is not associated with a program in any existing programming language. All equivalence results proved over more than the last 70 years, however, amount to convincing evidence that this is impossible. In the mid-1930s, Alonzo Church proposed a principle (which since then has become known as Church's, or the Church-Turing, Thesis) that states exactly this impossibility. We can formulate Church's Thesis as: every intuitively computable function is computed by a Turing Machine.

In contrast to the equivalence results, Church's Thesis is not a theorem because it refers to a concept (that of intuitive computability) which is not amenable to formal reasoning. It is, rather, a philosophical principle which the computer science community assumes with considerable strength to be true so that it will not even be discredited by new computational paradigms, for example quantum computing.

---

a function (a sequence) which did not belong to the enumeration. Therefore the cardinality of $\mathcal{F}$ is strictly greater than that of $\mathbb{N}$.

It can be shown that $\mathcal{F}$ has the cardinality of the real numbers. This fact indicates that the set of programs (which is denumerable) is much smaller than that of all possible functions, and therefore of all possible problems.

3.5 Chapter Summary

The phenomenon of computation on which Computer Science is founded has its roots in the theory of computability which studies the formalisms in which one can express algorithms and their limits. The chapter has only presented the main result of this theory. This is a fact of the greatest importance, one that every computer scientist should know. The principal concepts which were introduced are:

- *Undecidability*: there exist many important properties of programs which cannot be determined in a mechanical fashion by an algorithm; amongst these is the halting problem.
- *Computability*: a function is computable when there exists a program which computes it. The undecidability of the halting problem assures us that there exist functions which are not computable.

- *Partiality*: the functions expressed by a program can be undefined on some arguments, corresponding to those data for which the program will fail to terminate.
- *Turing Completeness*: every general-purpose programming language computes the same set of functions as those computed by a Turing Machine.

3.6 Bibliographical Notes

The original undecidability result is in the paper by A.M. Turing [3] which ought to be necessary reading for every computer scientist with an interest in theory. More can be found on the arguments of this chapter in any good textbook on computability theory, among which, let us recommend [1], which we cited in Chap. 2, and the classic [2] which after more than 40 years continues to be one of the most authoritative references.

3.7 Exercises

1. Proof that the restricted halting problem is undecidable. That is, determine whether a program terminates when it is applied to itself. (Suggestion: if the problem were decidable, the program which decides it would have to have the same property as program K, which can be derived by contradiction in the usual fashion.)
2. Show that the problem of verifying whether a program computes a constant function is undecidable. Hint: given a generic program P, consider the program Q_P, with a single input, specified as follows:

$$Q_P(y) = \begin{cases} 1 & \text{if } P(P) \text{ terminates,} \\ \text{does not terminate} & \text{otherwise.} \end{cases}$$

   (i) Write the program Q_P;
   (ii) assume now that P is a program such that $P(P)$ terminates. What is the behaviour of Q_P, as y varies?
   (iii) what is, on other hand, the behaviour of Q_P, as y varies, if $P(P)$ does not terminate?
   (iv) from (ii) and (iii), it can be obtained that Q_P computes the constant function *one* if and only if $P(P)$ terminates;
   (v) if it were now decidable whether a program computes a constant function, the restricted halting problem would also be decidable, given that the transformation that, given P, constructs Q_P is completely general.

References

1. J. E. Hopcroft, R. Motwani, and J. Ullman. *Introduction to Automata Theory, Languages, and Computation*. Addison-Wesley, Reading, 2001.
2. H. Rogers. *Theory of Recursive Functions and Effective Computability*. McGraw Hill, New York, 1967.
3. A. Turing. On computable numbers, with an application to the Entscheidungsproblem. *Proc. Lond. Math. Soc.*, 42:230–365, 1936. *A Correction*, ibidem, 43 (1937), 544–546.

Chapter 4
Names and The Environment

The evolution of programming languages can be seen in large measure as a process which has led, by means of appropriate abstraction mechanisms, to the definition of formalisms that are increasingly distant from the physical machine. In this context, *names* play a fundamental role. A name, indeed, is nothing more than a (possibly meaningful) sequence of characters used to represent some other thing. They allow the abstraction either of aspects of data, for example using a name to denote a location in memory, or aspects of control, for example representing a set of commands with a name. The correct handling of names requires precise semantic rules as well as adequate implementation mechanisms.

In this chapter, we will analyse these rules. We will, in particular, look at the concept of *environment* and the constructs used to organise it. We will also look at visibility (or *scope*) rules. We leave until the next chapter treatment of the implementation of these concepts. Let us immediately observe how, in languages with procedures, in order to define precisely the concept of environment one needs other concepts, related to parameter passing. We will see these concepts in Chap. 7. In the case of object-oriented languages, finally, there are other specific visibility rules which we will consider in Chap. 10.

4.1 Names and Denotable Objects

When we declare a new variable in a program:

```
int fie;
```

or we define a new function:

```
int foo( ){
    fie = 1;
}
```

M. Gabbrielli, S. Martini, *Programming Languages: Principles and Paradigms*,
Undergraduate Topics in Computer Science,
DOI 10.1007/978-1-84882-914-5_4, © Springer-Verlag London Limited 2010

we introduce new names, such as fie and foo to represent an object (a variable and a function in our example). The character sequence fie can be used every time that we want to refer to the new variable, just as the character sequence foo allows us to call the function that assigns to fie the value 1.

A name is therefore nothing more than a sequence of characters used to represent, or denote, another object.[1]

In most languages, names are formed of identifiers, that is by alphanumeric tokens, moreover other symbols can also be names. For example, + and − are names which denote, in general, primitive operations.

Even though it might seems obvious, it is important to emphasise that a name and the object it denotes are *not* the same thing. A name, indeed, is just a character string, while its denotation can be a complex objects such as a variable, a function, a type, and so on. And in fact, a single object can have more than one name (in this case, one speaks of *aliasing*), while a single name can denote different objects at different times. When, therefore, we use, as we may, the phrase "the variable fie" or the phrase "the function foo", it should be remembered that the phrases are abbreviations for "the variable with the name fie" and "the function with the name foo". More generally, in programming practice, when a name is used, it is almost always meant to refer to the object that it denotes.

The use of names implements a first, elementary, *data abstraction* mechanism. For example, when, in an imperative language, we define a name using a variable, we are introducing a symbolic identifier for a memory location; therefore we are abstracting from the low-level details of memory addresses. If, then, we use the assignment command:

```
fie = 2;
```

the value 2 will be stored in the location reserved for the variable named fie. At the programming level, the use of the name avoids the need to bother with whatever this location is. The correspondence between name and memory location must be guaranteed by the implementation. We will use the term *environment* to refer to that part of the implementation responsible for the associations between names and the objects that they denote. We will see better in Sect. 6.2.1 what exactly constitutes a variable and how it can be associated with values.

Names are fundamental even for implementing a form of *control abstraction*. A procedure[2] is nothing more than a name associated with a set of commands, together with certain visibility rules which make available to the programmer its sole interface (which is composed of the procedure's name and possibly some parameters). We will see the specifics of control abstraction in Chap. 7.

---

[1] Here and in the rest of this chapter, "object" is intended in a wide sense, with no reference to technical terms used in the area of object-oriented languages.

[2] Here and elsewhere, we will use the generic term "procedure" for procedures as well as functions, methods and subprograms. See also Sect. 7.1.

4.1.1 Denotable Objects

The objects to which a name can be given are called *denotable objects*. Even if there are considerable differences between programming languages, the following is a non-exhaustive list of possible denotable objects:

- Objects whose names are defined by the user: variables, formal parameters, procedures (in the broad sense), user-defined types, labels, modules, user-defined constants, exceptions.
- Objects whose names are defined by the programming language: primitive types, primitive operations, predefined constants.

The association (or *binding*) between a name and an object it denotes can therefore be created at various times. Some names are associated with objects during the design of a language, while other associations are introduced only when a program is executed. Considering the entire process ranging from a programming language's definition to the execution of a specific program, we can identify the following phases for the creation of bindings of names to objects:

Design of language In this phase, bindings between primitive constants, types and operations of the language are defined (for example, + indicates addition, and int denotes the type of integers, etc.).

Program writing Given that the programmer chooses names when they write a program, we can consider this phase as one with the partial definition of some bindings, later to be completed. The binding of an identifier to a variable, for example, is defined in the program but is effectively created only when the space for the variable is allocated in memory.

Compile time The compiler, translating the constructs of the high-level language into machine code, allocates memory space for some of the data structures that can be statically processed. For example, this is the case for the global variables of a program. The connection between a variable's identifier and the corresponding memory location is formed at this time.

Runtime This term denotes the entire period of time between starting and termination of a program. All the associations that have not previously been created must be formed at runtime. This is the case, for example, for bindings of variable identifiers to memory locations for the local variables in a recursive procedure, or for pointer variables whose memory is allocated dynamically.

In the previous description we have ignored other important phases, such as linking and loading in which other bindings (for example for external names referring to objects in other modules). In practice, however, two principle phases are distinguished using the terms "static" and "dynamic". The term "static" is used to refer to everything that happens prior to execution, while "dynamic" refers to everything that happens during execution. Thus, for example, static memory management is performed by the compiler, while dynamic management is performed by appropriate operations executed by the abstract machine at runtime.

Fig. 4.1 A name denoting
different objects

```
{int fie;
 fie = 2;
   {char fie;
    fie = a;
   }
}
```

4.2 Environments and Blocks

Not all associations between names and denotable objects are fixed once and for all at the start of program execution. Many can vary during execution. To be able to understand how these associations behave, we need to introduce the concept of environment.

Definition 4.1 (Environment) The set of associations between names and denotable objects which exist at runtime at a specific point in the program and at a specific time during execution, is called the (*referencing*) *environment*.

Usually, when we speak of environments, we refer only to associations that are not established by the language definition. The environment is therefore that component of the abstract machine which, for every name introduced by the programmer and at every point in the program, allows the determination of what the correct association is. Note that the environment does not exist at the level of the physical machine. The presence of the environment constitutes one of the principle characteristics of high-level languages which must be simulated in a suitable fashion by each implementation of the language.

A *declaration* is a construct that allows the introduction of an association in the environment. High-level languages often have explicit declarations, such as:

```
int x;
int f (){
   return 0;
}
type T = int;
```

(the first is a declaration of a variable, the second of a function named f, the third is declaration of a new type, T, which coincides with type int). Some languages allow implicit declarations which introduce an association in the environment for a name when it is first used. The denoted object's type is deduced from the context in which the name is used for the first time (or sometimes from the syntactic form of the name).

As we will see in detail below, there are various degrees of freedom in associations between names and denotable objects. First of all, a single name can denote different objects in different parts of the program. Consider, for example, the code of Fig. 4.1. The outermost name fie denotes an integer variable, while the inner one is of type character.

It is also possible that a single object is denoted by more than one name in different environments. For example, if we pass a variable by reference to a procedure, the variable is accessible using its name in the calling program and by means of the name of the formal parameter in the body of the procedure (see Sect. 7.1.2). Alternatively, we can use pointers to create data structures in which the same object is then accessible using different names.

While different names for the same object are used in different environments, no particular problems arise. The situation is more complicated when a single object is visible using different names in the same environment. This is called *aliasing* and the different names for the same object called *aliases*. If the name of a variable passed by reference to a procedure is also visible inside the same procedure, we have a situation of aliasing. Other aliasing situations can easily occur using pointers. If X and Y are variables of pointer type, the assignment X = Y allows us to access the same location using both X and Y.

Let us consider, for example, the following fragment of C program where, as we will do in the future, we assume that write(Z) is a procedure which allows us to print the value of the integer variable Z:

```
int *X, *Y;          // X,Y pointers to integers
X = (int *) malloc (sizeof (int));
                     // allocate heap memory
*X = 5;              // * dereference
Y=X;                 // Y points to the same object as X
*Y=10;
write(*X);
```

The names X and Y denote two different variables, which, however, after the execution of the assignment command X = Y, allow to access the same memory location (therefore, the next print command will output the value 10).

It is, finally, possible that a single name, in a single textual region of the program, can denote different objects according to the execution flow of the program. The situation is more common than it might seem at first sight. It is the case, for example, for a recursive procedure declaring a local name. Other cases of this type, which are more subtle, will be discussed below in this chapter when will discuss dynamic scope (Sect. 4.3.2).

4.2.1 Blocks

Almost all important programming languages today permit the use of blocks, a structuring method for programs introduced by ALGOL60. Block structuring is fundamental to the organisation of the environment.

Definition 4.2 (Block) A block is a textual region of the program, identified by a start sign and an end sign, which can contain declarations local to that region (that is, which appear within the region).

The start- and end-block constructs vary according to the programming language: begin ... end for languages in the ALGOL family, braces { ... } for C and Java, round brackets (...) for LISP and its dialects, let ... in ... end in ML, etc. Moreover, the exact definition of block in the specific programming language can differ slightly from the one given above. In some cases, for example, one talks about block only when there are local declarations. Often, though, blocks have another important function, that of grouping a series of commands into a syntactic entity which can be considered as a single (composite) command. These distinctions, however, are not relevant as far as we are concerned. We will, therefore, use the definition given above and we distinguish two cases:

Block associated with a procedure This is a block associated with declarations local to a procedure. It corresponds textually to the body of the procedure itself, extended with the declarations of formal parameters.

In-line block This is a block which does not correspond to a declaration of procedure and which can appear (in general) in any position where a command can appear.

4.2.2 Types of Environment

The environment changes during the execution of a program. However, the changes occur generally at two precise times: on the entry and exit of a block. The block can therefore be considered as the construct of least granularity to which a constant environment can be associated.[3]

A block's environment, meaning by this terminology the environment existing when the block is executed, is initially composed of associations between names declared locally to the block itself. In most languages allowing blocks, blocks can be *nested*; that is, the definition of one block can be wholly included in that of another. An example of nested anonymous blocks is shown in Fig. 4.1. The overlapping of blocks so the last open block is not the first block to be closed is never permitted. In other words a sequence of commands of the following kind is not permitted in any language:

```
open block A;
    open block B;
close block A;
    close block B;
```

Different languages vary, then, in the type of nesting they permit. In C, for example, blocks associated with procedures cannot be nested inside each other (that is, there cannot be procedure declarations inside other procedures), while in Pascal and Ada this restriction is not present.[4]

---

[3]Declarations in the block are evaluated when the block is entered and are visible throughout the block. There exist many exceptions to this rule, some of which will be discussed below.

[4]The reasons for this restriction in C will be made clear in the next chapter when we will have discussed techniques for implementing scope rules.

Block nesting is an important mechanism for structuring the environment. There are mechanisms that allow the declarations local to a block to be visible in blocks nested inside it.

Remaining informal for the time being, we say that a declaration local to a block is *visible* in another block when the association created by such a declaration is present in the second block. Those mechanisms of the language which regulate how and when the declaration is visible are called *visibility rules*. The canonical visibility rule for languages with blocks is well known:

> A declaration local to a block is visible in that block and in all blocks listed within it, unless there is a new declaration of the same name in that same block. In this case, in the block which contains the redefinition the new declaration *hides* the previous one.

In the case in which there is a redefinition, the visibility rule establishes that only the last name declared will be visible in the internal block, while in the exterior one there is a visibility hole. The association for the name declared in the external block will be, in fact, deactivated for the whole of the interior block (containing the new declaration) and will be reactivated on exit from the inner block. Note that there is no visibility from the outside inwards. Every association introduced in the environment local to a block is not active (or rather the name that it defines is not visible) in an exterior block which contains the interior one. Analogously, if we have two blocks at the same nesting level, or if neither of the two contains the other, a name introduced locally in one block is not visible in the other.

The definition just given, although apparently precise, is insufficiently so to establish with precision what the environment will be at an arbitrary point in a program. We will assume this rule for the rest of this section, while the next will be concerned with stating the visibility rules correctly.

In general we can identify three components of an environment, as stated in the following definition.

Definition 4.3 (Type of environment) The environment associated with a block is formed of the following components:

Local environment This is composed of the set of associations for names declared locally to the block. In the case in which the block is for a procedure, the local environment contains also the associations for the formal parameters, given that they can be seen, as far as the environment is concerned, as locally declared variables.

Non-local environment This is the environment formed from the associations for names which are visible from inside a block but which have not been declared locally.

Global environment Finally, there is the environment formed from associations created when the program's execution began. It contains the associations for names which can be used in all blocks forming the program.

The environment local to a block can be determined by considering only the declarations present in the block. We must look outside the block to define the non-local environment. The global environment is part of the non-local environment. Names

Fig. 4.2 Nested blocks with
different environments

```
A:{int a =1;

  B:{int b = 2;
     int c = 2;

     C:{int c =3;
        int d;
        d = a+b+c;
        write(d)
     }

     D:{int e;
        e = a+b+c;
        write(e)
     }
  }
}
```

introduced in the local environment can be themselves present in the non-local environment. In such cases, the innermost (local) declaration hides the outermost one.

The visibility rules specify how names declared in external blocks are visible in internal ones. In some cases, it is possible to import names from other, separately defined modules. The associations for these names are part of the global environment.

We will now consider the example in Fig. 4.2, where, for ease of reference, we assume that the blocks can be labelled (as before, we assume also that write(x) allows us to print an integer value). The labels behave as comments as far as the execution is concerned.

Let us assume that block A is the outermost. It corresponds to the main program. The declaration of the variable a introduces an association in the global environment.

Inside block B two variables are declared locally (b and c). The environment for B is therefore formed of the local environment, containing the association for the two names (b and c) and from the global environment containing the association for a.

Inside block C, 2 local variables (c and d) are declared. The environment of C is therefore formed from the local environment, which contains the association for the two names (c and d) and from the non-local environment containing the same global environment as above, and also the association for the name b which is inherited from the environment of block B. Note that the local declaration of c in block C hides the declaration of c present in block B. The print command present in block C will therefore print the value 6.

In block D, finally, we have a local environment containing the association for the local name e, the usual global environment and the non-local environment, which, in addition to the association for a contains the association for the names b and c introduced in block B. Given that variable c has not been internally re-declared, in this case, therefore, the variable declared in block B remains visible and the value printed will be 5. Note that the association for the name d does not appear in the environment non-local to D, given that this name is introduced in an exterior block which does not contain D. The visibility rules, indeed, allows only the inheritance of names declared in exterior blocks from interior ones and not vice versa.

4.2.3 Operations on Environments

As we have seen, changes in the environment are produced at entry to and exit from a block. In more detail, during the execution of the program, when a new block is entered, the following modifications are made to the environment:

1. Associations between locally declared names and the corresponding denotable objects are created.
2. Associations with names declared external to and redefined inside the block are deactivated.

Also when the block is exited, the environment is modified as follows:

1. The associations for names declared locally to the block and the objects they denote are destroyed .
2. The associations are reactivated between names that existed external to the block and which were redefined inside it.

More generally, we can identify the following operations on names and on the environment:

Creation of associations between names and denoted object (naming) This is the elaboration of a declaration (or the connection of a formal to an actual parameter) when a new block containing local or parameter declarations is entered.

Reference to a denoted object via its name This is the use of the name (in an expression, in a command, or in any other context). The name is used to access the denoted object.

Deactivation of association between name and denoted object This happens when entering a block in which a new association for that name is created locally. The old association is not destroyed but remains (inactive) in the environment. It will be usable again when the block containing the new association is left.

Reactivation of an association between name and denoted object When leaving block in which a new association for that name is created locally, reactivation occurs. The previous association, which was deactivated on entry to the block, can now be used.

Destruction of an association between name and denoted object (unnaming)
This is performed on local associations when the block in which these associations were created is exited. The association is removed from environment and can no longer be used.

Let us explicitly note, however, that any environment contains both active and inactive associations (they correspond to declarations that have been hidden by the effects of the visibility rules). As far as denotable objects are concerned, the following operations are permitted:

Creation of a denotable object This operation is performed while allocating the storage necessary to contain the object. Sometimes, creation includes also the initialisation of the object.

Access to a denotable object Using the name, and hence the environment, we can access the denotable object and thus access its value (for example, to read the content of a variable). Let us observe that the set of rules which locate the environment has, as its aim, making the association between a name and the object which it refers one-to-one (at a given point in the program and during a given execution).

Modification of a denotable object It is always possible to access the denotable object via a name and then modify its value (for example, by assigning a value to a variable).

Destruction of a denotable object An object can be destroyed by reallocating the memory reserved for it.

In many languages, the operations of creating an association between the name and a denotable object and that of creating a denotable object take place at the same time. This is the case, for example, in a declaration of the form:

```
int x;
```

This declaration introduces into the environment a new association between the name x and an integer variable. At the same time, it allocates the memory for the variable.

Yet, this is not always the case and, in general, it is not stated that the *lifetime* of a denotable object, that is the time between the creation of the object and its destruction, coincides with the *lifetime* of the association between name and object. Indeed, a denotable object can have a lifetime that is greater than the association between a name and the object itself, as the case in which a variable is passed to a procedure by reference. The association between the formal parameter and associated variable has a lifetime less than that of the variable itself. More generally, a situation of this type occurs when a temporary name (for example, one local to a block) is introduced for an object which already has a name.

Note that the situation we are considering is *not* that shown in Fig. 4.2. In this case, indeed, the internal declaration of the variable, c, does not introduce a new name for an existing object, but introduces a new object (a new variable).

Even if, at first sight, this seems odd, it can also be the case that the lifetime of an association between name and a denoted object is greater than that of the object itself. More precisely, it can be the case that a name allows access to an object which no longer exists. Such an anomalous situation can occur, for example, if we call by reference an existing object and then deallocate the memory for it before the procedure terminates. The formal parameter to the procedure, in this case, will denote an object which no longer exists. A situation of this type, in which it is possible to access an object whose memory has been reallocated, is called a *dangling reference* and is a symptom of an error. We will return to the problem dangling references in Chap. 8, where we will present some methods to handle them.

4.3 Scope Rules

We have seen how, on block entry and exit, the environment can change as a result
of the operations for the creation, destruction, activation and the deactivation of
associations. These changes are reasonably clear for local environments, but are less
clear where the non-local environment is concerned. The visibility rules stated in
the previous section indeed lend themselves to at least two different interpretations.
Consider for example the following program fragment:

```
A:{int x = 0;

   void fie(){
      x = 1;
   }

   B:{int x;
      fie();
   }

   write(x);
}
```

Which value will be printed? To answer this question, the fundamental problem
is knowing which declaration of x refers to the non-local occurrence of this name
appearing in the assignment in procedure fie's body. On the one hand, we can
reasonably think that the value 1 is printed, given that procedure fie is defined in
block A and, therefore, the x which appears in the body of the procedure could be
that defined on the first line of A. On the other hand, however, we can also reason as
follows. When we call procedure fie, we are in block B, so the x that we are using
in the assignment present in the body of the procedure is the one declared locally
to block B. This local variable is now no longer visible when we exit block B, so
write(x) refers to the variable x declared and initialised to 0 in block A and never
again modified. Therefore the procedure prints the value 0.

Before the reader tries to find possible tricks in the above reasoning, we must
assert that they are both legitimate. The result of the program fragment depends on
the *scope rule* being used, as will become clear at the end of the section. The visibility rule that we have stated above establishes that a "declaration local to a block is
visible in that block and all the blocks nested within it" but does not specify whether
this concept of nesting must be considered in a static (that is based on the text of
the program) or dynamic (that is based on the flow of execution) fashion. When
the visibility rules, also called *scope rules*, depend only on the syntactic structure
of the program, we will talk of a language with *static* or *lexical* scope. When it
is influenced also by the control flow at runtime, we are dealing with a language
with *dynamic* scope. In the following sections we will analyse these two concepts
in detail.

4.3.1 Static Scope

In a language with static (or lexical) scope, the environment in force at any point of the program and at any point during execution depends uniquely on the syntactic structure of the program itself. Such an environment can then be determined completely by the compiler, hence the term "static".

Obviously there can be different static scope rules. One of the simplest, for example, is that of the first version of the Basic language which allowed a single global environment in which it was possible to use only a small number of names (some hundreds) and where declarations were not used.

Much more interesting is the static scope rule that is used in those block-structured languages that allow nesting. This was introduced in ALGOL60 and is retained, with few modifications, by many modern languages, including Ada, Pascal and Java. The rule can be defined as follows:

Definition 4.4 (Static Scope)   The static scope rule, or the rule of nearest nested scope, is defined by the following three rules:

  (i) The declarations local to a block define the local environment of that block. The local declarations of a block include only those present in the block (usually at the start of the block itself) and not those possibly present in blocks nested inside the block in question.
 (ii) If a name is used inside a block, the valid association for this name is the one present in the environment local to the block, if it exists. If no association for the name exists in the environment local to the block, the associations existing in the environment local to the block immediately containing the starting block are considered. If the association is found in this block, it is the valid one, otherwise the search continues with the blocks containing the one with which we started, from the nearest to the furthest. If, during this search, the outermost block is reached and it contains no association for the name, then this association must be looked up in the language's predefined environment. If no association exists here, there is an error.
(iii) A block can be assigned a name, in which case the name is part of the local environment of the block which immediately includes the block to which the name has been assigned. This is the case also for blocks associated with procedures.

It can be immediately seen that this definition corresponds to the informal visibility rules that we have already discussed, suitably completed by a static interpretation of the concept of nesting.

Among the various details of the rule, the fact should not escape us that the declaration of a procedure introduces an association for name of a procedures in the environment local to the block containing the declaration (therefore, because of nesting, the association is also visible in the block which constitutes the body of the procedure, a fact which permits the definition of recursive procedures). The procedure's formal parameters, moreover, are present only in the environment local to

Fig. 4.3 An example of
static scope

```
{int x = 0;
  void fie(int n){
     x = n+1;
  }
  fie(3);
  write(x);
     {int x = 0;
       fie(3);
       write(x);
     }
  write(x);
}
```

the procedure and are not visible in the environment which contains the procedure's declaration.

In a language with static scope, we will call the *scope of a declaration* that portion of the program in which the declaration is visible according to Definition 4.4.

We conclude our analysis of static scope by discussing the example in Fig. 4.3. The first and third occurrences of write print the value 4, while the second prints the value 0. Note that the formal parameter, n, is not visible outside of the body of the procedure.

Static scope allows the determination of all the environments present in a program simply by reading its text. This has two important consequences of a positive nature. First, the programmer has a better understanding of the program, as far as they can connect every occurrence of a name to its correct declaration by observing the textual structure of the program and without having to simulate its execution. Moreover, this connection can also be made by the compiler which can therefore determine each and every use of a name. This makes it possible, at compile time, to perform a great number of correctness tests using the information contained in types; it can also perform considerable number of code optimisations. For example, if the compiler knows (using declarations) that the variable x which occurs in a block is an integer variable, it will signal an error in the case in which a character is assigned to this variable. Similarly, if the compiler knows that the constant fie is associated with the value 10, it can substitute the value 10 for every reference to fie, so avoiding having to arrange for this operation to be performed at runtime, therefore, it updates the code. If, instead, the correct declaration for x and for fie can be determined only at execution time, it is clear that these checks and this optimisation are not possible as compilation time.

Note that, even with the static scope rules, the compiler cannot know in general which memory location will be assigned to the variable with name x nor what its value might be, given that this information depends on the execution of the program. When using the static scope rule, moreover, the compiler is in possession of some important information about the storage of variables (in particular it knows the offsets relative to a fixed position, as we will see in detail in the next chapter), that it uses to compile efficient accesses to variables. As we will see, this information is not available using dynamic scope, which, therefore, leads to less efficient exe-

Fig. 4.4 An example of
dynamic scope

```
{const x = 0;
  void fie(){
     write(x);
  }
  void foo(){
     const x =1;
     fie();
  }
  foo();
}
```

cution. For these reasons, most current languages (for example ALGOL, Pascal, C,
C++, Ada, scheme and Java) use some form of static scope.

4.3.2 Dynamic Scope

Dynamic scope was introduced in some languages, such as, for example, APL, LISP
(some versions), SNOBOL and PERL, mainly to simplify runtime environment
management. In fact it is true that static scope imposes a fairly complicated runtime
regime because the various non-local environments are involved in a way that does
not reflect the normal flow of activation and deactivation of blocks. We seek to understand the problem by considering the fragment of code in Fig. 4.4 and following
its execution. First, the outermost block is entered and the association between the
name x and the constant 0 is created, as well as that between the names fie, foo
and associated procedures (as we said above, this association can be performed by
the compiler). Next the call to the procedure foo is executed and control enters the
block associated with the procedure. In this block, the link between the name x and
the constant 1 is created; then the call to procedure fie is executed which causes
entry to a new block (the one for the latter procedure). It is at this point that the
command write(x) is executed and given that x is not a name local to the block
introduced by the procedure fie, the association for the name x must be looked
up in outer blocks. However, according to the rules of static scope, as presented in
the last section, the first external block in which to look for the association for x is
not the last block to be activated (it is the one for procedure foo in our example);
such an external block depends on the structure of the program. In this case, then,
the correct association for the name x used by fie is the one located in the first
block and consequently the value 0 is printed. The block belonging to procedure
foo, even if it contains a declaration for x and is still active, is not considered.

Generalising from the previous example, we can say that, under static scope,
the sequence of blocks that must be considered to resolve references to non-local
names is different from the sequence of blocks that is opened and exited during
the program's normal flow of control. The opening and closing can be handled in a
natural manner using the LIFO (Last In First Out) discipline, that is using a stack.
The sequence of blocks that need examining to implement static scope depends on

Fig. 4.5 Another example of dynamic scope

```
{const x = 0;
 void fie(){
    write(x);
 }
 void foo(){
    const x = 1;
    {const x = 2;
    }
    foo();
 }
 foo();
}
```

the syntactic structure of the program and being able to handle it correctly at runtime depends upon the use of additional data structures, as we will see in detail in the next chapter.

To simplify the management of the runtime environment some languages use then the *dynamic scope* rule. This rule determines the associations between names and denoted objects using the backward execution of the program. In such languages, resolving non-local names requires only a stack dedicated to handling blocks at runtime. In our example, this means that, when the command write(x) is executed, the association for the name and x is sought in the second block (relative to procedure foo), rather than in the first block, because this is the last block, different from the current one, in which we entered and from which we have not yet exited. Given that in the second block, we find the declaration const x = 1, in the case of dynamic scope the preceding program prints the value 1.

With more precision the dynamic scope rule, also called the rule of the most recent association, can be defined as follows.

Definition 4.5 (Dynamic Scope) According to the rule of dynamic scope, the valid association for a name X, at any point P of a program, is the most recent (in the temporal sense) association created for X which is still active when control flow arrives at P.

It is appropriate to observe that this rule does not contradict the informal visibility rule that we stated in Sect. 4.2.2. A moment's reflection shows, indeed, that the dynamic scope rule expresses nothing other than the same visibility rule but the concept of block nesting is understood in a dynamic sense.

Let us again note how the difference between static and dynamic scope enters only into the determination of the environment which is currently *not local and not global*. For the local and global environment, the two rules coincide.

Let us conclude by discussing the example in Fig. 4.5. In a language with dynamic scope, the code prints the value 1 because when the command write(x) is executed, the last association created for x *which is still active* associates x with 1. The association which associates x to 2, even if it is the most recent one to be created, is no longer active when procedure fie is executed and is therefore not considered.

Note that dynamic scope allows the modification of the behaviour of procedure or subprogram without using explicit parameters but only by redefining some of the non-local variables used. To explain this point, assume that we have a procedure `visualise(text)` which can visualise text in various colours, according to the value of the non-local variable `colour`. If we assume that in the majority of cases, the procedure visualises text in black, it is natural to assume that we do not wish to introduce another parameter to the procedure in order to determine the colour. If the language uses dynamic scope, in the case in which the procedure has to visualise a text in red, it will be enough to introduce the declaration for the variable `colour` before the *call* of the procedure. We can therefore write:

```
...
{var colour = red;
 visualise(head);
}
```

Then the call to procedure *visualise* now will use the colour red, because of the effect of dynamic scope.

This flexibility of dynamic scope, is, on the one hand, advantageous, yet, on the other, it often makes programs more difficult to read, given that the same procedure call, in conditions differing by only one non-local variable can produce different results. If the variable (`colour` in our example) is modified in an area of program that is distant from the procedure call, understanding what has happened will probably turn out to be difficult.

For this reason, as well as for low runtime efficiency, dynamic scope remains little used in modern general-purpose languages, which instead use the static scope rule.

4.3.3 Some Scope Problems

In this section, we will discuss some questions about static scope. The major differences between the rules for static scope in various languages are based on where declarations can be introduced and what will be the exact visibility of the local variables. The scope rules just introduced, lend themselves to more than one interpretation and, in some cases, they can also be the cause of anomalous behaviour. Let us discuss here some different and important situations that can happen.

Let us, first, take the case of Pascal in which the static scope rule that we have already seen is extended with the following additional rules:

1. Declarations can appear only at the start of a block.
2. The scope of a name extends from the start to the end of the block in which the declaration of the name itself appears (excluding possible holes in scope) independent of the position of that declaration.

3. All names not predefined by the language must be declared before use.

It is an error therefore to write:

```
begin
    const fie = value;
    const value = 0;
...
end
```

This is because `value` is used before its definition. It could be assumed that such a fragment might be correct if it were inserted into a block already containing a definition of `value`. Also in this case, though, an error is produced. In fact, let us write:

```
begin
    const value = 1;
    procedure foo;
        const fie = value;
        const value = 0;
        ...
        begin
        ...
        end
...
end
```

Now, the rules that we have seen tell us that the declaration of the procedure `foo` introduces an internal block in which the local declaration of *value* (which initialises to the constant to 0) covers the external declaration (which initialises the constant to 1). Therefore the name `value` appearing in the declaration

```
const fie = value;
```

must refer to the declaration

```
const value = 0;
```

in the internal block. However this declaration occurs after the use of the name, therefore contravening Rule 3. In such a case, therefore, the more correct behaviour for a Pascal compiler is to raise a static semantic error as soon as it has analysed the declaration of `fie`. Some compilers, though, assign to `fie` the value 1; this is clearly incorrect for the reason that it violates the visibility rule.

To avoid this type of problem, some languages with static scope, such as C and Ada, limit the scope of declarations to that portion of the block between the point at which the declarations occur and the end of the book itself (excluding, as usual, holes in scope).

In these languages, therefore, we do not encounter the above problem where the name `value` appearing in the declaration

Fig. 4.6 A list

```
const fie = value;
```

would refer to the declaration in the external block, given that the name internally declared is no longer visible. However, also in these languages names must be declared before being used. So also in this case the following declarations

```
const fie = value;
const value = 0;
```

produce an error if value is not declared in an external block.

Rule 3, which prescribes declaration *before* use, is particularly burdensome in some cases. Indeed, it forbids the definition of recursive types or mutually recursive procedures.

Let us assume, for example, that we want to define a data type like a list which, as we know, is a variable-length data structure formed of a (possibly empty) ordered sequence of elements of some type and in which it is possible to add or remove elements. In a list, only the first element can be directly accessed (to access an arbitrary element, it is necessary to traverse the list sequentially). A list, as shown in Fig. 4.6, can be implemented using a sequence of elements, each of which is formed of two fields: the first will contain the information we want to store (for example, an integer); the second will contain a pointer to the next element of the list, if it exists, otherwise it stores the value nil if the list has ended. We can access the list using the pointer of the first element of the list (which is usually called the *head*). In Pascal, we can define the list type as follows:

```
type list = ^element;
type element = record
                    information: integer;
                    successor: list
                end
```

Here ^T denotes the type of pointers to objects of type T. A value of type list is a pointer to an arbitrary element of the list. The value of type element corresponds to an element of the list, which is composed of an integer and by a field the type list which allows it to connect to the next element. This declaration is incorrect according to Rule 3. In fact, whatever the order of the declarations of list and element may be, it can be seen that we use a name which has not yet been defined. This problem is resolved in Pascal by relaxing Rule 3. For data of a pointer type, and only for them, is it permitted to refer to a name that has not yet been declared. The declaration given above for list are therefore correct in Pascal.

In the case of C and Ada, on the other hand, the analogues of the previous declarations are not permitted. To specify mutually recursive types, it is necessary to use *incomplete* declarations which introduce a name which will later be specified in full. For example, in Ada we can write:

```
type element;
type list is access element;
type element is record
                 information: integer;
                 successor: list;
                 end record;
```

This solves the problem of using a name before its declaration.

The problem presents itself in the analogous case of the definition of mutually recursive procedures. Here, Pascal uses incomplete definitions. If procedure f i e is to be defined in terms of procedure foo and vice versa, in Pascal, we must write:

```
procedure fie(A:integer); forward;
procedure foo(B: integer);
    begin
    ...
    fie(3);
    ...
    end
procedure fie;
    begin
    ...
    foo(4);
    ...
    end
```

In the case of function names, it is strange to observe that C, on the other hand, allows the use of an identifier before its declaration. The declaration of mutually recursive functions does not require any special treatment.

Rule 3 is relaxed in as many ways as there are programming languages. Java, for example, allows a declaration to appear at any point in a block. If the declaration is of a variable, the scope of the name being declared extends from the point of declaration to the end of the block (excluding possible holes in scope). If, on the other hand, the declaration refers to a member of a class (either a field or a method), it is visible in all classes in which it appears, independent of the order in which the declarations occur.

4.4 Chapter Summary

In this chapter we have seen the primary aspects of name handling in high-level languages. The presence of the environment, that is of a set of associations between names and the objects they represent, constitute one of the principal characteristics that differentiate high-level from low-level languages. Given the lack of environment in low-level languages, name management, as well as that of the environment, is an important aspect in the implementation of a high-level language. We will see implementation aspects of name management in the next chapter. Here we are interested in those aspects which must be known to every user (programmer) of a high-level language so that they fully understand the significance of names and, therefore, of the behaviour of programs.

In particular, we have analysed the aspects that are listed below:

- *The concept of denotable objects.* These are the objects to which names can be given. Denotable objects vary according to the language under consideration, even if some categories of object (for example, variables) are fairly general.
- *Environment.* The set of associations existing at runtime between names and denotable objects.
- *Blocks.* In-line or associated with procedures, these are the fundamental construct for structuring the environment and for the definition of visibility rules.
- *Environment Types.* These are the three components which at any time characterise the overall environment: local environment, global environment and non-local environment.
- *Operations on Environments.* Associations present in the environment in addition to being created and destroyed, can also be deactivated, a re-activated and, clearly, can be used.
- *Scope Rules.* Those rules which, in every language, determine the visibility of names.
- *Static Scope.* The kind of scope rule typically used by the most important programming languages.
- *Dynamic Scope.* The scope rule that is easiest to implement. Used today in few languages.

In an informal fashion, we can say that the rules which define the environment are composed of rules for visibility between blocks and of scope rules, which characterise how the non-local environment is determined. In the presence of procedures, the rules we have given are not yet sufficient to define the concept of environment. We will return to this issue in Chap. 7 (in particular at the end of Sect. 7.2.1).

4.5 Bibliographical Notes

General texts on programming languages, such as for example [2, 3] and [4], treat the problems seen in this chapter, even if they are almost always viewed in the context of the implementation. For reasons of clarity of exposition, we have chosen to consider in this chapter only the semantic rules for name handling and the environment, while we will consider their implementation in the next chapter.

For the rules used by individual languages, it is necessary to refer to the specific manuals, some of which are mentioned in bibliographical notes for Chap. 13, even if at times, as we have discussed in Sect. 4.3.3, not all the details are adequately clarified.

The discussion in Sect. 4.3.3 draws on material from [1].

4.6 Exercises

Exercises 6–13, while really being centred on issues relating to scope, presuppose knowledge of parameter passing which we will discuss in Chap. 7.

1. Consider the following program fragment written in a pseudo-language which uses static scope and where the primitive read(Y) allows the reading of the variable Y from standard input.

```
   . . .
   int X = 0;
   int Y;
void fie(){
     X++;
}
void foo(){
     X++;
     fie();
}
read(Y);
if Y > 0{int X = 5;
         foo();}
else foo();
write(X);
```

State what the printed values are.

2. Consider the following program fragment written in a pseudo-language that uses dynamic scope.

```
   . . .
int X;
X = 1;
int Y;
void fie() {
    foo();
    X = 0;
}
void foo(){
    int X;
    X = 5;
}
read(Y);
if Y > 0{int X;
         X = 4;
         fie();}
else      fie();
write(X);
```

State which is (or are) the printed values.

3. Consider the following code fragment in which there are gaps indicated by (*) and (**). Provide code to insert in these positions in such a way that:

a. If the language being used employs static scope, the two calls to the procedure `foo` assign the same value to x.

b. If the language being used employs dynamic scope, the two calls to the procedure `foo` assign different values to x.

The function `foo` must be appropriately declared at (*).

```
{int i;
(*)
for (i=0; i<=1; i++){
    int x;
    (**)
    x= foo();
    }
}
```

4. Provide an example of a denotable object whose life is longer than that of the references (names, pointers, etc.) to it.

5. Provide an example of a connection between a name and a denotable object whose life is longer than that of the object itself.

6. Say what will be printed by the following code fragment written in a pseudo-language which uses static scope; the parameters are passed by a value.

```
{int x = 2;
 int fie(int y){
     x = x + y;
    }

    {int x = 5;
     fie(x);
     write(x);
    }
 write(x);
}
```

7. Say what is printed by the code in the previous exercise if it uses dynamic scope and call by reference.

8. State what is printed by the following fragment of code written in a pseudo-language which uses static scope and passes parameters by reference.

```
{int x = 2;
 void fie(reference int y){
     x = x + y;
     y = y + 1;
    }
    {int x = 5;
     int y = 5;
     fie(x);
     write(x);
    }
    write(x);
}
```

9. State what will be printed by the following code fragment written in a pseudo-language which uses static scope and passes its parameters by value (a command of the form foo(w++) passes the current value of w to foo and then increments it by one).

```
{int x = 2;
 void fie(value int y){
     x = x + y;
 }
 {int x = 5;
  fie(x++);
  write(x);
 }
 write(x);
}
```

10. State what will be printed by the following fragment of code written in a pseudo-language which uses static scope and call by name.

```
{int x = 2;
 void fie(name int y){
     x = x + y;
 }
 {int x = 5;
     {int x = 7
     }
  fie(x++);
  write(x);
 }
 write(x);
}
```

11. State what will be printed by the following code written in a pseudo-language which uses dynamic scope and call by reference.

```
{int x = 1;
 int y = 1;
 void fie(reference int z){
     z  = x + y + z;
 }
 {int y = 3;
   {int x = 3
   }
   fie(y);
   write(y);
 }
 write(y);
}
```

12. State what will be printed by the following fragment of code written in a pseudo-language which uses static scope and call by reference.

```
{int x = 0;
 int A(reference int y) {
        int x =2;
        y=y+1;
        return B(y)+x;
 }
 int B(reference int y){
        int C(reference int y){
            int x = 3;
            return A(y)+x+y;
        }
        if (y==1) return C(x)+y;
        else return x+y;
 }
 write (A(x));
}
```

13. Consider the following fragment of code in a language with static scope and parameter passing both by value and by name:

```
{int z= 0;
 int Omega(){
     return Omega();
 }
 int foo(int x, int y){
     if (x==0) return x;
     else return x+y;
 }
 write(foo(z, Omega()+z));
}
```

   (i) State what will be the result of the execution of this fragment in the case in which the parameters to foo are passed by *name*.
   (ii) State what will be the result of the execution of this fragment in the case in which the parameters to foo are passed by *value*.

References

1. R. Cailliau. How to avoid getting schlonked by Pascal. *SIGPLAN Not.*, 17(12):31–40, 1982. doi:10.1145/988164.988167.
2. T.W. Pratt and M.V. Zelkowitz. *Programming Languages: Design and Implementation*. Prentice-Hall, New York, 2001.
3. M. L. Scott. *Programming Language Pragmatics*. Morgan Kaufmann, San Mateo, 2000.
4. R. Sethi. *Programming Languages: Concepts and Constructs*. Addison-Wesley, Reading, 1996.

Chapter 5
Memory Management

An important component of an abstract machine's interpreter is the one dealing with memory management. If this component can be extremely simple in a physical machine, memory management in an abstract machine for a high-level language is fairly complicated and can employ a range of techniques. We will see both static and dynamic management and will examine activation records, the system stack and the heap. One section in particular is dedicated to the data structures and mechanisms used to implement scope rules.

Conceptually, garbage-collection techniques, techniques for the automatic recovery of memory allocated in a heap, are included in memory management. However, to make the presentation more coherent, these techniques will be explained in Sect. 8.12, after having dealt with data types and pointers.

5.1 Techniques for Memory Management

As we said in Chap. 1, memory management is one of the functions of the interpreter associated with an abstract machine. This functionality manages the allocation of memory for programs and for data, that is determines how they must be arranged in memory, how much time they may remain and which auxiliary structures are required to fetch information from memory.

In the case of a low-level abstract machine, the hardware, for example, memory management is very simple and can be entirely *static*. Before execution of the program begins, machine language program and its associated data is loaded into an appropriate area of memory, where it remains until its execution ends.

In the case of a high-level language, matters are, for various reasons, more complicated. First of all, if the language permits recursion, static allocation is insufficient.[1] In fact, while we can statically establish the maximum number of active procedures at any point during execution in the case of languages without recursion,

---

[1] We will see below an exception to this general principle. This is the case of so-called tail recursion.

M. Gabbrielli, S. Martini, *Programming Languages: Principles and Paradigms*, Undergraduate Topics in Computer Science, DOI 10.1007/978-1-84882-914-5_5, © Springer-Verlag London Limited 2010

when we have recursive procedures this is no longer true because the number of simultaneously active procedure calls can depend on the parameters of the procedures or, generally, on information available only at runtime.

Example 5.1 Consider the following fragment:

```
int fib (int n) {
    if (n == 0) return 1;
    else if (n == 1) return 1;
        else return fib(n-1) + fib(n-2);
}
```

which, if called with an argument n, computes (in a very inefficient way) the value of the nth Fibonacci number. Let us recall that Fibonacci numbers are the terms of the sequence[2] defined inductively as follows: $Fib(0) = Fib(1) = 1$; $Fib(n) = Fib(n-1) + Fib(n-2)$, for $n > 1$. It is clear that the number of active calls to Fib depends, other than on the point of execution, on the value of the argument, n. Using a simple recurrence relation, it can be verified that the number, $C(n)$, of calls to Fib necessary to calculate the value of the term $Fib(n)$ (and, therefore, the simultaneously active calls) is exactly equal to this value. From a simple inspection of the code, indeed, it can be seen that $C(n) = 1$ for $n = 0$ and $n = 1$, while $C(n) = C(n-1) + C(n-2)$ for $n > 1$. It is known that the Fibonacci numbers grow exponentially, so the number of calls to fib is of the order of $O(2^n)$.

Given that every procedure call requires its own memory space to store parameters, intermediate results, return addresses, and so on, in the presence of recursive procedures, static allocation of memory is no longer sufficient and we have to allow *dynamic* memory allocation and deallocation operations, which are performed during the execution of the program. Such dynamic memory processing can be implemented in a natural fashion using a *stack* for procedure (or in-line block) activations since they follow a LIFO (Last In First Out) policy—the last procedure called (or the last block entered) will be the first to be exited.

There are, however, other cases which require dynamic memory management for which a stack is not enough. These are cases in which the language allows explicit memory allocation and deallocation operations, as happens, for example, in C with the malloc and free commands. In these cases, given that the allocation operation (malloc) and the one for deallocation (free) can be alternated in any order whatsoever, it is not possible to use a stack to manage the memory and, as we will better see as the chapter unfolds, a particular memory structure called a *heap* is used.

---

[2]The sequence takes the name of the Pisan mathematician of the same name, known also as Leonardo da Pisa (ca., 1175–1250), who seems to have encountered the sequence by studying the increase in a population of rabbits. For information on inductive definition, see the box on page 153.

5.2 Static Memory Management

Static memory management is performed by the complier before execution starts. Statically allocated memory objects reside in a fixed zone of memory (which is determined by the compiler) and they remain there for the entire duration of the program's execution. Typical elements for which it is possible statically to allocate memory are *global variables*. These indeed can be stored in a memory area that is fixed before execution begins because they are visible throughout the program. The *object code instructions* produced by the compiler can be considered another kind of static object, given that normally they do not change during the execution of the program, so in this case also memory will be allocated by the compiler. *Constants* are other elements that can be handled statically (in the case in which their values do not depend on other values which are unknown at compile time). Finally, various *compiler-generated tables*, necessary for the runtime support of the language (for example, for handling names, for type checking, for garbage collection) are stored in reserved areas allocated by the compiler.

In the case in which the language does not support recursion, as we have anticipated, it is possible statically to handle the memory for other components of the language. Substantially, this is done by statically associating an area of memory in which is stored the information local to the procedure with each procedure (or subroutine)[3] itself. This information is composed of local variables, possible parameters of the procedure (containing both arguments and results), the return address (or the address to which control must pass when the procedure terminates), possible temporary values used in complex calculations and various pieces of "bookkeeping" information (saved register values, information for debugging and so on).

The situation of a language with only static memory allocation is shown in Fig. 5.1.

It will be noted that successive calls to the same procedure share the same memory areas. This is correct because, in the absence of recursion, there cannot be two different calls to the same procedure that are active at the same time.

5.3 Dynamic Memory Management Using Stacks

Most modern programming languages allow block structuring of programs.[4]

Blocks, whether in-line or associated with procedures, are entered and left using the LIFO scheme. When a block A is entered, and then a block B is entered, before leaving A, it is necessary to leave B. It is therefore natural to manage the memory

---

[3] It would be more correct to speak of subroutines because this was the term used in languages that used static memory allocation, such as, for example, the first versions of FORTRAN from the 1960s and 70s.

[4] We will see below that important languages, such as C, though, do not offer the full potential of this mechanism, in that they do not permit the declaration of local procedures and functions in nested blocks.

Fig. 5.1 Static memory management

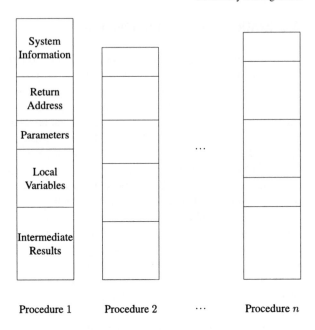

| System Information |
| Return Address |
| Parameters |
| Local Variables |
| Intermediate Results |

Procedure 1   Procedure 2   ⋯   Procedure n

space required to store the information local to each block using a stack. We will see an example.

Example 5.2 Let us consider the following program:

```
A:{int  a = 1;
   int  b = 0;

   B:{int  c = 3;
      int  b = 3;
      }
   b=a+1;
   }
```

At runtime, when block A is entered, a push operation allocates a space large enough to hold the variables a and b, as shown in Fig. 5.2. When block B is entered, we have to allocate a new space on the stack for the variables c and b (recall that the inner variable b is different from the outer one) and therefore the situation, after this second allocation, is that shown in Fig. 5.3. When block B exits, on the other hand, it is necessary to perform a pop operation to deallocate the space that had been reserved for the block from the stack. The situation after such a deallocation and after the assignment is shown in Fig. 5.4. Analogously, when block A exits, it will be necessary to perform another pop to deallocate the space for A as well.

The case of procedures is analogous and we consider it in Sect. 5.3.2.

The memory space, allocated on the stack, dedicated to an in-line block or to an activation of a procedure is called the *activation record*, or *frame*. Note that an acti-

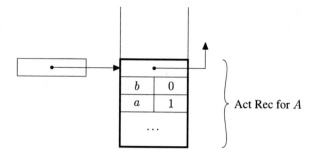

Fig. 5.2 Allocation of an activation record for block A in Example 5.2

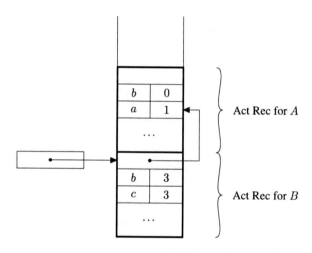

Fig. 5.3 Allocation of activation records for blocks A and B in Example 5.2

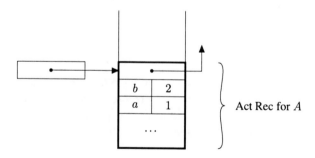

Fig. 5.4 Organisation after the execution of the assignment in Example 5.2

vation record is associated with a specific activation of a procedure (one is created when the procedure is called) and not with the declaration of a procedure. The values that must be stored in an activation record (local variables, temporary variables, etc.) are indeed different for the different calls on the same procedure.

The stack on which activation records are stored is called the *runtime (or system) stack*.

Fig. 5.5 Organisation of an
activation record for an
in-line block

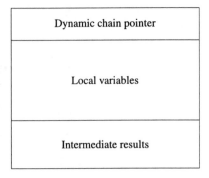

| Dynamic chain pointer |
| Local variables |
| Intermediate results |

It should finally be noted, that to improve the use of runtime memory, dynamic memory management is sometimes also used to implement languages that do not support recursion. If the average number of simultaneously active calls to the same procedure is less than the number of procedures declared in the program, using a stack will save space, for there will be no need to allocate a memory area for each declared procedure, as must be done in the case of entirely static management.

5.3.1 Activation Records for In-line Blocks

The structure of a generic activation record for an in-line block is shown in Fig. 5.5. The various sectors of the activation record contain the following information:

Intermediate results When calculations must be performed, it can be necessary to store intermediate results, even if the programmer does not assign an explicit name to them. For example, the activation record for the block:

```
{int a =3;
 b= (a+x)/ (x+y);}
```

could take the form shown in Fig. 5.6, where the intermediate results (a+x) and (x+y) are explicitly stored before the division is performed. The need to store intermediate results on the stack depends on the compiler being used and on the architecture to which one is compiling. On many architectures they can be stored in registers.

Local variables Local variables which are declared inside blocks, must be stored in a memory space whose size will depend on the number and type of the variables. This information in general is recorded by the compiler which therefore will be able to determine the size of this part of the activation record. In some cases, however, there can be declarations which depend on values recorded only at runtime (this is, for example, the case for dynamic arrays, which are present in some languages, whose dimensions depend on variables which are only instantiated at execution time). In these cases, the activation record also contains a variable-length

Fig. 5.6 An activation record
with space for intermediate
results

a	3
$a + x$	value
$x + y$	value

part which is defined at runtime. We will examine this in detail in Chap. 8 when
discussing arrays.

Dynamic chain pointer This field stores a pointer to the previous activation record
on the stack (or to the last activation record created). This information is necessary
because, in general, activation records have different sizes. Some authors call this
pointer the *dynamic link* or *control link*. The set of links implemented by these
pointers is called the *dynamic chain*.

5.3.2 Activation Records for Procedures

The case of procedures and functions[5] is analogous to that of in-line blocks but with
some additional complications due to the fact that, when a procedure is activated,
it is necessary to store a greater amount of information to manage correctly the
control flow. The structure of a generic activation record for a procedure is shown
in Fig. 5.7. Recall that a function, unlike a procedure, returns a value to the caller
when it terminates its execution. Activation records for the two cases are therefore
identical with the exception that, for functions, the activation record must also keep
tabs on the memory location in which the function stores its return value.

Let us now look in detail at the various fields of an activation record:

Intermediate results, local variables, dynamic chain pointer The same as for
in-line blocks.

Static chain pointer This stores the information needed to implement the static
scope rules described in Sect. 5.5.1.

Return address Contains the address of the first instruction to execute after the call
to the current procedure/function has terminated execution.

Returned result Present only in functions. Contains the address of the memory
location where the subprogram stores the value to be returned by the function when
it terminates. This memory location is inside the caller's activation record.

Parameters The values of actual parameters used to call the procedure or function
are stored here.

The organisation of the different fields of the activation record varies from implementation to implementation. The dynamic chain pointer and, in general, every

---

[5]Here and below, we will almost always use the terms "function" and "procedure" as synonyms.
Although there are is no agreement between authors, the term "procedure" should denote a subprogram which does not directly return a value, while a function is a subprogram that returns one.

Fig. 5.7 Structure of the
activation record for a
procedure

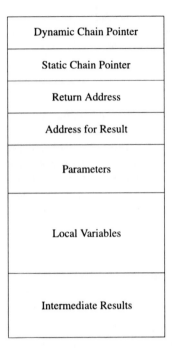

| Dynamic Chain Pointer |
| Static Chain Pointer |
| Return Address |
| Address for Result |
| Parameters |
| Local Variables |
| Intermediate Results |

pointer to an activation record, points to a fixed (usually central) area of the activation record. The addresses of the different fields are obtained, therefore, by adding a negative or positive offset to the value of the pointer.

Variable names are not normally stored in activation records and the compiler substitutes references to local variables for addresses relative to a fixed position in (i.e., an offset into) the activation record for the block in which the variables are declared. This is possible because the position of a declaration inside a block is fixed statically and the compiler can therefore associate every local variable with an exact position inside the activation record.

In the case of references to non-local variables, also, as we will see when we discuss scope rules, it is possible to use mechanisms that avoid storing names and therefore avoid having to perform a runtime name-based search through the activation-record stack in order to resolve a reference.

Finally, modern compilers often optimise the code they produce and save some information in registers instead of in the activation record. For simplicity, in this book, we will not consider these optimisations. In any case for greater clarity, in the examples, we will assume that variable names are stored in activation records.

To conclude, let us note that all the observations that we have made about variable names, their accessibility and storage in activation records, can be extended to other kinds of denotable object.

5.3.3 Stack Management

Figure 5.8 shows the structure of a system stack which we assume growing down-
wards (the direction of stack growth varies according to the implementation). As
shown in the figure, an external pointer to the stack points to the last activation
record on the stack (pointing to a predetermined area of the activation record which
is used as a base for calculating the offsets used to access local names). This pointer,
which we call the activation record pointer, is also called the frame or current environment pointer (because environments are implemented using activation records).
In the figure, we have also indicated where the first free location is. This second
pointer, used in some implementations, can, in principle, also be omitted if the
activation-record pointer always points to a position that is at a pre-defined distance
from the start of the free area on the stack.

Activation records are stored on and removed from the stack at runtime. When a
block is entered or a procedure is called, the associated activation record is pushed
onto the stack; it is later removed from the stack when the block is exited or when
the procedure terminates.

The runtime management of the system stack is implemented by code fragments
which the compiler (or interpreter) inserts immediately before and after the call to a
procedure or before the start and after the end of a block.

Let us examine in detail what happens in the case of procedures, given that the
case of in-line blocks is only a simplification.

First of all, let us clarify the terminology that we are using. We use "caller" and
"callee" to indicate, respectively, the program or procedure that performs a call (of
a procedure) and the procedure that has been called.

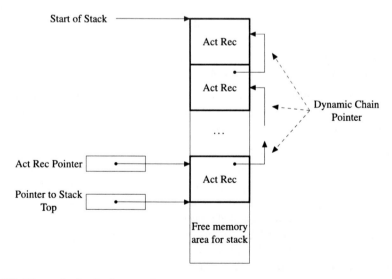

Fig. 5.8 The stack of activation records

Stack management is performed both by the caller and by the callee. To do this, as well as handling other control information, a piece of code called the *calling sequence* is inserted into the caller to be executed, in part, immediately before the procedure call. The remainder of this code is executed immediately after the call. In addition, in the callee two pieces of code are added: a *prologue*, to be executed immediately after the call, and an *epilogue*, which is executed when the procedure ends execution. These three code fragments manage the different operations needed to handle activation records and correctly implement a procedure call. The exact division of what the caller and callee do depends, as usual, on the compiler and on the specific implementation under consideration. Moreover, to optimise the size of code produced, it is preferable that the larger part of the activity is given to the callee, since the code is added only once (to the code associated with the declaration of the call) instead of many times (to the code associated with different calls). Without therefore further specifying the division of activities, they consist of the following tasks:

Modification of program counter This is clearly necessary to pass control to the called procedure. The old value (incremented) must be saved to maintain the return address.

Allocation of stack space The space for the new activation record must be pre-allocated and therefore the pointer to the first free location on the stack must be updated as a consequence.

Modification of activation record pointer The pointer must point to the new activation record for the called procedure; the activation record will have been pushed onto the stack.

Parameter passing This activity is usually performed by the caller, given that different calls of the same procedure can have different parameters.

Register save Values for control processing, typically stored in registers, must be saved. This is the case, for example, with the old activation record pointer which is saved as a pointer in the dynamic chain.

Execution of initialisation code Some languages require explicit constructs to initialise some items stored in the new activation record.

When control *returns to the calling program*, i.e. when the called procedure terminates, the *epilogue* (in the called routine) and the *calling sequence* (in the caller) must perform the following operations:

Update of program counter This is necessary to return control to the caller.

Value return The values of parameters which pass information from the caller to the called procedure, or the value calculated by the function, must be stored in appropriate locations usually present in the caller's activation record and accessible to the activation record of the called procedure.

Return of registers The value of previously saved registers must be restored. In particular, the old value of the activation record pointer must be restored.

Execution of finalisation code Some languages require the execution of appropriate finalisation code before any local objects can be destroyed.

Deallocation of stack space The activation record of the procedure which has terminated must be removed from the stack. The pointer to (the first free position on) the stack must be modified as a result.

It should be noted that in the above description, we have omitted the handling of the data structures necessary for the implementation of scope rules. This will be considered in detail in Sect. 5.5 of this chapter.

5.4 Dynamic Management Using a Heap

In the case in which the language includes explicit commands for memory allocation, as for example do C and Pascal, management using just the stack is insufficient. Consider for example the following C fragment:

```
int *p, *q; /* p,q  NULL pointers to integers */
p =  malloc (sizeof (int));
          /* allocates the memory pointed to by p */
q =  malloc (sizeof (int));
          /* allocates the memory pointed to by  q */
*p = 0;      /* dereferences and assigns */
*q = 1;      /* dereferences and assigns */
free(p);     /* deallocates the memory pointed to by p */
free(q);     /* deallocates the memory pointed to by q */
```

Given that the memory deallocation operations are performed in the same order as allocations (first p, then q), the memory cannot be allocated in LIFO order.

To manage explicit memory allocations, which can happen at any time, a particular area of memory, called a *heap*, is used. Note that this term is used in computing also to mean a particular type of data structure which is representable using a binary tree or a vector, used to implement efficiently priorities (and used also in the "heap sort" sorting algorithm, where the term "heap" was originally introduced). The definition of heap that we use here has nothing to do with this data structure. In the programming language jargon, a heap is simply an area of memory in which blocks of memory can be allocated and deallocated relatively freely.

Heap management methods fall into two main categories according to whether the memory blocks are considered to be of *fixed* or *variable* length.

5.4.1 Fixed-Length Blocks

In this case, the heap is divided into a certain number of elements, or blocks, of fairly small fixed length, linked into a list structure called the *free list*, as shown in Fig. 5.9. At runtime, when an operation requires the allocation of a memory block from the heap (for example using the `malloc` command), the first element of the free list is removed from the list, the pointer to this element is returned to the operation that

Fig. 5.9 Free list in a heap with fixed-size blocks

LL Start

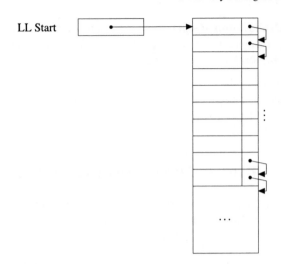

Fig. 5.10 Free list for heap of fixed-size blocks after allocation of some memory. *Grey blocks* are allocated (in use)

LL Start

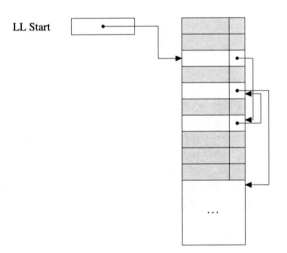

requested the memory and the pointer to the free list is updated so that it points to the next element.

When memory is, on the other hand, freed or deallocated (for example using `free`), the freed block is linked again to the head of the free list. The situation after some memory allocations is shown in Fig. 5.10. Conceptually, therefore, management of a heap with fixed-size blocks is simple, provided that it is known how to identify and reclaim the memory that must be returned to the free list easily. These operations of identification and recovery are not obvious, as we will see below.

5.4.2 *Variable-Length Blocks*

In the case in which the language allows the runtime allocation of variable-length memory spaces, for example to store an array of variable dimension, fixed-length blocks are no longer adequate. In fact the memory to be allocated can have a size greater than the fixed block size, and the storage of an array requires a contiguous region of memory that cannot be allocated as a series of blocks. In such cases, a heap-based management scheme using variable-length blocks is used.

This second type of management uses different techniques, mainly defined with the aim of increasing memory occupation and execution speed for heap management operations (recall that they are performed at runtime and therefore impact on the execution time of the program). As usual, these two characteristics are difficult to reconcile and good implementations tend towards a rational compromise.

In particular, as far as memory occupancy is concerned, it is a goal to avoid the phenomenon of memory *fragmentation*. So-called *internal fragmentation* occurs when a block of size strictly larger than the requested by the program is allocated. The portion of unused memory internal to the block clearly will be wasted until the block is returned to the free list. But this is not the most serious problem. Indeed, so-called *external fragmentation* is worse. This occurs when the free list is composed of blocks of a relatively small size and for which, even if the sum of the total available free memory is enough, the free memory cannot be effectively used. Figure 5.11 shows an example of this problem. If we have blocks of size x and y (words or some other unit—it has no relevance here) on the free list and we request the allocation of a block of greater size, our request cannot be satisfied despite the fact that the total amount of free memory is greater than the amount of memory that has been requested. The memory allocation techniques tend therefore to

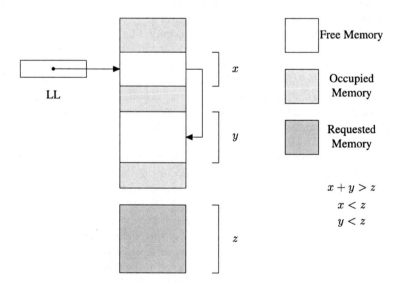

Fig. 5.11 External fragmentation

"compact" free memory, merging contiguous free blocks in such a way as to avoid external fragmentation. To achieve this objective, merging operations can be called which increase the load imposed by the management methods and therefore reduce efficiency.

Single free list   The first technique we examine deals with a single free list, initially composed of a single memory block containing the entire heap. It is indeed convenient to seek to maintain blocks of largest possible size. It makes no sense, therefore, initially to divide the heap into many small blocks as, on the other hand, we did in the case of fixed-size blocks. When the allocation of a block of n words of memory is requested, the first n words are allocated and the pointer to the start of the head is incremented by n. Successive requests are handled in a similar way, in which deallocated blocks are collected on a free list. When the end of the heap's memory space is reached, is necessary to reuse deallocated memory and this can be done in the two following ways:

(i) **Direct use of the free list**   In this case, a free list of blocks of variable size is used. When the allocation of a memory block n words in length is requested, the free list is searched for a block of size k words, where k is greater than or equal to n. The requested memory is allocated inside this block. The unused part of the block (of size $k - n$) if longer than some predefined threshold, is used to form a new block that is inserted into the free list (internal fragmentation is permitted below this threshold). The search for a block of sufficient size can be performed using one of two methods. Using *first fit*, the search is for the first block of sufficient size, while using *best fit*, the search is for a block whose size is the least of those blocks of sufficient size. The first technique favours processing time, while the second favours memory occupation. For both, however, the cost of allocation is linear with respect to the number of blocks on the free list. If the blocks are held in order of increasing block size, the two schemes are the same, because the list is traversed until a large enough block is found. Moreover, in this case, the cost of insertion of a block into the free list increases (from constant to linear), because is necessary to find the right place to insert it. Finally, when a deallocated block is returned to the free list, in order to reduce external fragmentation, a check is make to determine whether the physically adjacent blocks are free, in which case they are compacted into a single block. This type of compaction is said to be *partial* because it compacts only adjacent blocks.

(ii) **Free memory compaction**   In this technique, when the end of the space initially allocated to the heap is reached, all blocks that are still active are moved to the end; they are the blocks that cannot be returned to the free list, leaving all the free memory in a single contiguous block. At this point, the heap pointer is updated so that it points to the start of the single block of free memory and allocation starts all over again. Clearly, for this technique to work, the blocks of allocated memory must be movable, something that is not always guaranteed (consider blocks whose addresses are stored in pointers on the stack). Some compaction techniques will be discussed in Sect. 8.12, when we discuss garbage collection.

Multiple free lists   To reduce the block allocation cost, some heap management techniques use different free lists for blocks of different sizes. When a block of size n is requested, the list that contains blocks of size greater than or equal to n is chosen and a block from this list is chosen (with some internal fragmentation if the block has a size greater than n). The size of the blocks in this case, too, can be static or dynamic and, in the case of dynamic sizes, two management methods are commonly used: the *buddy system* and the *Fibonacci heap*. In the first, the size of the blocks in the various free lists are powers of 2. If a block of size n is requested and k is the least integer such that $2^k \geq n$, then a block of size 2^k is sought (in the appropriate free list). If such a free block is found it is allocated, otherwise, a search is performed in the next free list for a block of size 2^{k+1} and it is split into two parts. One of the two blocks (which therefore has size 2^k) is allocated, while the other is inserted into the free list for blocks of size 2^k. When a block resulting from a split is returned to the free list, a search is performed for its "buddy", that is the other half that was produced by the split operation, and it is free, the two blocks are merged to re-form the initial block of size 2^{k+1}. The *Fibonacci heap* method is similar but uses Fibonacci numbers instead of powers of 2 as block sizes. Given that the Fibonacci sequence grows more slowly than the series 2^n, this second method leads to less internal fragmentation.

5.5 Implementation of Scope Rules

The possibility of denoting objects, even complex ones, by names with appropriate visibility rules constitutes one of the most important aspects that differentiate high-level languages from low-level ones. The implementation of environments and scope rules discussed in Chap. 4 requires, therefore, suitable data structures. In this section, we analyse these structures and their management.

Given that the activation record contains the memory space for local names, when a reference to a non-local name is encountered, the activation records that are still active must be examined (that is, the ones present on the stack) in order to find the one that corresponds to the block where the name in question was declared; this will be the block that contains the association for our name. The order in which to examine the activation records varies according to the kind of scope under consideration.

5.5.1 Static Scope: The Static Chain

If the static scope rule is employed, as we anticipated in Chap. 4, the order in which activation records are consulted when resolving non-local references is not the one defined by their position on the stack. In other words, the activation record directly connected by the dynamic chain pointer is not necessarily the first activation record in which to look in order to resolve a non-local reference; the first activation record within which to look is defined by the textual structure of the program. Let us see an example.

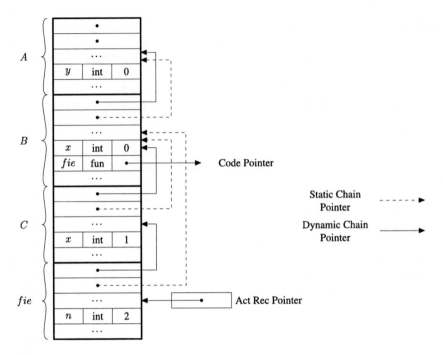

Fig. 5.12 Activation stack with static chain (see Example 5.3)

Example 5.3 Consider the following code (as usual, for ease of reference, we have labelled the blocks):

```
A:{int y=0;
   B:{int x = 0;
      void (int n){
          x = n+1;
          y = n+2;
      }
      C:{int x = 1;
         fie(2);
         write(x);
         }
      }
   write(y);
   }
```

After executing the call `fie(2)`, the situation on the activation-record stack is that shown in Fig. 5.12. The first activation record on the stack (the uppermost one in the figure) is for the outermost block; the second is the one for block B; the third is for C and finally the fourth is the activation record for the call to the procedure. The non-local variable, x, used in procedure `fie`, as we know from the static scope rule is not the one declared in block C but the one declared in block B. To be able

Fig. 5.13 A block structure

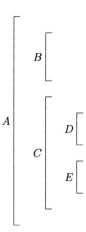

to locate this information correctly at runtime, the activation record for the call to the procedure is connected by a pointer, called the *static chain* pointer, to the record for the block containing the declaration of the variable. This record is linked, in its turn, by a static chain pointer to the record for block A, because this block, being the first immediately external to B, is the first block to be examined when resolving references non-local to B. When inside the call to procedure fie, the variables x and y are used, to access the memory area in which they are stored the static chain pointers are followed from fie's activation record until first the record for B is encountered (for x) and then that for A (when searching for y).

Generalising this example, we can say that, for the runtime management of static scope, the activation of the generic block B is linked by the *static chain pointer* to the record for the block immediately enclosing B (that is the nearest block that contains B). It should be noted that in the case in which B is the block for a procedure call, the block immediately enclosing B is the one containing the declaration of the procedure itself. Moreover if B is active, that is if its activation record is on the stack, then also the blocks enclosing B must be active and therefore can be located on the stack.

Hence, in addition to the *dynamic chain*, which is formed from the various records present on the system stack (linked in the order of the stack itself), there must exist a *static chain*, formed from the various static chain pointers used to represent the static nesting structure of the blocks within the program.

As an example, consider Fig. 5.13 which shows a generic structure of blocks which results from nested procedures. Consider now the sequence of calls: A, B, C, D, E, C, where it is intended that each call remains active when the next call is made. The situation on the activation-record stack, with is various static chain pointers, after such a sequence of calls is that shown in Fig. 5.14.

The runtime management of the static chain is one of the functions performed by the calling sequence, prologue and epilogue code, as we saw above. Such a management of the static chain can be performed by the caller and the callee in various ways. According to the most common approach, when a new block is entered, the caller calculates the static chain pointer and then passes it to the called routine. This

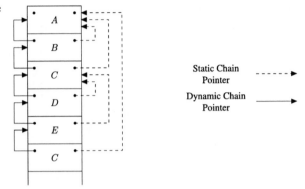

Fig. 5.14 Static chain for the previous structure and the sequence of calls A, B, C, D, E, C

computation is fairly simple and can be easily understood by separating the two cases:

The called routine is external to the caller In this case, by the visibility rules defined by static scope, for the called routine to be visible, it must be located in an outer block which includes the caller's block. Therefore, the activation record for such an outer block must already be stored on the stack. Assume that among the caller and the called routines, there are k levels of nesting in the program's block structure; if the caller is located on nesting level n and the called routine is on level m, we can assume therefore that $k = n - m$. This value of k can be determined by the compiler, because it depends only on the static structure of the program and therefore can be associated with the call in question. The caller can then calculate the static chain pointer for the called procedure simply by dereferencing its own static chain pointer k times (that is, it runs k steps along its own static chain).

Called inside calling routine In this case, the visibility rules ensure that the called routine is declared in same the block in which the call occurs and therefore the first block external to the called one is precisely that of the caller. The static chain pointer of the called routine must point to the caller's activation record. The caller can simply pass to the called routine the pointer to its own activation record as a pointer to the static chain.

Once the called routine has received the static chain pointer, it need only store it in the appropriate place in its activation record, an operation that can be performed by the prologue code. When a block exit occurs, the static chain requires no particular management actions.

We have hinted at the fact that the compiler, in order to perform runtime static-chain management, keeps track of the nesting level of procedure calls. This is done using the *symbol table*, a sort of dictionary where, more generally, the compiler stores all the names used in the program and all the information necessary to manage the objects denoted by the names (for example to determine the type) and to implement the visibility rules.

In particular, a number is maintained that depends on the nesting level and indicates the scope that contains the declaration of a name; this allows to associate to each name a number indicating the scope when the declaration for such a name is made. Using this number, it is possible to calculate, at compile time, the distance between the scope of the call and that of the declaration which is necessary at runtime to handle the static chain.

It should be noted that this distance is calculated statically and it also allows the runtime resolution of non-local references without having to perform any name searches in the activation record on the stack. Indeed, if we use a reference to the non-local name, x, to find the activation record containing the memory space for x it suffices to start at the activation record corresponding to the block that contains the reference and follow the static chain for a number of links equal to the value of the distance. Inside the activation record that is thus found, the memory location for x is also fixed by the compiler and, therefore, at runtime, there is no need for a search but only the static offset of x with respect to the activation record pointer is needed.

However, it is clear that, in a static model, the compiler cannot completely resolve a reference to a non-local name and it is always necessary to follow the static-chain links at runtime. This is why, in general, it is not possible to know statically what the number of activation records present on the stack is.

As a concrete example of what has just been said, consider the code in Example 5.3. The compiler "knows" that to use variable y in procedure fie, it is necessary to pass two external blocks (B and A) to arrive at the one containing the declaration of the variable. It is enough, therefore, to store this value at compilation time so that it can subsequently be known, at runtime, that to resolve the name y, it is necessary to follow two pointers in the static chain. It is not necessary to store the name y explicitly because its position inside the activation record for the block A is fixed by the compiler. Analogously, the type information that we, for clarity, have included in Fig. 5.12, is stored in the symbol table, and after appropriate compile-time checks, can, in a large part, be omitted at runtime.

5.5.2 Static Scope: The Display

The implementation of static scope using the static chain has one inconvenient property: if we have to use a non-local name declared in an enclosing block, k levels of block away from the point at which we currently find ourselves, at runtime we have to perform k memory accesses to follow the static chain to determine the activation block that contains the memory location for the name of interest. This problem is not all that severe, given that in real programs it is rare that more than 3 levels of block and procedure nesting are required. The technique called the *display*, however, allows the reduction of the number of accesses to a constant (2).

This technique uses a vector, called the *display*, containing as many elements as there are levels of block nesting in the program, where the kth element of the vector contains the pointer to the activation record at nesting level k that is currently active. When a reference is made to a non-local object, declared in an block

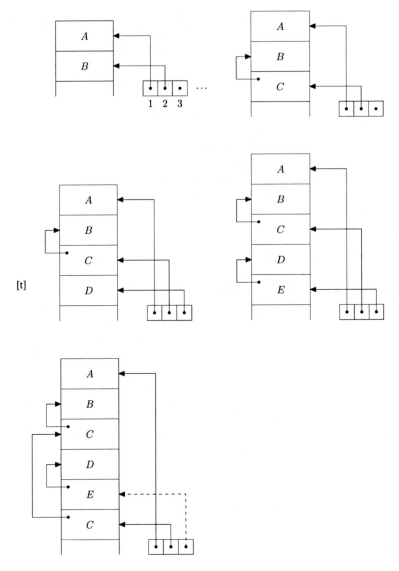

Fig. 5.15 Display for the structure in Fig. 5.13 and the call sequence A, B, C, D, E, C

external to level k, the activation record containing this object can be retrieved simply by accessing the kth position in the vector and following the pointer stored there.

Display processing is very simple, even if it is slightly more costly than static chain handling; when an environment is entered or left, in addition to updating the pointer stored in the vector, it is also necessary to save the old value. More precisely, when a procedure is called (or an in-line block is entered) at level k, position k in the display will have to be updated with the value of the pointer to the activation record for the call, because this has become the new active block at level k. Before this update, however, it is necessary to save the preceding contents of the kth position of the display, normally storing it in the activation record of the call.

The need to save the old display value can be better understood by examining the following 2 possible cases:

The called routine is external to the caller Let use assume that the call is at nesting level n and the called routine is at level m, with $m < n$. The called routine and the caller therefore share the static structure up to level $m - 1$ and also the display up to position $m - 1$. Display element m is updated with the pointer to the activation record of the called routine and until the called routine terminates, the active display is the one formed of the first m elements. The old value contained in position m must be saved because it points to the activation record of the block which will be re-activated when the called routine terminates; thereafter, the display will go back to being the one used before the call.

The called routine is located inside the caller The nesting depth reached this far is incremented. If the caller is located at level n, caller and called routine share the whole current display up to position n and it is necessary to add a new value at position $n + 1$, so that it holds the pointer to the activation record for the caller.

When we have the first activation of a block at level $n + 1$, the old value stored in the display is of no interest to us. However, in general, we cannot know if this is the case. Indeed, we could have reached the current call by a series of previous calls that also use level $n + 1$. In this case, as well, it will be necessary therefore to store the old value in the display at position $n + 1$.

Both display update and the saving of the old value can be performed by the called procedure. Figure 5.15 shows the handling of the display for the call sequence A, B, C, D, E, C, using the block structure described in Fig. 5.13. The pointers on the left of the stack denote storage of the old display value in the activation record of the called routine, while the dotted pointer denotes a display pointer that is not currently active.

5.5.3 Dynamic Scope: Association Lists and CRT

Conceptually, the implementation of the dynamic scope rule is much simpler than the one for static scope. Indeed, given that non-local environments are considered in the order in which they are activated at runtime, to resolve a non-local reference to a name x, it suffices, at least in principle, to run backwards down the stack, starting with the current activation record until the activation record is found in which the name x is declared.

The various associations between names and the objects they denote which constitute the various local environment can be stored directly in the activation record. Let us consider, for example, the block structure shown in Fig. 5.16, where the

Fig. 5.16 A block structure
with local declarations

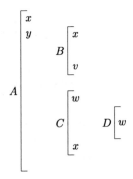

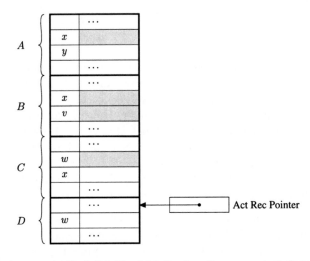

Fig. 5.17 Environment for block D in Fig. 5.16 after the call sequence A, B, C, D, with dynamic scope implemented using stored associations in the activation record. In *grey*: inactive associations

names denote local variable declarations (assuming the usual visibility rules). If we execute the call sequence A, B, C, D (where, as usual, all the calls remain active) when control reaches block D, we obtain the stack shown in Fig. 5.17 (the field on the right of each name contains the information associated with the object denoted by its name). The environment (local or otherwise) of D is formed from all the name-denoted object associations in which the information field is in white in the figure. The association fields that are no longer active are shown in grey. An association is not active either because the corresponding name is no longer visible (this is the case for v) or because it has been redefined in an inner block (this is the case for w and for the occurrences of x in A and B).

Other than direct storage in the activation record, name-object associations can be stored separately in an association list, called an *A-list*, which is managed like a stack. This solution is usually chosen for LISP implementations.

Fig. 5.18 Environment for
block D in Fig. 5.16, after the
call sequence A, B, C, D,
with dynamic scope
implemented using an A-list

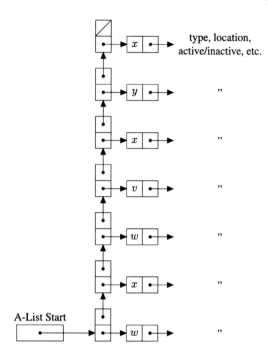

When the execution of a program enters a new environment, the new local associations are inserted into the A-list. When an environment is left, the local associations are removed from the A-list. The information about the denoted objects will contain the location in memory where the object is actually stored, its type, a flag which indicates whether the association for this object is active (there can also be other information needed to make runtime semantic checks). Figure 5.18 shows how dynamic scope is implemented for the example in Fig. 5.16 using an A-list (the fields in grey are implemented using the flags described above and are omitted from the figure). Both using A-list and using direct storage in the activation record, the implementation of dynamic scope has two disadvantages.

First, names must be stored in structures present at runtime, unlike in the scheme that we saw for static scope. In the case of the A-list, this is clear (it depends on its definition). In the case, on the other hand, in which activation records are used to implement local environments, the need to store names depends on the fact that the same name, if declared in different blocks, can be stored in different positions in different activation records. Given that we are using the dynamic scope rule, we cannot statically determine which is the block (and therefore the activation record) that can be used to resolve a non-local reference; we cannot know the position in the activation record to access in order to search for the association belonging the name that we are looking for. The only possibility is therefore explicitly to store the name and perform a search (based on the name itself) at runtime.

The second disadvantage is due to the inefficiency of this runtime search. It can often be the case that is necessary to scan almost all of the list (which is either an A-list or a stack of activation records) in the case reference is made to a name declared in one of the first active blocks (as for "global" names).

Central Referencing environment Table (CRT)   To restrict the effects of these two disadvantages, at the cost of a greater inefficiency in the block entry and exit operations, we can implement dynamic scope in a different way. This alternative approach is based on the *Central Referencing environment Table* (CRT).

Using the CRT-based technique, environments are defined by arranging for all the blocks in the program to refer to an single central table (the CRT). All the names used in the program are stored in this table. For each name, there is a flag indicating whether the association for the name is active or not, together with a value composed of a pointer to information about the object associated with the name (memory location, type, etc.). If we assume that all the identifiers used in the program are not known at compile time, each name can be given a fixed position in the table. At runtime, access to the table can, therefore, take place in constant time by adding the memory address of the start of the table to an offset from the position of the name of interest. When, on the other hand, all names are not known at compile time, the search for a name's position in the table can be make use of runtime hashing for efficiency. The block entry and exit operations now are, however, more complicated. When entering block B from block A, the central table must be modified to describe B's new local environment, and, moreover, deactivated associations must be saved so that they can be restored when block B exits and control returns to block A. Usually a stack is the best data structure for storing such associations.

It should be observed that the associations for a block are not necessarily stored in contiguous locations within the CRT. To perform the operations required of the CRT on block entry and exit, it is necessary, therefore,to consider the individual elements of the table. This can be done in a convenient fashion by associating with each entry in the table (i.e., with every name present) a dedicated stack that contains the valid associations at the top and, in successive locations, the associations for this name that have been deactivated. This solution is shown in Fig. 5.19 (the second column contains the flags).

Alternatively, we can use a single hidden stack separate from the central table to store the deactivated associations for all names. In this case, for every name, the second column of the table contains a flag which indicates whether the association for this name is active or not, while the third column contains the reference to the object denoted by the name in question. When an association is deactivated, it is stored in the hidden stack to be removed when it becomes active again. Considering the structure in Fig. 5.16 and the call sequence A, B, C, D, the development of the CRT is shown in the upper part of Fig. 5.20; the lower portion of the Figure depicts the evolution of the hidden stack.

Using the CRT, with or without the hidden stack. access to an association in the environment requires one access to the table (either direct or by means of a hash function) and one access to another memory area by means of the pointer stored in the table. Therefore, no runtime search is required.

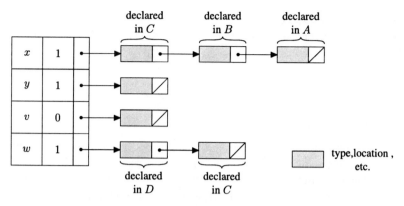

Fig. 5.19 Environment for block D in Fig. 5.16 after the call sequence A, B, C, D, with dynamic scope implemented using a CRT

Fig. 5.20 Environment for block D of Fig. 5.16 after the call sequence A, B, C, D, with dynamic scope implemented using a CRT and hidden stack

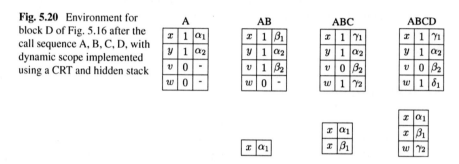

5.6 Chapter Summary

In this chapter, we have examined the main techniques for both static and dynamic memory management, illustrating the reasons for dynamic memory management using a stack and those that require the use of a heap. It remains to consider the important exception to this: in the presence of a particular type of recursion (called *tail recursion*) memory can be managed in a static fashion (this case will be given detailed consideration in the next chapter).

We have illustrated in detail the following on stack-based management:

- The format of activation records for procedures and in-line blocks.
- How the stack is managed by particular code fragments which are inserted into the code for the caller, as well as in the routine being called, and which act to implement the various operations for activation record allocation, initialisation, control field modification, value passing, return of results, and so on.

In the case of heap-based management, we saw:

- Some of the more common techniques for its handling, both for fixed- and variable-sized blocks.
- The fragmentation problem and some methods which can be used to limit it.

Finally, we discussed the specific data structures and algorithms used to implement the environment and, in particular, to implement scope rules. We examined the following in detail:

- The static chain.
- The display.
- The association list.
- The central referencing table.

This has allowed us better to understand our hint in Chap. 4 that it is more difficult to implement the static scope rules than those for dynamic scope. In the first case, indeed, whether static chain pointers or the display is used, the compiler makes use of appropriate information on the structure of declarations. This information is gathered by the compiler using symbol tables and associated algorithms, such as, for example, LeBlanc-Cook's, whose details fall outside the scope of the current text. In the case of dynamic scope, on the other hand, management can be, in principle, performed entirely at runtime, even if auxiliary structures are often used to optimise performance (for example the Central Referencing Table).

5.7 Bibliographic Notes

Static memory management is usually treated in textbooks on compilers, of which the classic is [1]. Determination of the (static) scopes to associate with the names in a symbol table can be done in a number of ways, among which one of the best known is due to LeBlanc and Cook [2]. Techniques for heap management are discussed in many texts, for example [4].

Stack-based management for procedures and for scope was introduced in AL-GOL, whose implementation is described in [3].

For memory management in various programming languages, the reader should refer to texts specific to each language, some which are cited at the end of Chap. 13.

5.8 Exercises

1. Using some pseudo-language, write a fragment of code such that the maximum number of activation records present on the stack at runtime is not statically determinable.
2. In some pseudo-language, write a recursive function such that the maximum number of activation records present at runtime on the stack is statically determinable. Can this example be generalised?
3. Consider the following code fragment:

```
A:{int X= 1;
   ....
```

```
B:{ X  = 3;
     ....
   }


....
  }
```

Assume that B is nested one level deeper that A. To resolve the reference to X present in B, why is it not enough to consider the activation record which immediate precedes that of B on the stack? Provide a counter-example filling the spaces in the fragment with dots with appropriate code.

4. Consider the following program fragment written in a pseudo-language using static scope:

```
void P1 {
   void P2 { body-ofi-P2
            }
   void P3 {
              void P4 { body-of-P4
                       }
              body-of-P3
            }
   body-of-P1
   }
```

Draw the activation record stack region that occurs between the static and dynamic chain pointers when the following sequence of calls, P1, P2, P3,P4,P2 has been made (is it understood that at this time they are all active: none has returned).

5. Given the following code fragment in a pseudo-language with goto (see Sect. 6.3.1), static scope and labelled nested blocks (indicated by A: { ... }):

```
A: { int x = 5;
     goto C;
        B: {int x = 4;
             goto E;
            }
        C: {int x = 3;
             D: {int x = 2;
                }
                  goto B;
             E: {int x = 1; // (**)
                }
            }
   }
```

The static chain is handled using a display. Draw a diagram showing the display and the stack when execution reaches the point indicated with the comment (**). As far as the activation record is concerned, indicate what the only piece of information required for display handling is.

6. Is it easier to implement the static scope rule or the one for dynamic scope? Give your reasons.
7. Consider the following piece of code written in a pseudo-language using static scope and call by reference (see Sect. 7.1.2):

```
{int x = 0;
 int A(reference int y) {
      int x =2;
      y=y+1;
      return B(y)+x;
 }
 int B(reference int y){
      int C(reference int y){
          int x = 3;
          return A(y)+x+y;
      }
      if (y==1) return C(x)+y;
      else return x+y;
 }
 write (A(x));
}
```

Assume that static scope is implemented using a display. Draw a diagram showing the state of the display and the activation-record stack when control enters the function A for the *second* time. For every activation record, just give value for the field that saves the previous value of the display.

References

1. A. V. Aho, R. Sethi, and J. D. Ullman. *Compilers: Principles, Techniques, and Tools.* Addison-Wesley, Reading, 1988.
2. R. P. Cook and T. J. LeBlanc. A symbol table abstraction to implement languages with explicit scope control. *IEEE Trans. Softw. Eng.*, 9(1):8–12, 1983.
3. B. Randell and L. J. Russell. *Algol 60 Implementation.* Academic Press, London, 1964.
4. C. Shaffer. *A Practical Introduction to Data Structures and Algorithm Analysis.* Addison-Wesley, Reading, 1996.

Chapter 6
Control Structure

In this chapter, we will tackle the problem of managing sequence control, an important part in defining the execution of program instructions in a generic abstract machine's interpreter.

In low-level languages, sequence control is implemented in a very simple way, just by updating the value of the PC (Program Counter) register. In high-level languages, however, there are special language-specific constructs which permit the structuring of control and the implementation of mechanisms that are much more abstract than those available on the physical machine. One thinks, for example, of the simple evaluation of an arithmetic expression: even if we find them obvious and natural, operations of this kind requires the use of control mechanisms that specify the order in which operands are evaluated, and operator precedence, and so on.

In this chapter, we will consider the constructs used in programming languages for the explicit or implicit specification of sequence control. We will first consider expressions, spending some time on the syntactic aspects of the usual notation for representing expressions, as well as the semantic aspects of their evaluation. We will then move on to commands and, after discussing the concepts of variable and assignment, we will see the main commands for sequence control present in modern languages, showing the difference between structured and unstructured control and briefly illustrating the principles of structured programming. We will finally examine some aspects that are significant to recursion and clarify an important terminological distinction between imperative and declarative languages.

We will leave the examination of those constructs that allow the implementation of mechanisms for control abstraction until the next chapter.

6.1 Expressions

Expressions, together with commands and declarations, are one of the basic components of every programming language. We can say that expressions are the essential component of every language because, although there exist declarative languages in

M. Gabbrielli, S. Martini, *Programming Languages: Principles and Paradigms,*
Undergraduate Topics in Computer Science,
DOI 10.1007/978-1-84882-914-5_6, © Springer-Verlag London Limited 2010

which commands are absent, expressions, numeric or symbolic, are present in every language.

First, let us try to clarify what sorts of object we are talking about.

Definition 6.1 (Expressions) An expressions is a syntactic entity whose evaluation either produces a value or fails to terminate, in which case the expression is undefined.

The essential characteristic of an expression, that which differentiates it from a command, is therefore that its evaluation produces a value. Examples of numerical expressions are familiar to all: 4+3*2, for example, is an expression whose evaluation is obvious. Moreover, it can be seen that, even in such a simple case, in order to obtain the correct result, we have made an implicit assumption (derived from the mathematical convention) about operator precedence. This assumption, which tells us that * has precedence over + (and that, therefore, the result of the evaluation is 10 and not 14), specifies a control aspect for evaluation of expressions. We will see below other more subtle aspects that can contribute to modify the result of the evaluation of an expression.

Expressions can be non-numeric, for example in LISP, we can write (cons a b) to denote an expression which, if it is evaluated, returns the so-called pair formed by a and b.

6.1.1 Expression Syntax

In general, an expression is composed of a single entity (constant, variable, etc.) or even of an operator (such as +, cons, etc.), applied to a number of arguments (or operands) which are also expressions. We saw in Chap. 2 how expression syntax can be precisely described by a context-free grammar and that an expression can be represented by a derivation tree in which, in addition to syntax, there is also semantic information relating to the evaluation of the expression. Tree structures are also often used to represent an expression internally inside the computer. However, if we want to use expressions in a conventional way in the text of a program, linear notations allow us to write an expression as a sequence of symbols. Fundamentally, the various notations differ from each other by how they represent the application of an operator to its operands. We can distinguish three main types of notation.

Infix Notation   In this notation, a binary operation symbol is placed between the expressions representing its two operands. For example, we write x+y to denote than the addition of x and y, or (x+y)*z to denote the multiplication by z of the result of the addition of x and y. It can be seen that, in order to avoid ambiguity in the application of operator to operands, brackets and precedence rules are required. For operators other than binary ones, we must basically fall back on their representation in terms of binary symbols, even if, in this case, this representation is not

Lisp and S-expressions

The programming language LISP (an acronym of LISt Processor), which was developed at the beginning of the 1960s by John McCarthy and by a group of researchers at MIT (Massachusetts Institute of Technology), is a language designed for symbolic processing, which has been particularly important in Artificial Intelligence. In particular, in the 1970s, the language Scheme was developed from a dialect of Lisp; Scheme is still in use in academic circles.

A Lisp program is composed of sequences of expressions to be evaluated by the language's interpreter. Some expressions are used to define functions which are then called in other expressions. Control is exercised using recursion (there is no iterative construct).

As the very name of the language implies, a LISP program mainly handles expressions constructed from lists. The basic data structures in LISP, in fact, is the dotted pair, or rather a pair of data items written with a dot separating the two components: for example, (A.B). A pair like this is implemented as a *cons* cell, or rather by the application of the cons operator to two arguments, as in (cons A B). As well as atomic types (integers, floating point numbers, character strings), the two arguments of cons can be other dotted pairs so this data structure allows the implementation of symbolic expressions, so-called S-expressions. S-expressions are binary trees which allow the representation of lists as a particular case. For example, it is possible to construct the list A B C as (cons A (cons B (cons C nil))), where nil is a particular value denoting the empty list. Among the many interesting characteristics of LISP, programs and data are represented using the same syntax and the same internal representation. This allows the evaluation of data structures as if they were programs and to modify programs as if they were data.

---

the most natural. A programming language which insists on infix notation even for user-defined functions is Smalltalk, an object oriented language.

Infix notation is the one most commonly used in mathematics, and, as a consequence is the one used by most programming languages, at least for binary operators and for user syntax. Often, in fact, this notation is only an abbreviation or, as we say, a *syntactic sugar* used to make code more readable. For example, in Ada, a + b is an abbreviation for +(a,b), while in C++ the same expression is an abbreviation for a.operator+(b).

Prefix Notation   Prefix notation is another type of notation. It is also called *prefix Polish notation.*[1] The symbol which represents the operation precedes the symbols representing the operands (written from left to right, in the same way as text). Thus, to write the sum of x and y, we can write +(x,y), or, without using parentheses,

---

[1]This terminology derives from the fact that the Polish mathematician W. Łukasiewicz was the person to make prefix notation without parentheses fashionable.

+ x y, while if we want to write the application of the function f to the operands a and b, we write f(a b) or fab.

It is important to note that when using this kind of notation, parentheses and operator precedence rules are of no relevance, provided that the arity (that is the number of operands) of every operator is already known. In fact there is no ambiguity about which operator to apply to any operands, because it is always the one immediately preceding the operands. For example if we write:

*(+(a b)+(c d))

or even

* + a b + c d

we mean the expression represented by (a+b) * (c+d) in normal infix notation.

The majority of regular languages use prefix notation for unary operators (often using parentheses to group arguments) and for user-defined functions. Some programming languages even use prefix notation for binary operators. LISP represents functions using a particular notation known as *Cambridge Polish*, which places operators inside parentheses. In this notation, for example the last expression becomes:

(*(+ a b)(+ c d)).

Postfix Notation   Postfix notation is also called *Reverse Polish*. It is similar to the last notation but differs by placing the operator symbol after the operands. For example, the last expression above when written in postfix notation is:

a b + c d + *.

Prefix notation is used in the intermediate code generated by some compilers. It is also used in programming languages (for example Postscript).

In general, an advantage of Polish notation (prefix or otherwise) over infix is that the former can be used in a uniform fashion to represent operators with any number of operands. In infix notation, on the other had, representing operators with more than two operands means that we have to introduce auxiliary operators. A second advantage, already stated, is that there is the possibility of completely omitting parentheses even if, for reasons of readability, both mathematical prefix notation f(a b) and Cambridge Polish (f a b) use parentheses. A final advantage of Polish notation, as we will see in the next subsection is that it makes the evaluation of an expression extremely simple. For this reason, this notation became rather successful during the 1970s and 80s when it was used for the first pocket-sized calculators.

6.1.2 Semantics of Expressions

According to the way in which an expression is represented, the way in which its semantics is determined changes and so, consequently, does its method of evaluation.
In particular, in infix representation the absence of parentheses can cause ambiguity problems if the precedence rules for different operators and the associativity of
every binary operator are not defined clearly. When considering the most common
programming languages, it is also necessary to consider the fact that expressions are
often represented internally in the form of a tree. In this section we will discuss these
problems, starting with the evaluation of expressions in each of the three notations
that we saw above.

Infix Notation: Precedence and Associativity   When using infix notation, we pay
for the facility and naturalness of use with major complication in the evaluation
mechanism for expressions. First of all, if parentheses are not used systematically,
it is necessary to clarify the precedence of each operator.

   If we write 4 + 3 * 5, for example, clearly we intend the value of 19 as the
result of the expression and not 35: mathematical convention, in fact, tells us that we
have to perform the multiplication first, and the addition next; that is, the expression
is to be read as 4 + (5 * 3) and not as (4 + 3) * 5. In the case of less familiar operators, present in programming languages, matters are considerably more
complex. If, for example, in Pascal one writes:

```
x=4 and y=5
```

where the and is the logical operator, contrary to what many will probably expect,
we will obtain an error (a static type error) because, according to Pascal's precedence rules, this expression can be interpreted as

```
x=(4 and y)=5
```

and not as

```
(x=4) and (y=5).
```

In order to avoid excessive use of parentheses (which, when in doubt it is good to
use), programming languages employ *precedence rules* to specify a hierarchy between the operators used in a language based upon the relative evaluation order.
Various languages differ considerably in their definition of such rules and the conventions of mathematical notation are not always respected to the letter.

   A second problem in expression evaluation concerns operator associativity. If we
write 15-5-3, we could intend it to be read as either (15-5)-3 or as 15-(5-3),
with clearly different results. In this case, too, mathematical convention says that the
usual interpretation is the first. In more formal terms, the operator "−" associates

from left to right.[2] In fact, the majority of arithmetic operators in programming languages associate *from left to right* but there are exceptions. The exponentiation operator, for example, often associates from right to left, as in mathematical notation. If we write 5^{3^2}, or, using a notation more familiar to programmers, 5 ** 3 ** 2, we mean $5^{(3^2)}$, or 5 ** (3 ** 2), and not $(5^3)^2$, or ((5 ** 3) ** 2). Thus, when an operator is used, it is useful to include parentheses when in doubt about precedence and associativity. In fact, there is no lack of special languages that in this respect have rather counter-intuitive behaviour.

In APL, for example, the expression 15−5−3 is interpreted as 15 − (5 − 3) rather than what we would ordinarily expect. The reason for this apparent strangeness is that in APL there are many new operators (defined to operate on matrices) that do not have an immediate equivalents in other formalisms. Hence, it was decided to abandon operator precedence and to evaluate all expressions from right to left.

Even if there is no difficulty in conceiving of a direct algorithm to evaluate an expression in infix notation, the implicit use of precedence and associativity rules, together with the explicit presence of parentheses, complicates matters significantly. In fact, it is not possible to evaluate an expression in a single left-to-right scan (or one from right to left), given that in some cases we must first evaluate the rest of the expression and then return to a sub-expression of interest. For example, in the case of 5+3*2, when the scan from left to right arrives at +, we have to suspend the evaluation of this operator but divert to the evaluation of 3*2 and then go back to the evaluation of +.

Prefix Notation   Expressions written in prefix Polish notation lend themselves to a simple evaluation strategy which proceeds by simply walking the expression from left to right using a stack to hold its components. It can be assumed that the sequence of symbols that forms the expression is syntactically correct and initially not empty. The evaluation algorithm is described by the following steps, where we use an ordinary stack (with the push and pop operations) and a counter C to store the number of operands requested by the last operator that was read:

1. Read in a symbol from the expression and push it on the stack;
2. If the symbol just read is an operator, initialise the counter C with the number of arguments of the operator and go to step 1.
3. If the symbol just read it is an operand, decrement C.
4. If $C \neq 0$, go to 1.
5. If $C = 0$, execute the following operations:
   (a) Apply the last operator stored on the stack to the operands just pushed onto the stack, storing the results in R, eliminate operator and operands from the stack and store the value of R on the stack.
   (b) If there is no operator symbol in the stack go to 6.

---

[2]A binary operator, op, is said to be associative if x op (y op z) = (x op y) op z holds; that is, whether it associates from the right to the left or left to right makes no difference.

(c) Initialise the counter C to $n - m$, where n is the number of the argument of the topmost operator on the stack, and m is number of operands present on the stack above this operator.

(d) Go to 4.

6. If the sequence remaining to be read is not empty, go to 1.

The result of the evaluation is located on the stack when the algorithm finishes. It should be noted that the evaluation of an expression using this algorithm assumes that we know in advance the number of operands required by each operator. This requires that we syntactically distinguish unary from binary operators. Furthermore, it is generally necessary to check that the stack contains enough operands for the application of the operator (Step 5.(c) in the algorithm above). This check is not required when using postfix notation, as we see below.

Postfix Notation   The evaluation of expression in Polish notation is even simpler. In fact, we do not need to check that all the operands for the last operator have been pushed onto the stack, since the operands are read (from left to right) before the operators. The evaluation algorithm is then the following (as usual, we assume that the symbol sequence is syntactically correct and is not empty):

1. Read the next symbol in the expression and push it on the stack.
2. If the symbol just read is an operator apply it to the operands immediately below it on the stack, store the result in R, pop operator and operands from the stack and push the value in R onto the stack.
3. If the sequence remaining to be read is not empty, go to 1.
4. If the symbol just read is an operand, go to 1.

This algorithm also requires us to know in advance the number of operands required by each operator.

6.1.3 Evaluation of Expressions

As we saw the start of the Chap. 2 and as we extensively discussed in that chapter, expressions, like the other programming language constructs, can be conveniently represented by trees. In particular, can be represented by a tree (called the expression's *syntax tree*) in which:

• Every non-leaf node is labelled with an operator.
• Every subtree that has as root a child of a node N constitutes an operand for the operator associated with N.
• Every leaf node is labelled with a constant, variable or other elementary operand.

Trees like this can be directly obtained from the derivation trees of an (unambiguous) grammar for expressions by eliminating non-terminal symbols and by appropriate rearrangement of the nodes. It can be seen also that, given the tree representation, the linear infix, prefix and postfix representations can be obtained by traversing

Fig. 6.1 An expression

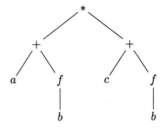

the tree in a symmetric, prefix or postfix order, respectively. The representation of expressions as trees clarifies (without needing parentheses) precedence and associativity of operators. The subtrees found lower in the tree constitute the operands and therefore operators at lower levels must be evaluated before those higher in the tree. For example the tree shown in Fig. 6.1 represents the expression:

```
(a+f(b))*(c+f(b))
```

This expression can be obtained (parentheses apart) from the symmetric-order traversal of the tree (f is here an arbitrary unary operation).

For languages with a compilative implementation, as we have seen, the parser implements syntactic analysis by constructing a derivation tree. In the specific case of expressions then, infix representation in the source code is translated into a tree-based representation. This representation is then used by successive phases of the compilation procedure to generate the object code implementing runtime expressions evaluation. This object code clearly depends on the type of machine for which the compiler is constructed. In the case in which we have a traditional physical machine, for example, code of a traditional kind (i.e. in the form opcode operand1 operand2) is generated which uses registers as well as a temporary memory locations to store intermediate results of evaluation.

In some particular cases, on the other hand, object code can be represented using a prefix or postfix form which is subsequently evaluated by a stack architecture. This is the case for example in the executable code for many implementations of SNOBOL4 programs.

In the case of languages with an interpretative implementation, it is also convenient to translate expressions, normally represented in the source code in infix notation, into a tree representation which can then be directly evaluated using a tree traversal. This is the case, for example, in interpreted implementations of LISP, where the entire program is represented as a tree.

It is beyond the scope of the present text to go into details on mechanisms for generating code or for evaluating expression in an interpreter. However, it is important to clarify some difficult points which often cause ambiguity. For convenience, we will fix on the evaluation of expressions represented in infix form. We will see that what we have to say applies equally to the direct evaluation of expressions represented as a tree, as well as to code generation-mechanisms.

Subexpression Evaluation Order Infix notation precedence and associativity rules (or the structure, when expressions are represented as trees) do not hint at the order to evaluate an operator's operands (i.e., nodes at the same level). For example, in the expression in Fig. 6.1, nothing tells us that it is necessary first to evaluate either a+f(b) or c+f(b). There is also nothing explicit about whether the evaluation of operands or operator should come first; nor, in general, whether expressions which are mathematically equivalent can be inter-substituted without modifying the result (for example, (a-b+c) and (a+c-b) could be considered equivalent).

While in mathematical terms these differences are unimportant (the result does not change), from our viewpoint these questions are extremely relevant and for the following five reasons.

Side effects In imperative programming languages, expression evaluation can modify the value of any variables through so-called side effects. A side effect is an action that influences the result (partial or final) of a computation without otherwise explicitly returning a value in the context in which it is found. The possibility of side effects renders the order of evaluation of operands relevant to the final result. In our example in Fig. 6.1, if the evaluation of the function f were to modify the value of its operand through side effects, first executing a+f(b) rather than c+f(b), could change the value produced by the evaluation (see Exercise 1). As far as side effects are concerned, languages follow various approaches. On the one hand, pure declarative languages do not permit side effects at all, while languages which do allow them in some cases forbid the use in expressions of functions that can cause side effects. In other, more common cases where the presence of side effects is permitted, the order with which expressions are evaluated is, though, clearly stated in the definition of the language. Java, for example, imposes left-to-right evaluation of expressions (while C fixes no order at all).

Finite arithmetic Given the set of numbers represented in a computer is finite (see also Sect. 8.3), reordering expressions can cause overflow problems. For example, if a has, as its value, the maximum integer representable and b and c are positive numbers such that b > c, right-to-left evaluation of (a-b+c) does not produce overflow, while we have an overflow resulting from the evaluation from left to right of (a+c-b). Moreover, when we do not have overflow, the limited precision of computer arithmetic implies that changing the order of the operands can lead to different results (this is particularly relevant in cases of floating point computation).

Undefined operands When the application of operator to operands is considered, two evaluation strategies can be followed. The first, called *eager evaluation*, consists of first evaluating all the operands and then applying the operator to the values thus obtained. The strategy probably seems the most reasonable when reasoning in terms of normal arithmetic operators. The expressions that we use in programming languages, however, pose problems over and above those posed by arithmetic expressions, because some can be defined even when some of the operands are missing. Let us consider the example of a conditional expression of the form:

```
a == 0 ? b : b/a
```

We can write this in C to denote the value of b/a when a is non-zero and b, other-wise. This expression results from the application of a single operator (expressed in infix notation using two binary operators ? and :) to three operands (the boolean expression, a==0, and the two arithmetic expressions b and b/a). Clearly here we cannot use eager evaluation for such conditional expressions because the expression b/a would have to be evaluated even when a is equal to zero and this would produce an error.

In such a case, it is therefore better to use a *lazy evaluation* strategy which mainly consists of *not* evaluating operands before the application of the operator, but in passing the un-evaluated operands to the operator, which, when it is evaluated, will decide which operands are required, and will only evaluate the ones it requires.

The lazy evaluation strategy, used in some declarative languages, is much more expensive to implement than eager evaluation and for this reason, most languages use eager evaluation (with the significant exception of conditional expressions as we will see below). There are languages which use a mix of both the techniques (ALGOL, for example). We will discuss the various strategies for evaluating ex-pressions in greater detail when we consider functional languages in Chap. 11.

Short-circuit evaluation The problem detailed in the previous point presents itself with particular clarity when evaluating Boolean expressions. For example, consider the following expression (in C syntax):

```
a == 0 || b/a > 2
```

If the value of a is zero and both operands of || are evaluated at the same time, it is clear that an error will result (in C, "||" denotes the logical operation of dis-junction). To avoid this problem, and to improve the efficiency of the code, C, like other languages uses a form of lazy evaluation, also called *short-circuiting evalua-tion*, of boolean expressions. If the first operand of a disjunction has the value *true* then the second is not evaluated, given that the overall result will certainly have the value *true*. In such a case, the second expression is *short-circuited* in the sense that we arrive at the final value before knowing the value of all of the operands. Analogously, if the first operand of a conjunction has the value *false*, the second is not evaluated, given that the overall result can have nothing other than the value *false*.

It is opportune to recall that not all languages use this strategy for boolean ex-pressions. Counting on the presence of a short-circuited evaluation, without being certain that the language uses it, is dangerous. For example, we can write in Pascal

```
p := list;
while (p <> nil ) and (p^.value <> 3) do
    p := p^.next;
```

The intention of this code is to traverse a list until we have arrived at the end or until we have encountered the value 3. This is badly written code that can produce a runtime error. Pascal, in fact, does not use short-circuit evaluation. In the case in which we have $p = nil$, the second operand of the conjunction ($p^.value <> 3$) yields an error when it dereferences a null pointer. Similar code, on the other hand, *mutatis mutandis*, can be written in C without causing problems. In order to avoid ambiguity, some languages (for example C and Ada), explicitly provide different boolean operators for short-circuit evaluation. Finally, it should be noted that this kind of evaluation can be simulated using a conditional command (see Exercise 2).

Optimisation Frequently, the order evaluation of subexpressions influences the efficiency of the evaluation of an expression for reasons relating to the organisation of the physical machine. For example, consider the following code:

```
a = vector[i];
b = a*a + c*d;
```

In the second expression, it is probably better first to evaluate $c*d$, given that the value of a has to be read from memory (with the first instruction) and might not be yet available; in such a case, the processor would have to wait before calculating a * a. In some cases, the compiler can change the order of operands expressions to obtain code that is more efficient but semantically equivalent.

The last point explains many of the semantic problems that appear while evaluating expressions. Given the importance of the efficiency of the object code produced by the compiler, it is given considerable liberty in the precise definition of its expression evaluation method, without it being specified at the level of semantic description of the language (as we have already said, Java is a rare exception). The result of this kind of approach is that, sometimes, different implementations of the same language produce different results for the same expression, or have errors at runtime whose source is hard to determine.

Wishing to capitalise in a pragmatic prescription, given what has been said so far, if we do not know the programming language well and the specific implementation we are using, if we want to write correct code, it is wise to use all possible means at our disposal to eliminate as many sources of ambiguity as possible in expression evaluation (such as brackets parentheses, specific boolean operations, auxiliary variables in expressions, etc.).

6.2 The Concept of Command

If, as we were saying above, expressions are present in all programming languages, the same is not true for commands. They are constructs that are typically present (but not entirely restricted to them) in so-called imperative languages.

Definition 6.2 (Command) A command is a syntactic entity whose evaluation does not necessarily return a value but can have a side effect.

A command, or more generally, any other construct, has a side-effect if it influences the result of the computation but its evaluation returns no value to the context in which it is located.

This point is fairly delicate and merits clarification with an example. If the print command in a hypothetical programming language can print character strings supplied as an argument, when the command print "pippo" is evaluated, we will not obtain a value but only a side-effect which is composed of the characters "pippo" appearing on the output device.

The attentive reader will be aware that the definition of command, just as the previous definition of expression, it is not very precise, given that we have referred to an informal concept of evaluation (the one performed by the abstract machine of the language to which the command or the expression belongs). It is clear that we can always modify the interpreter so that we obtain some value as a result of the evaluation of the command. This is what happens in some languages (for example in C assignment also returns the value to the right of =, see Sect. 6.2.2).

A precise definition and, equally, an exact distinction, between expressions and commands on the basis of their semantics is possible only in the setting of a formal definition of the semantics of language. In such a context, the difference between the two concepts derives from the fact that, once a starting state has been fixed, the result of the evaluation of an expression is a value (together with possible side-effects). On the other hand, the result of evaluating a command is a new state which differs from the start state precisely in the modifications caused by the side-effects of the command itself (and which are due principally to assignments). Command is therefore a construct whose purpose is the modification of the *state*. The concept of state can be defined in various ways; in Sect. 2.5, we saw a simple version, one which took into account the value of all the variables present in the program.

If the aim of a command is to modify the state, it is clear that the assignment command is the elementary construct in the computational mechanism for languages with commands. Before dealing with them, however, it is necessary to clarify the concept of variable.

6.2.1 The Variable

In mathematics, a variable is an unknown which can take on all the numerical values in a predetermined set. Even if we keep this in mind, in programming languages, it is necessary to specify this concept in more detail because, as we will see also in Sects. 11.1 and 12.3, the imperative paradigm uses a model for variables which is substantially different from that employed the in logic and functional programming paradigms.

The classical imperative paradigm uses *modifiable variables*. According to this model, the variable is seen as a sort of container, or location (clearly referring to physical memory), to which a name can be given and which contains values (usually of a homogeneous type, for example integers real, characters etc.). These values can

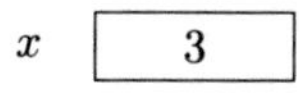

Fig. 6.2 A modifiable
variable

$$x \quad \boxed{ 3 }$$

be changed over time, by execution of assignment commands (whence comes the adjective "modifiable"). This terminology might seem tautological to the average computer person, who is almost always someone who knows an imperative language and is therefore used to modifiable variables. The attentive reader, though, will have noted that, in reality, variables are not always modifiable. In mathematics a variable represents a value that is unknown but when such a value is defined the link thus created cannot be modified later.

Modifiable variables are depicted in Fig. 6.2. The small box which represents the variable with the name x can be re-filled with a value (in the figure, the value is 3). It can be seen that the variable (the box) is different from the name x which denotes it, even if it is common to say "the variable x" instead of "the variable with the name x".

Some imperative languages (particularly object-oriented ones) use a model that is different from this one. According to this alternative model, a variable is not a container for a value but is a *reference* to (that is a mechanism which allows access to) a value which is typically stored in the heap. This is a new concept analogous to that of the pointer (but does not permit the usual pointer-manipulation operations). We will see this in the next section after we have introduced assignment commands. This variable model is called, in [8], the "reference model", while in [6], where it is discussed in the context of the language CLU, is called the "object model". Henceforth, we will refer to this as the *reference model* of variables.

(Pure) functional languages, as we will see in more detail in Sect. 11.1, use a concept of variable similar to the mathematical one: a variable is nothing more than an identifier that stands for a value. Rather, it is often said that functional languages "do not have variables", meaning that (in their pure forms) they do not have any modifiable variables.

Logic languages also use identifiers associated with values as variables and, as with functional languages, once a link between a variable identifier and a value is created, it can never be eliminated. There is however a mode in which the value associated with a variable can be modified without altering the link, as will be seen in Sect. 12.3.

6.2.2 Assignment

Assignment is the basic command that allows the modification of the values associated with modifiable variables. It also modifies the state in imperative languages. It is an apparently very simple command. However, as will be seen, in different programming languages, there are various subtleties to be taken into account.

Let us first see the case that will probably be most familiar to the reader. This is the case of an imperative language which uses modifiable variables and in which assignment is considered only as a command (and not also as an expression). One example is Pascal, in which we can write

```
X := 2
```

to indicate that the variable X is assigned the value 2. The effect of such a command is that, after its execution, the container associated with the variable (whose name is) X will contain the value 2 in place of the value that was there before. It should be noted that this is a side effect, given that the evaluation of the command does not on its own, return any kind of value. Furthermore, every access to X in the rest of the program will return the value 2 and not the one previously stored.

Consider now the following command:

```
X := X+1
```

The effect of this assignment, as we know, is that of assigning to the variable X its previous value incremented by 1. Let us observe the different uses of the name, X, of the variable in the two operands of the assignment operator. The X appearing to the left of the : = symbol is used to indicate the container (the location) inside which the variable's value can be found. The occurrence of the X on the right of the : = denotes the value inside the container. This important distinction is formalised in programming languages using two different sets of values: *l-values* are those values that usually indicate locations and therefore are the values of expressions that can be on the left of an assignment command. On the other hand, *r-values* are the values that can be stored in locations, and therefore are the values of expressions that can appear on the right of an assignment command. In general, therefore, the assignment command has the syntax of a binary operator in infix form:

```
exp1 OpAss exp2
```

where OpAss indicates the symbol used in the particular language to denote assignment (:= in Pascal, = in C, FORTRAN, SNOBOL and Java, ← in APL, etc.). The meaning of such a command (in the case of modifiable variables) is as follows: compute the l-value of exp1, determining, thereby, a container *loc*; compute the r-value of exp2 and modify the contents of *loc* by substituting the value just calculated for the one previously there.[3] Which expressions denote (in the context on the left of an assignment) an l-value depends on the programming language: the usual cases are variables, array elements, record fields (note that, as a consequence, calculation of an l-value can be arbitrarily complex because it could involve function calls, for example when determining an array index).

In some languages, for example C, assignment is considered to be an operator whose evaluation, in addition to producing a side effect, also returns the r-value thus computed. Thus, if we write in C:

---

[3]Some languages, e.g., Java, allow the left-hand side to be evaluated before the right-hand side; others (e.g., C), leave this decision to the implementer.

```
x = 2;
```

the evaluation of such a command, in addition to assigning the value 2 to x, returns the value 2. Therefore, in C, we can also write:

```
y = x = 2;
```

which should be interpreted as:

```
(y = (x = 2));
```

This command assigns the value 2 to x as well as to y. In C, as in other languages, there are other assignment operators that can be used, either for increasing code legibility or avoiding unforeseen side effects. Let us take up the example of incrementing a variable. Once again we have:

```
x = x+1;
```

This command, unless optimised by the compiler, requires, in principle, two accesses to the variable x: one to determine the l-value, and one to obtain the r-value. If, from the efficiency viewpoint, this is not serious (and can be easily optimised by the compiler), there is a question which is much more important and which is again related to side-effects. Let us then consider the code:

```
b = 0;
a[f(3)] = a[f(3)]+1;
```

where a is a vector and f is a function defined as follows:

```
int f (int n){
    if b == 0{
        b=1;
        return 1;
        }
    else return 2;
}
```

This function is defined in such a way that the non-local reference to b in the body of f refers to the same variable b that is cleared in the previous fragment.

Given that f modifies the non-local variable b, it is clear that the assignment

```
a[f(3)] = a[f(3)]+1
```

does not have the effect of incrementing the value of the element a[f(3)] of the array, as perhaps we wanted it to do. Instead, it has the effect of assigning the value of a[1]+1 to a[2] whenever the evaluation of the left-hand component of the assignment precedes the evaluation of the right-hand one. It should be noted, on the other hand, that the compiler cannot optimise the computation of r-values, because the programmer might have wanted this apparently anomalous behaviour.

To avoid this problem we can clearly use an auxiliary variable and write:

```
int j = f(3);
a[j]   = a[j]+1;
```

Doing this obscures the code and introduces a variable which expresses very little. To avoid all of this, languages like C provide assignment operators which allow us to write:

```
a[f(3)] += 1;
```

This add to the r-value of the expression present on the left the quantity present on the right of the += operator, and then assigns the result to the location obtained as the l-value of the expression on the left. There are many specific assignment commands that are similar to this one. The following is an incomplete list of the assignment commands in C, together with their descriptions:

- X = Y: assign the r-value of Y to the location obtained as the l-value of X and return the r-value of X;
- X += Y (or X -= Y): increment (decrement) X by the quantity given by the r-value of Y and return of the new r-value;
- ++X (or -X): increment (decrement) X by and return the new r-value of X;
- X++ (or X-): return the r-value of X and then increment (decrement) X.

We will now see how the reference model for variables differs from the traditional modifiable-variable one. In a language which uses the reference model (for example, CLU and, as we will see, in specific cases, Java) after an assignment of the form:

```
x=e
```

x becomes a reference to an object that is obtained from the evaluation of the expression e. Note that this does not copy the value of e into the location associated with x. This difference becomes clear if we consider an assignment between two variables using the reference model.

```
x=y
```

After such an assignment, x and y are two references to the same object. In the case in which this object is modifiable (for example, record or array), a modification performed using the variable x becomes visible through variable y and vice versa. In this model, therefore, variables behave in a way similar to variables of a pointer type in languages which have that type of data. As we will more clearly see in Sect. 8.4.5, a value of a pointer type is no more than the location of some data item (or, equivalently, its address in some area of memory). In many languages which have pointer types, the values of such types can be explicitly manipulated (which causes several problems as we will also see in Chap. 8). In the case of the reference model, however, these values can be manipulated only implicitly using assignments

Environment and Memory

In Chap. 2, we defined the semantics of a command by referring to a simple notion of state, which we defined as a function associating with every variable present in the program, the value it takes. This concept of state, although adequate for didactic purposes in mini-languages, is not sufficient when we want to describe the semantics of real programming languages which use modifiable variables and assignments. In fact, we have already seen in Chap. 4 (and will see in more detail in the next two chapters) that parameter-passing mechanisms as well as pointers can easily create situations in which two different names, for example X and Y, refer to the same variable, or rather the same location in memory. Such case of aliasing cannot be described using a simple function *State: Names* → *Values* because with a simple function it is not possible to express the fact that a modification of the value associated with (the variable denoted by) X also reflects on the value associated with Y. To correctly express the meaning of modifiable variables, we therefore use two separate functions. The first, called the *environment*, mostly corresponds to the concept of environment introduced in Chap. 4: in other words, it is a function *Environment: Names* → *DenotableValues* which maps names to the values they denote. The set (or, as one says in semantics jargon, the *domain*) of names often coincides with that of identifiers. The domain *DenotableValues*, instead, includes all values to which a name can be given; what these values are depends on the programming language but if the language provides modifiable variables then this domain certainly includes memory locations.

The values associated with locations are, on the other hand, expressed by a function *Memory: Locations* → *StorableValues* which (informally) associates every location with the value stored in it. In this case also, what exactly is a storable value depends on the specific language.

Therefore, when we say that "in the current state the variable X has the value 5", formally we mean to say that we have an environment ρ and a memory σ such that $\sigma(\rho(X)) = 5$. Note that when a variable is understood to be an l-value, we are interested only in the location denoted by the name and, therefore, only in the environment is specified, while when we understand it as an r-value the store is also used. For example given environment ρ, and a store σ, the effect of the command X=Y is to produce a new state in which the value of $\rho(\sigma(Y))$ is associated with $\rho(X)$. Let us recall, for completeness, that a third value domain important in the language semantics is formed from *ExpressibleValues*: these are those values which can be the result of the evaluation of a complex expression.

between variables. Java (which does not have pointers) adopts the reference model for variables for all class types, but uses the traditional modifiable-variable model for primitive types (integers, reals floating point, booleans and characters).

Below, unless otherwise specified, when we talk about variables, we mean the modifiable variable.

6.3 Sequence Control Commands

Assignment is the basic command in imperative languages (and in "impure" declarative languages); it expresses the elementary computation step. The remaining commands serve to define sequence control, or rather serve to specify the order in which state modifications produced by assignments, are to be performed. These other commands can be divided into three categories:

Commands for explicit sequence control These are the sequential command and goto. Let us consider, in addition, the composite command, which allows us to consider a group of commands as a single one, as being in this category.

Conditional (or selection) commands These are the commands which allow the specification of alternative paths that the competition can take. They depend on the satisfaction of specific conditions.

Iterative commands These allow the repetition of a given command for a predefined number of times, or until the satisfaction of specific conditions.

Let us consider these command typologies in detail.

6.3.1 Commands for Explicit Sequence Control

Sequential Command   The *sequential command*, indicated in many languages by a ";", allows us directly to specify the sequential execution of two commands. If we write:

```
C1 ; C2
```

the execution of C2 starts immediately after C1 terminates. In languages in which the evaluation of a command also returns a value, the value returned by the evaluation of the sequential command is that of the second argument.

Obviously we can write a sequence of commands such as:

```
C1 ; C2 ; ... ; Cn
```

with the implicit assumption that the operator ";" associates to the left.

Composite Command   In modern imperative languages, as we have already seen in Chap. 4, it is possible to group a sequence of commands into a *composite command* using appropriate delimiters such as those used by Algol:

```
begin
...
end
```

or those in C:

```
{
...
}
```

Imperative and Declarative Languages

Denotable, storable and expressible values, even if they have a non-empty intersection, are conceptually distinct sets. In effect, many important differences between various languages depend on how these domains are defined. For example, functions are denotable but not expressible in Pascal, while they are expressible in Lisp and ML. A particularly important difference between various languages concerns the presence of storable value and the *Memory* semantic function which we saw in the previous box. In fact, in a rather synthetic fashion, we can classify as *imperative* those languages which have environments as well as memory functions; those languages which have only environments are *declarative*. Imperative languages, while they are high-level languages, are inspired by the physical structure of the computer. In them the concept of memory (or state) is interpreted as the set of associations between memory locations and values stored in those locations. A program, according to this paradigm, is a set of *imperative* commands and computation consists of a sequence of steps which modify the state, using as its elementary command the assignment. The terminology "imperative" here has to do with natural language: as in an imperative phrase, we say "take that apple" to express a command, so with an imperative command we can say " assign to x the value 1". Most programming languages normally used belong to the imperative paradigm (Fortran, Algol, Pascal, C, etc.).

Declarative languages were introduced with the aim of offering a higher level programming paradigms, close to the notations of mathematics and logic, abstracting from the characteristics of the physical machine on which the programs are executed. In declarative languages (or at least in "pure" versions of them) there are no commands to modify the state, given that there are neither modifiable variables nor a semantic memory function. Programs are formed from a set of declarations (from which the name is derived) of functions or relations which define new values. According to the elementary mechanism used to specify the characteristics of the result, declarative languages are divided into two classes: functional and logic programming languages (the latter, also called logic languages for short). In the first case, computation consists of the evaluation of functions defined by the programmer using rules of a mathematical kind (mostly composition and application). In the second form of declarative language, on the other hand, computation is based on first-order logical deduction. Let us recall that, in actuality, there exist "impure" functional and logic languages that also have imperative characteristics (in particular, they include assignment). We will encounter both functional and logic languages in two next chapters.

Such a composite command, also called a *block*, can be used in any context in which a simple command is expected and therefore, in particular, can be used inside another composite command to create a tree-like structure of arbitrary complexity.

A Quibble about ";"

Being rigorous, the ";" used to separate commands is not always a sequential command. In C, C++ and Java, for example, it is a command *terminator* more than an operator expressing concatenation. In fact, this can be easily seen when we deal with the last command in a block. In these languages, the ";" is always required, even if the command is not followed by another as in

```
{x=1;
 x=x+1;
}
```

In languages like Pascal, on the other hand, ";" is really an operator that sequentialises commands. The same example as above can be written as:

```
begin
    x:=1;
    x:=x+1
end
```

To insert a ";" without there being a command to follow it is, however, a venial programming sin which the compiler absolves by inserting an *empty command* between the ";" and the end. An empty command is denoted by nothing syntactically and corresponds to no action.

Goto   A unique place is occupied in the panorama of sequential control commands by the goto. It was included in the first programming languages and continues to be included in languages. It has 2 different forms (conditional or direct). This command is directly inspired by jump instructions in assembler languages and therefore by the sequence control of the hardware machine. The execution of the command

```
goto A
```

transfers control to the point in the program at which the label A occurs (different languages differ in what exactly constitutes a label but these differences are not relevant to us).

Despite its apparent simplicity and naturalness, the goto command has been at the centre of a considerable debate since the start of the 1970s (see, for example, the famous article by Dijkstra referred to in the bibliography), and, after about 30 years of debate, we can say that it is the detractors who have beaten the supporters of this command. To clarify the sense of this debate, let us, first of all, observe that the goto is not essential to the expressiveness of a programming language. A theorem due to Böhm and Jacopini in fact shows that any program can be translated into an equivalent one which does not use the goto (the formulation of the theorem, obviously, is much more precise than our account). This result, moreover, does not come down on one side or the other. If, on the one hand, we can assert that, in principle, the goto is useless, on the other, it is possible to object (as has been done) that even this result shows that it is permissible to use the goto in programs. If just we wish to eliminate this command, in fact, it can be done using the Böhm and Jacopini transformation (which, in particular, completely destroys the structure of the reformulated program).

The nexus of the question really is not of a theoretical nature but of a pragmatic one. Using goto, it is easily possible to write code which soon becomes incomprehensible and which still remains incomprehensible when all gotos are eliminated. We can think, for example, of a program of some considerable size where we have inserted jumps between points which are some of thousands of lines of code apart. Or, we can think of a subprogram in which exits are made at different points based on some condition and the exits are performed by gotos. These and other arbitrary uses of this construct make the code hard to understand, and therefore hard to modify, correct and maintain; this has the obvious negative consequences in terms of cost. To all of this, we can add the fact that the goto with its primitive method of transferring control, does not accord well with other mechanisms present in high-level languages. What happens, for example, if we jump *inside* of a block? When and how is the activation record for this block initialised so that everything works correctly?

If goto were used in an extremely controlled fashion, locally to small regions of code, the majority of these disadvantages would disappear. However, the cases in which it can be useful to use this command, such as exit from loops, return from a subprograms, handling of exceptions, can, in modern programming languages, be handled by specific, more appropriate, constructs. We can therefore assert that in modern high-level languages, the goto is a construct whose use is disappearing. Java is the first commercial language to have completely removed it from its set of admissible commands.

Other sequence control commands If goto is dangerous in its general form, there are local and limited uses which are useful in given circumstances. Many languages make available limited forms of jump to confront these pragmatic necessities without having to make use of the brute force of a goto. Among these commands (which take on different forms in different languages), we find constructs such as break (for terminating the execution of a loop, of a case, or, in some languages, of the current block), continue (for terminating the current iteration in an iterative command and force the starting of the immediately following command) or return (to terminate the evaluation of the function, returning control to the caller, sometimes also passing a value).

Finally, a more elaborate sequence control can be implemented using exceptions. We will deal with these in a more detailed fashion in Sect. 7.3 below.

6.3.2 Conditional Commands

Conditional commands, or selection commands, express one alternative between two or more possible continuations of the computation based on appropriate logical conditions. We can divide conditional commands into two groups.

If   The `if` command, originally introduced in the ALGOL60 language, is present in almost all imperative languages and also in some declarative languages, in various syntactic forms which, really, can be reduced to the form:

```
if Bexp then C1 else C2
```

where `Bexp` is a boolean expression, while `C1` and `C2` are commands. Informally, the semantics of such a command expresses an alternative in the execution of the computation, based on the evaluation of the expression `Bexp`. When this evaluation returns true, the command `C1` is executed, otherwise the command `C2` is executed. The command is often present in the form without the `else` branch:

```
if Bexp then C1
```

In this case, too, if the condition is false, the command `C1` is not executed and control passes to the command immediately after the conditional. As we saw in Chap. 2, the presence of a branching `if` as in the command

```
if Bexp1 if Bexp2 then C1 else C2
```

causes problems of ambiguity, which can be resolved using a suitable grammar which formally describes the rules adopted by the language (for example, the `else` branch belongs to the innermost `if`; this is the rule in Java and it is used in almost every language). To avoid problems of ambiguity, some languages use a " terminator" to indicate where the conditional command ends, as for example in:

```
if Bexp then C1 else C2 endif
```

Furthermore, in some cases, instead of using a list of nested `if then elses`, use is made of an `if` equipped with more branches, analogous to the following:

```
if Bexp1 then C1
   elseif Bexp2 then C2
   ...
   elseif Bexpn then Cn
   else  Cn+1
endif
```

The implementation of the conditional command poses no problems, and makes use of instructions for test and jump that are found in the underlying physical machine.[4] The evaluation of the boolean expression can use the shorter circuit technique that we saw above.

Case   The command is a specialisation of the `if` command, just discussed, with more branches. In its simplest form it is written as follows:

```
case Exp   of
    label1:  C1;
    label2:  C2;
    ...
    labeln:  Cn;
else Cn+1
```

where `Exp` is an expression whose value is of a type compatible with that of the labels `label1`, ..., `labeln`, while `C1`, ..., `Cn+1` are commands. Each label is represented by one or more constants and the constant used in different labels are different from each other. The type permitted for labels, as well as their form, varies from language to language. In most cases, a discrete type is permitted (see Sect. 8.3), including enumerations and intervals. So, for example, we can use the constants 2 and 4 to denote a label, but in some languages we can also write 2 , 4 to indicate either the value 2 or the value 4, or 2 .. 4 to indicate all values between 2 and 4 (inclusive).

The meaning of this command, as stated above, is analogous to that of a multi-branch `if`. Once the expression `Exp` has been evaluated, the command which occurs in the unique branch whose label includes the value to which `Exp` evaluated is executed. The `else` branch is executed whenever there is no other branch whose label satisfies the condition stated above.

It is clear that whatever can be done using a `case` can certainly be expressed using a nested series of `if`s. Even so, many languages include some form of case in their commands, either to improve the readability of the code, or because it is possible to compile a `case` much more efficiently than a long series of nested `if`s. A `case` is, in fact, implemented in assembly language using a vector of contiguous cells called a *jump table*, in which each element of the table contains the address of the first instruction of the corresponding command in the case's branches. The use of such a table is shown in Fig. 6.3, where, for simplicity, it is assumed that the labels `label1`,.., `labeln` are the consecutive constants $0, 1, \dots, n-1$. As should be clear in the figure, the expression which appears as an argument to the `case` is evaluated first of all. The value thus obtained is then used as an offset (index) to compute the position in the jump table of the instruction which performs the jump to the chosen branch. The extension of this mechanism to the general case in which labels are sets or intervals as simple (see Exercise 3).

---

[4]At the assembly language level, and therefore in the language of the physical machine, there are jump operations, conditional or not, analogous to the `goto` in high-level languages.

Fig. 6.3 Implementation of
case

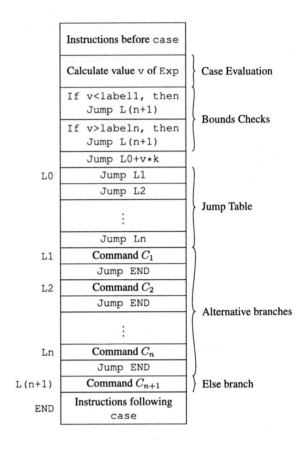

This implementation mechanism for case gives greater efficiency than a series of nested ifs. Using a jump table, once the value of the expression is calculated, two jump instructions are required to arrive at the code of the command to execute. Using nested ifs, on the other hand, for n alternative branches (in the worst case of an unbalanced if), it is necessary to evaluate $O(n)$ conditions and perform $O(n)$ jumps before arriving at the command of interest. The disadvantage of using a jump table is that, since it is a linear structure whose contiguous elements correspond to successive label values, it can consume a lot of space when the label values are dispersed over a fairly wide interval or when the individual labels are a type denoting a wide interval. In this case alternative methods can be used for calculating the jump address, such as sequential tests hashing or even methods based on binary search.

Different languages exhibit significant differences in their case commands. In C, for example, the switch has the following syntax (also to be found in C++ and in Java):

switch (Exp) *body*

where body can be any command that all. In general, though, the body is formed from a block in which some commands can be labelled; that is they are of the form:

```
case label : command
```

while the last command of the block is of the form:

```
default : command
```

When the expression Exp is evaluated and control is to be transferred to the command whose label coincides with the resulting value, if there are no labels with such a value, control passes to the command with the label default. If there is no default command, control passes to the first command following the switch. It can be seen that, once a the branch of the switch has been selected, control then flows into the immediately following branches. To obtain a construct with semantics analogous to that of the case we discussed above, it is necessary to insert an explicit control transfer at the end of the block, using a break:

```
switch (Exp){
    case label1: C1 break;
    case label2: C2 break;
    ...
    case labeln: Cn break;
    default: Cn+1 break;
}
```

It can be seen also that in a switch, the value returned by the evaluation of the expression might not appear in any label, in which case the entire command has no effect. Finally, lists or ranges of values are not permitted as labels. This however is no real limitation, given that lists of values can be implemented using the fact that control passes from one branch to its successor when break is omitted. If, for example, we write:

```
switch (Exp){
    case 1:
    case 2: C2 break;
    case 3: C3 break;
    default: C4 break;
}
```

in the case in which the value of Exp is 1, given that the corresponding branch does not contain a break command, control passes from the case 1 branch immediately to the case 2 branch and therefore it is as if we had used a list of values 1, 2 for the label of C2.

6.3.3 Iterative Commands

The commands that we have seen up to this point, excluding `goto`, only allow us to
express finite computations, whose maximum length is determined statically by the
length of the program text.[5] A language which had only such commands would be
of highly limited expressiveness. It would certainly not be Turing complete (recall
Sect. 3.3), in that it would not permit the expression of all possible algorithms (consider, for example, scanning a vector of n elements, where n is not known *a priori*).

In order to acquire the expressive power necessary to express all possible algorithms in low-level languages, jump instructions allowing the repetition of groups of
instructions by jumping back to the start of the code are needed. In high-level languages, given that, as has been seen, it is desirable to avoid commands like `goto`,
two basic mechanisms are employed to achieve the same effect: *structured iteration*
and *recursion*. The first, which we consider in this section, is more familiar from
imperative languages (and they almost always allow recursion as well). Suitable linguistic constructs (which we can regard as special versions of the jump command)
allow us compactly to implement loops in which commands are repeated or *iterated*.
At the linguistic level, it is possible to distinguish between *unbounded iteration* and
bounded iteration. In bounded iteration, repetition is implemented by constructs that
allow a determinate number of iterations. Unbounded iteration, on the other hand,
is implemented by constructs which continue until some condition becomes true.

Recursion which we will consider in the next section, allows, instead, the expression of loops in an implicit fashion, including the possibility that a function
(or procedure) can call itself, thereby repeating its own body an arbitrary number
of times. The use of recursion is more common in declarative languages (in many
functional and logic languages there does not, in fact, exist any iterative construct).

Unbounded iteration Unbounded iteration is logically controlled iteration. It is
implemented by linguistic constructs composed of two parts: a loop *condition* (or
guard) and a *body*, which is composed of a (possibly compound) command. When
executed, the body is repeatedly executed until the guard becomes false (or true,
according to the construct).

In its most common form, this type of iteration takes the form of the `while`
command, originally introduced in ALGOL:while

while (Bexp) **do** C

The meaning of this command is as follows: (1) the boolean expression `Bexp` is
evaluated; (2) if this evaluation returns the value *true*, execute the command `C` and
return to (1); otherwise the `while` command terminates.

In some languages there are also commands that test the condition *after* execution
of the command (which is therefore always executed at least once). This construct
is for example present in Pascal in the following form:

---

[5]It can easily be seen that the maximum length of the computation is a linear function of the length
of the program.

repeat C **until** Bexp

This is no more than an abbreviation for:

```
C;
while not Bexp do C
```

(not Bexp here indicates the negation of the expression Bexp). In C an analogous construct is do:

do C **while** (Bexp)

which corresponds to:

```
C;
while Bexp do C
```

(note that the guard is not negated as in the case of repeat.)

The while construct is simple to implement, given that it corresponds directly to a loop that is implemented on the physical machine using a conditional jump instruction. This simplicity of implementation should not deceive us about the power of this construct. Its addition to a programming language which contains only assignment and conditional commands immediately makes the language Turing complete. Our mini-language from Chap. 2 is therefore Turing complete (or: it allows the implementation of all computable functions). The same is not the case with bounded iteration which we will now turn to.

Bounded iteration Bounded iteration (sometimes also called numerically controlled iteration) is implemented by linguistic constructs that are more complex than those used for unbounded iteration; their semantics is also more elaborate. These forms are very different and not always "pure" as we will see shortly. The model that we adopt in this discussion is that of ALGOL, which was then adopted by many other languages of the same family (but *not* by C or Java).

Bounded iteration is implemented using some variant of the for command. Without wishing to use any specific syntax, it can be described as:

```
for I = start to end by step do
    body
```

where I is a variable, called the *index*, or counter, or *control variable*; start and end are two expressions (for simplicity we can assume that they are of integer type and, in general, they must be of a discreet type); step is a (compile-time) non-zero integer constant; *body* is the command we want to repeat. This construct, in the "pure" form we are describing, is subject to the important static semantic constraint that the control variable can not be modified (either explicitly nor implicitly) during the execution of the body.

The semantics of the bounded iteration construct can be described informally as follows (assuming that step is positive):

1. The expression start is evaluated, as is end. The values are frozen and stored in dedicated variables (which cannot be updated by the programmer). We denote them, respectively, as start_save and end_save.
2. I is initialised with the value of start_save.
3. If the value of I is strictly greater than the value of end_save, execution of the for command is terminated.
4. Execute *body* and increment I by the value of step.
5. Go to 3.

In the case in which step is negative, the test in step (3) determines whether I is strictly less than end_save.

It is worth emphasising the importance of step (1) above and the constraint that the control variable cannot be modified in the body. Their combined effect is to *determine* the number of times and the body will be executed *before* the loop begins execution. This number is given by the quantity, *ic* (*iteration count*), which is defined as:

$$ic = \left\lfloor \frac{\texttt{end} - \texttt{start} + \texttt{step}}{\texttt{step}} \right\rfloor$$

if *ic* is positive, otherwise it is 0. It can be seen, finally, that there is no way of producing an infinite cycle with this construct.

There are considerable differences, both syntactic and semantic, between the versions of this construct in different languages. First, not all languages require non-modifiability of the control variable and/or the freezing of the control expressions. Strictly speaking, such cases do not implement bounded iteration because they are unable to compute *ic* once and once only. It is common, though, to continue speaking of bounded iteration even when the language does not guarantee determinateness, but this is obtained on any loop, by the programmer (modifying neither directly nor indirectly the control variable and the start, end and step expressions). Also different other aspects constitute important differences between languages, of which we mention four:

Number of iterations According to the semantics which we have just given, when step is positive, if the value of start is initially (strictly) greater than the value of end, body is not executed at all. Even this is not the case in all languages, just the majority. Some languages execute the test in Step 3 after having executed body.

Step The requirement that step is a (non-zero) constant is necessary for statically determining its sign, so that the compiler can generate the appropriate code for the test in step 3. Some languages (such as Pascal and Ada) use a special syntax to indicate that step is negative, for example using downto or reverse in place of to. Other languages, such as, for example, some versions of Fortran, do not have a different syntax for the native step and their implementation of the for directly uses the iteration counter rather than the test of I and end. The value *ic* is computed and if this value is positive, it is used to control the loop, decrementing it by 1 until it reaches the value 0. If, on the other hand, *ic* has a negative value or is equal to 0, the loop is never repeated. It is the use of this implementation technique that suggests the name numerically controlled iteration.

Final index value The other subtle aspect concerns the value of the control variable I after the end of the loop. In many languages, I is a variable that is also visible outside of the loop. The most natural approach seems to be that of considering the value of I to be the last value assigned to it during execution of the `for` construct itself (in the case in which the loop terminates normally and the step is positive, the last value assigned to the index I is the first value greater than end). This approach, though, can generate type ambiguities or errors. Let us assume, for example, that I is declared as being of an interval type 1 .. 10 (from 1 to 10). If we use a command:

```
for I = 1 to 10 by 1 do
    body
```

The final value assigned to I would have to be the successor of 10, which is clearly not an admissible value. An analogous problem occurs for integer values when the calculation of I causes an overflow. To avoid this problem, some languages (for example Fortran IV or Pascal) consider the value of I to be indeterminate on termination of the loop (that is, the language definition does not specify what it should be). In other words, each implementation of these languages is allowed to behave how it wishes, with the imaginable consequence of the non-portability of programs. Other languages (for example: AlgolW, Algol 68, Ada, and, in certain circumstances, C++) cut the matter short, decreeing that the control variable is a variable that is *local* to the `for`; hence it is not visible outside the loop. In this case the header of the `for` implicitly declares the control variable with a type that is determined from that one of `start` and `end`.

Jump into a loop The last point which merits attention concerns the possibility of jumping into the middle of a `for` loop using a `goto` command. Most languages forbid such jumps for clear semantic reasons, while there are fewer restrictions on the possibility of using a `goto` for jumping out of a loop.

We have just considered a number of important aspects of the implementation of `for` loops. Particular tricks can be used by the compiler to optimise the code that is produced (for example, eliminating tests which involve constants) or by limiting overflow situations which could occur when the incrementing the index I (by inserting appropriate tests).

Expressiveness of bounded iteration Using bounded iteration, we can express the repetition of a command for n times, where n it is an arbitrary value not known when the program is written, but is fixed at when the iteration starts. It is clear that this is something that cannot be expressed using only conditional commands and assignment, because it is possible to repeat a command only by repeating the command in the body of the program syntactically. Given that every program has a finite length, we have a limit on the maximum number of repetitions that we can include in a specific program.

Despite this increase in expressive power, bounded iteration on its own is insufficient to make a programming language Turing complete. Think, for example, of a simple function f which can be defined as follows:

$$f(x) = \begin{cases} x & \text{if } x \text{ is even,} \\ \text{does not terminate} & \text{if } x \text{ is odd.} \end{cases}$$

Certainly such a function is computable. Every programmer would know how to implement it using a `while` or a `goto` or a recursive call so as to obtain a nonterminating computation. However such a function is not representable in a language only having assignment, sequential command, `if` and bounded iteration, given that, as can easily be verified in such a language, all programs terminate for every input. In other words, in such a language, only total functions can be defined while function f is partial.[6] In order to obtain a language that is Turing complete, it is necessary to include unbounded iteration. The complication of the informal semantics of `for` is only apparent, and the easy translation into machine language of `while` should not deceive us. In fact, from a formal viewpoint, `while` is semantically more complicated than `for`. As we saw in Chap. 2, the semantics of the `while` command is defined in terms of itself, something which, if at first sight it appears a little strange, finds its formal justification in fix point techniques which are beyond the scope of this text (and to which we will mention in the section on recursion, below). Even if we have not formally defined the semantics of `for`, the reader can convince themselves that this can be given in simpler terms (see Exercise 4). The major complication in the semantics of `while` with respect to `for` corresponds to the greater expressiveness of the first construct. It is in fact clear that every `for` command can easily be translated into a `while`.

It can now be asked why a language provides a bounded iteration construct when unbounded iteration constructs allow the same things to be done. The reply is principally of a pragmatic nature. The `for` it is a much more compact form of iteration, putting the three components of the iteration (initialisation, control and increment of the control variable) on the same line makes understanding what the loop does a lots easier; it can also prevent some common errors, such as forgetting the initialisation or increment of the control variable. The use of a `for` instead of a `while` can therefore be an important way to improve understanding and, therefore testing and maintenance of a program. There is also the implementation motive in some languages and on some architectures. A `for` a loop can often be compiled in a more efficient way (and, in particular, be optimised better) than a `while`, particularly as far as register allocation is concerned.

The for in C   In C (and in its successors, among them Java), the `for` is far from being, the in a general case, a bounded iteration construct. The general version is:

---

[6]In reality there are other *total* functions that are not definable using only assignment, sequential composition, `if` and `for`. A famous example is the Ackerman function, for whose definition the reader is referred to texts on computability theory for example [3].

```
for (exp₁; exp₂; exp₃)
    body
```

Its semantics is the following:

1. Evaluate `exp1`;
2. Evaluate `exp2`; if it is zero, terminate execution of the `for`;
3. Execute `body`;
4. Evaluate `exp3` and go to (2).

As can be seen, there is no way to freeze the value of the control expressions, nor is there any ban on the possibility of modifying the value of index (which, in the general case, need not even exist). It is clear how the semantics expresses the fact that in C, `for` is, when all is said and done, an abbreviation for a `while`.

Making use of the fact that, in C, a command is also an expression, we obtain the most usual form in which the `for` appears in C programs:

```
for (i = initial; i <= final; i += step){
    body
}
```

This is an abbreviation (which is very important pragmatically) of:

```
i = initial;
while (i <= final){
    body
    i += step;
}
```

For-each   One of the most common iterative constructions performs the sequential scanning of all the elements of the data structure. A typical example is the following which contains a function which computes the sum of the values in an array of integers:

```
int sum(int[] A){
    int acc = 0;
    for(int i=0; i<length(A); i++)
        acc += A[i];
    return acc;
}
```

This function is full of details that the compiler knows: the first and last index of A, the specific check for `i` reaching its limit. The more detail that has to be added in a construct, the easier it is to make an error and much more difficult to understand at a glance what the construct does. In the case of `sum`, what we want to express is simply the application of the body to *every element of* A.

Hence, some languages use a special construct, called *for-each*, to perform this kind of operation. The *for-each* has the following general syntax:

```
foreach (FormalParameter : Expression) Command
```

The for-each construct expresses the application of Command (in which the *FormalParameter* can clearly appear) to each element of *Expression*.

Using such a construct, the operation of summing a vector can be written as:

```
int sum(int[] A){
    int acc = 0;
    foreach(int e : A)
        acc += e;
    return acc;
}
```

Here, we can read the header for the for-each as "for every element e in A". The vector index, together with all of the vector's limits, is hidden in a more synthetic and elegant construct.

The use of the for-each construct is not limited to vectors, but can also be applied to all collections over which the notion of iteration can be defined in a natural way. In addition to enumerations and sets (which we will see in Chap. 8), let us mention the particularly important case of languages which allow the user to define types which are " iterable".

Among the more common languages, Java Version 5 supports the for-each construct. The key word used is simply for[7] but the syntax is different and allows the construct to be disambiguated without problem. In Java the for-each (also called *enhanced for* in the documentation) is applicable to all subtypes of the library type Iterable.

6.4 Structured Programming

The rejection of the goto command of the 1970s was not an isolated phenomenon. The goto's rejection was due to its properties, yet it was only one issue among many that contributed to a much wider debate which brought so-called *structured programming* to the fore. This can be considered as the antecedent of modern programming methodology. As the name itself suggests, it consists of a series of prescriptions aimed at allowing the development of software that has a certain structure in code and, correspondingly, in the flow of control. These prescriptions have both a methodological nature, providing precise development methods for programs, and a linguistic component, indicating appropriate typologies for the commands used (in substance, all those seen here so far, with the exception of goto). Let us see in more detail some salient points about structured programming and its associated linguistic implications.

---

[7]The for-each construct has been added on the fly when the language was already distributed and in use for some years. In a case like this, the modification of the set of reserved words is not a good design decision. Old programs which used the new keyword would stop working.

Top-down or hierarchical design of programs The program is developed by successive refinements, starting from a first (fairly abstract) specification adding successively extra detail at each step.

Code modularisation It is appropriate to group the commands which correspond to the specific functions in the algorithm that is to be implemented. To do this, all the linguistic mechanisms made available by the language are used; these range from compound commands to constructs for abstraction, such as procedures, functions, and real modules, where the language supports them.

Use of meaningful names The use of meaningful names for variables, as well as for procedures, etc., greatly simplifies the process of understanding the code and therefore eases making any changes required during maintenance. Even if this appears (and is) obvious, in practice it is too often ignored.

Extensive use of comments Comments are essential for understanding, testing, verification, correction and modification of code. A program with no comments, becomes rapidly incomprehensible, once it has reached a certain length.

Use of structured data types The use of appropriate datatypes, for example records, to group and structure information, even if it is of an heterogeneous type, eases both the design of code and its later maintenance. For example, if we can use the single variable, of type *student record*, to store the information about family name, registration number and a subscription year for a student, then the structure of the program will be much clearer than it would be if one had to use four different variables to hold the information about a single student.

Use of structured control constructs This, from a linguistic viewpoint, is the essential aspect. To implement structured programming, it is necessary to use structured control constructs, or rather constructs which, typically, have a single entry and a single exit point.

The last point is the one which interests us the most and merits extra study. The essential idea behind structured control constructs is that, by having a single entry and a single exit point, they allow structuring of the code in which the linear scanning of the program text corresponds to execution flow. If command C2 textually a follows command C1, at the (unique) exit of command C1, when C1 terminates, control passes to the (unique) entry point of command C2. Each command internally can have complex structure: branching (as in an if) or loops (as in for) with a non-linear control structure or internal jumps. The important thing is that each elementary component, externally, is visible in terms only of an entry point and an exit. This property, which is fundamental for the understanding of code, is violated in the presence of a command such as goto which allows jumps forward and backwards in the program. In such a case, the code can rapidly reach a state which is called "spaghetti code", where the control flow between the various program components, instead of being a simple graph with few the edges (which connect the output of a command to the input of the following one), is described by a graph in which the edges resemble a plate of spaghetti.

The control constructs seen so far, except the goto, are all structured and are the ones left in the modern programming languages. From a theoretical position, they allow programs for all computable functions to be written, as we have already observed. From the pragmatic point of view they are sufficient to express all types of control flow present in real applications. In particular, the constructs that were discussed at the end of Sect. 6.3.1 enable us to handle those cases in which we have to exit from a loop, a procedure, or, in some way, interrupt processing before "normal" termination occurs. All of these cases could be handled in a natural manner using a goto. For example, if we wished to process all the elements of a file that we have read from an external device, we could use code of the form:[8]

```
while true do{
    read(X);
    if X = end_of_file then goto end;
    elaborate(X);
}
end: ...
```

It can be observed that this use of goto does not violate the single entry, single exit principle because the jump only anticipates the exit, which happens at a single point in the overall construct. The structured command break (or its analogues) is the canonical form of this "jump to end of loop". When written in place of goto end, it makes the program clearer, and omits the label (the destination of the jump implicit in the break is the unique exit from the construct).

Let us finally recall that structured programming constituted a first reply to the demands of so-called programming in the large,[9] given that it requires the decomposition of a system of vast dimensions into different components, each of which is assigned a certain level of independence. The amount of independence depends on the abstraction mechanisms being used. For example, if procedures are used, communication between the various components can happen only through parameters. More significant answers to the needs of programming in the large cannot, though, be given solely at the linguistic level of programming languages. Software engineering has studied many methodologies for managing projects and implementing big software systems. Some of these methodologies also have linguistic implications, which, however, cannot be completely accounted for in this book. The object-oriented paradigm, together with some specification formalisms for object-oriented projects (like UML), are some of the more recent replies to issues we consider in this text.

6.5 Recursion

Recursion is another mechanism, an alternative to iteration, for obtaining Turing-equivalent programming languages. In empirical terms, a function (or procedure)

---

[8]Wishing to avoid goto and using only while and if, we find that we have to write code that is much less natural.

[9]This term denotes the implementation of large-scale software systems.

Inductive Definitions

Using an axiomatic presentation due to Giuseppe Peano, the natural numbers (non-negative integers) 0, 1, 2, 3, . . ., can be defined as the least set X, satisfying the following rules:

1. $0 \in X$
2. If $n \in X$, then $n + 1 \in X$,

where we assume as primitive the concept of 0 (zero), that of number (denoted by n) and that of successor of n (written $n + 1$). This definition of the naturals clearly provides an intuitive justification of the principle of induction, a fundamental tool in mathematics and also, in some ways, in computer science. This principle can be stated as follows. To prove that a property, $P(n)$, is true for all natural numbers, it is necessary to show that the following two conditions are satisfied:

1. $P(0)$ is true;
2. For every natural, n, if $P(n)$ is true, then so is $P(n + 1)$.

In addition to the proof of properties, induction is a powerful tool for the definition of functions. In fact, it can be shown that if $g : (\mathbb{N} \times X) \to X$ is a total function, $\mathbb{N}$ denotes natural numbers and a is an element of X, then there exists a unique (total) function $f : \mathbb{N} \to X$, such that:

1. $f(0) = a$
2. $f(a + 1) = g(n, f(n))$

Such a pair of equations then provide an *inductive definition* of the function f.

What has so far been said about induction over the naturals can be generalised to arbitrary sets over which a well-founded ordering relation $<$ is defined, i.e. a relation which does not admit infinite descending chains $\cdots x_m < \cdots < x_1 < x_0$. In this case, the induction principle, called well-founded induction, can be expressed as follows. Let $<$ be a well-founded relation defined on a set A. To show that $P(a)$ has a value for every a belonging to A, it is necessary to show the following implication:

For all $a \in A$,   if $P(b)$ is true for every $b < a$,   then $P(a)$ is true.

that is recursive is a procedure in whose body a call to itself is included. One can have indirect recursion as well (it is best called *mutual recursion*) when a procedure P calls another procedure, Q, which, in its turn, calls P. In Chap. 5, we have already seen the example of the recursive function `fib` which compute the nth value of the Fibonacci function.

```
int fib (int n){
   if (n == 0)
      return 1;
   else
      if (n == 1)
```

```
        return 1;
    else
        return fib(n-1) + fib(n-2);
}
```

The fact that a function like `fib` can be defined in terms of itself can evoke some doubt about the nature of the function being defined. In reality, recursive definition, also called inductive definition, is fairly common in mathematics. As the box on page 153 shows in more detail, the idea is that of describing the result of the application of a function f to an argument X in terms of the application of f itself to arguments which are "smaller" than X. The domain on which f is defined must be such that it does not allow infinite chains of successively smaller elements, thus ensuring that, after a finite number of applications of the function f, we arrive at a terminal case, by the definition of which we can reconstruct the value of f applied to X. For example, recalling that the factorial of a natural number, n, is given by the product $1 \cdot 2 \cdots n - 1 \cdot n$, we can inductively define the function computing the factorial as follows:

$$factorial(0) = 1,$$

$$factorial(n + 1) = (n + 1) \cdot factorial(n).$$

Here n is an arbitrary natural number. In an analogous fashion, we can define the function which computes the nth term in the Fibonacci series, for which we have first provided a recursive program.

If, then, inductive definitions in mathematics and recursive functions in programming languages are similar, there is still a fundamental difference. In the case of inductive definitions, not all possible definitions of function in terms of itself will work. If for example we write:

$$foo(0) = 1,$$

$$foo(n) = foo(n) + 1 \quad \text{for } n > 0$$

it is clear that no total function over the naturals will satisfy this equation, so we cannot define such a function. If, on the other hand, we write:

$$fie(1) = fie(1)$$

the problem is now the opposite. Many functions satisfy these equations, so once again this does not constitute a valid definition.

On the other hand it is perfectly legitimate to write the following function in any programming language supporting recursion:

```
int foo1 (int n){
    if (n == 0)
        return 1;
    else
        return foo1(n) + 1;
}
```

And also:

```
int fie1 (int n){
   if (n == 1) return fie1(1);
}
```

These are functions which, in some case, do not terminate (when $n > 0$ for fool(n) and for $n = 1$ in the case of fie1(n)), but from the semantic viewpoint there is no problem because, as we saw in Chap. 3, programs define partial functions.

6.5.1 Tail Recursion

In Chap. 5, we saw how, in general, the presence of recursion in a programming language makes it necessary to include dynamic memory management since it is not possible statically to determine the maximum number of instances of a single function that will be active at the same time (and, therefore, to determine the maximum number of activation records required). For example, we have seen that for the call fib(n) in our Fibonacci function, this number is equal to the nth element of the Fibonacci series, and obviously, n cannot be known as compilation time. If, on the other hand, we more carefully consider the nature of the recursive calls, we notice that in some cases we can avoid the allocation of new activation records for successive calls of a single function, since we can always reuse the same memory space. To understand this point let us look at two recursive functions which compute the factorial of a natural number. The first is the usual:

```
int fact (int n){
   if (n <= 1)  return 1;
   else
      return n * fact(n-1);
}
```

The activation record for a call fib(n) is shown in a slightly simplified form in Fig. 6.4. The field n contains the value of the actual parameter to the procedure; the field *Intermediate Result* will contain the intermediate result produced by the evaluation of fact(n-1); the field *Result address*, finally, contains the address of the memory area in which the result must be returned (that is, the address the *Intermediate Result* of the caller for all calls after the first). It is important to note that the value of the *Intermediate Result* field present in the activation record of fact(n), can be determined only when the reclusive call to fact(n-1) terminates and the value of this field, as a result of the code of fact, is used in the computation of n * fact(n-1) to obtain the value of fact(n). In other words, when we have the call fact(n), before it can terminate, we must know the value of fact(n-1); in its turn, for the call to fact(n-1) to terminate we have to know the value of fact(n-2) and so on, recursively, right back to the terminal

Fig. 6.4 Activation record
for the `fact` function

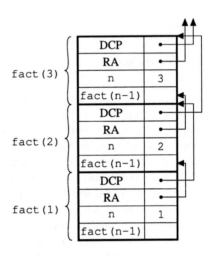

| Dynamic Chain Pointer (DCP) |
| Result Address (RA) |
| n |
| Intermediate Result (`fatt (n-1)`) |

Fig. 6.5 Activation record
stack and for the call
`fib(3)` and the two
recursive calls `fact(2)` and
`fact(3)`

case `fact(1)`. Therefore all activation records for the recursive calls `fact(n)`, `fact(n-1)`,...,`fact(1)`, must reside at the same time on the stack, in distinct memory areas.

Figure 6.5 shows the stack of activation records created by the call to `fact(3)`, as well as the by the following calls to `fact(2)` and `fact(1)`. When we reach the final case, the call to `fact(1)`, terminates immediately and returns the value 1, which, using the pointer contained in the *Result Address* of the activation record for `fact(1)`, will be returned to the *Intermediate result* field of the activation record for `fact(2)`, as is shown in Fig. 6.6. At this point, too, the call to `fact(2)` can terminate, returning the value $2 \cdot fact(1) = 2 \cdot 1$ to the call `fact(3)`, as shown in Fig. 6.7. Finally, too, the call to `fact(3)` will terminate, returning to the calling program the value $3 \cdot fact(2) = 3 \cdot 2 = 6$.

Consider now another function:

```
int factrc (int n, int res){
    if (n <= 1)
        return res;
    else
        return factrc(n-1, n * res)
}
```

Fig. 6.6 Stack of activation records after termination of the call fact (2)

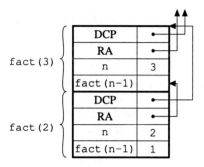

Fig. 6.7 Activation record stack after the termination of the call fact (2)

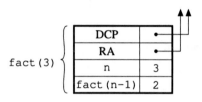

This, if called with factrc (n,1) also returns the factorial of *n*.

In this case, also, the initial call factrc (n,1) produces $n - 1$ following recursive calls

```
factrc(n-1,n*1),
factrc(n-2,(n-1)*n*1),
...,
factrc(1,2*...*(n-1)*n*1).
```

However, let us now observe that for $n > 1$, the value returned by the generic call factrc (n, res) is *exactly the same* as the value returned by the next recursive call factrc (n-1,n+res) without there being any additional computation. The value finally returned from the initial call factrc (n, 1) is therefore the same as that returned by the last recursive call factrc (1, 2*...*(n-1)*n*1) (and is therefore $n \cdot (n - 1) \cdot (n - 2) \cdots 1$), without there being any requirement to "climb back up" the call chain using then the intermediate results to compute the final value, as on the other hand happens in the case of fact.

From what has been said, it appears clear that, once factrc (n, res) has recursively called factrc (n-1,n*res), there is no need to continue maintaining the information present in the activation record for the call factrc (n, res), given that all the information necessary to perform the calculation of the final result is passed to factrc (n-1,n*res). This means that the activation record for the recursive call factrc (n-1,n*res) can simply reuse the memory space allocated to the activation record for factrc (n, res). So the consideration is valid also for successive calls and, therefore, in short, the function factrc will need a single memory area to allocate a single activation record, independent of the number of recursive calls to be made. We have therefore obtained a recursive function for which the memory can be allocated statically!

Recursion of the kind illustrated by the function factrc is said to be *tail recursion* since the recursive call is, so to speak, the last thing that happens in the body of the procedure. After the recursive call, no other computation is performed. More generally we can give the following definition.

Definition 6.3 (Tail recursion) Let f be a function which, in its body, contains a call to a function g (different from f or equal to f). The call of g is said to be a *tail call* if the function f returns the value returned by g without having to perform any other computation. We say that the function f is tail recursive if all the recursive calls present in f are tail calls.

For example, in the function:

```
int f (int n){
   if (n == 0)
      return 1;
   else
      if (n == 1)
         return f(0);
      else
         if (n ==  2)
            return f(n-1);
         else
            return f(1)*2;
}
```

The first two recursive calls are tail calls, the third is not a tail call. Therefore the function f is not tail recursive.

Our interest in tail recursion lies in the possibility of implementing it using a single activation record and therefore using constant memory space. Our investigation of the `factrc` function, in fact, is completely general, and does not depend on the specific form of this function; it depends only on the fact that we are dealing with a tail recursive function. All of this, however, does not hold in the case in which we also consider higher-order functions (i.e. when they are functions that are passed as parameters), as we will see later in this section.

In general, it is always possible to transform a function which is not tail recursive into an equivalent one which is, by complicating the function. The idea is that all the computations which have to be made after the recursive call (and make the function non-tail recursive) should, as far as possible, be performed before the call. The part of the work which cannot be done before the recursive call (because, for example, it uses its results) is "passed" with appropriate additional parameters, to the recursive call itself. This technique is exactly the same as the one we used in the case of the tail-recursive function `factrc`, where, instead of recursively calculating the product `n*fact(n-1)` in the body of the call to `fact(n-1)`, we have added a parameter `res` which allows us to pass to the product $n \cdot (n - 1) \cdot (n - 2) \cdots j$ to the generic recursive call `factrc(j- 1,j* res)`. Therefore, in this case, the calculation of the factorial is performed incrementally by the successive recursive calls, in a way analogous to that performed by an *iterative* function such as the following:

```
int fact-it (int n, int res){
   res=1;
   for (i=n; i>=1; i--)
      res = res*i;
}
```

In an analogous fashion to this, we can also transform the `fib` function into a function with tail recursion `fibrc`, by addition of two additional parameters:

```
int fibrc (int n, int res1, int res2){
   if (n == 0)
      return res2;
   else
      if (n == 1)
         return res2;
      else
         return fibrc(n-1,res2,res1+res2);
}
```

The call `fibrc(n,1,1)` returns the nth value in the Fibonacci series. Clearly, both in the case of `fibrc` and in that of `factrc`, if we want to make the additional parameters invisible, we can encapsulate the functions inside others which have only the parameter n. For example the scope of the declaration of `fibrc`, we can define:

```
int fibrctrue (int n){
   return fibrc(n,1,1);
}
```

The transformation of one function into an equivalent one with tail recursion can be done automatically using a technique called *continuation passing style*, which basically consists of representing, at all points in a program, that part of the program that remain using a function called a *continuation*. If we want to convert a function into a tail-recursive one, it suffices to use a continuation to represent everything remains of the computation and passing this continuation to the recursive call. This technique however does not always produce functions which can be executed with constant memory requirement because the continuation, since it is a function, could contain the variables which will be evaluated in the environment of the caller and therefore require the caller's activation record.

6.5.2 Recursion or Iteration?

Without going into detail on theoretical results (which are, in any case, extremely important and interesting), let us recall that recursion and iteration (in its most general form) are alternative methods for achieving the same expressive power. The use of the one or the other is often due more to the predisposition of the programmer than to the nature of the problem. For the elaboration of data using rigid structures (matrices, tables, etc.), as normally happens in numerical or data processing applications, it is often easier to use iterative constructs. When, on the other hand, processing structures of a symbolic nature which naturally lend themselves to being defined in a recursive manner (for example, lists, trees, etc.), it is often more natural to use recursion.

Recursion is often considered much less efficient than iteration and therefore declarative languages are thought much less efficient than imperative ones. The argument presented above about tail recursion make us understand that recursion is not necessarily less efficient than iteration, both in terms of memory occupation and in terms of execution time. Certainly naive implementations of recursive functions, such as those often resulting from the direct translation of inductive definitions, can be fairly inefficient. This is the case, for example, for our procedure `fib(n)` which has execution time and memory occupation that are exponential in n. However, as was seen, using recursive functions that are more "astute", such as those with tail recursion, we can obtain performance similar to that of the corresponding iterative program. The function `fibrc` in fact uses a space of constant size and runs in time linear in n.

Regarding then, the distinction between imperative and declarative languages, things are more complex and will be analysed in the chapters dedicated to the functional and logic programming paradigms.

6.6 Chapter Summary

In this chapter, we have analysed the components of high-level languages relating to the control of execution flow in programs. We first considered expressions and we have analysed:

- The types of syntax most used for their description (as trees, or in prefix, infix and postfix linear form) and the related evaluation rules.
- Precedence and associativity rules required for infix notation.
- The problems generally related to the order of evaluation of the subexpressions of an expression. For the semantics of expressions to be precisely defined, this order must be precisely defined.
- Technical details on the evaluation (short-circuit, or lazy evaluation) used by some languages and how they can be considered when defining the correct value of an expression.

We then passed to commands, seeing:

- Assignment. This is the basic command in imperative languages. Even though it is fairly simple, we had to clarify the notion of variable in order to understand its semantics.
- Various commands which allow the management of control (conditionals and iteration) in a structured fashion.
- The principles of structured programming, stopping to consider age-old questions about the `goto` command.

The last section, finally, dealt with recursion, a method that stands as an alternative to iteration for expressing algorithms. We concentrated on tail recursion, a form of recursion that is particularly efficient both in space and time. This must clear up the claim that recursion is a programming method that is necessarily less efficient than iteration.

In the various boxes, we examined an historic theme that has been extremely important in the development of modern programming languages, as well as a semantic issue which precisely clarifies the difference that exists between imperative, functional and logic programs.

We still have to deal with important matters concerning control abstraction (procedures, parameters and exceptions) but this will be the subject of the next chapter.

6.7 Bibliographical Notes

Many texts provide an overview of the various constructs present in programming languages. Among these, the most complete are [7] and [8].

Two historical papers, of certain interest to those who want to know more about the goto question are [4] (in which Böhm and Jacopinin's theorem is proved) and Dijkstra's [5] (where the "dangerousness" of the jump command is discussed).

An interesting paper, even though not for immediate reading, which delves into themes relating to inductive definitions is [2]. For an introduction to recursion and induction that is more accessible, [9] is a very good book.

According to Abelson and Sussman [1], the term "syntactic sugar" is due to Peter Landin, a pioneer in Computer Science who made fundamental contributions in the area of programming language design.

6.8 Exercises

1. Define, in any programming language, a function, f, such that the evaluation of the expression $(a + f(b)) * (c + f(b))$ when performed from left-to-right has a result that differs from that obtained by evaluating right-to-left.
2. Show how the if then else construct can be used to simulate short-circuit evaluation of boolean expressions in a language which evaluates all operands before applying boolean operators.
3. Consider the following case command:

```
case Exp of
    1:    C1;
    2,3:  C2;
    4..6: C3;
    7:    C4
    else: C5
```

Provide an efficient pseudocode assembly program that corresponds to the translation of this command.

4. Define the operational semantics of the command

```
for I = start to end by step do body
```

using the techniques introduced in Chap. 3. Suggestion: using values of the expressions, start, end and step, the following can be computed before executing the for: the number, *ic*, of repetitions which must be performed (it is assumed, as already stated in the chapter, that the possible modification of I, start, end and step in the body of the for have no effect upon their evaluation). Once this value, *n*, has been computed, the for can be replaced by a sequence of *ic* commands.

5. Consider the following function:

```
int ninetyone (int x){
    if (x>100)
     return x-10;
    else
     return ninetyone(ninetyone(x+11));
    }
```

Is this tail recursive? Justify your answer.

6. The following code fragment is written in a pseudo-language which admits bounded iteration (numerically controlled) expressed using the for construct.

```
z=1;
for i=1 to 5+z by 1 do{
    write(i);
    z++;
}
write(z);
```

What is printed by write?

7. Say what the following code block prints. This code is written in a language with static scope and call by name. The definition of the language contains the following phrase: "The evaluation of the expression $E_1 \circ E_2$ where $\circ$ is any operator, consists of (i) the evaluation of E_1; (ii) then the evaluation of E_2; (iii) finally, the application of the operator $\circ$ to the two values previously obtained."

```
{int x=5;
 int P(name int m){
      int x=2;
      return m+x;
 }
 write(P(x++) + x);
}
```

References

1. H. Abelson and G. J. Sussman. *Structure and Interpretation of Computer Programs*. MIT Press, Cambridge, 1996.
2. P. Aczel. An introduction to inductive definitions. In J. Barwise, editor, *Handbook of Mathematical Logic*, pages 739–782. North-Holland, Amsterdam, 1977.
3. M. Aiello, A. Albano, G. Attardi, and U. Montanari. *Teoria della Computabilità, Logica, Teoria dei Linguaggi Formali*. ETS, Pisa, 1976 (in Italian).
4. C. Böhm and G. Jacopini. Flow diagrams, Turing machines and languages with only two formation rules. *Commun. ACM*, 9(5):366–371, 1966.
5. E. Dijkstra. Go to statement considered harmful. *Communications of the ACM*, 11(3):147–148, 1968.
6. B. Liskov and J. Guttag. *Abstraction and Specification in Program Development*. MIT Electrical Engineering and Computer Science Series. MIT Press, Cambridge, 1986.
7. T. Pratt and M. Zelkowitz. *Programming Languages: Design and Implementation*. Prentice-Hall, New York, 2001 (quarta edizione).
8. M. L. Scott. *Programming Language Pragmatics*. Morgan Kaufmann, San Mateo, 2000.
9. G. Winskel. *The Formal Semantics of Programming Languages*. MIT Press, Cambridge, 1993.

Chapter 7
Control Abstraction

The concept of abstraction is a recurrent theme in this text. Right from the first chapter, we have encountered *abstract* machines and their hierarchies. For them, we used the terms "abstract" rather than "physical", denoting by abstract machine, a set of algorithms and data structures not directly present in any specific physical machine, but executable on it by means of interpretation. Moreover, the fact that the concept of abstract machine, to some extent, hides the underlying machine is fundamental.

"To abstract" means simply to hide something. Often, abstracting from some concrete data relating to some object, one succeeds in bringing out with more clarity a concept common to that object. Each description of a phenomenon (natural, artificial, physical, etc.) is not based on the set of *all* data relating to the phenomenon itself, otherwise it would be like a geographical map of scale 1:1, extremely precise but useless. Every scientific discipline describes a certain phenomenon, concentrating only on some aspects, those which have been found to be the most relevant to the agreed aims. It is for this reason that scientific language uses appropriate mechanisms to express these "abstractions". Programming languages, themselves the abstractions of the physical machine, are no exception. Rather, expressiveness depends in an essential way on the mechanisms of abstraction which the languages provide. These mechanisms are the principal instruments available to the designer and programmer for describing in an accurate, but also simple and suggestive, way the complexity of the problems to be solved.

In a programming language, in general, two classes of abstraction mechanisms are distinguished. That which provides *control abstraction* and that which provides *data abstraction*. The former provides the programmer the ability to hide procedural data; the latter allow the definition and use of sophisticated data types without referring to how such types will be implemented. In this chapter we will be concerned with the mechanisms for control abstraction, while data abstraction will be the subject of Chap. 9, after we have seen mechanisms for data structuring in the next chapter.

M. Gabbrielli, S. Martini, *Programming Languages: Principles and Paradigms*, Undergraduate Topics in Computer Science, DOI 10.1007/978-1-84882-914-5_7, © Springer-Verlag London Limited 2010

Fig. 7.1 Definition and use
of a function

```
int foo (int n, int a) {
    int tmp=a;
    if (tmp==0) return n;
    else return n+1;
}
...
int x;
x = foo(3,0);
x = foo(x+1,1);
```

7.1 Subprograms

Every program of any complexity is composed of many components, each of which serves to provide part of a global solution. The decomposition of a problem into subproblems allows better management of complexity. A more restrictive problem is easier to solve. The solution to the global problem is obtained by appropriate composition of the solutions to these subproblems.

In order for all of this to be efficient, however, it is necessary that the programming language provides linguistic support which facilitates and makes possible such subdivisions and, therefore, re-composition. This linguistic support allows the expression of decomposition and re-composition directly in the language, transforming these concepts from simple methodological suggestions into real and genuine instruments for design and programming.

The key concept provided by all modern languages is that of the subprogram, procedure, or function.[1] A *function* is a piece of code identified by name, is given a local environment of its own and is able to exchange information with the rest of the code using *parameters*. This concept translates into two different linguistic mechanisms. The first, *definition* (or declaration) of function, and its *use* (or call). In Fig. 7.1, the first five lines constitute the definition of the function named foo, whose local environment is composed from three names n, a and tmp.[2] The first line is the *header*, while the remaining lines constitute the *body* of the function. The last two lines of Fig. 7.1 are the uses (or calls) of foo.

A function exchanges information with the rest of the program using three principal mechanisms: parameters, return value, nonlocal environment.

Parameters   We distinguish between *formal parameters*, which appear in the definition of a function, and *actual parameters*, which appear, instead, in the call. The formal parameters are always names which, as far as the environment is concerned, behave as declarations local to the function itself. They behave, in particular, as *bound variables*, in the sense that their consistent renaming has no effect on the

---

[1]These three terms assume different meanings in different languages. For example, "subprogram" is usually the most general term. In languages of the Algol family and their descendants, a procedure is a subprogram which modifies the state, while a function is a subprogram that returns a value. In this chapter, at least, we will use the three terms as synonyms.

[2]The name foo is part of the nonlocal environment of the function.

Fig. 7.2 Renaming of formal
parameters

```
int foo (int m, int b){
    int tmp=b;
    if (tmp==0) return m;
    else return m+1;
}
```

semantics of the function. For example, the function `foo` in Fig. 7.1 and that in
Fig. 7.2 are indistinguishable, even though the second has different names for its
formal parameters.

The number and type of actual and formal parameters must, in general, coincide,
although many type compatibility rules can be brought into play (see Sect. 8.7).
There is sometimes also the possibility of declaring functions with a variable number of parameters.

Return value   Some functions exchange information with the rest of the program
by returning a value as a result of the function itself, as well as through the use of
parameters. Our function, `foo`, for example, returns an integer. The language makes
available, in this case, the mechanism which allows the "return of value" to be expressed (for example the `return` construct which has also the effect of terminating the execution of the current function). In some languages, the name "function"
is reserved for subprograms which return a value, while those subprograms which
interact with the caller just via parameters or the non-local environment are called
"procedures".

In languages which derive their syntax from C, all subprograms are, linguistically, functions. If the result type of a function is `void`, the function returns no
meaningful value (the command to return such a value and to terminate execution is
`return`).

Nonlocal environment   This is a less sophisticated mechanism with which a function can exchange information with the rest of the program. If the body of the function modifies a nonlocal variable, it is clear that such a modification is felt in all
parts of the program where this variable is visible.

7.1.1 Functional Abstraction

From a pragmatic viewpoint, subprograms are mechanisms which allow the software designer to obtain *functional abstraction*. A software component is an entity
which provides services to its environment. The clients of such a component are not
interested *how* the services are provided, only how to use them. The possibility of
associating a function with every component allows separation of what the client
needs to know (expressed in the header of the function: its name, its parameters, its
result type, if present) from what it does not need to know (which is in the body).
We have real functional abstraction when the client does not depend on the body

"Static" variables

In all we have said, we have always assumed that the local environment of a function has the same lifetime as the function itself. In such a case, there is no primitive mechanism which one instance of a function can use for communicating information to another instance of the *same* function. The only way for this to happen is through the use of a nonlocal variable.

In some languages, though, it is possible to arrange for that a variable (which must be local to a function) to maintain its value between one invocation of the function and another. In C, for example, this is achieved using the static modifier (Fortran uses save, Algol own, etc.). A static variable allows programmers to write functions with memory. The following function, for example, returns the number of times it has been called:

```
int how_many_times(){
    static int count;
            /* C guarantees that static variables are
               initialised to zero by the first
               activation of the function */
    return count++;
}
```

The declaration of a static variable introduces an association with unlimited lifetime into the environment (in the lifetime of the program, clearly).

It should be observed that a static variable provides greater data abstraction than a global variable. It is not, in fact, visible from outside the function. The visibility mechanisms guarantee, therefore, that it is only modifiable inside the function body.

of a function, only on its header. In this case, the substitution (for example for efficiency reasons) of the body by another one with the same semantics is transparent to the system software in its entirety. If a system is based on functional abstraction, the three acts of specification, implementation and use of a function can occur independent of one another without knowledge of the context in which the other actions are performed.

Functional abstraction is a methodological principle, whose functions provide linguistic support. It is clear that this is not a definitive support. It is necessary that the programmer correctly uses these functions, for example by limiting the interactions between function and call to parameter passing, because use of the nonlocal environment to exchange information between functions and the rest of the program destroys functional abstraction. On the other hand, functional abstraction is increasingly guaranteed by greater limitation of interaction between components to external behaviour, as expressed by function headers.

7.1.2 Parameter Passing

The way in which actual parameters are paired with formal parameters, and the semantics which results from this, is called the *parameter passing discipline*. According to what is now traditional terminology, a specific mode is composed of the kind of communication that it supports, together with the implementation that produces this form of communication. The mode is fixed when the function is defined and can be different for each parameter; it is fixed for all calls of the function.

From a strictly semantic viewpoint, the classification of the type of communication permitted by a parameter is simple. From a subprogram's viewpoint, three parameter classes can be discerned:

- Input parameters.
- Output parameters.
- Input/output parameters.

A parameter is of input type if it allows communication which is only in the direction from the caller to the function (the "callee"). It is of output type if it permits communication only in direction from the callee to the caller. Finally, it is input/output when it permits bidirectional communication.

Note that this is a linguistic classification, part of the definition of the language; it is not derived from the use to which parameters are put. An input/output parameter remains that way even if it is used only in a unidirectional fashion (e.g., from caller to callee).

It is clear that each of these types of communications can be obtained in different ways. The specific implementation technique constitutes, exactly, the "call mode", which we will now subject to analysis, describing for each mode:

- What type of communication it allows.
- What form of actual parameter is permitted.
- The semantics of the mode.
- The canonical implementation.
- Its cost.

Of the modes that we will discuss, the first two (by value and by reference) are the most important and are widely used. The others are little more than variations on the theme of call by value. An exception is call by name, which we will discuss last. Although call by name is now disused as a parameter-passing mechanism, nevertheless, it allows us to present a simple case of what it means to "pass an environment" into a procedure.

Call by value   Call by value is a mode that corresponds to an input parameter. The local environment of the procedure is extended with an association between the formal parameter and a new variable. The actual parameter can be an expression. When called, the actual parameter is evaluated and its r-value obtained and associated with the formal parameter. On termination of the procedure, the formal parameter is destroyed, as is the local environment of the procedure itself. During the execution of

Fig. 7.3 Passing by value

```
int y = 1;
void foo (int x) {
    x = x+1;
    }
    . . .
y = 1;
foo(y+1);
    // here y =  1
```

the body, there is no link between the formal and the actual parameter. There is no way of make use of a value parameter to transfer information from the callee to the caller.

Figure 7.3 shows a simple example of passing by value. Like in C, C++, Pascal and Java, when we do not explicitly indicate any parameter-passing method for a formal parameter, it is to be understood that parameter is to be passed by value. The variable y never changes its value (it always remains 1). During the execution of foo, x assumes the initial value 2 by the effect of passing the parameter. It is then incremented to 3, finally it is destroyed with the entire activation record for foo.

If we assume a stack-based allocation scheme, the formal parameter corresponds to a location in the procedure's activation record in which the value of the actual parameter is stored during the calling sequence of the procedure.

Let us note how this is an expensive method when the value parameter is bound to a large data structure. In such a case, the entire structure is copied to the formal.[3] On the other hand, the cost of accessing the formal parameter is minimal, since it is the same as the cost of accessing a local variable in the body.

Passing by value is a very simple mechanism with clear semantics. It is the default mechanism in many languages (e.g., Pascal) and is the only way to pass parameters in C and Java.

Call by reference   Call by reference (also called *by variable*) implements a mechanism in which the parameter can be used for both input and output. The actual parameter *must* be an expression with l-value (recall the definition of l-value on page 132). At the point of call, the l-value of the actual parameter is evaluated and the procedure's local environment is extended with an association between the formal parameter and the actual parameter's l-value (therefore creating an *aliasing* situation). The most common case is that in which the actual parameter is a variable. In this case, the formal and the actual are two names for the same variable. At the end of the procedure, the connection between the formal parameter and the actual parameter's l-value is destroyed, as is the environment local to the procedure. It is clear that call by reference allows bidirectional communication: each modification of the formal parameter is a modification of the actual parameter.

---

[3]The reader who knows C should not be misled. In a language with pointers, as we will discuss below, often the passing of a complex structure consists of passing (by value) a pointer to the data structure. In such a case, it is the pointer that is copied, not the data structure.

Fig. 7.4 Passage by
reference

```
int y = 0;
void foo (reference int x) {
    x = x+1;
    }
y=0;
foo(y);
    // here y = 1
```

Fig. 7.5 Another example of
passage by reference

```
int[] V = new V[10];
int i=0;
void foo (reference int x) {
    x = x+1;
    }
...
V[1] = 1;
foo(V[i+1]);
    // here V[1] = 2
```

Figure 7.4 shows a simple example of call by reference (which we have notated
in the pseudocode with the `reference` modifier). During the execution of foo, x
is a name for y. Incrementing x in the body is, to all effects, the incrementing of y.
After the call, the value of y is therefore 1.

It can be seen that, as shown in Fig. 7.5, the actual parameter need not necessarily
be a variable but can be an expression whose l-value is determined at call time. In a
way similar to the first case, during the execution of foo, x is a name for v[1] and
the increment of x in the body, is an increment of v[1]. After the call, the value of
v[1] is, therefore, 2.

In the stack-based abstract machine model, each formal is associated with a location in the procedure's activation record. During the calling sequence, the l-value of
the actual is stored in the activation record. Access to the formal parameter occurs
via an indirection which uses this location.

This is a parameter passing mode of very low cost. At the point of call, only
an address need be stored; every reference to the formal is achieved by an indirect
access (implemented implicitly by the abstract machine) which can be implemented
at very low cost on many architectures.

Call by reference is a low-level operation. It is possible in Pascal (`var` modifier)
and in many other languages. It has been excluded from more modern languages.
In these languages, however, some form of bidirectional communication between
caller and callee can be obtained by exploiting the interaction between parameter passing and other mechanisms (the most important being the model chosen for
variables) or the availability of pointers in the language. Two boxes show simple
examples in C (and C++) and Java. The moral of the examples is that in an imperative language, passing by value is always accompanied by other mechanisms so that
procedures are really a versatile programming technique.

Call by constant   We have already seen how call by value is expensive for large-
sized data. When, however, the formal parameter is not modified in the body of

Call by reference in C

C admits only call by value but also allows the free manipulation of pointers and addresses. Making use of this fact, it is not difficult to simulate call by reference. Let us consider the problem of writing a simple function which swaps the values of two integer variables which are passed to the function as parameters. With only call by value, there is no way to do this. We can, though, combine call by value with pointer manipulation, as in the following example:

```
void swap (int *a, int *b) {
    int tmp = *a; *a=*b; *b=tmp;
    }
int v1 = ...;
int v2 = ...;
swap(&v1, &v2);
```

The formal parameters to swap (both by value) are of type pointer to integer (int *). The values of the actual parameters are the addresses (that is, the l-value) of v1 and v2 (obtained using the operator &). In the body of swap, the use of the * operator performs dereferencing of the parameters. For example, we can paraphrase the meaning of *a = *b as: take the value contained in the location whose address is contained in b and store it in the location whose address is stored in a. Our swap therefore simulates call-by-reference.

the function, we can imagine maintaining the semantics of passing by value, implementing it using call by reference. This is what constitutes the *read-only* parameter method.

This is a method that establishes an input communication and in which arbitrary expressions are permitted as actual parameters. The formal parameters passed by this method are subject to the static constraint that they cannot be modified in the body, either directly (by assignment) or indirectly (via calls to functions that modify them). From a semantic viewpoint, call by constant coincides completely with call by value, while the choice of implementation is left to the abstract machine. For data of small sizes, call by constant can be implemented as call by value. For larger structures, an implementation using a reference, without copy, will be chosen.

Call by constant is an optimum way to "annotate" a given parameter to a procedure. By reading the header, one immediately has information about the fact that this parameter is input only. Furthermore, one can count on static semantic analysis to verify that this annotation is really guaranteed.

Call by result Call by result is the exact dual of call by value. This a mode which implements *output-only* communication. The procedure's local environment is extended with an association between the formal parameter and a new variable. The actual parameter must be an expression that evaluates to an l-value. When the procedure terminates (normally), immediately before the destruction of the local environ-

---

Bidirectional communication in Java

A function like `swap` (in the box "Call by reference in C") cannot be written in Java. However, we can make use of the fact that Java uses a reference-based model for variables (of class type) to obtain some form of bidirectional communication. Let us consider for example the following simple definition of a class:

```
class A {
    int v;
    }
```

We can certainly write a method which swaps the values of the field `v` in two objects of class A:

```
void swap (A a, A b) {
    int tmp = a.v; a.v= b.v; b.v=tmp;
    }
```

In this case, what is passed (by value) to `swap` are two references to objects of class A. Using the reference model for variables of class type, `swap` effectively swaps the values of the two fields. It can be seen, however, that a true simulation of call by reference is not possible, as it was with C.

---

ment, the current value of the formal parameter is assigned to the location obtained using the l-value from the actual parameter. It should be clear that, as in call by value, the following questions about evaluation order must be answered. If there is more than one result parameter, in which order (for example, from left to right) should the corresponding "backward assignment" from the actual to formal be performed? Finally, when is the actual parameter's l-value determined? It is reasonable to determine it both when the function is called and when it terminates.[4]

It can be seen that, during the execution of the body, there is no link between the formal and actual parameter. There is no way to make use of a result parameter to transfer information from the caller to the callee. An example of call by result is shown in Fig. 7.6. The implementation of call by result is analogous to call by value, with which it shares its advantages and disadvantages. From a pragmatic viewpoint, the by-result mode simplifies the design of functions which must return (that is provide as result) more than one value, each in a different variable.

Call by value-result   The combination of call by value and call by result produces a method called call by value-result. This is a method that implements bidirectional communication using the formal parameter as a variable local to the procedure.

---

[4]Construct an example which gives different results if the l-value of the actual is determined at call time or when the procedure terminates.

Fig. 7.6 Call by result

```
void foo (result int x) {x = 8;}
...
int y = 1;
foo(y);
   // here y is 8
```

Fig. 7.7 Call by value-result

```
void foo (valueresult int x) {
   x = x+1;
}
...
y = 8;
foo(y);
   // here y is 9
```

Fig. 7.8 Call by value-result
is not call by reference

```
void foo (reference/valueresult int x,
          reference/valueresult int y,
          reference int z) {
   y = 2;
   x = 4;
   if (x == y) z = 1;
}
...
int a = 3;
int b = 0;
foo(a,a,b);
```

The actual parameter must be an expression that can yield an l-value. At the call, the actual parameter is evaluated and the r-value thus obtained is assigned to the formal parameter. At the end of the procedure, immediately before the destruction of the local environment, the current value of the formal parameter is assigned to the location corresponding to the actual parameter. An example of call by value-result is shown in Fig. 7.7.

The canonical implementation of call by value-result is analogous to that of call by value, even if some languages (Ada, for example) choose to implement it as call by reference in the case of large-sized data, so that the problems of cost of call by value can be avoided.

The implementation of call by value-result using a reference is, however, not semantically correct. Consider, for a moment, the fragment in Fig. 7.8. At first sight, the conditional command present in the body of foo seems useless, for x and y have just received distinct values. The reality is that x and y have different values only *in the absence of aliasing*. If, on the other hand, x and y are two different names for the same variable, it is clear that the condition x == y is always true.

If, therefore, x and y are passed by value-result (there is no aliasing), the call foo(a,a,b) terminates without the value of b being modified. If, on the other hand, x and y are passed by reference (where there *is* aliasing), foo(a,a,b) terminates by assigning the value 1 to b.

Fig. 7.9 Which environment
should be used to evaluate
x+1 in the body of foo?

```
int x=0;
int foo (name int y) {
    int x = 2;
    return x + y;
}
...
int a = foo(x+1);
```

Call by name   Call by name, introduced in ALGOL60, is a semantically cleaner
way of passing parameters than by reference. It is no longer used by any major imperative language. However, it is a conceptually important method worth the effort
of studying in detail because of its properties and its implementation.

The problem that the designers of ALGOL60 set themselves was to give a *precise*
semantics. The semantics should specify in an elementary fashion what the effect of
a call to a function with specified parameters would be. The solution that they chose
was to define the semantics of function call using the so-called *copy rule*. Without
loss of generality, we will state it in the case of a function of one argument:

> Let f be a function with a single formal parameter, x, and let a be an expression of a
> type that is compatible with that of x. A call to f with an actual parameter a is semanti-
> cally equivalent to the execution of the body of f in which all occurrences of the formal
> parameter, x, have been replaced by a.

As can easily be seen, it is a very simple rule. It reduces the semantics of function
call to the syntactic operation of expanding the body of the function after a textual
substitution of the actual for the formal parameter. This notion of substitution, however, is not a simple concept because it must take into account the fact it might have
to deal with several different variables with the same name. Consider, for example,
the function in Fig. 7.9. If we blindly apply the copy rule, the call foo(x+1) results in the execution of return x+x+1. This command, executed in the local
environment of foo, returns the value 5. But it is clear that this is an incorrect application of the copy rule because it makes the result of the function depend on what
the name of the local variable is. If the body of foo had been:

`{int z=2; return z+y; }`

the same call would result in the execution of return z+x+1, with the result 3.

In the first substitution that we suggested, we say that the actual parameter, x,
was *captured* by the local declaration. The substitution of which the copy rule talks
must therefore be a substitution that *does not capture variables*. It is not possible
to avoid having different variables with the same name, so we can obtain a non-
capturing substitution by requiring that the formal parameter, even after substitution,
is evaluated in the environment of the caller and not in that of the callee.

We can therefore define call by name as that method whose semantics is given
by the copy rule, where the concept of substitution is always understood without
capture. Equivalently, we can say that what is substituted is not merely the actual
parameter, but the actual parameter *together with* its own evaluation environment
which is fixed at the moment of call.

Fig. 7.10 Side effects of call
by name

```
int i = 2;
int fie (name int y) {
    return y+y;
}
...
int a = fie(i++);
    // here  i has value 4; a has value 5
```

```
void fiefoo (valueresult/name int x, valueresult/name int y) {
    x = x+1;
    y = 1;
}
...
int i = 1;
int[] A = new int[5];
A[1]=4;
fiefoo(i,A[i]);
```

Fig. 7.11 Call by name is not call by value-result

Note how the copy rule requires that the actual parameter must be evaluated *every time* that the formal parameter is encountered during execution. Consider the example of Fig. 7.10, where the construct i++ has the semantics of returning the current value of the variable i and then incrementing the value of the variable by 1.

The copy rule requires that the i++ construct must be evaluated twice. Once for every occurrence of the formal parameter y in fie. The first time, its evaluation returns the value 2 and increments the value of i by one. The second time, it returns the value 3 and increments i again.

The example we have just discussed shows how it is an error to consider call by name as a complicated way of describing call by value-result. The two modes are semantically different, as Fig. 7.11 shows.

Let us assume, first, that we are to execute fiefoo with parameters passed by value-result. On termination, we will have A[1] with value 1 and i with value 2, while the rest of the array A has not been touched. If, on the other hand, we execute the same procedure with the two parameters passed by name, on termination, we will have A[1] with value 4, i with value 2 and, what is more important, the element A[2] will have been updated to the value 1. It can be seen that, in this case, value-result and call by reference will have exhibited the same behaviour.

It remains to describe how call by name can be implemented. We have already discussed the necessity for the caller to pass not only the textual expression forming its actual parameter but also the environment in which this expression must be evaluated. We call a pair, (expression, environment), in which the environment includes (at least) all the free variables in the expression a *closure*.[5] We can therefore

---

[5]The term "closure" comes from mathematical logic. A formula is closed when it does not contain free variables. A closure is a canonical method for transforming a piece of code containing nonlocal (that is, "free") variables in a completely specified code.

Fig. 7.12 Implementation of
call by name

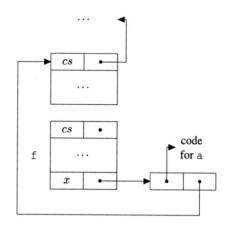

say that, in the case of call by name, the caller passes a closure, formed from the
actual parameter (in the form of a textual expression) and the current environment.
When the callee encounters a reference to the formal parameter, it is resolved using
the evaluation of the first component of the closure in the environment given by the
second component. Figure 7.12 describes this situation in the particular case of an
abstract machine with a stack. In this case, a closure is a pair formed from two pointers: the first points to the code that evaluates the expression of the formal parameter,
the second is a pointer to the static chain, which indicates the block which forms the
local environment in which to evaluate the expression. When a procedure f with a
formal name parameter, x, is called with actual parameter a, the call constructs a
closure whose first component is a pointer to the code for a and whose second component is a pointer to the (caller's) actual activation record. It then binds this closure
(for example, using another pointer) to the formal parameter x which resides in the
called procedure's activation record.

We can finally summarise what we know on call by name. It is a method which
supports input and output parameters. The formal parameter does *not* correspond
to a variable that is local to the procedure; the actual parameter can be an arbitrary
expression. It is possible that the actual and formal parameters can be aliased. The
actual parameter must evaluate to an l-value if the formal parameter appears on the
left of an assignment, The semantics of call by name was established by the copy
rule which allows the maintenance of a constant link between formal and actual parameters during execution. The canonical implementation uses a closure. The procedure's local environment is extended with an association between the formal and
a closure, the latter being composed of the actual parameter and the environment
in which the call occurs. Every access to the formal parameter is performed via the
ex novo evaluation of the actual parameter in the environment stored in the closure.
This is a very expensive parameter-passing method, both because of the need to
pass a complex structure and, in particular, because of the repeated evaluation of the
actual parameter in an environment that is not the current one.

Jensen's Device

Call by name allows side effects to be exploited to obtaining elegant and compact code, even though it often results in code that is difficult to understand and maintain. This is the case with the so-called Jensen's Device which makes use of pass by name to pass a complex expression and, at the same time, a variable which appears in the same expression, in such a way that modifications to variable change the value of the expression. Let us consider the following example:

```
int summation (name int exp; name int i;
               int start; int stop) {
   int acc = 0;
   for (i=start, i<= stop, i++)
      acc = acc + exp;
   return acc;
}
int x = ...;
...
int y = summation(2*x*x - 2*x + 1, x, 1, 10);
```

The side effects of passing a parameter by name are such that, in the body of the loop in summation, the value of exp can depend upon the value of i. A moment's reflection shows that the call on the last line is equivalent to the calculation of the sum:

$$y = \sum_{x=1}^{10} 2x^2 - 2x + 1.$$

Jensen's Device allows call by name to be used as a way to derive powerful and specialisable "higher-order" procedures at call time (in the case of the example, by indicating the expression in which to calculate the sum).

7.2 Higher-Order Functions

A function is *higher order* when it accepts as parameters, or returns another function as its result. Although there is no unanimous agreement in the literature, we will say that a programming language is higher-order when it allows functions either as parameters or as results of other functions. Languages with functions as parameters are fairly common. On the other hand, languages that allow functions to return functions as a result are less common. This last type of operation, however, is one of the fundamental mechanisms of *functional* programming languages (which we will deal with extensively in Chap. 11). We will, in this section, discuss linguistic and implementation problems in these two cases. We treat each of them separately.

Fig. 7.13 Functional
parameters

```
{int x = 1;
int f(int y){
       return x+y;
}
void g (int h(int b)){
       int x = 2;
       return h(3) + x;
}
...
 {int x = 4;
  int z = g(f);
 }
}
```

7.2.1 Functions as Parameters

The general case, the one we want to analyse, is that of a language with functional
parameters, nested environments and the ability to define functions at every nesting
level.[6] Let us consider the example shown in Fig. 7.13.

Using the notation void g (int h(int n)){ ... }, we mean, in our
pseudo-language, the declaration of the function g with a single formal parameter,
h, which, in its turn, is specified to be a function returning an int with its own formal parameter of type int.[7] The two key points of the example are: (i) the fact that
f is passed as an actual parameter to g and later called through the formal parameter
h; and (ii) the name x is defined more than once, so it is necessary to establish which
is the (nonlocal) environment in which f will be evaluated. Concerning this second
question, the reader will not be surprised if we observe that there are two possibilities for selecting the nonlocal environment to use when executing a function f
invoked using a formal parameter h:

- Use the environment that is active at the time when the *link between h and f is
  created* (which happens on line 11). We say, in this case, that the language uses a
  deep binding policy.
- Use the environment that is active when the *call* of f using h occurs (which
  happens on line 7). In this case, we say that the language uses a *shallow binding*
  policy.[8]

Although the two alternatives for binding immediately recall the distinction between static and dynamic scope, we emphasise that the binding policy (in the case

---

[6]C allows functions as parameters, but it is possible to define a function only in the global environment. With this limitation, the problem becomes considerably simplified (and this simplicity is
just one of the reasons why C does not allow nested functions).

[7]The name of the formal parameter of h (in this case n), is of no relevance and there is no way in
which the programmer can use it in the body of g.

[8]The terminology, however, is not uniform across the literature. In particular, the terms deep and
shallow binding are also used, in a special way, in the LISP community to indicate two different
implementation techniques for dynamic scope.

of higher-order functions) should be considered independent of scope policy. All common languages that use static scope also use deep binding (because the choice of a shallow policy appears contradictory at the methodological level). The matter is not as clear for languages with dynamic scope, among which there are languages with deep as well as shallow binding.

Returning to the example of Fig. 7.13, the different scope and binding policies yield the following behaviours:

- Under static scope and deep binding, the call h(3) returns 4 (and g returns 6). The x in the body of f when it is called using h is the one in the outermost block;
- Under dynamic scope and deep binding, the call h(3) returns 7 (and g returns 9). The x in the body of f when it is called using h is the one local to the block in which the call g(f) occurs;
- Under dynamic scope and shallow binding, the call h(3) returns 5 (and g returns 7). The x in the body of f at the moment of its call through h is the one local to g.

Implementation of deep binding Shallow binding does not pose additional implementation problems to the technique used to implement dynamic scope. It is enough, at least conceptually, to look for every name's last association in the environment. Things are different, though, for deep binding, which requires auxiliary data structures in addition to the usual static and dynamic chains.

So as to fix our ideas, let us consider the case of a language with static scope and deep binding (the case of dynamic scope is left to the reader, see Exercise 6). From Sect. 5.5.1, we already know that to any direct invocation (one that is not of a call to a formal parameter) of a function f, there is statically associated information (an integer) which expresses the nesting level of the definition of f with respect to the block in which the call occurs. This information is used dynamically by the abstract machine to initialise the static chain pointer (that is, the nonlocal environment) in the activation record for f. When, on the other hand, a function f is invoked using a formal parameter, h, no information can be associated to the call because it is called via a formal parameter. Indeed, in the course of different activations of the procedure in which it is located, the formal can be associated with different functions (this is the case, for example, with the call h(3) in Fig. 7.13).

In other words, it is clear that with deep binding, the information about the static chain pointer must be determined at the moment the association between the formal and actual parameters is created. With the formal h must be associated not only the code for f but also the nonlocal environment in which the body of f is to be evaluated. Such a nonlocal environment can be determined in a simple fashion: corresponding to a call of the form g(f) (the procedure g is called with the functional actual parameter f), we can statically associate with the parameter f the information about the nesting level of the definition of f within the block in which the call g(f) occurs. When this call is performed, the abstract machine will use this information to associate with the formal parameter corresponding to f *both* the code for f, *and* a pointer to the activation record of the block inside which f is declared (this pointer is determined using the same rules that were discussed in Sect. 5.5.1).

Fig. 7.14 Closure and static chain

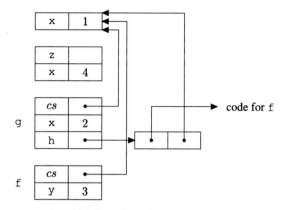

The formal function parameter is therefore associated logically with a (text, environment) pair, represented at the implementation level by a pair (pointer to code, pointer to an activation record). We have already seen when we discussed the implementation of call by name that such a data structure is called a *closure*. Therefore, a closure is associated with the formal functional parameter. When the formal parameter is used to invoke a function (that is statically unknown), the abstract machine finds in the first component of the pair the code to which to transfer control and assigns the content of the second component of the closure to the static chain pointer of the activation record for the new invocation.

Figure 7.14 shows the situation on the activation stack for the code in Fig. 7.13 at the moment at which the function f is entered (it is called using h from the body of g). When the function g is called with actual parameter f, a closure is linked to h. f is declared at distance 1 from the place in which it appears as an actual parameter (it is in fact declared inside the block which *contains* the one in which it appears as an actual parameter). The second component of the closure is therefore determined by 1 step along the static chain (obtaining a pointer to the outer block). When f is called through the name h, the corresponding activation record is pushed onto the stack. The value of the static chain pointer is taken from the second component of the closure.

The reader will recall, once more, that the problems we are discussing appear only when the language allows the definition of functions with nonlocal environments, that is allows the definition of functions *inside nested blocks*. In the contrary case, for example in C, there is no nonlocal environment, so there is no need for closures. To pass a function as a parameter, it is enough to pass a pointer to its code. All nonlocal references in the body of the function will be resolved in the global environment.

Binding policy and static scope We have already observed how all languages with static scope use deep binding. At first sight it could rather seem that deep or shallow binding make no difference in the case of static scope. After all, the nonlocal environment of a function is determined from the (static) position of its declaration and not by the way in which it is invoked. In the case in Fig. 7.13, it is the scope

Fig. 7.15 The binding policy
is necessary for determining
the environment

```
{void foo (int f(), int x){
    int fie(){
        return x;
    }
    int z;
    if (x==0) z=f();
    else foo(fie,0);
}
int g(){
    return 1;
}
foo(g,1);
}
```

Thunks

The parameter-passing rule required for functional parameters is similar to call by name. In fact, a formal name parameter can be considered as a kind of functional parameter (without arguments). Analogously, the corresponding actual parameter can be considered as the definition of an anonymous argumentless function. During execution of the body, every occurrence of the name parameter corresponds to an *ex novo* evaluation of the actual parameter in the environment fixed at the moment the association between the actual and formal name parameter is made. A process that is analogous to a new call to the anonymous function corresponding to the actual parameter.

In ALGOL60 jargon, the name *thunk* was used for a structure like this. A function without arguments and associated evaluation environment. In call by name, therefore a connection between the formal parameter and a thunk is introduced.

(and not binding) rule that establishes that every invocation of f (whether direct, using its name, or indirect, using a formal parameter) is evaluated in the outermost nonlocal environment.

In general, however, it is not like this. The reason for this is that there can be many activation records for the same function simultaneously present on the stack (this clearly happens when we have recursive or mutually recursive functions). If a procedure is passed out from one of these activations, it is possible to create a situation in which the scope rules alone are not enough to determine which nonlocal environment to use in invoking the functional parameter. As an example, we will discuss the code in Fig. 7.15, which, as usual, we assume was written in a pseudo-language with static scope.

The heart of the problem is the (nonlocal) reference to x inside fie. The scope rules tell us that such an x refers to the formal parameter to foo (which, as it happens, is the only x declared in the program). But when fie is called (using the formal f), there are two active instances of foo (and therefore two instances of its local environment). A first activation from the call foo(g,1), in which x is

The environment in C

The structure of the environment in C is particularly simple. A C program consists, in fact, of a sequence of variable and function declarations. The variables declared in this way (which in C jargon are called *external* variables) are visible at any point in the program. They are global variables, according to the terminology of Sect. 4.2.2. Functions are structured internally as blocks, and in each block local variables can be declared, but the definition of functions inside other functions is not permitted.

The environment of a function, therefore, is composed of a local and a global part. Each reference to a nonlocal name is resolved in a unique fashion in the global environment. With this simplified structure, environment handling is very simple. The static chain does not have to be maintained and to pass a function as a parameter to another function, it is sufficient to pass a pointer to its code.

For reasons of efficiency, furthermore, there is no management of in-line blocks. Variables declared in any block in a function are allocated in the activation record of the function.

Execution efficiency is one of the primary objectives for C. To avoid the cost of activation record stacks, the compiler can choose to translate a function call using the expansion of its body (in the case of a recursive function, the expansion happens once only).

---

associated (to a location which contains) the value 1, and a second one from the (recursive) call `foo(fie, 0)`, in which x is associated with the value 0. It is inside this second activation that the call to `fie` through `f` is made. The scope rules say nothing about which of the instances of x should be used in the body of `f`. It is at this point that the binding policy intervenes. Using deep binding, the environment is established when the association between `fie` and `f` is created, that is when x is associated with the value 1. The variable z will therefore be assigned the value 1. To help in understanding this example, Fig. 7.16 shows the stack and the closures when `fie` is executed.

In the case of shallow binding (which, let us repeat, is not used with static scope), the environment would be determined at the time `f` is invoked and z would be assigned the value 0.

What defines the environment   Before closing this section, let us consider again the problem encountered in Chap. 4, of which rules are used to determine the environment. We can finally complete the ingredients which contribute to the correct determination of the evaluation environment for a block-structured language. The following are necessary:

- Visibility rules, normally guaranteed by block structure.
- Exceptions to the visibility rules (which take into account, for example, redefinitions of names and the possibility or not of using a name before its declaration).
- Scope rules.

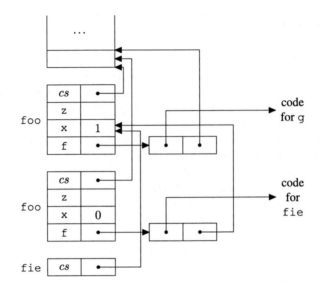

Fig. 7.16 Activation stack for Fig. 7.15

- The rules for the parameter passing method.
- The binding policy.

7.2.2 Functions as Results

The possibility of generating functions as the results of other functions allows the dynamic creation of functions at runtime. It is clear how, in general, a function returned as a result cannot be represented at execution time by its code alone, it will also be necessary to include the environment in which the function will be evaluated. Let us consider a first simple example in Fig. 7.17. Let us fix, first of all, the notation: by void->int we denote the *type* of the functions which take no argument (void) and return a value of type integer (int). The second line of the code is therefore the declaration of a function F which returns a function of no arguments which also returns an integer (note that return g returns the "function", not its application). The first line after the body of F is the declaration of the name gg with which the result of the evaluation of F is dynamically associated.

It should not be difficult to convince ourselves that the function gg returns the successor of the value of x. Using the static scope regime, this x is fixed by the structure of the program and not by the position of the call to gg, which could appear in an environment in which another definition of the name x occurs.

We can, therefore, say that, in general, when a function returns a function as result, this result is a *closure*. In consequence, the abstract machine must be appropriately modified to take into the account calls to closures. Analogous to what happens

Fig. 7.17 Functions as
results

```
{int x = 1;
void->int  F () {
    int g () {
        return x+1;
    }
    return g;
}
void->int gg = F();
int z = gg();
}
```

Fig. 7.18 Functions as result
and stack discipline

```
void->int  F () {
    int x = 1;
    int g () {
        return x+1;
    }
    return g;
}
void->int gg = F();
int z = gg();
```

Fig. 7.19 Activation records
for Fig. 7.18

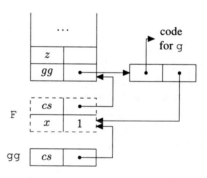

when a function is called via a formal parameter, when a function whose value is
obtained dynamically (like gg), the static chain pointer of its activation record is
determined using the associated closure (and not the canonical rules discussed in
Sect. 5.5.1, which would be of no help).

The general situation, moreover, is much more complex. If it is possible to return a function from the inside of a nested block, it is possible to arrange that its
evaluation environment will refer to a name that, according to stack discipline, is
going to be destroyed. Let us consider, indeed, the code in Fig. 7.18, where we
have moved the declaration of x to the inside of F. Figure 7.19 shows the activation
record arrangement when gg() is called.

When the result of F() is assigned to gg, the closure which forms its value
points to an environment containing the name x. But this environment is local to F
and will therefore be destroyed on its termination. How is it possible, then, to call
gg later than this without producing a dangling reference to x? The reply can only
be drastic: abandon stack discipline for activation records, so that they can then stay

alive indefinitely, because they could constitute the environments for functions that will be evaluated subsequently. In languages with the characteristics that we have just discussed, local environments have an *unlimited* lifetime.

The most common solution in this case is to allocate all activation records in the heap and to leave it to a garbage collector to deallocate them when it is discovered that there are no references to the names they contain.

Every functional language is constructed around the possibility of returning functions as results. They must therefore take this problem head on. On the contrary, returning functions as results in imperative languages is rare; this is purely to maintain a stack discipline for activation records. In imperative languages which do permit functions as results, there are, generally, many restrictions aimed at guaranteeing that it is never possible to create a reference to an environment that has become deactivated (for example: no nested functions (C, C++), return only non-nested functions (Modula-2, Modula-3), appropriately restrict the scope of those nested functions that are returned (Ada), etc.).

7.3 Exceptions

An exception is an event that is checked during the execution of a program and which must not (or cannot) be handled in the normal flow of control. Such events could be checking that a dynamic semantic error has occurred (e.g., a division by zero, overflow, etc.) or checking that a situation has occurred for which the programmer explicitly decides to terminate the current computation and transfer control to another point in the program, often outside the currently executing block.

First-generation languages did not provide structures for handling such situations. They typically treat them by means of jumps (`goto`s). On the other hand, many modern languages such as C++, Ada and Java have *structural* mechanisms for exception handling which appear as real abstraction constructs. These constructs allow the interruption of a computation and the shifting of control outside of the current construct, block or procedure. Often, this mechanism also allows data to be passed across the jump, resulting in a very flexible (and also often efficient) tool for handling those cases of exceptional termination of a computation which the normal control constructs (loops and conditionals) are unable to handle properly. Devised for handling the unusual or exceptional cases which can present themselves in a program, exceptions are also useful, as we will see, when giving compact and efficient definitions of some ordinary algorithms.

The mechanisms for handling exceptional situations vary greatly from language to language. We will restrict ourselves here to describing some common approaches and we do not pretend to be exhaustive. In general, we can say that, in order to correctly handle exceptions, a language must:

1. Specify *which* exceptions can be handled and how they can be defined.
2. Specify how an exception can be *raised*, that is which mechanisms cause the exceptional termination of a computation.

```
class EmptyExcp extends Throwable {int x=0;};

int average(int[] V) throws EmptyExcp(){
    if (length(V)==0) throw new EmptyExcp();
    else {int s=0; for (int i=0, i<length(V), i++) s=s+V[i];}
    return s/length(V);
};
...
try{...
    average(W);
    ...
}
catch (EmptyExcp e) {write('Array_empty);_}
```

Fig. 7.20 Exception handling

3. Specify how an exception can be *handled*, that is what are the actions to perform to determine an exception has occurred and where to transfer control of execution.

On the first point, we find both exceptions raised directly by the abstract machine (when some dynamic semantic condition is violated) and exceptions defined by the user. The latter can be values of a special type (as is the case in Ada and in ML), or any value whatsoever (as in C++) or something in the middle (in Java, an exception is an instance of some subclass of Throwable). When an exception is of any type whatsoever, in general it can contain a dynamically generated value which is passed to the handler.

Once an exception is defined, it can be raised implicitly if it is an abstract machine exception, or explicitly by the programmer using an appropriate construct.

Finally, for point (3), the handling of an exception in general requires two different constructs:

- A mechanism that defines a capsule around a portion of code (the *protected block*), with the aim of intercepting the exceptions that are to be handled inside the capsule itself.
- The definition of a handler for the exception, statically linked to the protected block. Control is transferred to the handler when the capsule intercepts the exception.

Let us examine the example in Fig. 7.20 (written in the usual pseudo-language inspired by Java and C++). The first line is the definition of the exception. In the case we are considering, all instances of class EmptyExcp can be an exception. To an approximation, we can imagine an instance of such a class as a record with a single internal field, labelled by x. Passing an exception involves the creation of a such a value and then raising the exception proper.

The second line is the definition of the average function. The keyword throws introduces the list of exceptions that *can* be thrown in the body of the function (in our case EmptyExcp). This clause (necessary in Java but optional in C++) has an important function as documentation: it shows the clients of the function that, in addition to the integer result, it could result in anomalous termination as signalled by the exception itself.

The construct that raises an exception is throw. A protected block is introduced by the keyword try, while the handler is contained in a block introduced by catch. The average function computes the arithmetic mean of the elements of the vector V. In the case in which the vector is empty, the function, instead of returning something arbitrary, raises an exception of class EmptyExcp. In checking such an event, the language's abstract machine interrupts the execution of the current command (in this case, the conditional command) and propagates the exception. All blocks entered during execution are exited until a try block trapping (catch) *this* exception is found. In the case of Fig. 7.20, the average function would be terminated, as would every block appearing between the only try present and the call to average. When the exception is intercepted by a try, control passes to the code in the catch block. If no explicit try trapping the exception is encountered, it is captured by a default handler which then terminates execution of the program and prints some error message or other.

The handler (the code in the catch) block is statically linked to the protected block. When an exception is detected, execution of the handler replaces the part of the protected block which has still to be executed. In particular, after execution of the handler, control flows normally to the first instruction which follows the handler itself.[9]

As far as these questions are strongly dependent on the language, let us make two important observations:

1. An exception is not an anonymous event. It has a name (often, rather, as in our case, it is a value in one of the language's types) which is explicitly mentioned in the throw construct and is used by constructs of the form try-catch to trap a specific class of exception.
2. Although the example does not show it, the exception could include a value which the construct that raised the exception passes in some way to the handler as an argument on which to operate in order to react to the exception that has just occurred (in our case, when it is raised, the value of the field x in the exception could be modified).

It is easy to convince ourselves that the propagation of an exception is not a simple jump. Let us assume that the exception is detected inside some procedure. If the exception is not handled inside the currently executing procedure, it is necessary to terminate the current procedure and to re-raise the exception at the point at which the current procedure was invoked. If the exception is not handled by the caller either, the exception is propagated along the procedure's call chain until it reaches

---

[9]This way of working is, in the literature, called "handling with termination" (because the construct where the exception is determined is terminated). Some older languages, PL/1 for example, (one of the first languages to introduce exception-handling mechanisms) follow a different approach, called "handling with resumption". In this case, the handler can arrange that control returns to the point where the exception was raised. The scheme with resumption can lead to flagging errors that are very difficult to locate.

Fig. 7.21 Exceptions
propagate along the dynamic
chain

```
{
  void f() throws X {
      throw new X();
  }

  void g (int sw) throws X {
      if (sw == 0) {f();}
      try {f();} catch (X e) {write("in_g");}
  }
  ...
  try {g(1);}
  catch (X e)  {write("in_main");}
}
```

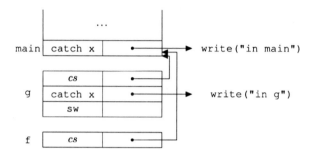

Fig. 7.22 System stack for Fig. 7.21

a compatible handler or reaches the highest level which provides a default handler
(which results in an error termination).

A subtle aspect which is worth explicitly considering is that exceptions propagate along the dynamic chain, even if the handler is statically associated with the
protected block. To illustrate this point, let us consider the code in Fig. 7.21, where
we have assumed that we have already declared an exception class X.

The exception X is raised inside two protected blocks. The outer try is the one in
the body of g. This is the one that traps the exception. The program prints the string
"in g". Figure 7.22 shows the stack of activation records and handlers when the body
of function f is executed. Considering Fig. 7.21, note that, in the case in which
the argument of g in the protected block is a variable whose value is execution-
dependent, it is not statically determinable which will be the handler to invoke.

Summarising, an exception is handled by the last handler that has been placed on
the execution stack. This is a reasonable behaviour. The exception is trapped at the
closest possible point to the one at which it was detected.

Pragmatics   We have discussed the use of exceptions in handling error cases.
There are ordinary cases, though, in which the cautious use of exceptions makes
for more elegant and efficient programs. We will limit ourselves to presenting one
example, that of walking a binary tree where it is desired to calculate the product of
the integers which label the nodes. The most obvious code is that shown in Fig. 7.23,

```
type Node = {int key;
             Node FS;
             Node FD;
             }

int mul (Node alb){
    if (alb == null) {return 1;}
    return alb.key * mul(alb.FS) * mul(alb.FD);
}
```

Fig. 7.23 Anticipated visit to a binary tree

```
int mulAus (Node alb) throws Zero{
    if (alb == null) {return 1;}
    if (alb.key == 0) {throw new Zero();}
    return alb.key * mulAus(alb.FS) * mulAus(alb.FD);
}

int mulEff (Node alb){
    try {return mulAus (alb);}
    catch (Zero e) {return 0;};
}
```

Fig. 7.24 A more efficient traversal

where a depth-first search of the tree is used and it is assumed that the type `Tree` is a structure (a record or a class) with three fields of which the first is an integer and the others are of type `Tree` and which link the structure together. The generic null value is represented by `null`.

The function `mul` correctly returns the product of the nodes, but is inefficient in the cases of very large trees where there is significant chance that some nodes are zero, given that in such a case the function could immediately terminate with the result zero. We can make use of the exception mechanism to force this expected termination without needing to produce the traversal code.

Figure 7.24 shows the function `mulAus` which raises an exception (of class `Zero`, which we assume to be defined elsewhere) when it encounters a node labelled with zero. `mullAus` is called by `mulEff`[10] inside to the protected block which handles the exception returning zero.

7.3.1 Implementing Exceptions

The simplest and intuitive way in which an abstract machine can implement exceptions is one that uses the stack of activation records. When a block is entered at

---

[10]The function `mulEff` is the function "exported" to clients in this program. In jargon, we say that `mulEff` is a *wrapper* of `mulAus`.

runtime, a pointer to the corresponding handler (together with the type of exception to which it refers) is inserted into the activation record (of the current procedure or of the current anonymous block). When a normal exit is made from a protected block (that is, because control transfers from it in the usual way and not through raising an exception), the reference to the handler is removed from the stack. Finally, when an exception is raised, the abstract machine looks for a handler for this exception in the current activation record. If one is not found, it uses the information in the record to reset the state of the machine, removes the record from the stack and rethrows the exception. This is a conceptually very simple solution but it has a not insignificant defect: each time that a protected block is entered, or is left, the abstract machine must manipulate the stack. This implementation, therefore, requires explicit work even in the normal (and more frequent) case in which the exception *is not* raised.

A more efficient runtime solution is obtained by anticipating a little of the work at compile time. In the first place, each procedure is associated with a hidden protected block formed from the entire procedure body and whose hidden handler is responsible only for clearing up the state and for rethrowing the exception unchanged. The compiler then prepares a table, *EH*, in which, for each protected block (including the hidden ones) it inserts two addresses (ip, ig) which correspond to the start of the protected block and the start of its handler. Let us assume that the start of the handler coincides with the end of the protected block. The table, ordered by the first component of the address, is passed to the abstract machine. When a protected block is entered or exited normally, nothing need be done. When, on the other hand, an exception is raised, a search is performed in the table for a pair of addresses (ip, ig) such that ip is the greatest address present in *EH* for which $ip \leq pc \leq ig$, where pc is the value of the program counter when the exception is detected. Since *EH* is ordered, a binary search can be performed. The search locates a handler for the exception (recall that a hidden handler is added to each procedure). If this handler re-throws the exception (because it does not capture this exception or because it is a hidden handler), the procedure starts again, with the current value of the program counter (if it was a handler for another exception) or with the return address of the procedure (if it was a hidden handler). This solution is more expensive than the preceding one when an exception is detected, at least by a logarithmic factor in the number of handlers (and procedures) present in the program (the reduction in performance depends on the need to perform a search through a table every time; the cost is logarithmic because a binary search is performed). On the other hand, it costs nothing at protected block entry and exit, where the preceding solution imposed a constant overhead on both of these operations. Since it is reasonable to assume that the detection of an exception is a rarer event than simple entry to a protected block, we have a solution that is on average more efficient than the preceding one.

7.4 Chapter Summary

The chapter has dealt with a central question for every programming language: mechanisms for functional abstraction. It has discussed, in particular, two of the

```
class X extends Exception {};
class P{                                                          2
    void f() throws X{
        throw new X();                                            4
    }
}                                                                 6

class Q{                                                          8
    class X extends Exception {};
    void g(){                                                     10
        P p = new P();
        try {p.f();} catch (X e){                                 12
                System.out.println("in_g");
                }                                                 14
    }
}                                                                 16
```

Fig. 7.25 Static scope and exception names

Exceptions and Static Scope

Languages like Java and C++ combine static scope for name definitions (and therefore also for exception names) with the dynamic association of handlers with protected blocks, as we have just seen. Such a combination is sometimes the cause of confusion, as the Java code in Fig. 7.25 shows. On a superficial reading, the code seems syntactically correct. Moreover, it could be said that an invocation of g results in the string "in g" being printed.

Yet, if the compilation of the code is attempted, the compiler finds two static semantic errors around line 12: (i) the exception X which must be caught by the corresponding catch is not raised in the try; (ii) the exception X, raised by f, is not declared in the (absent) throws clause of g.

The fact is that exception names (X in this case) have normal static scope. Method f raises the exception X declared on line 1; while the catch on line 12 traps the exception X declared on line 9 (and which is more correctly denoted by Q.X, since it is a nested class within Q). Just so as to avoid errors caused by situations of this kind, Java imposes the requirement on every method that it must declare all the exceptions that can be generated in its body in its throws clause.

The analogous situation can be reproduced in C++, *mutatis mutandis*. In C++, however, the throws clause is optional. If we compile the C++ code corresponding to that in Fig. 7.25, in which throws clauses are omitted, compilation terminates properly. But clearly, an invocation of the method f throws an exception different from that caught in the body of g. An invocation of g results in an exception X (of the class declared on line 1) which is then propagated upwards.

---

most important linguistic mechanisms to support functional abstraction in a high-level language: procedures and constructs for handling exceptions. The main concepts introduced are:

- *Procedures*: The concept of procedure, or function, or subprogram, constitutes the fundamental unit of program modularisation. Communication between procedures is effected using return values, parameters and the nonlocal environment.
- *Parameter passing method*: From a semantic viewpoint, there are input, output and input-output parameters. From an implementation viewpoint, there are different ways to pass a parameter:
    - By value.
    - By reference.
    - By means of one of the variations on call by value: by result, by constant or by value-result.
- *Higher-order functions*: Functions that take functions as arguments or return them as results. The latter case, in particular, has a significant impact on the implementation of a language, forcing the stack discipline for activation records to be abandoned.
- *Binding policy*: When functions are passed as arguments, the binding policy specifies the time at which the evaluation environment is determined. This can be when the link between the procedure and the parameter is established (deep binding) or when the procedure is used via the parameter (shallow binding).
- *Closures*: Data structures composed of a piece of code and an evaluation environment, called *closures*, are a canonical model for implementing call by name and all those situations in which a function must be passed as a parameter or returned as a result.
- *Exceptions*: Exceptional conditions which can be detected and handled in high-level languages using *protected blocks* and a *handler*. When an exception is detected, the appropriate handler is found by ascending the dynamic chain.

7.5 Bibliographical Notes

All the principal modes for parameter passing originate in the work of the Algol committee and were subsequently explored in other languages such as Algol-W and Pascal. The original definition of Algol60 [1] is a milestone in programming language design. The preparatory work on Algol-W can be seen in [10] and its mature form in the reference manual [7]. Algol-W included call by name (as default), call by value, by result and by value-result, as well as pointers and garbage collection. Pascal, which adopts as default call by reference, was first defined in [9]; the reference manual for the ISO Standard is [4].

The problems with determining the environment in the case of higher-order functions are often known as the *funarg problem* (the *fun*ctional *arg*ument problem). The *downward* funarg problem refers to the case of functions passed as arguments and therefore to the necessity of handling deep binding. The *upward* funarg problem refers to the case in which a function can be returned as a result [6]. The relations between binding policy and scope rules are discussed in [8].

One of the first languages with exceptions was PL/1 which used resumption handling (see [5]). More modern handling with termination (which anticipates the static link between protected blocks and handling) descends from Ada, which, in its turn, was inspired by [3].

7.6 Exercises

1. On page 166, commenting on Fig. 7.1, it can be seen that the environment of the function foo includes (as a nonlocal) the name foo. What purpose does the presence of this name serve inside the block?
2. State what will be printed by the following code fragment written in a pseudo-language permitting reference parameters (assume Y and J are passed by reference).

```
int X[10];
int i = 1;
X[0] = 0;
X[1] = 0;
X[2] = 0;
void foo (reference int Y,J){
      X[J] = J+1;
      write(Y);
      J++;
      X[J]=J;
      write(Y);
}
foo(X[i],i);
write(X[i]);
```

3. State what will be printed by the following code fragment written in a pseudo-language which allows *value-result* parameters:

```
int X = 2;
void foo (valueresult int Y){
      Y++;
      write(X);
      Y++;
}
foo(X);
write(X);
```

4. The following code fragment, is to be handed to an *interpreter* for a pseudo-language which permits constant parameters:

```
int X = 2;
void foo (constant int Y){
      write(Y);
      Y=Y+1;
```

```
    }
    foo(X);
    write(X);
```

What is the most probable behaviour of the interpreter?

5. Say what will be printed by the following code fragment which is written in a pseudo-language allowing *name* parameters:

```
int X = 2;
void foo (name int Y){
    X++;
    write(Y);
    X++;
}
foo(X+1);
write(X);
```

6. Based on the discussion of the implementation of deep binding using closures, describe in detail the case of a language with dynamic scope.

7. Consider the following fragment in a language with exceptions and call by value-result and call by reference:

```
{int y=0;
 void f(int x){
    x = x+1;
    throw E;
    x = x+1;
 }
 try{ f(y); } catch E {};
 write(y);
}
```

State what is printed by the program when parameters are passed: (i) by value-result; (ii) by reference.

8. In a pseudo-language with exceptions, consider the following block of code:

```
void ecc() throws X {
    throw new X();
}
void g (int para) throws X {
    if (para == 0) {ecc();}
    try {ecc();} catch (X) {write(3);}
}
void main () {
    try {g(1);} catch (X) {write(1);}
    try {g(0);} catch (X) {write(0);}
}
```

Say what is printed when main() is executed.

9. The following is defined in a pseudo-language with exceptions:

```
int f(int x){
   if (x==0) return 1;
   else if (x==1) throw E;
       else if (x==2) return f(1);
           else try {return f(x-1);} catch E {return x+1;}
}
```

What is the value that is returned by f(4)?

10. The description of the implementation of exceptions in Sect. 7.3.1 assumes that the compiler has access (direct or through the linkage phase) to the entire code of the program. Propose a modification to the implementation scheme based on the handler table for a language in which separate compilation of program fragments is possible (an example is Java, which allows separate compilation of classes).

References

1. J. W. Backus, F. L. Bauer, J. Green, C. Katz, J. McCarthy, A. J. Perlis, H. Rutishauser, K. Samelson, B. Vauquois, J. H. Wegstein, A. van Wijngaarden, and M. Woodger. Report on the algorithmic language ALGOL 60. *Commun. ACM*, 3(5):299–314, 1960.
2. M. Broy and E. Denert, editors. *Software Pioneers: Contributions to Software Engineering.* Springer, Berlin, 2002.
3. J. B. Goodenough. Exception handling: issues and a proposed notation. *Commun. ACM*, 18(12):683–696, 1975.
4. K. Jensen and N. Wirth. *Pascal-User Manual and Report.* Springer, Berlin, 1991.
5. M. D. MacLaren. Exception handling in PL/I. In *Proc. of an ACM Conf. on Language Design for Reliable Software*, pages 101–104, 1977.
6. J. Moses. The function of FUNCTION in LISP, or why the FUNARG problem should be called the environment problem. Technical report, MIT AI Memo 199, 1970. Disposable online at http://hdl.handle.net/1721.1/5854.
7. R. L. Sites. ALGOL W reference manual. Technical report, Stanford, CA, USA, 1972.
8. T. R. Virgilio and R. A. Finkel. Binding strategies and scope rules are independent. *Computer Languages*, 7(2):61–67, 1982.
9. N. Wirth. The programming language Pascal. *Acta Informatica*, 1(1):35–63, 1971. Reprinted in [2].
10. N. Wirth and C. A. R. Hoare. A contribution to the development of ALGOL. *Commun. ACM*, 9(6):413–432, 1966.

Chapter 8
Structuring Data

Each programming language contains constructs and mechanisms for structuring data. Instead of just the simple sequences of bits in the physical machine, a high-level language provides complex, structured data which more easily lends itself to describing the structure of the problems that are to be solved. These constructs and mechanisms are formed from what is called the *type system* of a language. Far from being an auxiliary aspect, types represent one of the salient characteristics of a programming language and which substantially differentiate one language from another.

In this chapter, we will examine type systems in the general sense, discussing primitive types and the mechanisms used to define new ones. Central to our presentation will be the concept of *type safety*, which will be introduced in Sect. 8.2. We will then tackle the questions of type equivalence and compatibility of types, that is mechanisms which will allow us to use a value of some type in a context requiring another type. We will then discuss polymorphism and overloading. We will conclude the chapter with some questions about storage management (*garbage collection*), which is not, strictly speaking, a topic about data types but which well complements the examination of pointers which we must undertake.

8.1 Data Types

Data types are present in programming languages for at least three different reasons:

1. At the design level, as support for the conceptual organisation;
2. At the program level, as support for correctness;
3. At the translation level, as support for the implementation.

Before entering into detailed discussion of these aspects, which we will do in the coming sections, we give a definition which, as is often the case with programming languages, is not formally precise but suffices to explain the phenomena which we intend studying.

M. Gabbrielli, S. Martini, *Programming Languages: Principles and Paradigms*,
Undergraduate Topics in Computer Science,
DOI 10.1007/978-1-84882-914-5_8, © Springer-Verlag London Limited 2010

Definition 8.1 (Data Type) A *data type* is a homogeneous collection of values, effectively presented, equipped with a set of operations which manipulate these values.

We will try to clarify the various terms used in the previous definition. A type is a collection of values, like the integers, or an integral interval. The adjective "homogeneous", for all its informality, suggests that these values must share any structural property which makes them similar to each other. For example, let us take as an example the integers between 5 and 10, inclusive, while we will not consider as a type the collection composed of the integer number 2, the truth value `true` and the rational number 3/4. Next, such values "come with" the operations which manipulate them. For example, together with the integers, we can consider the usual operations of addition, subtraction, multiplication and division; otherwise, also consider the less common operations such as remainder after integer division and raising to a power. According to our definition, the same set of values, equipped with two distinct sets of operations, forms another data type. The final component of the definition is that it must be "effectively presented", which refers to values. Since we are speaking of languages for describing algorithms, we are interested in values which it is possible to present (write, name) in a finite manner. Real numbers (the "true" ones in mathematics, that is the only complete archimedian ordered field) are *not* effectively presentable because there are real numbers with infinite decimal expansion which cannot be obtained by means of any algorithm. Their approximations in programming languages (`real` or `float`) are only subsets of the rationals.

8.1.1 Types as Support for Conceptual Organisation

The solution to every complex problem has a conceptual structure which often reflects that of the problem. The presence of different types allows the designer to use the type that is most appropriate to each class of concept. For example, a program handling hotel reservations, will handle concepts such as client, date, price, rooms, etc. Each of these concepts can be described as a different type, with its own set of operations. The designer can define new types and associate them with different concepts, even if they are represented by the same values. For example, rooms and prices could be both represented by integers within specified intervals, but their representation as distinct types makes their conceptual difference explicit.

The use of distinct types can be seen both as a design and a documentation tool. When reading a program, it is clear from the declaration of the type that a variable of type "room" has a different role from that of a variable of type "price". In this sense, types are similar to comments, with the important difference that we are dealing with *effectively controllable* comments, as we will see in the next section.

8.1.2 Types for Correctness

Every programming language has its own type-checking rules which regulate the use of types in a program. The most common example is that of an assignment; for a command of the form x := exp; to be correct, the majority of languages require that the type of exp coincides (or better, is compatible) with the (declared) type of x. In a similar fashion, it is forbidden to add integers and records or to call (that is, transfer control to) an object which is not a function or a procedure.

Such constraints are present in languages both to avoid runtime hardware errors (for example, a call to an object that is not a function might cause an address error), and, more likely, to avoid the kinds of logic error frequently hidden beneath type-rule violations. The sum of an integer and a string rarely corresponds to anything sensible.

Programming languages, then, assume that the violation of a type constraint corresponds to a possible semantic error (a design error). The crucial point is that many languages determine that type constraints must all be satisfied before the execution (or to code generation) of a program. This is the role of the *type checker*, a very important component of the static semantic checking phase of a compiler (Sect. 2.3). We have talked about types as if they were effectively controlled comments, because through them, the programmer communicates the legal ways with which the given objects can be used; but (unlike comments), the compiler (or the language's abstract machine) detects and signals every attempted incorrect use of these objects.

It is clear that a program that is correct with respect to the type rules can still be logically incorrect. Types ensure a minimal correctness, which, however, is of considerable help during the development phase of a program. A fairly powerful analogy is that of dimensional control in physics: when a physicist writes a formula, before verifying its correctness using laws, they verify that the dimensions are correct. If the formula is to express velocity, there must be distance over a time; if there is an acceleration, there must be distance over time squared, and so on. If the formula is dimensionally incorrect, no more time should be spent on it because it is certainly incorrect. If, on the other hand, it is dimensionally correct, it *might* be incorrect and must be handled semantically.

Sometimes, however, the type rules can appear too restrictive. A C programmer is used to the free handling of pointers (which are, in C, actual memory locations) and they can find the restrictions on performing arbitrary pointer arithmetic such as those in languages like Java or Pascal unnecessarily restrictive. In this case, the reply by the designers of these two languages is that the benefits of strict control over types considerably outweighs the loss of expressiveness and conciseness.

A more apt example is that of a subprogram that sorts a vector. In many languages, because of the presence of types, it will be necessary to write one routine to order an integer vector, another to order vectors of characters, and still another for vectors of reals, and so on. All these functions are identical as far as algorithm goes and differ only in the declaration of the types of the parameters and variables. The way out, in this case, is to adopt more sophisticated typing rules, which, without renouncing any control, allow one to write a single function which is parameterised by type. We will see below that languages which allow this kind of *polymorphism* are becoming common.

Let us finally observe that the rules pertaining to types are not always sufficient to guarantee that the constraints they express are satisfied. We give just a single example here. In a language that permits the explicit deallocation of store in a heap, it is possible that references (pointers) are generated that refer to memory that is no longer allocated to the program (*dangling references*). An attempted access using such a reference is an error that can be classified as a type error, but it is not guaranteed that it will be detected and reported by the abstract machine. Let us therefore classify programming languages as existing somewhere between *secure* and *insecure* with respect to types, according to how possible it is that there can be type-constraint violations during program execution that go undetected by the abstract machine.

8.1.3 Types and Implementation

The third principal motivation for the use of types in programming languages is that they are important sources of information for the abstract machine. The first kind of information, clearly, is about the amount of memory to be allocated to various objects. The compiler can allocate one word for an integer, one byte for a boolean value, n words for a vector of integers, and so on. When we have types, all of this information is available statically and does not change during execution.

As a consequence of this kind of static allocation during compilation, it is possible to optimize the operations that access an object. In Sect. 5.3, we discussed how access to an allocated variable in an activation record is performed using an offset from the pointer to an activation record, without a runtime search by name. This form of optimisation is possible because the information carried by types allows the static determination of the allocation sizes for almost every object, even for heap-allocated objects. We will soon see that a record is formed from a collection of fields, each of which is characterised by its own name and its own type. For example, using the same notation as in C, the following declaration introduces the Professor type, a record with two fields:

```
struct Professor{
    char Name[20];
    int Course_code;
}
```

If now we have a variable, p, of type Professor, we can access its fields using either the name p.Name or the name p.Course_Code. However the object p is allocated (in the heap or on the stack), access to its fields will always be possible through the use of offsets from the start address of p in memory.

8.2 Type Systems

Before going into the detailed treatment, in this section, we introduce a little terminology which we will illustrate in detail in the following sections.

As argued in the previous section, every programming language has its own *type
system*, or rather the complex of information and rules which govern the types in
that language. More precisely, a type system consists of the following:[1]

1. The set of predefined types of the language.
2. The mechanisms which permit the definition of new types.
3. The mechanisms for the control of types, among which we distinguish the following:

   - Equivalence rules which specify when two formally different types correspond
     to the same type.
   - Compatibility rules specifying when a value of a one type can be used in a
     context in which a different type would be required.
   - Rules and techniques for type inference which specify how the language as-
     signs a type to a complex expression based on information about its compo-
     nents.

4. The specification as to whether (or which) constraints are statically or dynamically checked.

A type system (and, by extension, a language) is *type safe*[2] when no program can
violate the distinctions between types defined in that language. In other words, a type
system is safe when no program, during its execution, can generate an unsignalled
error derived from a type violation. Once more, it is not always clear what a type
violation is, at least in general. We have already given many examples, such as
access to memory that is not allocated to the program, or the call of a non-functional
value. We will see below other examples of errors of this kind.

We have defined a type as a pair composed of a set of values and a set of operations. In any particular language, the values of a type can correspond to different
syntactic entities (constants, expressions, etc.). Having fixed a programming language, we can classify its types according to how the values of a type can be manipulated and the kinds of syntactic entity that corresponds to these values. Following
the classification that we have already seen in the box on page 135, we have values:

- *Denotable*, if they can be associated with a name.
- *Expressible* if they can be the result of a complex expression (that is different
  from a simple name).
- *Storable* if they can be stored in a variable.

---

[1]"A type system is a tractable syntactic method for proving the absence of certain program behav-
iors by classifying phrases according to the kinds of values they compute" [13].

[2]Much of the literature uses the term *strongly typed* in place of type safe.

Let us give some examples. The values of the type of functions from int to int are denotable in almost all languages because a name can be given using a declaration. For example:

```
int succ (int x){
    return x+1;
}
```

This assigns a name succ to the function which computes the successor. Functional values are not in general expressible in common imperative languages because there are no complex expressions returning a function as the result of their evaluation. In the same way, they are not, in general, storable values because it is not possible to assign a function to a variable. The situation is different in languages from other paradigms, for example functional languages (Scheme, ML, Haskell, etc.) in which functional values are both denotable, and expressible or, in some languages, storable. Values of type integer are in general denotable (they can be associated with constants), expressible, and storable.

8.2.1 Static and Dynamic Checking

A language has *static typing* if its checking of type constraints can be conducted on the program text at compile time. Otherwise, it has *dynamic typing* (that is if checking happens at runtime).

Dynamic type checking assumes that every object (value) have a runtime descriptor specifying its type. The abstract machine is responsible for checking that every operation is applied only to operands of the correct type. Often, this can be done by making the compiler generate appropriate checking code that is executed before each operation. It is not difficult to see that dynamic type checking locates type errors but is not efficient, given that operations are intermixed with type checking. In addition, a possible type error is revealed only during execution when the program might be in operation with its end user.

In static type checking, on the other hand, checks are made during compilation. In this scheme, checks are performed and reported to the programmer before the program is sent to the user. When checking is completely static, moreover, the explicit maintenance of type information at execution time is useless because correctness is guaranteed statically *for every execution sequence*. Execution is therefore more efficient, given that checks are not required at runtime. There is, clearly, a price to pay. In the first place, the design of a statically-typed language is more complex than that of a dynamic language, especially if, together with static checking, guaranteed type safety is also desired. In the second place, compilation takes longer and is more complex, a price that one pays willingly, given that compilation takes place only a few times (with respect to the number of times that the program will be executed) and, above all because type checking shortens the testing and debugging phases.

There is, in the end, a third price to pay. This is less clear than the others but is intimately connected with the nature of static type checking. Static types can decree as erroneous, programs that, in reality, do not cause a runtime type error. By way of a simple example, let us consider the following fragment in our pseudocode:

```
int x;
if (0==1) x = "pippo";
else x = 3+4;
```

The first branch of the conditional assigns the integer variable, x, to a value that is incompatible with its type but the execution of the fragment causes no error because the condition is never satisfied. However, every static type checker will signal that this fragment is incorrect because the types of the two conditional branches are not the same. Static checking is therefore more *conservative* than dynamic checking. The motivation for this statement is found in the considerations of Chap. 3 on the existence of undecidable problems. In addition to the halting problem, the problem of determining whether a program causes a type error at execution time is undecidable (see the box on p. 204). It follows from this that there exists no static check that can determine all and only those programs that produce errors at runtime. Static typing therefore adopts a prudential position: that of excluding more programs than strictly necessary with the justification that it can therefore guarantee correctness.

As we have already seen more than once in other contexts, static and dynamic type checking represent the two extremes of a spectrum of solutions in which the two methods coexist. Almost every high-level language combines static and dynamic type checks. We promise to return to this topic in due course; meanwhile let us just give a simple example from Pascal, a language traditionally classified as one that uses static type checking. Pascal allows the definition of interval types (see Sect. 8.3.9). For example, 1..10 is the type of the integers between 1 and 10 (inclusive). An expression of an interval type must be checked dynamically to guarantee that its value is properly contained within the interval. More generally, if a language with arrays want to check that the index of an array lies between the bounds of that array, must perform checks at runtime.

8.3 Scalar Types

Scalar (or simple) types are those types whose values are not composed of aggregations of other values. In this section, we will undertake a quick review of the main scalar types found in most common programming languages, while, in the next section, we will be concerned with the types that result from aggregating different values. The details (which we will not give) clearly depend on specific languages. In order to fix our notation, let us assume that we have in our pseudo-language the following way of defining (or declaring) new types:

```
type newtype = expression;
```

Type errors are undecidable

It is not difficult to prove that the problem of determining whether a program will cause a type error during its execution is undecidable. Let us, in fact, make use of what we already know, the undecidability of the halting problem.

Let us consider the following fragment, where P is an arbitrary program:

```
int x;
P;
x = "pippo";
```

Under what conditions will this fragment produce a type error as it runs? Only if P terminates, in which case it will try to execute the assignment:

```
x = "pippo";
```

which clearly violates the type system. If, on the other hand, P does not terminate, it will produce no error because control remains always inside P without ever reaching the critical assignment. Therefore, the fragment generates a type error if and only if P terminates. If there now existed a general method for deciding whether an arbitrary program causes an type error while executing, we could apply this method to our fragment. Such a method, though, would also be a method for deciding the termination of the (arbitrary) program P, something we know to be impossible.

This introduces the name of the type, newtype, whose structure is given by expression. In C, we would write, for the same meaning:

```
typedef expression newtype;
```

8.3.1 Booleans

The type of logical values, or booleans, is composed of:

- *Values*: The two truth values, *true* and *false*.
- *Operations:* an appropriate selection from the main logical operations: conjunction (and), disjunction (or) and negation (not), equality, exclusive or, etc.

If present (C for example has no type constructed in this fashion), its values can be stored, expressed and denoted. For reasons of addressing, the memory representation does not consist of a single bit but a byte (or possibly more if alignment is required).

8.3.2 Characters

The character type is composed of:

- *Values*: a set of character codes, fixed when the language is defined; the most common of these are ASCII and UNICODE.
- *Operations*: strongly dependent upon the language; we always find equality, comparison and some way to move from a character to its successor (according to the fixed encoding) and/or to its predecessor.

Values can be stored, expressed and denoted. The representation in store will consist of a single byte (ASCII) or of two bytes (UNICODE).

8.3.3 Integers

The type of integer numbers is composed of:

- *Values*: A finite subset of the integers, usually fixed when the language is defined (but there are cases in which it is determined by the abstract machine which can be the cause of some portability problems). Due to representation issues, the interval $[-2^t, 2^t - 1]$ is commonly used.
- *Operations*: the comparisons and an appropriate selection of the main arithmetic operators (addition, subtraction,, multiplication, integer division, remainder after division, exponentiation, etc.).

The values can be stored, expressed and denoted. The representation in memory consists of an even number of bytes (usually 2, 4, or 8), in two's complement form. (Some languages include support for arbitrary-length integers.)

8.3.4 Reals

The so-called real type (or floating point numbers) is composed of:

- *Values:* an appropriate subset of the rational numbers, usually fixed when the language is defined (but there are case in which it is fixed by the specific abstract machine, a matter that deeply affects portability); the structure (size, granularity, etc.) of such a subset depends on the representation adopted.
- *Operations*: comparisons and an appropriate selection of the main numeric operations (addition, subtraction, multiplication, division, exponentiation, square roots, etc.).

The values can be stored, expressed and denoted. The memory representation consists of four, eight and also ten bytes, in floating point format as specified by the IEEE 754 standard (for languages and architectures from 1985).

8.3.5 Fixed Point

The so-called fixed point type for reals is composed of:

Empty or singleton

At first sight, one might be confused by the statement that `void` has one (a single) element rather than none. Let us think a little. We are used to defining a function which "returns nothing" as:

```
void f (...){...}
```

If `void` were the empty set, we could not write a function such as `f`. There exist no functions with an empty codomain, with the unique exception of the function that is everywhere divergent. It is, instead, sensible to assume that in `void`, there is a single element and that this (implicitly) is returned by `f`. Since such an element is unique, we have no (and we must not have any) interest in explicitly saying what it is.

- *Values:* an appropriate subset of the rational numbers, usually fixed when the language is defined; the structure (size, granularity, etc.) of such a subset depends on the representation adopted.
- *Operations:* comparisons and an appropriate selection of the main numeric operations (addition,subtraction, multiplication, division, exponentiation, extraction of square roots, etc.).

The values can be stored, expressed and denoted. The representation in memory consists of four or eight bytes. Values are represented in two's complement, with a fixed number of bits reserved for the decimal part. Reals in fixed point permit compact representation over a wide interval with few precision places.

8.3.6 Complex

The so-called complex type is composed of:

- *Values*: an appropriate subset of the complex numbers, usually fixed by the definition of the language; the structure (size, granularity, etc.) of this subset depends on the adopted representation.
- *Operations*: comparisons and an appropriate selection of the main numerical operations (sum, subtraction, multiplication, division, exponentiation, taking of square roots, etc.).

The values can be stored, expressed and denoted. The representation consists of a pair of floating-point values.

8.3.7 Void

In some languages, there exists a primitive type whose semantics is that of having a single value. It is sometimes denoted `void` (even if, semantically, it would be better to call it `unit`, given that it is not the empty set but a singleton):

- *Values*: only one, which can be written as ().
- *Operations*: none.

What is the purpose of a type of this kind? It is used to denote the type of operations that modify the state but return no value. For example, in some languages, (but not in C or Java), assignments have type `void`.

8.3.8 Enumerations

In addition to the predefined types, such as those introduced above, we also find in some languages different ways to define new types. Enumerations and intervals are scalar types that are defined by the user.

An enumeration type consists of a fixed set of constants, each characterized by its own name. In our pseudo-language, we could write the following definition

```
type Dwarf = {Bashful, Doc, Dopey, Grumpy, Happy, Sleepy, Sneezy};
```

which introduces a new type with the name `Dwarf` and is a set of seven elements, each one denoted by its own name.

The operations available over an enumeration consist of comparisons and of a mechanism to move from a value to its successor and/or predecessor value (this should be compared with what was said about the character type; in Pascal, the `char` type is, basically, a predefined enumeration).

From a pragmatic viewpoint, enumerations permit the creation of highly legible programs insofar as the names for values constitute a fairly clear form of self documentation of the program. Type checking moreover can be exploited to check that a variable of an enumeration type assumes only the correct values.

Introduced for the first time in Pascal, enumeration types are present in many other languages; the box discusses those in C.

A value of an enumeration type is typically represented by a one-byte integer. The individual values are represented by contiguous values, starting at zero. Some languages (C and Ada for example) allow the programmer to choose the values corresponding to the different elements of an enumeration.

Enumerations in C

In C, our definition of Dwarf takes the form:

```
enum Dwarf {Bashful, Doc, Dopey, Grumpy, Happy, Sleepy, Sneezy};
```

Apart from notational variants, the essential point is that in C (but not in C++), such a declaration is substantially equivalent to the following:

```
typedef int Dwarf;
const Dwarf Bashful=0, Doc=1, Dopey=2,
       Grumpy=3, Happy=4, Sleepy=5, Sneezy=6;
```

The type equivalence rules for the language, in other words, allow an integer to be used in place of a Dwarf and vice versa. Type checking does not distinguish between the two types and, therefore, better documentation is all that is obtained by the use of an enumeration; stronger type checking is not obtained. In languages derived from Pascal, on the other hand, enumerations and integers are completely different types.

8.3.9 Intervals

The values of an interval type form a contiguous subset of the values of another scalar type (the *base type* of the interval). Two examples in Pascal (which was the first language to introduce intervals as well as enumerations) are:

```
type Bingo = 1..90;
     SomeDwarves = Grumpy..Sleepy;
```

In the first case, the Bingo type is an interval of 90 elements whose base type is the integer type. The interval SomeDwarves is formed from the values Grumpy, Happy and Sleepy and has Dwarf as its base type.

As in the case of enumerations, the advantage of using an interval type rather than the corresponding base type is both that it is better for documentation and because it provides a stronger type check. It can be seen that verifying that a value of a certain expression really belongs to the interval must necessarily be made dynamically, even in those languages whose type system is designed for the static checking of type constraints.

As far as representation goes, a compiler can represent a value of an interval type as a one- or two-byte integer according to the number of elements in the interval. In reality, usually an abstract machine will represent the values of an interval in the same way (and in the same number of bytes) in which the base type is represented.

8.3.10 Ordered Types

The boolean, character, integer, enumeration and interval types are examples of *ordered types* (or *discrete* types). They are equipped with a well-defined concept of total order and, above all, possess a concept of predecessor and successor for every element, except for the extreme values. Ordered types are a natural choice for vector indices and for control variables of definite iterations (see Sect. 6.3.3).

8.4 Composite Types

Non-scalar types are said to be *composite* since they are obtained by combining other types using appropriate *constructors*. The most important and common composite types are:

- *Record* (or structure), an collection of values in general of different type.
- *Array* (or vector), a collection of values of the same type.
- *Set*: subsets of a base type, generally ordinal types.
- *Pointer*: l-values which permit access to data of another type.
- *Recursive types*: types defined by recursion, using constants and constructors; particular cases of recursive types are lists, trees, etc.

In the following subsections, we will analyse these types in the same order as in the above list.

8.4.1 Records

A record is a collection formed from a finite number of (in general ordered) elements called *fields*, which are distinguished by name. Each field can be of a type that is different from the others (records are a *heterogeneous* data structure). In the majority of imperative languages, each field behaves like a variable of the same type.[3] The terminology is not, as usual, universal. In Pascal, one talks about records, in C (C++, Algol68, etc.), one talks about *structures* (`struct`); in Java, they do not exist because they are subsumed by the concept of class.

A simple example in our pseudo-language (which is inspired by C's notation) is the following:

```
type Student = struct{
    int year;
    float height;
};
```

---

[3]In many non-imperative languages, a record is, instead, a finite set of values each of which is accessed by name. Ignoring the question of name-based access, a record type, in such a case, is the cartesian product of the types of its fields.

Fig. 8.1 Possible storage
arrangement for a record of
type Hall

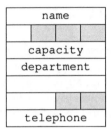

Each record of type Student is composed of a pair whose first component is
an integer, while the second is a real (float).

The only operation usually permitted on a value of a record type is the selection
of a component, which can be obtained using the name of the fields. For example,
if s is a variable that refers to a Student, we can assign values to its fields as
follows:

```
s.year = 12345;
s.height = 1.85;
```

In many languages, records can be nested, that is the field of a record is permitted
to be of a record type.

```
type Hall = struct{
                char name[5];
                int capacity;
                struct{
                    char department[10];
                    int telephone;
                } manager;
};
```

The third field (manager) of a record of type Hall is a record with two fields
(whose type, anonymous, is therefore also a struct; the convention is observed
that the type occurs before the name being declared). The selection of fields is
performed by an obvious extension of the dot notation: if h refers to a Hall,
with h.manager.telephone, we can denote the second field of the third field
(manager) of h.

Equality of records is not always defined (Ada permits it but Pascal, C, C++ do
not). Similarly, assignment of entire records is not always permitted. In the case in
which these operations are not permitted, the language user must explicitly program
them, for example by comparing (or assigning) one field at a time.

The order of fields is, in general, significant and is reflected in the way in which
records are stored. The fields of a record are stored in contiguous locations, even if
reasons of alignment can insert a hole between one field and another. For example,
in a 32-bit architecture a record of type Hall could be represented by as shown
in Fig. 8.1. The name field is represented by 5 bytes. The following field, however,
being an integer, must be aligned on a word boundary and therefore between name

Fig. 8.2 A variant record in
C using union

```
struct Stud{
    char name[6];
    int reg_no;
    int graduated;
    union{
        int lastyear;
        struct{
            int major;
            int year;
        } major_student;
    } variantfields;
};
```

and `capacity`, 3 empty bytes must be left. A similar thing happens with fields
`department` and `telephone`. A record of type `Hall` is therefore represented
by 7 words each of 4 bytes, even though only 23 bytes are significant.[4] To avoid
these problems, some languages do not ensure that the order of fields will be maintained by the abstract machine, thus allowing the compiler to re-organise fields in
order to minimise the number of holes required to enforce alignment. Our record of
type `Hall` could be represented in 6 words, with the waste of a single byte. This
is a good implementation if the language guarantees a significant level of abstraction between the user and the implementation. In some applications, on the other
hand, there is the need to allow users to manipulate the implementation of types.
Languages such as C allow designers to allow this kind of operation as well. In such
cases, the reorganisation of fields would not be a good design decision.

8.4.2 Variant Records and Unions

A particular form of record is that in which some fields are mutually exclusive.
We talk of *variant record* in this case. It is a feature that, with different names and
with different syntax and constraints, is provided by many languages (as we will
see very shortly, this is also the cause of much complication). In a way different
from our usual method of working (which uses one, neutral pseudo-language), we
will start with an example in Pascal, one of the languages in which the concept
of variant record is present in its clearest form (but is also accompanied by all of
the associated problems). In Pascal, we can declare a type `Stud` as follows (the
corresponding definition in C, which we will discuss next, is shown in Fig. 8.2):

```
type Stud = record
    name : array [1..6] of char;
    reg_no : integer;
```

---

[4]The presence of holes is often the reason for which some languages do not permit equality between entire records. A bit-by-bit comparison of two records would distinguish two records which
are in reality equal apart from the irrelevant information present in the holes.

```
case graduated : boolean of
   true: (lastyear : 2000..maxint);
   false:(major : boolean;
          year : (first,second,third)
          )
end;
```

The first two fields of the record are a vector of 6 characters (name) and an integer reg_no. The third field, major is preceded by the reserved work case, which is called the *tag* or *discriminant* of the variant record. A tag true indicates that the record has another field: lastyear of interval type. A tag false indicates, on the other hand, that the record has two more fields: major of type boolean and year of an enumeration type. The two possibilities which appear between round brackets are the *variants* of the record. In general, the tag can be of any ordinal type and can, therefore, be followed by a number of variants equal in number to the cardinality of this type.

From a semantic viewpoint, in a variant record, only one of the two variants is significant, never both. Which of the two variants is significant is indicated by the value of the tag. The tag and variants can be accessed as if they were any other field. For example, if s is one Stud,

```
s.graduated := true
```

assigns a value to the tag, while

```
s.lastyear := s.lastyear+1
```

increments by one the first variant.

As far as representation in memory is concerned, all variants share the same region of memory, given that they cannot be active at the same time. In effect, memory saving was one of the reasons for introduction of this data type, even if today this is not so important. Figure 8.3 shows the way in which a Stud is allocated.

Unions in C The primitive concept of variant record is not present in C, where we find instead the concept of *union*. A union is analogous to a record (struct) in definition and in selection of its fields but with the fundamental difference that only one of the fields of a union can be active at any particular time, given that the fields (which can be of different types) share the same area of storage. It can thus be immediately seen that Fig. 8.2 corresponds exactly to the variant record in Pascal that we just discussed.[5] The single difference (which, from the pragmatic viewpoint, is considerable) is in the necessity in C to add an extra level of naming: the fourth field

---

[5]Let us observe that, from a notational viewpoint, the outermost struct (the one immediately followed by the name Stud) is a definition of *type* (precisely the Stud type), while the innermost struct (which has no name before the braces) is a type expression which determines the type of the field major_student.

Fig. 8.3 Possible storage allocations for a variant record

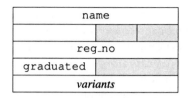

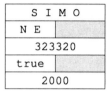

of the structure, named `variantfields`, is of union type and serves to enable access to the real variants. Notice, moreover, that the second variant (which is a pair) must be explicitly declared as a structure with its own name (`major_student`). To access the `major` field, if s refers to a `Stud`, it is necessary to write

```
s.variantfields.major_student.major
```

which is certainly much more demanding than Pascal's simple `s.major`.

From the linguistic viewpoint, however, the most revealing difference between Pascal's variant records and their simulation in C using unions is the fact that in C the tag is completely unrelated to the union. As can be seen in Fig. 8.2, `graduated` is a field like all the others and only the programmer's discipline makes it significant with respect to the fields of the union that follows it. The following fragment, for example, is completely legal:

```
s.graduated = 0; // 0 = false: C has no primitive boolean type
s.variantfields.lastyear = 2001;
if (s.graduated) printf("%d", s.variantfields.lastyear);
else print("%d", s.variantfields.major_student.year);
```

Despite being syntactically legal, it is clear that this can pose some semantic problems. The "tag" is false (to indicate that the second union component is active), but a value is assigned to the union's first field, yet then the second component is accessed (for printing).

Variants and Security The above discussion of C unions might seem to suggest that Pascal variant records are to be preferred to the "struct + union" solution adopted for C. There is no doubt that Pascal is more elegant. By merging the two concepts of record and union into the single concept of variant record, the language defines a clearer mechanism, which is more compact and which, one would like to say, is more secure. Unfortunately, this last adjective cannot be used in this context, with reference to type safety; here, Pascal behaves exactly like C.

The fact is that, in Pascal too, the language does not succeed in guaranteeing that there is a formal, verified connection between the value of the tag and the meaning of one of the variants which follow it. The crucial point is that the tag is accessible through an ordinary assignment.

One might think of requiring that the abstract machine should check that every access to a variant happens only if the tag has the correct value (signalling a dynamic error otherwise). Apart from the fact that the language definition does not require such checks, the problem is that this solution would catch some semantic errors but not all. Let us assume, in fact, that we have the following declaration:

```
type Three = 1..3;
var tmp : record
                case which : Three of
                    1 : (a : integer);
                    2 : (b : boolean);
                    3 : (c : char)
          end
```

A hypothetical abstract machine checking the tag prior to access would be able to signal (dynamically) the error in the following program (the error context is analogous to that one we discussed for C above):

```
tmp.which := 1;
tmp.a := 123;
writeln(tmp.c); (* dynamic error *)
```

But the following fragment, on the other hand, would pass unnoticed by all checks, despite the fact that it contains an access to the field c that has not yet been assigned a meaningful value:

```
tmp.which := 1;
tmp.a := 123;
tmp.which := 3;
writeln(tmp.c); (* no error, but c not meaningful! *)
```

The situation is even worse, because the tag is not obligatory. The following variant record definition is completely legal:

```
var tmp : record
                case Three of
                    1 : (a : integer);
                    2 : (b : boolean);
                    3 : (c : char)
          end
```

The variants are discriminated with respect to the type Three, but in this record, no space is reserved to store the tag. In this case, even the limited form of access check that we have just discussed turns out to be impossible.

Secure union: Algol68

Is it possible to design secure variant records such that they do not threaten the very roots of the language's type system? The reply is certainly yes, provided we are willing to pay the price both linguistically and in terms of efficiency. Let us discuss here in summary form the Algol-68 solution which antedates Pascal's design by some years (Ada is another language with secure variants). Algol-68 allows the definition of union types and requires the abstract machine to follow the evolution of the type of any variable of union type. It does not require an explicit tag:

```
union (int, bool, char) tmp; # tmp of union type #
...
tmp := true; # now tmp is of type boolean #
...
tmp := 123; # now tmp is an integer #
```

For every variable of union type, the abstract machine maintains a hidden type tag which is implicitly set when an assignment occurs. The crucial point is that a union can be used only through a "conformity clause" (a case) which specifies what to do with this variable in all cases. For example:

```
case tmp in
    (int a)  : a := a+1,
    (bool b) : b := not b,
    (char c) : print(c)
esac
```

A conformity clause is the only construct in the language that generate type checks for dynamic types. Beyond the efficiency penalty, it is clear what the linguistic burden of a similar solution would be.

The consequence of all this is that the presence of variant records destroys the security of Pascal's type system. One could then ask if it is worth the effort including such a construct that is so expensive in terms of security in a language which considers typing as one of its primary goals. The reply, given today's climate, is negative: the saving in memory (as well as in conceptual elegance) that variant records provide is not justified by the problems that they cause to the type system.[6] Variant records (or unions) are not present in Modula-3 or in Java.

---

[6]But it should be noted that Pascal is a language designed at the end of the sixties when the problem of runtime central-memory occupancy was a central concern.

8.4.3 Arrays

An array (or vector) is a finite collection of *elements* of the same type, indexed by an interval of ordinal type.[7] Each element behaves as if it were a variable of the same type. The ordinal interval of the indices is the index type, or the type of the array indices. The type of the elements is the *component type*, or even, with a little imprecision, the *array type*. Since all elements are of the same type, arrays are homogeneous data types.

Arrays are doubtless the most common composite type found in programming languages; they first appeared in FORTRAN, the progenitor of all high-level languages. The syntax and various characteristics of arrays, however, vary considerably from language to language. The fundamental ingredients of array declarations are its name, its index type and the type of its elements. Let us begin with one of the simplest examples we can produce in C:

```
int V[10];
```

The square brackets after the name of the variable indicate that we are dealing with an array formed from 10 elements, each of which is a variable of type integer (from now on, we will simply say: an array of 10 integers). The element type is therefore int, while the index type is an interval of 10 elements; using the convention adopted in many languages (C, C++, Java, etc.), this interval starts at 0. In this case, therefore, the index type is the interval 0 to 9. In general, we can assume that a language allows the declaration of the index type to be an arbitrary interval of an ordinal type, for example:

```
int W[21..30];
type Dwarf = {Bashful, Doc, Dopey, Grumpy, Happy, Sleepy,
              Sneezy};
float Z[Dopey..Sneezy];
```

In the first declaration, W is an array of 10 integers, with integer indices from 21 to 30. The last line declares Z, an array of 4 reals, with indices taken from the Dwarf type that run Dopey to Sneezy.

All languages permit the definition of *multidimensional* arrays, that is arrays indexed by two or more indices:

```
int V[1..10,1..10];
char C[Dopey..Sleepy,0..10,1..10];
```

The array V is a 10×10 square integer matrix, with row and column indices running from 1 to 10; C is a matrix whose elements are characters and whose bounds are $4 \times 11 \times 10$.

---

[7]From a semantic viewpoint, an array is a function which has, as domain, an interval for the indices and, as codomain, a type for the array elements.

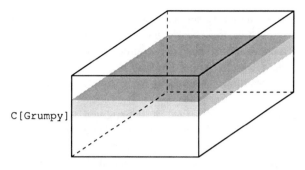

C[Grumpy]

Fig. 8.4 A slice through an array

In some languages, a multidimensional array can be obtained by declaring that the type of the array elements is, at the same time, an array. A possible syntax in our pseudo-language could be the following, so we can declare the above as:

```
int V[1..10][1..10];
char C[Dopey..Sleepy][0..10][1..10];
```

In some languages, the two models (multidimensional array and array of array) are equivalent (one is an abbreviation for the other). This is the case in Pascal. In other languages, only one of the two possibilities is admitted. In C, a multidimensional array is an array of arrays and must be declared as such. Other languages, finally, allow both models, but arrays of arrays support additional operations (*slicing*, as will shortly be seen) that are only defined over multidimensional arrays.

Operations on Arrays   The simplest operation permitted on an array is *element selection*. It is performed using an index variable. The most common notation uses square brackets: W[e] indicates the element of W corresponding to the index denoted by the value of the expression e. For multidimensional arrays, it is possible to find C[Grumpy,1,2] or C[Grumpy][1][2], depending on whether the emphasis is on multidimensional or arrays of arrays.

Some languages, furthermore, allow operations on arrays in their entirety: assignment, equality, comparisons and also arithmetic operations (performed, in general, elementwise). In other languages, these global operations are just one particular case of operations that allow the selection of interior parts of an array, which is operated on in a global fashion. An *array slice* is a portion of an array composed of contiguous elements. With the declarations above, V[3] could indicate the third row of the matrix V, and C[Grumpy] the plane of the 3-dimensional matrix C which is obtained by selecting only its first component (Fig. 8.4). Other languages may allow the selection of more sophisticated slices: diagonals, frames, etc.

Checking   The specification of the index type of an array is an integral of its definition. Type checking in the language, therefore, would have to verify that every access of an element of a vector really happens "between the bounds" of the array and that there is no attempt to access elements that do not exist. With the exception of some special cases, this check can occur only at runtime. A secure language, therefore, will have to ensure that the compiler generates appropriate checks for *every access*. Since this checking will affect the efficiency of the program, some languages, while permitting such checks to be generated, allow their deactivation (for example, Pascal).

Let us observe, by the way, that we are dealing with a of matter of not insignificant importance to the security of a system, understood not just as "type safety", but as "security" in a real sense. One of the most common attacks, which is also one of the most serious for the security of a system, is called *buffer overflow*. A malicious agent sends messages across the network with the aim of having them read into the buffers of the destination. If the destination does not check that the length of messages does not exceed the capacity of the buffer, the malicious sender can write into an area of memory that is not allocated to the buffers. If the buffer is allocated in an activation record and the sender succeeds in writing into the area the activation record reserves for saving the procedure's return address, a "return" to any instruction can be made, in particular it can be made to jump to malicious code loaded by the attacker on purpose (for example in the same buffer that caused the overflow). In almost all cases, a buffer overflow attack can be stopped by an abstract machine that checks that every access to an array happens "between the bounds".

Storage and Calculation of Indices   An array is usually stored as a contiguous portion of memory (see Exercise 2 for a non-contiguous allocation technique). For a single-dimensional array, allocation follows the order of the indices. In the case of a multidimensional array, there are two alternative techniques, referred to as storage in *row order* and in *column order*. In row order, two elements are contiguous when they differ in their last index (except in the case of elements at the extremes of a row, or on a plane, etc.). In column order, two elements are contiguous if they differ in the first index (except in the case of extremal elements). Row order is a little more common than column order; the fact that the elements of a row are stored contiguously makes the selection of a row slice easier (this is the slicing operation that is most often provided).

The two storing techniques are not equivalent as far as efficiency is concerned, particularly when there is a cache. Programs that manipulate large multidimensional arrays are often characterised by nested loops that run over such arrays. If the array cannot be stored entirely in a cache, it is important that its elements are accessed "along" the cache, such that the first miss brings into the cache the elements that will be accessed immediately after. If the loop works by row, the cache must also be loaded by row, that is, row order is more convenient; if the loop is columnwise, column order should be preferred.

Once an array is stored in a contiguous fashion, the calculation of the address corresponding to an arbitrary element is not difficult, even if it requires a little arithmetic. Let us consider the generic array of n dimensions, with elements of type T.

T V$[L_1 . . U_1]...[L_n . . U_n]$;

Let S_n be the number of the addressable units (typically a byte) necessary to store a single element of type T. Starting from this value, we can successively calculate a series of values which express the quantity of memory required to store increasingly larger slices of V. Let us assume we are working in row order, so we have:

$$S_{n-1} = (U_n - L_n + 1)S_n,$$

$$\dots$$

$$S_1 = (U_2 - L_2 + 1)S_2.$$

For example, for $n = 3$, S_2 is the amount of memory required to store a row, while S_1 is the amount of memory required for an entire plane of V.

The address of element $V[i_1, \dots, i_n]$ is now obtained by adding to the first address used to store V the quantity:

$$(i_1 - L_1)S_1 + \cdots + (i_n - L_n)S_n.$$

In the case in which the number of dimensions (that is, n), and the value of the L_j and U_j are all known at compile time (that is the *form* of the array is static, see next section), it is convenient to reformulate the addressing expression as:

$$i_1 S_1 + \cdots + i_n S_n - (L_1 S_1 + \cdots + L_n S_n). \tag{8.1}$$

Here, the second part (in parentheses), and *a fortiori*, all the S_j are constants that can be determined at compile time. Making use of this formulation, an address is calculated (dynamically) with n multiplications and n additions. The final subtraction disappears whenever all the L_j are zero (which explains why some languages use zero as lower bound for indices).

Form of an Array: Where an Array is Allocated   The *shape* of an array is determined by the number of its dimensions and by the interval within which each of them can vary. An important aspect of the definition of a language is the decision about when the form of an array is fixed. Corresponding to the three principal cases, we also have three different models for allocating arrays in memory:

- *Static* shape. Everything is decided at compile time; the array can be stored in the activation record of the block in which its declaration appears (or in the static memory allocated for globals, if used). Let us observe that in this case, the total dimension required for an array is a constant that is known at compile time. The offset from the address of the array's start and the fixed point in the activation record to which the activation record pointer points is also therefore a constant (this was explained in Sect. 5.3.3). Access to an element of the array is differentiated from access to an ordinary (scalar) variable only by the quantity determined by (8.1).
- Shape *fixed at declaration time*. In this case, the shape is not defined at compile time but is recorded and fixed when execution reaches the array declaration (for example, the interval of the index depends on the value of a variable). In this case,

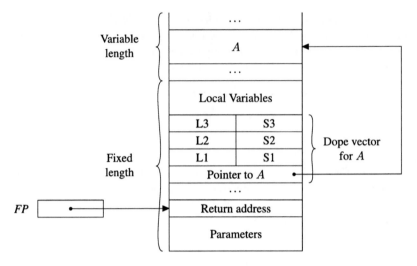

Fig. 8.5 Structure of an activation record with a dope vector

too, the array can be allocated in the activation record of the block in which its declaration appears, but the compiler has no way of knowing what the offset is between the start of the array and the fixed point of the activation record to which the frame pointer refers. This is an unpleasant position because it could have repercussions for other, completely static, data structures. To avoid this problem, an activation record is divided into two parts: one part for fixed-length data, and the other for variable-length data. Access to all the data allocated in the fixed-length part is performed in the usual fashion. On the other hand, when accessing a variable-length data item, an indirection through a variable-length data descriptor is performed. The descriptor is contained in the fixed-length part which is accessed by offset and contains, amongst other things, a pointer to the start of the data structure (in our case, an array). Figure 8.5 shows a scheme for allocation inside an activation record for this. The descriptor for an array is known as a *dope vector*. We will describe dope vectors in a little more detail in a short while.

- *Dynamic* shape. In this case, an array can change shape after its creation as a result of the effects of execution. Stack allocation is no longer possible because the size and structure of an activation record would have to be dynamically modified. Dynamic arrays must therefore be allocated on the heap, while a pointer to the start of the array remains stored in the fixed-length part of the activation record.

To conclude the argument, let us argue that, in addition to the static or dynamic nature of the shape, the decision on allocation of an array must also take its lifetime into account. An array allocated in an activation record has a lifetime limited to that of the block in which it is declared. In languages that allow the creation of arrays with unlimited lifetimes (for example, Java) they must be allocated on the heap.

Dope Vectors The descriptor of an array whose shape is not known statically (and which can either be fixed at execution time or be completely dynamic) is called a

Arrays in Java

In Java, an array is not created at the same time as the declaration of a variable of array type. The declaration int [] v; introduces only the name v. It is not associated with any data structure (more precisely, this is the same as for any declaration of a variable of class type). The data structure is created on the heap using the pre-defined new operation: V = new int[10]; creates in the heap a new array of 10 integers and assigns a reference to them to the name v.

An array in Java is an object in the strict sense of the term as understood for that language. It has unlimited lifetime.

dope vector. A dope vector, which is usually allocated in the fixed-length part of an activation record contains the following components:

- A pointer to the first location at which the array is stored;
- All the dynamic information required to perform the calculation in expression (8.1): the number of dimensions (also called the *rank* of the array), the value of the lower limit of each dimension (the L_j), the occupation of each dimension (the S_j).

If some of these values are known statically, they are not explicitly stored. The dope vector is initialised when the array is created (using appropriate calculations of the values S_j). To access an element of the array, the dope vector is accessed (by an offset from the frame pointer), expression (8.1) is computed and is added (via an indirect access) to the address of the start of the array.

8.4.4 Sets

Some programming languages (in particular Pascal and its descendants) allow the definition of set types, whose values are composed of subsets of a base type (or universe), usually restricted to an ordinal type. Based on Pascal's syntax but adapting it somewhat, we have:

```
set of char S;
set of Dwarf N;
```

We have a variable S which is a subset of the characters and a variable N which will contain a subset of the type Dwarf, as defined on page 207. Languages allowing sets provide appropriate syntax for assigning a specific subset to a variable, for example:

```
N = (Grumpy, Sleepy);
```

The possible operations on values of set type set are the membership test (the test that an element belongs to a set) and the usual set-theoretic operations of union, intersection and difference; complement is not always provided.

A set is usually represented as a bit vector (the *characteristic* vector of the set) whose length is the same as the cardinality of the base type. For example, a subset of char, in an implementation that uses the ASCII 7-bit code, would be represented as 128 bits. If, in the characteristic vector, the jth bit is set, it indicates that the jth element of the base type (in the standard enumeration) is in the set; otherwise, a bit equal to zero indicates that the corresponding element is not in the set. Although this representation permits the highly efficient execution of set-theoretic operations (as bitwise operations on the physical machine), it is clear that it is completely inappropriate for subsets of types whose base type has a cardinality greater than a few hundred. To obviate this problem, languages often limit the types that can be used as base for set types. Or rather, they select other representations (for example, hash tables), which will support the representation of the set in a more compact fashion, even if this reduces the efficiency of the operations performed upon it.

8.4.5 Pointers

Some languages permit the direct manipulation of l-values. The corresponding type is called a pointer type. In general, languages permit the definition of a pointer type for every type: if T is a type, it is possible to define the type of "pointers to (variables of type) T". It should be noted that, in this context, we will be interested in pointers as far as they are explicitly present in the language, in contrast to the obvious presence of pointers in the abstract machine.

In a language with a reference model for variables, pointer types are not necessary (or required). Every variable is always a reference, or rather it is considered as an l-value, even if this value cannot explicitly be manipulated. In languages with modifiable variables, on the other hand, pointers provide a way of referring to an l-value without automatically dereferencing it. In such languages, one of main uses for pointers is to construct values of recursive type (as linked structures) which are not in general provided as primitives of the language itself.

In our pseudo-language, we use T* to indicate a pointer type to objects of type T and therefore we declare a pointer as:[8]

```
T* p;
```

---

[8]The mother tongue C programmer would write the example with a different distribution of spaces: T *p, which is read as *p is a pointer to T. In C, * is a modifier of the variable and not of the type (which is apparent when you introduce two pointers in the same declaration: C requires int *p, *q;, while we would write int* p,q; for uniformity with the other types). Although the C approach seems simpler (particularly when considered with the dereferencing operator), it is semantically more correct (and more uniform with respect to other languages) to see * as a type modifier and not a variable modifier.

The values of type `T*` are pointers (from an implementation viewpoint: addresses) to memory locations (that is modifiable variables) which contain values of type `T`. It is not always the case such pointers can refer to arbitrary locations; some languages require that pointers point only to objects allocated in the heap (this is the case with Pascal, in its descendants and in some earlier versions of Ada). Other languages, on the other hand, allow pointers also to point to locations on the system stack or into the global area (this is the case with C++ and later versions of Ada).

There usually exists a canonical value, which is an element of type `T*`, for every `T`, which indicates the null pointer, that is which points to no value. We write `null` for this value. The operations permitted on values of pointer type are usually creation, equality (in particular, equality to `null`), dereferencing (access to the object begin pointed to).

The commonest way of creating a value of pointer type is to use a predefined construct or a library function which allocates an object of an appropriate type on the heap and also returns a reference to the object. This is the purpose of `malloc` in C:

```
int* p;
p = (int *) malloc (sizeof (int));
```

or of `new` in Pascal. For heap management in the presence of explicit allocation, we refer to our discussion in Sect. 5.4.

In some languages, it is possible also to create pointers by applying special operators which return the storage address of an object stored in memory. Again we use C as the model for our examples. C uses the `&` operator to obtain the address of an entity:

```
float r = 3.1415;
float* q;
q = &r;
```

The pointer `q` now points to the location that contains the variable `r`. This is also an example of a pointer pointing to a location on the stack and not in the heap.

Dereferencing a pointer is often indicated by some operator, for example, the `*` in C. Continuing the example above:

```
*p = 33;
r = *q + 1;
```

Here, the first line assigns the value 33 to the object pointed by `p` (which is in the heap). The second line assigns to `r` the value 4.1415 (on the stack). It can be seen that, as a side-effect, the second assignment also modifies the value pointed by `q` (but not `q` itself). It can also be observed that the l-value/r-value distinction for variables in an assignment still remains valid even for a dereferenced pointer. When `*p` is on the left of an assignment, it indicates the l-value that is obtained by dereferencing `p` (that is, the assignment will work on the address contained in the pointer); when *p is on the right of an assignment, it indicates the r-value of the same location.

From the pragmatic viewpoint, pointers play a key role in the definition of so-called *recursive* structures such as lists, trees, etc. Some languages directly allow the definition of recursive types, as will be seen in Sect. 8.4.7. In languages with pointers, recursive data structures can be defined in a natural fashion. For example, the type for the lists of integers[9] can be defined as:

```
type int_list = element*;
type element  = struct {int val;
                        int_list next;};
```

It can be seen that, in order for such a definition to be legal in a hypothetical language, problems related to the use of a name before its definition (which we mentioned in Sect. 4.3.3) must be solved.

Pointer Arithmetic   In C and in its descendants, in addition to the operations that we have just discussed, it is possible to perform some arithmetic operations on pointers. It is possible to increment a pointer, subtract one pointer from another (so obtain an offset constant), add an arbitrary value to a pointer. This complex of operations goes under the name of pointer arithmetic. The semantics of these operations, although denoted by the standard arithmetic operators, must be understood with reference to the pointer type on which they operate. By means of an example, let us consider the following fragment:

```
int* p;
int* c;
p = (int *) malloc(sizeof(int));
c = (char *) malloc(sizeof(char));
p = p+1;
c = c+1;
```

If the two mallocs return addresses (i for p and j for c), at the end of the fragment, the value of the two pointers is *not* $i + 1$ and $j + 1$, but, rather, $i+$sizeof(int) and $j +$sizeof(char). And thus, analogously, for other increment and decrement operations.

It should be clear that pointer arithmetic destroys every hope of type safety in a language. There is no guarantee whatsoever that, at any time during the execution of a program, a variable declared as a pointer to an object of type T will still point to an area of store in which a value of type T is actually stored.

---

[9] As we saw in Sect. 4.3.3, a list is a variable-length data structure formed from a possibly empty ordered sequence of elements of some type, in which it is possible to add or remove elements and where only the first element can be directly accessed.

Deallocation   We have already seen that one of the most common methods for creating values of a pointer type is to use a function defined as standard in the language to allocate an object on the heap and also return a pointer to it. The deallocation of memory can be explicit or implicit.

In the case of implicit deallocation, the language does not provide the programmer with mechanisms to reclaim memory. The programmer continues to request allocations while there is still available heap. When the heap memory is full, however, the computation need not abort: already allocated values might not be accessible so they can be reused. Consider indeed the following fragment:

```
int* p = (int *) malloc(sizeof(int));
*p = 5;
p = null;
```

The last command, which assigns null to p, destroys the only pointer through which this previously allocated area can be accessed. It is possible to equip the abstract machine with a mechanism to recoup such pieces of memory. This technique, which is called garbage collection, is a subject that has been studied a great deal when implementing programming languages. We will examine it in Sect. 8.12.

In the case of explicit deallocation, the language makes available a mechanism with which the programmer can release the memory referred to by a pointer. In C, for example, if p points to an object on the heap that was previously allocated by malloc, calling the function free on p, will deallocate the object pointed to by p (the store will be put back on the free list if the technique described in Sect. 5.4 is used). It is good practice to assign the value null to p when this is done. It is a semantic error (with unpredictable result) to invoke free on a pointer which does not refer to an object allocated using malloc (this can happen if either pointer arithmetic has been used or if the pointer was created using the operator &).[10] As we saw in Chap. 4, the most important problem that is raised by deallocation is that it is possible to generate dangling references; that is pointers with a value other than null which point to storage that is no longer allocated. The simplest example is probably the following:

```
int* p;
int* q;
p = (int *) malloc(sizeof(int));
*p = 5;
q = p;
free(p);
p = null;
...          //
...          // series of commands not modifying  p or q
```

---

[10]The point is that malloc does not only allocate the space required for the object required, but also a descriptor to the data. The descriptor contains the size of the allocated block and possibly other information. It is by accessing such data that free (which takes a single pointer as parameter) can determine what is to be deallocated.

after line 5   after line 7

Fig. 8.6 Dangling references

```
...            //
print(*p);  // error that may be trapped
print(*q);  // error that cannot be trapped
```

Figure 8.6 shows the situation in memory as well as the pointers immediately after lines 5 and 7. The pointer q has a value that is not null. It points to an area of memory that could by now be allocated to other data. We can certainly assume that the abstract machine checks and signals an error every time a pointer dereferences to null (as on line 11),[11] while the de-referencing of q in line 12 will not be signalled and can be the cause of errors that are as devastating as they are difficult to find.

In languages which allow pointers to refer to objects on the stack, dangling references can also be generated without explicit deallocation. It is sufficient to store the address of a variable local to a function in a nonlocal environment.

```
{int* p;
 void foo(){
    int n;
    p = &n;
 }
 ...
 foo();
 ...     // here p is a dangling reference
}
```

If a language allows dangling references to happen, it is obvious that it cannot be type safe. If a language does not allow pointers to data on the stack, dangling references can be avoided by not having deallocation, both at the level of program design (by using a language with implicit pointer deallocation and garbage collection), or by deallocating nothing even if the programmer requests it: this is the case with some early implementations of Pascal, where the deallocation function dispose was implemented as a function with an empty body.

If, though, a language provides explicit deallocation, or pointers to the stack, some techniques are discussed in Sect. 8.11 with which dangling pointers can be rendered harmless, thereby restoring type safety.

---

[11] This can happen often without affecting efficiency, by making use of mechanisms for protecting addresses on the underlying physical machine.

Arrays and pointers in C

In C, arrays and pointers are considered under certain circumstances to be equivalent. The declaration of an array introduces a name which can be used as a pointer to the whole array. Conversely, if an integer pointer refers to an array, it can also be used as the name of an array:

```
int V[10];
int* W;
W = V;            // W points to the start of array V
V[1] = 5;
W[1] = 5;
*(W+1) = 5;
*(V+1) = 5;
```

The last four assignments in this example are all equivalent. They assign the value 5 to the second element of the array pointed to by both V and W. (It can be seen how pointer arithmetic is natural here.) In the case of a multidimensional array (stored in row order), pointer arithmetic allows various combinations of operation. In the scope of the declaration int Z[10][10], the following expressions are equivalent: Z[i][j], (*(Z+1))[j]), *(Z[i]+j) and *(*(Z+i)+j).

The equivalence of arrays and pointers is essential when passing parameters. It will be recalled that C has only call by value. When it passes a vector, it always passes a pointer (by value), never the array itself. The formal parameter can be declared as an array (int A[]) or as a pointer (int *A). In the case of multidimensional arrays, it is required only to specify the number of elements of the dimensions other than the first in the formal parameter (for example A[][10], or even (*A)[10]). This information is necessary for the static generation of the correct code for accessing elements of the vector.

Finally, C permits storage of multidimensional array as a vector of pointers to arrays; for this organisation by row-pointer, see Exercise 2.

8.4.6 Recursive Types

A recursive type is a composite type in which a value of the type can contain a (reference to a) value of the same type. In many languages recursive types can be assimilated to (and in effect are) records in which a field is of the same type as the record itself. The simplest example is perhaps that of a list of integers, which we present in our pseudo-language (adapting Java's notation):

```
type int_list = {int val;
                 int_list next;};
```

To end the recursion, the language can provide a special value, for example null, which belongs to any (recursive) type and which we can imagine as having

$$\{2,\{33,\{1,\{4,\{3,\{1,\{21,\text{null}\}\}\}\}\}\}\}$$

Fig. 8.7 A value of type int_list

```
type char_tree = {char val;
                  char_tree left;
                  char_tree right;};
```
$$\{A,\{B,\{C,\text{null},\text{null}\},\{D,\{E,\text{null},\text{null}\},\text{null}\}\},\{F,\text{null},\text{null}\}\}$$

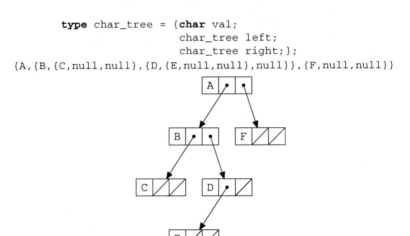

Fig. 8.8 Binary tree over char

the empty value. A value of type int_list is therefore a pair: the first element is an integer, the second is a value of type int_list, and so on, until one of these int_list values is null (see the example in Fig. 8.7).

Figure 8.8 shows the definition of a recursive type for binary trees of characters. It also shows a value and the usual graphical representation for trees.

As can be seen from these very simple examples, the possibility of defining recursive types makes the type system of a language flexible and powerful (see Exercise 4). The operations permitted on the values of recursive types are the selection of a component and equality test for null.

If the language admits modifiable variables (which is the case in all imperative languages), it is also possible to construct circular values. In purely functional languages, the values of a recursive type are always in the form a tree.

Recursive types are usually represented as structures in the heap. A value of a recursive type corresponds to a linked structure. Every element of the structure is composed of a record in which the recursive reference is implemented as an address to the next record (the one created in the previous recursive step). The representation in the heap of a binary tree shown in Fig. 8.8 corresponds exactly to its graphical representation.

The creation of values of a recursive type (so that they can be associated with a name) is an operation which varies considerably from language to language. In many functional languages, the values of a recursive type are expressible. There exist explicit syntactic constructs for designating their values. An example could be the expression in Fig. 8.7 or in Fig. 8.8 (see, also, the box an ML). In imperative languages, on the other hand, the values of recursive types are constructed by explicit allocation of their components in the heap. To continue our analogy with Java, we have a predefined constructor, `new`, which allows us to allocate instance of the type in the heap:

```
int_list l = new int_list();
```

The part on the right of the assignment symbol creates on the heap a record of the form specified by `int_list` and assigns the name `l` to a reference to this record. At this point, its fields can be initialised. For example:

```
l.val = 2;
l.next = null;
```

It remains to discuss the management of the heap when there are values of recursive type. They are in fact dynamically allocated (explicitly as in Java, or implicitly as in ML) but languages which admit recursive types as primitive do not in general permit explicit deallocation of the values thus created. As in the case of implicit allocation that we discussed in the context of pointers, it is necessary to provide the abstract machine with mechanisms for garbage collection in order to reclaim the chunks of memory that can no longer be accessed.

8.4.7 Functions

Every high-level programming language supports the definition of functions (or procedures). Few traditional languages permit the denotation of function types (that is, give them a name in the language). Let `f` be a function defined as:

```
T f(S s){...}
```

It has the type `S -> T`; more generally, a function with header

```
T f(S₁ s₁, ..., Sₙ sₙ){...}.
```

is of type $S_1 \times \cdots \times S_n -> T$.

The values of a functional type are therefore denotable in every language but are rarely expressible (or storable). In addition to definition, the principal operation permitted on a value of functional type is *application*, that is the invocation of a function on some arguments (actual parameters).

In some languages, moreover, the type of functions has the same status of any other type: it is possible to pass functions as arguments to other functions, and to define functions which return functions as results. Such *higher order* languages belong, in particular, to the functional paradigm (which includes, to name but a few: ML, Haskell, Scheme). In these languages, a function is not just a piece of code equipped with its local environment, but may be handled like other data. We will see in Chap. 11, the outline of a possible abstract machine for doing this.

Recursive Types in ML

ML is an important functional language. It is equipped with an extended type system. It is a type-safe language with many interesting properties. The language allows the definition of explicitly recursive types using *constructors*, which are introduced as part of the definition of the type. By way of an example, our definition of list of integers can be written as (ignoring the fact that ML has lists as a predefined type):

```
datatype int_list = Null | CONS of int * int_list;
```

In this definition, `Null` and `CONS` are constructors, that is function symbols to which there corresponds no code, but which serve only to construct, syntactically, terms of the desired type (in this case `int_list`). The vertical line is read as "or". A value of type `int_list` is the constant `Null`, or is a pair (denoted by the constructor `CONS`) composed of an `int` and an `int_list`. Therefore `CONS(2,Null)` is a simple value of type `int_list`. Figure 8.9 shows the ML expression which corresponds to the value in Fig. 8.7.

The language permits the definition of ill-founded recursive types. For example the following definition introduces the type `empty`; it is so-called because it is impossible to construct values of this type:

```
datatype empty =  Void of empty;
```

Indeed, there is no basic constructor which will allow us to construct a value of type `empty` without presupposing another such value.

```
CONS(2,CONS(33,CONS(1,CONS(4,CONS(3,CONS(1,CONS(21,Null)))))))
```

Fig. 8.9 A value of type `int_list` in ML

8.5 Equivalence

Having analysed the principal types that we find in programming languages, the time has come to discuss the rules which govern the correctness of programs with respect to types. The first class of these rules deals with the definition of when two types, which are formally different, are to be considered interchangeable. The rules define an equivalence relation between types. If two types are equivalent, every expression or value of one type is also an expression or value of the other, and vice versa. In the next section, we will discuss compatibility rules which specify when a value of one type can be used in a context in which the value of another type would be expected (but not conversely).

Let us recall that a type is defined in the following form (the details will vary from language to language):

```
type newtype = expression;
```

Relations of preorder and equivalence

A binary relation, $*$, on a set, D, is a subset of the cartesian product of D with itself: $* \subseteq D \times D$. We write $c * d$ for $(c, d) \in *$. A relation is *reflexive* when, for every $d \in D$, it is true that $d * d$. It is symmetric if, for all $c, d \in D$, if $c * d$ holds, then also $d * c$ holds. It is transitive if, for every $c, d, e \in D$, if $c * d$ and $d * e$, then $c * e$. It is antisymmetric if, for every $c, d \in D$, if $c * d$ and $d * c$, then c coincides with d.

If a relation is reflexive and transitive, it is said to be a *preorder*. If a preorder is also symmetric, it is an *equivalence*. If, on the other hand, a preorder is also antisymmetric, it is a *partial order*.

Different languages interpret a definition like this in two different ways which lead to two distinct rules for type equivalence:

- The definition of a type of can be *opaque*, in which case we have equivalence *by name*.
- The definition of the type can be *transparent*, in which case we have *structural* equivalence.

8.5.1 Equivalence by Name

If a language uses opaque type definitions, each new definition introduces a new type which is different from every preceding one. In this case, then, we have equivalence by name, as defined below.

Definition 8.2 (Equivalence by name) Two types are equivalent by name only if they have the same name (so a type is equivalent only to itself).

By way of example, let us consider the following definitions of types:

```
type T1 = 1..10;
type T2 = 1..10;
type T3 = int;
type T4 = int;
```

Four distinct types are introduced. There is no equivalence between them.

However, equivalence by name is too restrictive. Some languages (Pascal for example) adopt the rule of *weak* (or *lax*) equivalence by name. The simple renaming of a type does not generate a new type but only an alias for the same one. In the example above, using a weak equivalence by name, the types T3 and T4 are equivalent, but types T1 and T2 remain distinct.

Under equivalence by name, each type has a unique definition which occurs at a unique point in the program, a fact which simplifies maintenance. Despite its simplicity, from the programming point of view, equivalence by name is the choice that

Equivalence by Name in Pascal

An aspect of equivalence by name that is not always pleasant is that two expressions of "anonymous" type correspond to two different types (because they do not have names, they cannot have the same name!). In the two following Pascal declarations:

```
var V : array [1..10] of integer;
    W : array [1..10] of integer;
```

V and W do *not* have the same type. The situation is particularly bad when we declare a formal parameter to a procedure using an expression of anonymous type:

```
procedure f (Z : array [1..10] of integer);
```

In this example, neither V nor W can be passed as actual parameters to f because the formal parameter Z is of a (third) type which is distinct from the two previous ones.

most respects the intentions of the designer. If the programmer has introduced two different names for the same type, they will have their reasons which the language respects by maintaining two different types.

Note that equivalence by name is defined with reference to a specific, fixed program and it does not make sense to ask whether two types are equivalent by name "in general".

8.5.2 Structural Equivalence

A type definition is transparent when the name of the type is just an abbreviation for the expression defining the type. In a language with transparent declarations, two types are equivalent if they have the same structure, that is if, substituting names for the relevant definitions, identical types are obtained. If a language uses transparent type definitions, the equivalence between types that is obtained is said to be *structural equivalence*.

We can give a more precise recursive definition of structural equivalence.

Definition 8.3 (Structural Equivalence) Structural equivalence of types is the (least) equivalence relation satisfying the following properties:

- The name of a type is equivalent to itself;
- If a type T is introduced with the definition `type T = expression`, T is equivalent to `expression`;
- If two types are constructed by applying the same type constructor to equivalent types, then the two types are equivalent.

By way of example, consider the following definitions:

```
type T1 = int;
type T2 = char;
type T3 = struct{
            T1 a;
            T2 b;
          }
type T4 = struct{
            int a;
            char b;
          }
```

T3 and T4 are structurally equivalent. Some aspects of the definition of equivalence that we have given are deliberately vague or imprecise. For example, it is not clear whether the three following types are equivalent:

```
type S = struct{
           int a;
           int b;
         }
type T = struct{
           int n;
           int m;
         }
type U = struct{
           int m;
           int n;
         }
```

They result from the application of the same constructors, but they have been given names (or field order) that are different. A further subtle question concerns structural equivalence and recursive types:

```
type R1 = struct{
            int a;
            R2  p;
          }
type R2 = struct{
            int a;
            R1  p;
          }
```

Intuitively, we can think that R1 and R2 equivalent, but the type checker will be unable to solve the mutual recursion involved in these definitions (showing the equivalence between R1 and R2 requires a mathematical argument of some sophistication).

Structural equivalence allows us to speak about equivalent types in general, not just those in a specific program. In particular, two equivalent types can always be substituted for each other in any context without altering the meaning of the program in which the substitution occurs (this general property of substitution is often known as *referential transparency*).

It will come as no surprise to the reader to learn that existing languages almost always use some form of combination or variant of the two equivalence rules that we have just defined. We have already seen that Pascal uses (weak) equivalence by name; Java uses equivalence by name, except for arrays, for which it uses structural equivalence; C uses structural equivalence for arrays and for types defined using typedef, but not when it involves records (structs) and unions, for which it always uses equivalence by name; C++ uses equivalence by name (except when it inherits from C); ML uses structural equivalence, except for types defined using datatype; Modula-2 inherits from Pascal its use of equivalence by name, but Modula-3 uses structural equivalence; and so on.

8.6 Compatibility and Conversion

The relation of compatibility between types, which is weaker than equivalence, allows the use of one type in a context in which another has been requested.

Definition 8.4 (Compatibility)   We say that type T is compatible with type S, if a value of type T is permitted in any context in which a value of type S would be admissible.

In many languages, it is the rule of compatibility (and not that of equivalence) which controls the correctness of assignment (the type of the right-hand component must be compatible with that of the left-hand one), parameter passing (the type of the actual parameter must be compatible with that of the formal parameter), etc. It is clear that two equivalent types are also compatible with each other but in general the relation of compatibility is not symmetric: the canonical example is the compatibility that exists in many languages (but not in all: ML and Java, for example, do not admit it) between int and float (but not vice versa). The compatibility relation is therefore a pre-order (that is a reflexive and transitive relation) that is not symmetric, but almost never an ordering (that is it is not symmetric, but not anti-symmetric either). In fact, in a language which admits structural equivalence, two types that are structurally equivalent are compatible but not equal.

The compatibility relation, more than that of equivalence, varies enormously between languages. Without pretending to be complete, let us list some of the possible concepts that we can encounter in order of generality (that is, of the "generosity" of the compatibility relation). A type T can be compatible with S when:

1. Types T and S are equivalent; it is the most restrictive version of compatibility.
2. The values of T form a subset of the values of S: this is a case of an interval type, contained in its own base type (and therefore compatible with it).
3. All the operations on the values of S are also permitted on values of T. The simplest example (which however the does not correspond to compatibility in any of the principal commercial languages) is that of two record types. We assume that we have declared

```
type S = struct{
            int a;
         }
type T = struct{
            int a;
            char b;
         }
```

The only possible operation on values of type S is the selection of a field with name a; this also makes sense for values of type T. There is no inclusion relation between values of T and those of S, but there is a canonical way to obtain a value of S from a value of T: take the first component and forget the second. This interpretation of compatibility leads to a particular notion of compatibility based on the concept of *subtype* in object-oriented languages (we will discuss this below in Sect. 10.2.4).

4. The values of T correspond *in a canonical fashion* to values of S. In addition to the case outlined in the previous point, this is the case that we have already mentioned of int being compatible with float. (This is not an instance of point (2), above, because, as far as the implementation is concerned, the values of the two types are distinct).

5. Values of T can be made to correspond with some values of S. Once the requirement of the canonicality of correspondence has been dropped, every type can be made to be compatible with another defining a (conventional) way to transform one value of T into one of S. Using this very broad notion of compatibility, float can be made compatible with int by arbitrarily defining the conversion procedure (for example, rounding, truncation, etc.).

In order to manage this collection of different interpretations as a unified whole, we introduce the notion of *type conversion*. This notion will be stated in two distinct ways:

- *Implicit conversion* (also called *coercion* or forced conversion). This is the case in which the abstract machine inserts a conversion when there is no such indication in the high-level language;
- *Explicit conversion* (or *cast*). This is when the conversion is indicated in the text of the program.

Coercions   In the presence of compatibility between the types T and S, the language allows a value of type T to occur where a value of type S is expected. When this happens, the compiler and/or abstract machines inserts a type conversion between T and S. We will call this a *type coercion*.

From a syntactic viewpoint, coercion has no significance other than annotating a compatibility. From the implementation viewpoint, however, a coercion can correspond to different things depending upon the notion of compatibility adopted:

1. Type T is compatible with S and have the same storage representation (at least for values of T). In such a case, coercion remains a syntactic matter and causes no code to be generated.

Casts which do not modify representation

In some situations, especially in systems programming, it is useful to be able to change the type of an object without changing its representation in memory. This kind of conversion is obviously forbidden in type-safe languages, but is, though, permitted in many languages (these are often said to be "unchecked" (ADA) or "non-converting type casts").

An example in C using the addressing (&) and de-reference (*) operators is:

```
int a = 233;
float b = *((float*) &a);
```

First of all, the address of the integer variable a is taken, then it is converted explicitly into a pointer to a float using the cast (float *); finally, it is dereferenced and assigned to the real value b. The entire example is merely annotation for the compiler which does not result in any action by the machine. The bits, which in twos complement represents 233, are now interpreted as an the IEEE 754 representation for floating point numbers (provided that integer and float are represented by the same number of bytes).

It is clear that a conversion which does not modify the stored representation is always an extremely delicate operation, as well as being a potential source of hard-to-fix errors.

2. Type T is compatible with S but there exists a canonical way to transform values of T into values of S. In this case, the coercion is executed by the abstract machine, which applies precisely the canonical conversion. For example, in the case of int and float, the abstract machine inserts code to transform (at runtime) the representation in twos complement that is required for integers to that for floating point.
3. The compatibility of T with S is based on an arbitrary correspondence between values of T with those of S. In this case, too, the abstract machine inserts code that performs the transformation. This is the case, also, of all those situations where T and S have the same representation , but T is a superset of S. For example, T is int and S is an integer interval[12] (note that we are in the symmetric case to the "canonic" case, considered in point 1, in which $T \subseteq S$). Coercion in this case does not transform the representation but dynamically checks (at least if the language is supposed to be type safe) that the value of T belong to S.

Languages with strong type checking tend to have few coercions (that is few compatibilities) of the last kind. On the other hand, in a language like C, the type system is designed to be by-passed and so permits numerous coercions (from char-

---

[12] Almost all languages with interval types allow this kind of compatibility for the obvious reason of programming flexibility.

acters to integers, from long reals to short, from long integers to short reals, and so on).

Explicit Conversions   Explicit conversions (or *casts*, using the name by which they are known in C and in other languages) are annotations *in the language* which specify that a value of one type must be converted to that of another type. In this case, as well, such a conversion can be either just a syntactic marking or can correspond to code that is executed by the abstract machine, using the scheme for coercions that we have already discussed. In our pseudo-language, we will follow the conventions of the C language family and will denote a cast using brackets:

```
S s = (S) t;
```

Here we are assigning a value t, having converted it into type S, to a variable of type S. Not every explicit conversion is permitted, only those for which the language knows how to implement the conversion. It is clear that we can insert a cast where a compatibility exists. In this case explicit conversion is syntactically useless but must be advised for documentation purposes. Languages with few compatibilities make available, in general, many explicit conversions, which the programmer can use to annotate the program where a change of type is necessary.

Generally, modern languages tend to prefer casts over coercions. They are more useful as far as documentation is concerned; they do not depend upon the syntactic context in which they appear, and, most importantly, they behave better in the presence of overloading and polymorphism (which we will consider shortly).

8.7 Polymorphism

A type system in which any language object (value, function, etc.) has a unique type is said to be *monomorphic*.[13] Here we will be interested in the more general concept given in the next definition.

Definition 8.5 A type system in which the same object can have more than one type is said to be polymorphic.[14] By analogy, we will say that the object is polymorphic when the type system assigns more than one type to it.

Even the more conventional languages contain limited forms of polymorphism. The name + in many languages is of type $int \times int \rightarrow int$, as well as of type $float \times float \rightarrow float$. The value null has the type T* for every type T. The function length (which returns the number of elements of an array) is of type $T[] \rightarrow int$ for every type T. The list could be continued. In conventional languages,

---

[13]This is a word derived from the Greek and means "has only a single (*mono*) form (*morphos*)"

[14]"Which has many (*poly*) forms."

however, it is not in general permitted for the user to define polymorphic objects. Let us take as an example, a language with a type system that is fairly inflexible (for example, Pascal or Java but to some extent C also) and let us assume that we want to write a function that sorts a vector of integers. The resulting function could have the signature:

```
void int_sort(int A[])
```

If we now need to sort a vector of characters, we need to define *another* function

```
void char_sort (char C[])
```

which is wholly identical to the previous example except in the type annotations. A polymorphic language would allow the definition of a single function

```
void sort(<T> A[])
```

where <T> denotes a generic type which will be specified at a later stage.

In this section, we will analyse the phenomenon of polymorphism. We will start by distinguishing three different forms:

- *Ad hoc polymorphism*, also called *overloading*.
- *Universal polymorphism*, which can be further divided into:
  - Parametric polymorphism, and
  - Subtyping or inclusion polymorphism.

8.7.1 Overloading

Overloading, as its other name (*ad hoc* polymorphism) suggests, is really polymorphism in appearance only. A name is *overloaded* when it corresponds to more than one object and context information must be used to determine which object is denoted by a specific instance of that name. The most common examples of this are:

- The use of the name + to indicate either integer or real addition (and sometimes it also denotes concatenation of character sequences).
- The ability to define more than one function (or constructor) with the same name but whose instances differ in the number or type of their parameters.

In the case of overloading, therefore, a single name corresponds to more than one object (in fact, to a finite number of objects). If it is the name of a function, it will be associated with different pieces of code. The ambiguity of the situation is solved statically using type information that is present in the context. From the conceptual viewpoint, we can imagine a kind of pre-analysis of the program which solves cases of overloading by substituting a unambiguous name which uniquely denotes a unique object for each symbol that is overloaded. Overloading is therefore

Polymorphic types and universal quantification

Rather than writing a polymorphic type between angle brackets, a more uniform notation (one which is more suggestive, as well as mathematically more accurate) is that which uses universal quantification. Instead of `<T> -> void`, we write $\forall T. T[]\text{->void}$.

This is a notation that is well-suited to the description of all the variations on polymorphism which have been proposed; in Sect. 8.7.3 (and again in Sect. 10.4.1) it will be used to analyse subtype polymorphism.

---

a sort of abbreviation at the syntactic level. It vanishes as soon as we introduce additional information.

Overloading should not be confused with coercion. They are two different mechanisms which solve different problems. On the other hand, in the presence of coercions, it might be not at all clear how a case of overloading should be solved. Consider for example the following expressions:

```
1 + 2
1.0 + 2.0
1 + 2.0
1.0 + 2
```

This quartet of expressions can be interpreted in several ways. First, + is overloaded with four different meanings. Second, + is overloaded with two meanings (integer and real) and coercion is inserted in the final two cases. Next, + merely denotes real addition and in the other three cases, coercions are employed. It is up to the definition of the language to determine which of these interpretations is correct.

8.7.2 Universal Parametric Polymorphism

We begin with a definition that is relatively imprecise but adequate for our needs.

Definition 8.6 A value exhibits universal parametric polymorphism (or parametric polymorphism, more briefly) when it has is an infinite number of different types which can be obtained by instantiating a single schema of general type.

A universal polymorphic function is therefore composed of a single piece of code which operates uniformly on all the instances of its general type (because information about the type is not exploited by the algorithm which the function implements).

Among the examples that we discussed at the start of the section, there are some that fall into this category: the value `null`, which belongs to every type $T*$ (that is to every type that can be obtained by substituting an actual type for T); the function `void sort(<T> A[])`, which sorts an array of *any type whatsoever*.

Before presenting more examples, we need to extend the notation. Following on from what was suggested in Sect. 8.4.7, we can write the polymorphic type of sort as <T>[]→void. In this notation, we use angle brackets to indicate that <T> is not a usual type but a sort of parameter. By substituting any "concrete" type for the parameter, we obtain a specific type for sort. Each way to substitute a type for <T> corresponds to one of the infinite number of ways to apply the function: int[] -> void, char[]-> void, etc. With this notation, the type of null should be more correctly given as <T>*.

Let us give another example. A function which exchanges two variables of any type. As with sort, if it is written in a language without polymorphism, we would need a swap function for every possible variable type. Using universal polymorphism, and assuming that we have at our disposition call by reference, we can write:

```
void swap (reference <T> x, reference <T> y){
    <T> tmp = x;
    x = y;
    y = tmp;
    }
```

A polymorphic object can be *instantiated* to a specific type. The instantiation can happen in many different ways, according to the specific mechanism(s) for polymorphism provided by the language. The simplest model is that in which instantiation occurs automatically and is performed by the compiler or the abstract machine:

```
int* k = null;                                                              1
char v,w;
int i,j;                                                                    3
...
swap(v,w);                                                                  5
swap(i,j);
```

Without requiring additional annotations, on line 1, using information from the context (the assignment is performed on the variable of type int*), the type checker instantiates the type of null as int*. On line 5, swap is instantiated to character and, on line 6, to integer.

Parametric polymorphism is general and flexible. It is present in programming languages in two notationally different forms called explicit and implicit parametric polymorphism.

Explicit polymorphism Explicit polymorphism is the kind we have discussed thus far. In the program, there are explicit annotations (our <T>) which indicate the types to be considered parameters. This is the kind of polymorphism present in C++ (using the concept of "template") and in Java (from version J2SE 5.0 using the "generic" notion).

Implicit Polymorphism Other languages (in particular functional languages like ML) adopt implicit parametric polymorphism, in which the programmer need not provide any type indications and instead the type checker (or rather, more properly, the module performing type inference—see Sect. 8.9) tries to determine for each object the most general type from which the other types can be obtained by instantiation. The simplest example of a polymorphic function is that of the identity which, using a notation as close as possible to that which we have used this far, can be written as:

```
fun Ide(x){return x;}
```

We will use the word `fun` to indicate that we are defining a function. The rest is totally analogous to the definitions we have already seen, except that there are no type annotations, either for parameters or results. Type inference will assign to the function `Ide`, the type `<T>-><T>`. If the actual parameter is of type `X`, the result will be of type `X`, for any type `X`. The application of a polymorphic function obviously takes place without type indication. `Ide(3)` will be correctly typed as a value of type `int`, while `Ide(true)` be typed as `bool`.

Let us consider here a final example of implicit parametric polymorphism combined with higher order:

```
fun Comp(f,g,x){return f(g(x));}
```

`Comp` applies the composition of its first two parameters (the functions) to the argument `x`. What is the type that can be inferred for `Comp`? Here is the most general possible:

```
(<S>-><T>) x (<R>-><S>) x <R> -> <T>
```

The inferred type is perhaps more general than the reader would have thought.

8.7.3 Subtype Universal Polymorphism

Subtype polymorphism is typically present in object-oriented languages. It is a more limited form of universal polymorphism than parametric polymorphism.

Indeed, here as well, a single object can be assigned an infinite number of different types. They are obtained by instantiating a single most general type. In this case, too, since it is a case of true polymorphism (i.e., universally quantified polymorphism), there is (at least conceptually) a single algorithm which is *uniform in the type*—that is, it does not depend upon the particular structure of the type—that can be instantiated to each of the infinite number of possible types.

However, in the case of subtype polymorphism, not all of the possible instantiations of the schema for the most general type are admissible. Instantiations are limited by a notion of *structural* compatibility between types, that is, using the concept of subtype.

Templates in C++

Parametric polymorphism is obtained in C++ by means of *templates*. These are program schemata which include parameters (of class or of type). The function `swap` could take the following form:

```
template<typename T>
void swap (T& x, T& y){
    T tmp = x;
    x = y;
    y = tmp;
}
```

The operator, &, attached to the type of a formal parameter indicates that the parameter is passed by reference, a primitive parameter-passing mode in C++ (in which it differs from C). The instantiation of a template is automatic. The call `swap(x,y)` is instantiated to the common type of x and y.

To be more precise, let us assume that a subtype relation is defined over the language's types. We denote this relation by the symbol <:. Therefore, we read C <: D as "C is a subtype of D". For the time being, we can be content with an abstract concept, but in Sect. 10.2.4, we will flesh out this concept in terms of relations between classes in object-oriented languages.

Definition 8.7 A value exhibits subtype (or bounded) polymorphism when there is an infinity of different types which can be obtained by instantiating a general type scheme, substituting for a parameter the subtypes of an assigned type.

To express subtype polymorphism, it is useful to make use of the notation with universal quantifiers that we introduced in the box on page 239. A polymorphic function of type

```
∀T<:D.T-> void
```

can be applied to all the values of any subtype of D. Polymorphism therefore is not general but is *limited to subtypes of* D.

8.7.4 Remarks on the Implementation

In this book, we cannot possibly explain the implementation of universal polymorphism in detail. We will limit ourselves to two paradigmatic examples of the problems which can be encountered.

Implicit polymorphism in ML

The majority of compilers for ML are interactive. The user enters one expression (or definition) at a time. First of all, the system verifies the correctness of the typing of the input expression and then derives the most general type for it. If the types are correct, the expression is evaluated and the result is displayed (in the case of a definition, its evaluation will extend the environment with the new association). We can define the identity function as:

```
- fun Ide(x) = x;
val Ide = fn : 'a -> 'a
```

In this example, the first line is what is entered by the user ("–" is the prompt), while the following line is the system's reply. The name Ide is added to the environment and associated with a functional value of type 'a -> 'a. The identifiers prefixed by ' ' are *type variables* in ML, that is they can be instantiated. We can request the evaluation of Ide as follows:

```
- Ide(4);
val it = 4 : int
- Ide(true);
val it = true : bool
```

Now the functions:

```
- fun Comp(f,g,x) = f(g(x));
val Comp = fn : ('a->'b)*('c->'a)*'c -> 'b
- fun swap(x,y) = let tmp = !x in
                      (x:=!y; y=tmp;);
val swap = fn : ('a ref)*('a ref) -> unit
```

In the case of swap, type inference finds that the two arguments cannot be generic values but *variables* (or *references*) of any type whatsoever ('a ref). The exclamation mark, "!", is the explicit dereferencing operator. The identifier, unit, is the singleton type that is used for expressions with side effects.

```
- val v = ref 0;
val v = ref 0 : int ref
- val w = ref 2;
val w = ref 0 : int ref
- swap(v,w);
val it = () : unit
- !w;
val it = 0 : int
```

In the example, v and w are initialised, respectively, to a reference to 0 and 2. Type inference correctly deduces that they must be variables of type int. After the swap, the dereferencing of w obviously yields 0.

The first way of handling polymorphism is that of solving it statically at link time[15] (this is the case with C++). When a polymorphic function is called in two different instances, its code is instantiated in two different ways, one for each of the different instances required. Taking again the concrete example of swap, there is a local variable, tmp, which must be allocated in the activation record when swap is called. But the space to allocate for tmp depends on its type which is not known when the template for swap is originally compiled. At link time, though, polymorphic functions can be identified and their code is modified (instantiated) so as to take into account the actual type(s) with which they are called. The resulting code can then be linked. It can be seen that there can be many copies of the same template (one per instantiation) in the executable code. On the other hand, the execution of a template-using program is as efficient as a program that does not use them, because that templates no longer exist at runtime.

In the case of other polymorphic languages (and ML is one of them), a single version of the code for a polymorphic function is maintained. It is this single piece of code that is executed when one of its instances is required. What is done about the type-dependent information (in the case of swap, this is the amount of store to allocate for tmp)? It is necessary to change the whole data representation. Instead of directly allocating the data in the activation record, a pointer is maintained that points to the actual data. The data also includes its own descriptors (representing dimensions, structure, etc.). In the case of swap, when it is necessary to store a value in tmp, a pointer to the variable x is accessed and its size (as recorded in the descriptor) is accessed. At this point, the memory necessary for tmp is allocated in the heap and a pointer to it is stored in the activation record. The flexibility, uniformity and the conciseness of the code (there are no repeated instances of the same function) are paid for by decreased efficiency—an indirect reference is always required to access a piece of data. We will see more implementation details for subtype polymorphism in Sect. 10.4 when considering object-oriented languages.

8.8 Type Checking and Inference

We have already seen how a language's type checker is responsible for verifying that a program respects the rules (in particular, the compatibility rules) imposed by the type system. In the case of a language with static checking, the type checker is one of the compiler's modules; when type checking is dynamic, the type checker is a module in the runtime system. To perform its task, the type checker must determine the type of the expressions occurring in the program (for example, it must determine whether the type of the expression on the right-hand side of an assignment is compatible with the variable on the left-hand side). To do this, it uses the

---

[15]Some authors hold that in cases of this kind, we should talk of *generics* rather than polymorphism. We think, on the contrary, that the phenomenon of polymorphism is a syntactic phenomenon of a language, that can be obtained through several different implementation approaches.

type information that the programmer has explicitly placed at critical points in the program (for example, declarations of local names, parameter declarations, explicit conversions, etc.), as well as information that is implicit in the program text (for example, the types of predefined constants, those of numerical constants and so on).

To determine the type of complex expressions, the type checker performs a simple traversal of the program's abstract syntax tree (see the start of Sect. 6.1.3). Starting at the leaves (which represent variables and constants whose types are known), it moves upwards through the tree towards the root, computing the type of the composite expressions on the basis of the information provided by the programmer and the information it obtains from the type system (for example, the type system could establish that + is an operator which, when applied to two expressions of type int, permits an expression also of type int to be derived, while =, when applied to two arguments of scalar type, gives an expression of type bool). In many cases, the information provided by the programmer can turn out to be redundant, for example:

```
int f(int n){return n+1;}
```

Starting with the fact that n is of type int, it can be easily inferred that the value returned by the function must be of type int. The explicit specification given by the programmer of the result type is a redundant specification that the language requires as a last resort so that it can report possible logical errors.

Instead of the simple type checking method we have merely outlined, some languages use a more sophisticated procedure which we might call *type inference*. The progenitor of this family of languages is ML (we have cited this language a number of times above), whose type system is sophisticated and refined. Some ideas presented in work on ML have inspired the design of many different languages, even those of a non-functional kind. In order to introduce the concept of inference in a simplified form, we will again use the definition of function f. It is clear that also the specification that the formal parameter, n, must be an int is redundant. This is because the constant 1 is an integer and + takes two integers and returns an integer, so n must be an integer. From a declaration of the form:

```
fun f(n){return n+1;}
```

it is certainly possible automatically to derive that f has type int -> int. Type inference is exactly this process of the attribution of a type to an expression in which explicit type declarations of its components do not occur. To perform this derivation, the algorithm also works on a syntax tree, again starting at the leaves but, this time, it must take into account the fact that it might not be immediately possible to determine a specific type for any atomic expression (n, in this case). In a case like this, the inference algorithm assigns a *type variable* which it might indicate by 'a (using ML notation). Climbing the tree again and using information present in the context, some constraints for type-variables will be collected. In our case, from the type of 1 and from that of + (which comes from looking up the table of predefined symbols), the constraint 'a = int is derived.

This form of inference is more general and powerful than the simple type checking algorithm used in languages like Pascal, C or Java. It is capable of determining
the most general type of a function, that is it can account for all the polymorphism
implicit in an expression. This is done as follows:

1. Assign a type to each node in the syntax tree. For predefined names and constants, use the type stored in the symbol table. For new (i.e., programmer-defined)
   identifiers, and for every composite expression (which are stored as the internal
   nodes of the tree), use a type variable (one new variable for every expression or
   name);
2. Rewalk the syntax tree, generating an (equality) constraint between types at every
   internal node. For example, if we apply the function symbol, f, to which we have
   previously assigned the type ' a to the argument v of type ' b, the constraint ' a
   = ' b -> ' c will be generated to indicate that f must really be a function and
   that its argument must be of the same type as v (' c is a new type variable).
3. Resolve the constraints thus gathered using the *unification* algorithm (a powerful,
   but conceptually simple, instrument for symbolic manipulation which we will
   discuss in the context of logic languages, in Sect. 12.3).

There are cases in which solving constraint equations does not remove all variables. If we apply the inference algorithm to

```
fun g(n){return n;}
```

we will obtain, as type, ' a -> ' a. We already know that this is not an error but
a positive characteristic: an expression whose most general type contains a type
variable is a polymorphic expression.

8.9 Safety: An Evaluation

We started our analysis of types in programming languages with the idea of safety
based on types. This same notion has guided us in our examination of the various
characteristics of type systems. The time has arrived to take into account what we
have understood, classifying programming languages according to their safeness.
Let us, then, distinguish between:

1. Non safe languages;
2. Locally safe languages;
3. Safe languages.

In the category of unsafe languages, we find all of those languages whose type
system is a more or less just a methodological suggestion to the programmer, in
the sense that the language allows the programmer to bypass type checking. Every
language that allows access to the representation of a data type belongs to this category, as does every language that allows access to the value of a pointer (pointer
arithmetic, that is). C, C++ and all the languages of their family are unsafe.

Locally unsafe languages are those languages whose type system is well regulated and type checked but which contain some, limited, constructs which, when used, allow insecure programs to be written. The languages Algol, Pascal, Ada and many of their descendants belong to this category, provided that the abstract machine really checks types that need dynamic checking, such as checking the limits of interval types (which, it should be recalled, can be used as an index type for arrays). The unsafe part results from the presence of unions (uncontrolled variants) and from the explicit deallocation of memory. Of these two constructs, it is the second that has the greater impact in practice (it is much more common to encounter programs which deallocate memory than those which make significant use of variant records), but it is the former that is the more dangerous. As we will see in the next section, it is possible to equip the abstract machine with appropriate mechanisms to allow it to detect and prevent dangling pointers, even if, for reasons of efficiency, they are almost never used. We have already seen different examples of type-system violations which are possible when using variant records. We have postponed until last the nastiest possibility: that variant records can be used to access and manipulate the value of a pointer. In Pascal, we can write:[16]

```
var v : record
        case bool of
            true  : (i:integer);
            false : (p:^integer)
        end
```

Here, ^integer is the Pascal notation for the type of pointers to integers. It is now possible to assign a pointer to the variant p, manipulate it as an integer using the variant i and then use it again as a pointer.

Finally, we have safe languages for which a theorem guarantees that the execution of a typed program can never generate a hidden error "induced by the violation of a type." In this category are languages with dynamic type checking like Lisp and Scheme, as well as languages with static checking such as ML, as well as languages with static checking but with many checks also performed at runtime (as in Java).

8.10 Avoiding Dangling References

In this section, we will tackle the question of which mechanisms can be included in an abstract machine that will dynamically prevent dereference of dangling pointers. This is a problem we first discussed in Sect. 8.4.5. We will first present a radical solution which works in the general case of pointers into the heap or into the stack. We will then consider a somewhat less demanding mechanism that, however, works only for pointers into a heap (and then under some probabilistic assumptions).

---

[16]In Pascal, pointers are allocated only on the heap by an allocation request (the new function).They can be assigned but there is no primitive method to access the value of a pointer.

8.10.1 Tombstone

Using tombstones, an abstract machine can detect every attempt at dereferencing a dangling reference. Every time an object is allocated in the heap (to be then accessed by pointer), the abstract machine also allocates an extra word in memory. This word is called the *tombstone*. In a similar fashion, a tombstone is allocated every time that a stack-referencing pointer is allocated (that is, to a certain approximation, every time that the "indirection-to" operator (&) is used). The tombstone is initialised with the address of the allocated object and the pointer receives the address of the tombstone. When a pointer is dereferenced, the abstract machine inserts a second level of indirection, so that it first accesses the tombstone and then uses what it finds there to access the object that is pointed to. When one pointer is assigned to another, it is the contents of the pointer (and not the tombstone) that is modified. Figure 8.10 shows this operation graphically.

On deallocation of an object, or when an indirection on the stack becomes invalid because it is part of an activation record that has been popped,[17] the associated tombstone becomes invalidated, and a special value is stored in it to signal that the data to which the pointer refers is dead (this is where the name of this technique derives from). An appropriate choice of such a value must be made so that every attempt to access the contents of an invalid tombstone is captured by the address-protection mechanism of the underlying physical machine.

Tombstones are allocated in a particular area of memory in the abstract machine (this, appropriately enough, is called the *cemetery*). The cemetery can be managed more efficiently than the heap because all tombstones are of the same size.

For all its simplicity, the tombstone mechanism imposes a heavy cost in terms both of time and space. As far as time is concerned, we must consider the time required for the creation of tombstones, that for their checking (which can be reduced, as we have seen, if an underlying hardware protection mechanism can be used) and, most importantly, the cost of two levels of indirection. Tombstones are also expensive in terms of storage. They require a word of memory for every object allocated on the heap; a word is also required every time a pointer into the stack is created. If there are lots of allocations of small objects, the percentage of memory required by tombstones can be significant. Moreover, invalid tombstones always remain allocated, with the consequence that they might exhaust the space available in the cemetery, even though there might a great deal of space available on the heap. To prevent this last problem, it is possible to reuse those tombstones that are no longer in use (that is, those to which no pointer points) using a small reference-counting garbage collector (Sect. 8.11.1); this further increases the time cost of the mechanism.

---

[17]The operation can be quite opaque. Consider the case of a variable passed by reference to a function. Inside the function, a pointer is created to point to the variable. The pointer will be created using an associated tombstone. The tombstone must be invalidated when the lifetime of the variable forming the actual parameter ends, not when the function terminates.

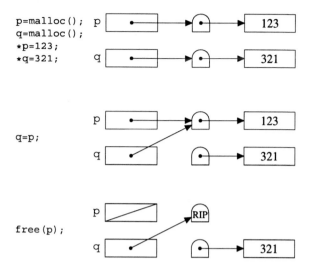

Fig. 8.10 Tombstones

8.10.2 Locks and Keys

An alternative to the tombstone technique is called *locks and keys*. This solves the problem of dangling references into a heap using a mechanism which does not suffer from the accumulated problems of tombstones.

Every time an object is created on the heap, the object is associated with a *lock* which is a word of memory in which an arbitrary value is stored. (Strictly speaking, it should be a value that can be sequentially incremented every time an object is allocated, but which avoids values such as 0 and 1, the code of frequently used characters, and so on.) In this approach, a pointer is composed of a pair: the address proper and a *key* (a word of memory that will be initialised with the value of the lock corresponding to the object being pointed to). When one pointer is assigned to another, the whole pair is assigned. Every time the pointer is dereferenced, the abstract machine checks that the key opens the lock. In other words, it verifies that the information contained in the key coincides with that in the lock. In the case in which the values are not the same, an error is signalled. When an object is deallocated, its lock is invalidated and some canonical value (for example, zero) is stored, so that all the keys which previously opened it now cause an error (see Fig. 8.11). Clearly, it can happen that the area of memory previously used as a key is reallocated (for another lock or for some other structure). It is statistically highly improbable that an error will be signalled as a result of randomly finding an ex-lock that has the same value that it had prior to being clearing.

Locks and keys also have a non-negligible cost. In terms of space, they cost even more than tombstones because it is necessary to associate an additional word with each pointer. On the other hand, locks as well as keys are deallocated at the same time as the object or the pointer of which they are a part. From an efficiency viewpoint, it is necessary to take into account both the cost of creation, and, more

Fig. 8.11 Locks and keys

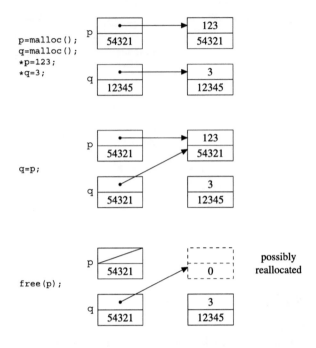

```
p=malloc();
q=malloc();
*p=123;
*q=3;
```

```
q=p;
```

```
free(p);
```

importantly, the high cost of pointer assignment and of determining whether the key opens a lock, something that happens every time a pointer is dereferenced.

8.11 Garbage Collection

In languages without explicit memory deallocation, it is necessary to equip the abstract machine with a mechanism which could automatically reclaim the memory allocated on the heap that is no longer used. This is done by a *garbage collector*, introduced for the first time in LISP around 1960, and since then included in many languages initially mostly functional, and later imperative. Java has a powerful and efficient garbage collector.

From the logical point of view, the operation of a garbage collector consists of two phases:

1. Distinguish those objects that are still alive from those no longer in use (*garbage detection*);
2. Collect those objects known no longer to be in use, so that the program can reuse them.

In practice these two phases are not always temporally separate, and the technique for reclaiming objects essentially depends on the one in which the objects no longer in use are discovered. We will see, then, that the "no longer in use" concept in a garbage collector is often a conservative approximation. For reasons of efficiency,[18] not all the objects that can be used again are, in reality, determined by the garbage collector to be so.

The educational aim of this text does not permit us to describe a garbage collector for a real language, or to provide an exhaustive overview of the different techniques available (there are bibliographic references to exhaustive treatments). We will limit ourselves to presenting in some detail the main points in the light of the most common techniques. Real garbage collectors are variations on these techniques. In particular the collectors that are of greatest interest today are based upon some form of incremental reclamation of memory and are beyond the scope of this book.

We can classify classical garbage collectors according to how they determine whether an object is no longer in use. We will have, therefore, collectors based on *reference counting*, as well as *marking* and *copying*. In the next few sections, we will present these collectors. We will discuss these techniques in terms of pointers and objects but the argument can equally be applied to languages without pointers which use the reference variable model.

Finally, we will see that all the techniques that we consider need to be able to recognize those fields inside an object that correspond to pointers. If objects are created as instances of statically-defined types (so it is statically known where pointers are inside instances), the compiler can generate a descriptor containing offsets to the pointers in each type. Each object in the heap is associated with the type of which it is an instance (for example, via a pointer to its type descriptor). When an object is to be deallocated, the garbage collector accesses the type descriptor to access the pointers inside the object. Similar techniques are used to recognise which words in an activation record are pointers. If types are only known dynamically, descriptors have to be completely dynamic and allocated together with the object.

8.11.1 *Reference Counting*

A simple way to tell whether an object is not in use is to determine whether there are any pointers to it. This is the reference counting technique. It defines what is probably the easiest way of implementing a garbage collector.

When an object is created on the heap, an integer is allocated at the same time. This integer is the *reference counter* or *reference count* for the object. The reference count is inaccessible to the programmer. For each object, the abstract machine must ensure that the counter contains the number of pointers to this object that are still active.

In order to do this, when an object is created (that is, a pointer for it is assigned for the first time), its counter is initialised to 1. When we have a pointer assignment:

```
p = q;
```

---

[18] As well as decidability.

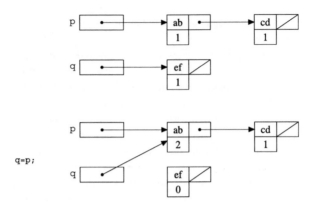

Fig. 8.12 Reference counting

the counter belonging the object pointed to by q is incremented by one, while the counter of object pointed to by p is decremented by one. When a local environment is exited, the counters of all the objects pointed to by pointers local to the environment are decremented. Figure 8.12 shows operation of this technique in diagrammatic form.

When a counter returns to the value 0, its associated object can be deallocated and returned to the free list. This object, moreover, might contain internal pointers, so before returning the memory occupied by an object to the free list, the abstract machine follows the pointers inside the object and decrements by one the counters of the objects they point to, recursively collecting all the objects whose counter has reached 0.

From the viewpoint of the abstract division into two phases of a garbage collector, the update and checking of counters implement the garbage-detection phase. The collection phase occurs when the counter reaches zero.

A clear advantage of this technique is that it is *incremental* because checking and collection are interleaved with the normal operation of the program. With a few adjustments, real-time systems (that is systems where there are absolute deadlines to response time) can employ this technique.

The biggest defect, at least in principle, of this technique is in its inability to deallocate circular structures. Figure 8.13 shows a case in which a circular structure has no more access paths. However it cannot be collected because, clearly, its counters are not zero. It can be seen that the problem does not reside so much in the algorithm, as in the definition of what a useless object is. It is clear that all objects in a circular structure are not usable any more, but this is not at all captured by the definition of not being pointed at.

Reference counting, despite its simplicity, is also fairly inefficient. Its cost is proportional to the combined work performed by the program (and not to the size of the heap or to the percentage of it in use or not in use at any time). One particular case is that of updating the counters of parameters of pointer type which are passed to functions that execute only for a short time. These counters are allocated and, after a particularly short time, have their value returned to zero.

Fig. 8.13 Circular structures
with reference counts

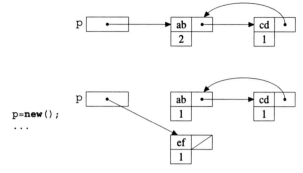

p=**new**();
...

8.11.2 Mark and Sweep

The *mark and sweep* method takes its name from the way in which the two abstract phases we mentioned at the start are implemented:

- *Mark*. To recognize that something is unused, all the objects in the heap are traversed, marking each of them has "not in use". Then, starting from the pointers which are active and present on the stack (the *root set*), all the data structures present in the heap are traversed recursively (the search is usually performed depth-first) and every object that is encountered is marked as "in use".
- *Sweep*. The heap is swept—all blocks marked "in use" are left alone, while those marked "not in use" are returned to the free list.

It can be seen that to implement both phases, it is necessary to be able to recognize allocated blocks in the heap. Descriptors might be necessary to give the size (and organisation) of every allocated block.

Unlike the reference-counting garbage collector, a mark and sweep collector is not incremental. It it will be invoked only when the free memory available in the heap is close to being exhausted. The user of the program can therefore experience a significant degradation in response time while waiting for the garbage collector to finish.

The mark and sweep technique suffers from three main defects. In the first place, and this is also true for reference counting, it is asymptotically the cause of external fragmentation (see Sect. 5.4.2): live and no longer live objects are arbitrarily mixed in the heap which can make allocating a large object difficult, even if many small blocks are available. The second problem is efficiency. It requires time proportional to the total length of the heap, independent of the percentages of used and free space. The third problem relates to locality of reference. Objects that are "in use" remain in their place, but it is possible that objects contiguous with them will be collected and new objects allocated in their place. During execution, we find that objects with very different ages appear next to each other. This, in general, drastically reduces locality of reference, with the usual degradation in performance observed in systems with memory hierarchies.

Fig. 8.14 A stack is necessary for depth-first traversal

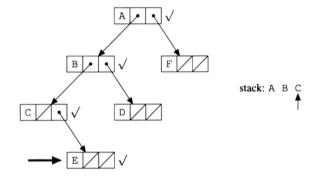

stack: A B C

8.11.3 Interlude: Pointer Reversal

Without some precautions, every marking technique runs the risk of being completely unusable in a garbage collector. The collector, indeed, goes into action when the memory is near to being exhausted, while the marking phase consists of the recursive traversal of a graph, which requires the use of a stack to store the return pointers.[19] It is necessary, when marking a graph under these circumstances, to use carefully the unused space present in pointers, using a technique called *pointer reversal*.

As shown in Fig. 8.14, when visiting a chained structure, it is necessary to mark a node and recursively visit the substructures whose pointers are part of that node. In this recursive scheme, it is necessary to store the addresses of blocks when they are visited in a stack, so that they can be revisited when the end of the structure is reached. In the Figure, using depth-first search, node E has been reached (marked blocks are indicated with a tick). The stack contains nodes A, B and C. After visiting E, it takes C from the stack and follows any pointers leading from this node; since there are none, it takes B from the stack and follows the remaining pointer, pushing B onto the stack, and visiting D. Using pointer reversal, this stack is stored in the pointers that form the structure, as shown in Fig. 8.15. When the end of a substructure is reached, (and a pop of the stack is required), the pointer is returned to its original value, so that at the end of the visit, the structure is exactly the same as it was at the start (apart from marking, clearly). In the figure, we are visiting node E. It can be seen how the stack in Fig. 8.14 is stored in space internal to the structure itself (pointers marked with a grey background). Only two pointers (p_prec and p_curr) are required to perform the visit. After visiting E, using p_prec, the structure is retraversed in a single step. Using the reversed pointer, we return to B, resetting the correct value of the pointer in C using p_curr.

---

[19]In many abstract machines, stack and heap are implemented in a single area of memory, with stack and heap growing in opposite directions starting from the two ends. In such a case, when there is no space in the heap, there is no space for the stack.

Fig. 8.15 Pointer reversal

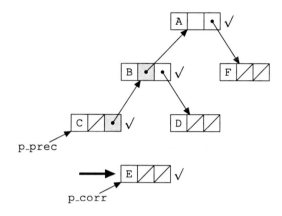

8.11.4 Mark and Compact

To avoid the fragmentation caused by the mark and sweep technique, we can modify the sweep phase and convert it into a compaction phase. Live objects are moved so that they are contiguous and thereby leave a contiguous block of free memory. Compaction can be performed by moving linearly across the heap, moving every live block encountered and making it contiguous with the previous block. At the end, all free blocks are contiguous, as are all unused blocks.

This is a technique which, like mark and sweep, requires more than one pass over the heap (and the time required is therefore proportional to the heap size). Compaction, on its own, requires two or three passes. The first is to compute the new position to be taken by the live blocks; a second updates the internal pointers and a third actually moves objects. It is, therefore, a technique that is substantially more expensive than mark and sweep if there are many objects to be moved.

On the other hand, compaction has optimal effect on fragmentation and on locality. It supports treating the free list as a single block. New objects are allocated from the free list by a simple pointer subtraction.

8.11.5 Copy

In garbage collectors based on copy there is no phase during which the "garbage" is marked. There is just the copying and compaction of live blocks. The lack of an explicit mark phase and the completely different way space is handled make its costs substantially different from those of algorithms based on marking.

In the simplest copy-base garbage collector (called a *stop and copy* collector), the heap is divided into two equally-sized parts (two *semi-spaces*). During normal execution, only one of the two semi-spaces is in use. Memory is allocated at one end of the semi-space, while free memory consists of a unique contiguous block which reduces its size every time there is an allocation (see Fig. 8.16). Allocation is extremely efficient and there is no fragmentation.

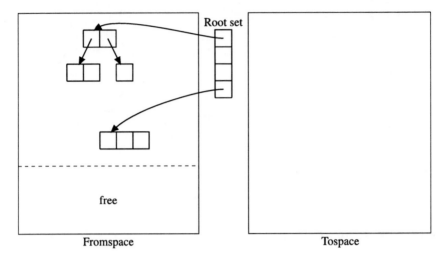

Fig. 8.16 Stop and copy before a call to the garbage collector

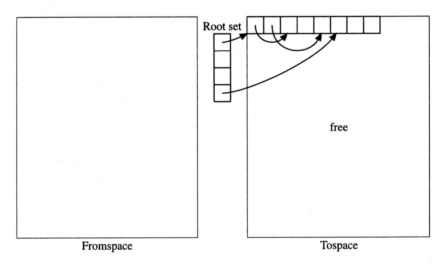

Fig. 8.17 Stop and copy after the execution of the garbage collector

When the memory in the semi-space is exhausted, the garbage collector is invoked. Starting with pointers in the stack (the root set), it begins visiting the chain of structures held in the current semi-space (the *fromspace*), copying the structures one by one into the other semi-space (the *tospace*), compacting them at one end of the latter (see Fig. 8.17). At the end of this process, the role of the two semi-spaces is swapped and execution returns to the user program.

The visit and copy of the live part can be executed in an efficient manner using the simple technique known as Cheney's algorithm (Fig. 8.18). Initially, all the objects which are immediately reachable from the root set are copied. This first set of

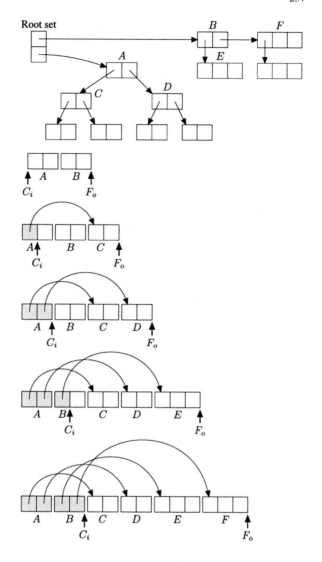

Fig. 8.18 Cheney's algorithm

objects is copied in a contiguous fashion into the tospace; it is handled as if it were a queue. Consider now the first of these objects, and add to the end of the queue (that is, copy into the tospace) the objects pointed to by the pointers present in the first object, while, at the same time, these pointers are modified. In this way, we have copied into the tospace all the first object's children. We keep processing the queue until it remains empty. At this point, in the tospace we have a copy of the live objects in the fromspace.[20]

---

[20]Some precautions must be taken to prevent objects accessible via multiple pointers being copied more than once.

A stop and copy garbage collector can be made arbitrarily efficient, provided that there is enough memory for the two semi-spaces. In fact, the time required for a stop and copy is proportional to the number of live objects present in the heap. It is not unreasonable to assume that this quantity will be approximately constant at any moment during the execution of the program. If we increase the memory for the two semi-spaces, we will decrease the frequency with which the collector is called and, therefore, the total cost of garbage collection.

8.12 Chapter Summary

This chapter has dealt with a crucial aspect in the definition of programming languages: the organisation of data in abstract structures called data types. The main points can be summarised as follows.

- *Definition of type* as a set of values and operations and the role of types in design, implementation and execution of programs.
- *Type systems* as the set of constructs and mechanisms that regulate and define the use of types in a programming language.
- The distinction between *dynamic* and *static* type checking.
- The concept of type-safe systems, that is safe with respect to types.
- The primary *scalar types*, some of which are *discrete* types.
- The primary *composite types*, among which we have discussed *records*, *variant records* and *unions*, *arrays* and *pointers* in detail. For each of these types, we have also presented the primary storage techniques.
- The concept of *type equivalence*, distinguishing between equivalence by name and structural equivalence.
- The concept of *compatibility* and the related concepts of coercion and conversion.
- The concept of *overloading*, when a single name denotes more than one object and static disambiguation.
- The concept of *universal polymorphism*, when a single name denotes an object that belongs to many different types, finally distinguishing between parametric and subtype polymorphism.
- *Type inference*, that is mechanisms that allow the type of a complex expression to be determined from the types of its elementary types.
- Techniques for runtime checking for *dangling references*: tombstones and locks and keys.
- Techniques for *garbage collection*, that is the automatic recovery of memory, briefly presenting collectors based on reference counters, mark and sweep, mark and compact and copy.

Types are the core of a programming language. Many languages have similar constructs for sequence control but are differentiated by their type systems. It is not possible to understand the essential aspects of other programming paradigms, such as object orientation, without a deep understanding of the questions addressed in this chapter.

8.13 Bibliographic Notes

Ample treatments of programming language types can be found in [14] and the rather older [4]. Review articles which introduce the mathematical formalisms necessary for research in this area are [2, 11]. A larger treatment of the same arguments is to be found in [13]. On overloading and polymorphism in type systems, a good, clear review is [3] (which we have largely followed in this chapter).

Tombstones originally appeared in [8] (also see, by the same author, [9]). Fisher and Leblanc [5] proposed locks and keys, as well as techniques so that an abstract Pascal machine can make variant records secure.

The official definition of ALGOL68 (which is quite a read) is [15]. A more accessible introduction can be found in [12]. The definition of ML can be found in [10], while an introductory treatment of type inference is to be found in [1].

There is a large literature on garbage-collection techniques. A detailed description of a mark and sweep algorithm can be found in many algorithm books, for example [6], while [16] is a good summary of classical techniques. For a book entirely devoted to the problem, that contains pseudocode and a more-or-less complete bibliography (up to the time of publication), [7] is suggested.

8.14 Exercises

1. Consider the declaration of the multi-dimensional array:

   ```
   int A[10][10][10]
   ```

   We know that an integer can be stored in 4 bytes. The array is stored in row order, with increasing memory addresses (that is, if an element is at address i, its successor is at $i + 4$, and so on). The element A[0][0][0] is stored at address 0. State the address at which element A[2][2][5] is stored.

2. Instead of the contiguous multidimensional array allocation that we discussed in Sect. 8.4.3, some languages allow (e.g., C), or adopt (Java), a different organisation, called *row-pointer*. Let us deal with the case of a 2-dimensional array. Instead of storing rows one after the other, every row is stored separately in some region of memory (for example on the heap). Corresponding to the name of the vector, a vector of pointers is allocated. Each of the pointers points to a proper row of the array. (i) Give the formula for accessing an arbitrary element A[i][j] of an array allocated using this scheme. (ii) Generalise this memory technique to arrays of more than 2 dimensions. (iii) Discuss the advantages and disadvantages of this organisation in the general case. (iv) Discuss the advantages and disadvantages of this technique for the storage of 2-dimensional arrays of characters (that is, arrays of strings).

3. Consider the following (Pascal) declarations:

   ```
   type string = packed array [1..16] of char;
   ```

```
type string_pointer =   ^string;
type person = record
                 name : string;
                 case student: Boolean of
                     true:   (year: integer);
                     false: (socialsecno: string_pointer)
              end;
```

and assume that the variable C contains a pointer to the string "LANGUAGES".
Describe the memory representation for the person record after each of the
following operations:

```
var pippo : person;
pippo.student := true;
pippo.year := 223344;
pippo.student := true;
pippo.socialsecno := C;
```

4. Show that the integer type can be defined as a recursive type starting with just
   the value null. Then write a function that checks if two integers defined in this
   way are equal.

5. Given the following type definitions in a programming language which uses
   structural type equivalence:

```
type T1 = struct{
            int a;
            bool b;
          };
type T2 = struct{
            int a;
            bool b;
          }
type T3 = struct{
            T2 u;
            T1 v;
          }
type T4 = struct{
            T1 u;
            T2 v;
          }
```

   In the scope of the declarations T3 a and T4 b, it is claimed that the assignment a = b is permitted. Justify your answer.

6. Which type is assigned to each of the following functions using polymorphic
   type inference?

```
fun G(f,x){return f(f(x));}
fun H(t,x,y){if (t(x)) return x;
         else return y;}
fun K(x,y){return x;}
```

7. Using tombstones, it is necessary to invalidate a tombstone when its object is no longer meaningful. The matter is clear if the object is on the heap and is explicitly deallocated. It is less clear when the tombstone is associated with an address on the stack. In this case, indeed, it is necessary for the abstract machine to be able to determine all the tombstones that are potentially associated with an activation record. Design a possible organisation which makes this operation reasonably efficient (recall that tombstones are not allocated in activation records but in the cemetery).

8. Consider the following fragment in a pseudo-language with reference-based variables and which uses locks and keys (C is a class whose structure is of no importance):

```
C foo = new C();   // object OG1
C bar = new C();   // object OG2
C fie = foo;
bar = fie;
```

Give possible values *after* the execution of the fragment for all the keys and all the locks involved.

9. Under the same assumptions as in Exercise 8, consider the following code fragment in which free(p) denotes the explicit deallocation of the object referred to by the pointer p:

```
class C { int n; C next;}
C foo = new C();   // object OG1
C bar = new C();   // object OG2
foo.next = bar;
bar.next = foo;
free(bar);
```

For all the pointers in the fragment, give possible key values. For each object in the fragment, give possible lock values. In both cases, the values should be those *after* execution of the fragment terminates. After execution of the fragment, also execute the code foo.n = 1; foo.next = 0;. State what a possible result of this execution might be.

10. Consider the following fragment which is written in a pseudo-language with a reference-model for variables and a reference-counting garbage collector. If OGG is an arbitrary object in the heap, indicate by OGG.cont its (hidden) contents:

```
class C { int n; C next;}
C foo(){
    C p = new C();        // object OGG1
    p.next = new C();     // object OGG2
    C q = new C();        // object OGG3
    q.next = p.next;
    return p.next;
    }
C r = foo();
```

State what are the values of the reference counters for the three objects after execution of line 6 and then of line 9.

11. Under the same assumptions as in Exercise 10, state what the values of the reference counters are for the two objects after the execution of the following fragment. Which of the two can be returned to the free list?

```
C foo = new C();   // object OG1
C bar = new C();   // object OG2
C fie = foo;
bar = fie;
```

12. Under the same assumptions as in Exercise 10, state what the reference-counter values for the three objects after execution of the following fragment are. Which of them can be returned to the free list?

```
class C { int n; C next;}
C foo = new C();   // object OG1
bar = new C();     // object OG2
foo.next = bar;
bar = new C();     // object OG3
foo = bar;
```

13. Using your favourite programming language, define the data structures required to represent a binary tree. Then write detailed code that performs a preorder traversal of a tree without using the system stack and instead using the pointer-reversal technique.

References

1. L. Cardelli. Basic polymorphic typechecking. *Science of Computer Programming*, 8(2):147–172, 1987. citeseer.ist.psu.edu/cardelli88basic.html.
2. L. Cardelli. Type systems. In A. B. Tucker, editor, *The Computer Science and Engineering Handbook*. CRC Press, Boca Raton, 1997. citeseer.ist.psu.edu/cardelli97type.html.
3. L. Cardelli and P. Wegner. On understanding types, data abstraction, and polymorphism. *ACM Computing Surveys*, 17(4):471–522, 1985. citeseer.ist.psu.edu/cardelli85understanding.html.
4. J. C. Cleaveland. *An Introduction to Data Types*. Addison-Wesley, Reading, 1986.
5. C. N. Fisher and R. J. LeBlanc. The implementation of run-time diagnostics in Pascal. *IEEE Trans. Softw. Eng.*, 6(4):313–319, 1980.
6. E. Horowitz and S. Sahni. *Fundamentals of Data Structures in Pascal*. Freeman, New York, 1994.
7. R. Jones and R. Lins. *Garbage Collection: Algorithms for Automatic Dynamic Memory Management*. Wiley, New York, 1996.
8. D. B. Lomet. Scheme for invalidating references to freed storage. *IBM Journal of Research and Development*, 19(1):26–35, 1975.
9. D. B. Lomet. Making pointers safe in system programming languages. *IEEE Trans. Softw. Eng.*, 11(1):87–96, 1985.
10. R. Milner, M. Tofte, R. Harper, and D. MacQueen. *The Definition of Standard ML—Revised*. MIT Press, Cambridge, 1997.

11. J. C. Mitchell. *Type Systems for Programming Languages*, pages 365–458, 1990. ISBN: 0-444-88074-7.
12. F. Pagan. *A Practical Guide to Algol 68*. Wiley Series in Computing. Wiley, London, 1976.
13. B. Pierce. *Types and Programming Languages*. MIT Press, Cambridge, 2002.
14. D. A. Schmidt. *The Structure of Typed Programming Languages*. MIT Press, Cambridge, 1994.
15. A. van Wijngaarden, B. J. Mailloux, J. E. L. Peck, C. H. A. Koster, M. Sintzoff, C. H. Lindsey, L. G. L. T. Meertens, and R. G. Fisker. Revised report on the algorithmic language ALGOL 68. *Acta Informatica*, 5:1–236, 1975.
16. P. R. Wilson. Uniprocessor garbage collection techniques. In *Proc. Int. Workshop on Memory Management*, LNCS, volume 637. Springer, Berlin, 1992. Extented version on-line ftp://ftp.cs.utexas.edu/pub/garbage/bigsurv.ps. citeseer.ist.psu.edu/wilson92uniprocessor.html.

Chapter 9
Data Abstraction

The physical machine manipulates data of only one type: bit strings. The types of a high-level language impose an organisation on this undivided universe, giving each value a sort of "wrapping". Each value is wrapped in an encapsulation (its type) which provides the operations that manipulate it. The type system for a language establishes how transparent this encapsulation is. In type-safe languages, the encapsulation is completely opaque, in the sense that it does not allow access to the representation (or better: every access can only take place using or by means of the encapsulation itself).

The last chapter presented in detail many of the predefined types and the principal mechanisms for defining new ones. The latter, however, are fairly limited: finite homogeneous aggregations (arrays) and heterogeneous ones (records), recursive types and pointers. The operations possible on these composite types are predefined by the language and the programmer is restricted to use them. It is clear that the programmer, using just the mechanisms we discussed in Chap. 8, cannot really define a *new* type, when it is understood, using our definition, as a collection of (homogeneous and effectively presented) values equipped with a set of operations. The user of a language can only make use of the existing capsules and only has highly limited ways to define new types: there are few *data abstraction* mechanisms.

In this chapter, we will present some of the main ways in which a language can provide more sophisticated mechanisms for defining abstractions over data. Among these, we will discuss the so-called abstract data type, which in different forms is provided by several languages. We then look at modules, a largely similar concept, but which mainly applies to programming in the large. These abstraction mechanisms also constitute an introduction to some themes that we will encounter again with object-oriented programming. The key concepts that we will investigate in this chapter are the separation between *interface* and *implementation* and the concepts associated with *information hiding*.

9.1 Abstract Data Types

The introduction of a new type using the mechanisms discussed in the last chapter

M. Gabbrielli, S. Martini, *Programming Languages: Principles and Paradigms,*
Undergraduate Topics in Computer Science,
DOI 10.1007/978-1-84882-914-5_9, © Springer-Verlag London Limited 2010

```
type Int_Stack = struct{
                   int P[100];   // the stack proper
                   int top;      // first readable element
}
Int_Stack create_stack(){
   Int_Stack s = new Int_Stack();
   s.top = 0;
   return s;
}
Int_Stack push(Int_Stack s, int k){
   if (s.top == 100) error;
   s.P[s.top] = k;
   s.top = s.top + 1;
   return s;
}
int top(Int_Stack s){
   return s.P[s.top];
}
Int_Stack pop(Int_Stack s){
   if (s.top == 0) error;
   s.top = s.top - 1;
   return s;
}
bool empty(Int_Stack s){
   return (s.top == 0);
}
```

Fig. 9.1 Stack of integers

does not permit the user of a language to define types at the same level of abstraction as that enjoyed by the predefined types in these languages.

By way of an example, Fig. 9.1 shows one possible definition in our pseudo-language of the stack of integers data type. We assume a reference model for variables. When defining a type of this kind, it is probably intended that a stack of integers will be a data structure that can be manipulated by the operations of creation, insertion, access to the top element, removal of the top element. However, the language does not guarantee that these are the *only* ways in which a stack can be manipulated. Even if we adopt a strict type equivalence by name discipline (so that a stack is introduced by a declaration of the type Int_Stack) nothing prevents us from directly accessing its representation as an array:

```
int second_from_top()(Int_Stack c){
   return c.P[s.top - 1];
}
```

From a general viewpoint, therefore, while languages provide predefined data abstractions (types) which hide implementations, the programmer cannot do this for themselves. To avoid this problem, some programming languages allow the definition of data abstractions which behave like predefined types as far as the (in)accessibility of representations is concerned. This mechanism is called an *abstract data type* (ADT). It is characterised by the following primary characteristics:

1. A name for the type.
2. An implementation (or representation) for the type.
3. A set of names denoting operations for manipulating the values of the type, together with their types.
4. For every operation, an implementation that uses the representation provided in point 2.
5. A security capsule which separates the name of the type and those of the operations from their implementations.

One possible notation for the stack of integers ADT in our pseudo-language could be that depicted in Fig. 9.2.

```
abstype Int_Stack{                                                        1
   type Int_Stack = struct{
                        int P[100];                                       3
                        int n;
                        int top;                                          5
   }
   signature                                                              7
      Int_Stack create_stack();
      Int_Stack push(Int_Stack s, int k);                                 9
      int top(Int_Stack s);
      Int_Stack pop(Int_Stack s);                                         11
      bool empty(Int_Stack s);
   operations                                                             13
      Int_Stack create_stack(){
         Int_Stack s = new Int_Stack();                                   15
         s.n = 0;
         s.top = 0;                                                       17
         return s;
      }                                                                   19
      Int_Stack push(Int_Stack s, int k){
         if (s.n == 100) error;                                           21
         s.n = s.n + 1;
         s.P[s.top] = k;                                                  23
         s.top = s.top + 1;
         return s;                                                        25
      }
      int top(Int_Stack s){                                               27
         return s.P[s.top];
      }                                                                   29
      Int_Stack pop(Int_Stack s){
         if (s.n == 0) error;                                             31
         s.n = s.n - 1;
         s.top = s.top - 1;                                               33
         return s;
      }                                                                   35
      bool empty(Int_Stack s){
         return (s.n == 0);                                               37
      }
}                                                                         39
```

Fig. 9.2 ADT for stacks of integers

A definition of this kind must be interpreted as follows. The first line introduces the name of the abstract data type. Line 2 provides the representation (or *concrete type*) for the abstract type Int_Stack. Lines 7 to 12 (introduced by signature) define the names and types of the operations that can manipulate an Int_Stack. The remaining lines (introduced by operations) provide the implementation of the operations. The important point of this definition is that inside the declaration of type, Int_Stack is a synonym for its concrete representation (and therefore the operations manipulate a stack as a record containing an array and two integer fields), while outside (and therefore in the rest of the program), there is no relation between an Int_Stack and its concrete type. The only possible ways to manipulate an Int_Stack are provided by its operations. The function second_from_top(), which we defined above, is now impossible because type checking does not permit the application of a field selector to an Int_Stack (which is *not* a record outside of its definition.)

An ADT is an opaque capsule. On the outside surface, visible to anyone, we find the name of the new type and the names and types of the operations. Inside, invisible to the outside world, there are the implementations of the type and its operations. Access to the inside is always controlled by the capsule which guarantees the consistency of the information it encloses. This external surface of the capsule is called the *signature* or *interface* of the ADT. On its inside is its *implementation*.

Abstract data types (in languages that support them, for example ML, and CLU[1]) behave just like predefined types. It is possible to declare variables of an abstract type and to use one abstract type in the definition of another, as has been done, by way of example, in Fig. 9.3. The code in Fig. 9.3 implements (very inefficiently) a variable of type integer using a stack. Inside the implementation of Int_Var, the implementation of Int_Stack is invisible because it was completely encapsulated when it was defined.

9.2 Information Hiding

The division between interface and implementation is of great importance for software development methods because it allows the separation a component's use from its definition. We also saw this distinction when we looked at control abstraction. A function abstracts (that is, hides) the code constituting its body (the implementation), while it reveals its interface, which is composed of its name and of the number and types of its parameters (that is, its signature). Data abstraction generalises this somewhat primitive form of abstraction. Not only is how an operation is implemented hidden but so is the way in which the data is represented, so that the language (with its type system) can guarantee that the abstraction cannot be violated. This phenomenon is called *information hiding*. One of the more interesting

---

[1] In object-oriented languages, we will see that it is possible to obtain the same abstraction goal using a similar but more flexible method.

Constructors, transformers and observers

In the definition of an abstract data type, T, the operations are conceptually divided into three separate categories:

- *Constructors.* These are operations which construct a new value of type T, possibly using values of other known types.
- *Transformers* or *operators.* These are operations that compute values of type T, possibly using other values (of the same ADT or of other types). A fundamental property of a transformer t of type $S_1 \times \cdots \times S_k \rightarrow Y$ is that, for every argument value, it must be the case that $t(s_1, \ldots, s_k)$ is a value constructable using only constructors.
- *Observers.* These are operations that compute a value of a known type that is different from T, using one or more values of type T.

An ADT without constructors is completely useless. There is no way to construct a value. In general, an ADT must have at least one operation in each of the above categories. It is not always easy to show that an operation is really a transformer (that is, that each of its values is in reality a value that can be obtained from a sequence of constructors).

In the integer stack example, create_stack and push are constructors, pop is a transformer and top and empty are observers.

```
abstype Int_Var{
    type Int_Var = Int_Stack;
    signature
        Int_Var create_var();
        int deref(Int_Var v);
        Int_Var assign(Int_Var v, int n);
    operations
        Int_Var create_var(){
            return push(create_stack(),0);
        }
        int deref(Int_Var v){
            return top(v);
        }
        Int_Var assign(Int_Var v, int n){
            return push(pop(v),n);
        }
}
```

Fig. 9.3 An ADT for an integer variable, implemented with a stack

consequences of information hiding is that, under certain conditions, it is possible to substitute the implementation of one ADT for that of another while keeping the interface the same. In the stack example, we could opt to represent the concrete type as a linked list (ignoring deallocation) allocated in the heap. This is de-

```
abstype Int_Stack{
   type Int_Stack = struct{
                          int info;
                          Int_stack next;
   }
   signature
      Int_Stack create_stack();
      Int_Stack push(Int_Stack s, int k);
      int top(Int_Stack s);
      Int_Stack pop(Int_Stack s);
      bool empty(Int_Stack s);
   operations
      Int_Stack create_stack(){
         return null;
      }
      Int_Stack push(Int_Stack s, int k){
         Int_Stack tmp = new Int_Stack(); // new element
         tmp.info = k;
         tmp.next = s;                     // chain on
         return tmp;
      }
      int top(Int_Stack s){
         return s.info;
      }
      Int_Stack pop(Int_Stack s){
         return s.next;
      }
      bool empty(Int_Stack s){
         return (s == null);
      }
}
```

Fig. 9.4 Another definition of the Int_Stack ADT

fined as in Fig. 9.4. Under certain assumptions, by substituting the first definition of Int_Stack by that in Fig. 9.4, there should be no *observable* effect on programs that use the abstract data type. These assumptions centre on what the clients of the interface expect from the operations. Let us say that the description of the semantics of the operations of an ADT is a *specification*, expressed not in terms of concrete types but general abstract relations. One possible specification for our ADT Int_Stack could be:

- create_stack creates an empty stack.
- push inserts an element into the stack.
- top returns the element at the top of the stack without modifying the stack itself. The stack must not be empty.
- pop removes the top elements from the stack. The stack must not be empty.
- empty is true if and only if the stack is empty.

Every client that uses Int_Stack making use of this specification *only*, will see no difference at all in the two definitions. This property has come to be called the *principle of representation independence*.

The specification of an abstract data type can be given in many different ways, ranging from natural language (which we have done) to semi-formal schemata, to completely formalised languages that can be manipulated by theorem provers. A specification is a kind of contract between the ADT and its client. The ADT guarantees that the implementation of the operations (which are unknown to the client) *matches* the specification; that is, all the properties stated in the specification are satisfied by the implementation. When this happens, it is also said that the implementation is *correct* with respect to the specification.

9.2.1 *Representation Independence*

We can state the representation independence property as follows:

> Two correct implementations of a single specification of an ADT are observationally indistinguishable by the clients of these types.

If a type enjoys representation independence, it is possible to replace its implementation by an equivalent (e.g., more efficient) one without causing any (new) errors in clients.

It should be clear that a considerable (and not at all obvious) part of representation independence consists of the guarantee that both implementations are correct with respect to the same specification. This can be hard to show, particularly when the specification is informal. There is, however, a weak version of the representation independence property that concerns only correctness with respect to the signature. In a type-safe language with abstract data types, the replacement of one ADT by another with the same signature (but different implementation) does not cause type errors. Under the assumptions we have made (of type safety and ADT), this property is a theorem which can be proved by type inference. Languages like ML and CLU enjoy this form of representation independence.

9.3 Modules

Abstract data types are mechanisms for programming in the small. They were designed to encapsulate *one* type and its associated operations. It is much more common, however, for an abstraction to be composed of a number of inter-related types (or data structures) of which it is desired to give clients a limited (that is, abstract) view (not all the operations are revealed and there is concealment of the implementation). The linguistic mechanisms which implement this type of encapsulation are called *modules* or *packages*. They belong to that part of a programming language dealing with programming in the large, that is with the implementation of complex systems using composition and assembly of simpler components. The module mechanism allows the static partitioning of a program into separate parts, each of which is equipped with data (types, variables, etc.) as well as with operations (functions, code, etc.). A module groups together a number of declarations (of data and/or functions) as well as defining visibility rules for these declarations by means of which a form of encapsulation and information hiding is implemented.

Considering semantic principles, there is not much of a difference between modules and ADTs, mostly the ability to define more than one type at a time (according to the definitions we have given, an ADT is a particular case of a module). Pragmatically, on the other hand, the module mechanism affords greater flexibility, both in the ability to state how permeable its encapsulation is (indeed, it is possible to indicate on an individual basis which operations are visible or to choose the level of visibility), or in the possibility of defining generic (polymorphic) modules (recall Sect. 8.8). Finally, module constructs are often related to separate compilation mechanisms for modules themselves.[2]

Even given the enormous variety among existing languages, we can state the important linguistic characteristics of a module by discussing the example shown in Fig. 9.5. It is expressed, as usual, in an suitable pseudo-language. First of all, a module is divided, as is an ADT, into a public part (which is visible to all the module's clients) and a private part (which is invisible to the outside world). The private part of a module can contain declarations that do not appear at all in the public part (for example, the bookkeep function inside Queue). A module can mention some of its own data structures in the public part, so that anyone can use or modify them (the variable c in Buffer, for example). A client module can use the public part of another module by *importing* it (the imports clause). In our example, Buffer has an additional import clause in its private part.

We will not continue with this discussion, both because we would have to go into the details of the mechanisms in a specific language, and because we will return to many points when considering object-oriented programming. To conclude, let us merely observe that the module mechanism is often associated with some form of parametric polymorphism which requires link-time resolution. In our example, we could have defined a buffer of type T, rather than a buffer of integer, making the definition generic and then suitably instantiating it when it is used. Figure 9.6 shows the generic version of the buffer example. It can be seen how the buffer and the code are both generic. When the private part of Buffer imports Queue, it specifies that it must be instantiated to the same type (which is not specified) as Buffer.

9.4 Chapter Summary

This short chapter has presented a first introduction to data abstraction, which turns on the key concepts of *interface, implementation, encapsulation, data hiding*.

---

[2]Keep in mind that modules and separate compilation are independent aspects of a language. In Java, for example, it is not the module (package, in Java terminology) which is the unit of compilation, rather the class is.

```
module Buffer imports Counter{
   public
      type Buf;
      void insert(reference Buf f, int n);
      int get(Buf b);
      Count c; // how many times buffer has been used
   private imports Queue{
      type Buf = Queue;
      void insert(reference Buf b, int n){
         inqueue(b,n);
         inc(c);
      }
      int get(Buf b){
         return dequeue(b);
         inc(c);
      }
      init_counter(c);     // module initialisation part
}
module Counter{
   public
      type Count;
      void init_counter(reference Count c);
      int get(Count c);
      void inc(reference Count c);
   private
      type Count = int;
      void init_counter(reference Count c){
         c=0;
      }
      int get(Count c){
         return c;
      }
      void inc(reference Count c){
         c = c+1;
      }
}
module Queue{
   public
      type Queue;
      inqueue(reference Queue q, int n);
      int dequeue(reference Queue q);
      ...
   private
      void bookkeep(reference Queue q){
         ...
      }
      ...
}
```

Fig. 9.5 Modules

```
module Buffer<T> imports Counter{
   public
      type Buf;
      void insert(reference Buf f, <T> n);
      <T> get(Buf b);
      Count c; //  how many times buffer has been used
   private imports Queue<T>{
      type Buf = Queue;
      void insert(reference Buf b, <T> n){
         inqueue(b,n);
         inc(c);
         }
      <T> get(Buf b){
         return dequeue(b);
         inc(c);
         }
}
module Counter{
   public
      type Count;
      void init_counter(reference Count c);
      int get(Count c);
      void inc(reference Count c);
   private
      type Count = int;
      void init_counter(reference Count c){
         c=0;
         }
      int get(Count c){
         return c;
         }
      void inc(reference Count c){
         c = c+1;
         }
      init_counter(c);     // module initialisation
}
module Queue<S>{
   public
      type Queue;
      inqueue(reference Queue q, <S> n);
      <S> dequeue(reference Queue q);
      ...
   private
      void bookkeep(reference Queue q){
         ...
         }
      ...
}
```

Fig. 9.6 Generic modules

From a linguistic viewpoint, we have presented the following:

- *Abstract data type* mechanisms.
- Mechanisms to hide information and their consequences; that is, the *Principle of representation independence*.
- *Modules* which apply the concepts of encapsulation to programming in the large.

All of these concepts are treated in more depth in texts on software engineering. As far as this book is concerned, they are devices to help understanding object-oriented programming which is the subject of the next chapter.

9.5 Bibliographical Notes

The concept of module probably appears for the first time in the Simula language [1, 4], the first object-oriented language (see Chap. 13). The development of modules in programming languages is due to the work of Wirth [6], which includes the Modula and Oberon [7] projects.

The concept of information hiding made its first appearance in the literature in a classic paper by Parnas [5]. Abstract data types originate in the same context, as a mechanism guaranteeing abstraction that is different from modules. Among the languages that include ADTs, the most influential is certainly CLU [3] which is also the basis for the book [2].

9.6 Exercises

1. Consider the following definition of an ADT in our pseudo-language:

```
abstype LittleUse{
   type LittleUse = int;
   signature
      LittleUse prox(LittleUse x);
      int get(LittleUse x);
   operations
      LittleUse prox(LittleUse x){
         return x+1;
         }
      int get(LittleUse x){
         return x;
         }
}
```

   Why this type is useless?

References

1. G. Birtwistle, O. Dahl, B. Myhrtag, and K. Nygaard. *Simula Begin*. Auerbach Press, Philadelphia, 1973.
2. B. Liskov and J. Guttag. *Abstraction and Specification in Program Development*. MIT Electrical Engineering and Computer Science Series. MIT Press, Cambridge, 1986.
3. B. Liskov, A. Snyder, R. Atkinson, and C. Schaffert. Abstraction mechanisms in CLU. *Commun. ACM*, 20(8):564–576, 1977.
4. K. Nygaard and O.-J. Dahl. The development of the SIMULA languages. In *HOPL-1: The First ACM SIGPLAN Conference on History of Programming Languages*, pages 245–272. ACM Press, New York, 1978.
5. D. L. Parnas. On the criteria to be used in decomposing systems into modules. *Commun. ACM*, 15(12):1053–1058, 1972.
6. N. Wirth. The module: A system structuring facility in high-level programming languages. In *Language Design and Programming Methodology*. LNCS, volume 79, pages 1–24. Springer, Berlin, 1979.
7. N. Wirth. From Modula to Oberon. *Softw. Pract. Exp.*, 18(7):661–670, 1988.

Chapter 10
The Object-Oriented Paradigm

In this chapter, we present the important aspects of object-oriented languages, a paradigm which has its roots in Simula (during the 60s) and Smalltalk (in the 70s). It achieved enormous success, including commercial success, in the two following decades (C++ and Java are only two of the most known languages among the many that are in use today). "Object oriented" is by now an abused slogan, which can be found applied to languages, to databases, operating systems, and so on. Here, we attempt to present the *linguistic* aspects which concern objects and their use, making the occasional reference to object-oriented design techniques (but we can only refer the reader to the (extended) literature for details).

Even after restricting the subject, there are many ways to proceed to the concepts that interest us. We will follow the approach we believe the simplest: we will present objects as a way to gain data abstraction in a way that is flexible and extensible. We will begin our study, then, by showing some limits to the techniques that we introduced in Chap. 9. These limits will suggest to us some concepts, which, in fact, form the basics of an object-oriented language. Having examined these characteristic aspects in detail, we will study some extensions to linguistic solutions that are available in commercial languages, referring, in particular, to the concepts of subtype, polymorphism and genericity.

Following the style that we have maintained thus far in this text, we will seek to remain independent of any specific programming language, even if this will not always be possible. The language that will mostly inspire us will be Java, for its coherence of design, which will allow us to discuss some concepts (and not linguistic details) in a clearer way and in a way that allows us to summarise the properties of other languages.

10.1 The Limits of Abstract Data Types

Abstract data types are a mechanism that guarantees the encapsulation and hiding of information in a clean and efficient manner. In particular, the have the excellent characteristic of uniting in a single construct both data and the methods for legally

M. Gabbrielli, S. Martini, *Programming Languages: Principles and Paradigms*,
Undergraduate Topics in Computer Science,
DOI 10.1007/978-1-84882-914-5_10, © Springer-Verlag London Limited 2010

manipulating it. This is a very important methodological principle, which is obtained at the cost of a certain rigidity of use, which shows up when it is wanted to extend or reuse an abstraction. We will discuss these problems using a simple and certainly not realistic example, but one which exposes the most important questions.

So that we do not overload the notation with the call-by-reference, it is convenient to use a language that uses a reference model for variables. The following ADR implements a simple counter:

```
abstype Counter{
   type Counter = int;
   signature
      void reset(Counter x);
      int get(Counter x);
      void inc(Counter x);
   operations
      void reset(Counter x){
         x = 0;
      }
      int get(Counter c){
         return x;
      }
      void inc(Counter c){
         x = x+1;
      }
}
```

The concrete representation of the Counter type is the integer type. The only operations possible are zeroing of a counter, reading and incrementing its value.

We want now to define a counter that is enriched by some new operations. For example, we want to take into account the number of calls the reset operation has had in a given counter. We have a choice of 2 approaches: the first is that of defining a completely new ADT which is similar in many respects to the one just defined with the addition of new operations, as in:

```
abstype NewCounter1{
   type NewCounter1 = struct{
                         int c;
                         int num_reset = 0;
                      }
   signature
      void reset(NewCounter1 x);
      int get(NewCounter1 x);
      void inc(NewCounter1 x);
      int howmany_resets(NewCounter1 x);
   operations
      void reset(NewCounter1 x){
         x.c = 0;
         x.num_reset = x.num_reset+1;
      }
      int get(NewCounter1 x){
         return x.c;
```

```
      }
      void inc(NewCounter1 x){
         x.c = x.c+1;
      }
      int howmany_resets(NewCounter1 x){
         return x.num_reset;
      }
}
```

This is a solution that is acceptable as far as encapsulation goes, but we were required to redefine the operations what we have already defined for a simple counter (they are operations with the same name but with different argument types; names are therefore overloaded which the compiler has to differentiate using the context). In this academic example, we have only a few lines of code but the negative effect on a real situation can be quite significant.[1] More important again is what happens when, for whatever reason, it is desired to change the implementation of a simple counter. There being no relationship between Counter and NewCounter, modifications such as these are not felt by another counter: a NewCounter will still continue to work perfectly. But if the modification were due to reasons of usefulness or efficiency (for example, we found an excellent new way to implement an inc), such a modification must be performed by hand on the definition of a New-Counter, with all the known problems that this brings (find all the places where a variant of the old inc is used, do not introduce any syntactic errors, etc.).

The second possibility that we have is one that makes use of Counter to define an enriched counter:

```
abstype NewCounter2{
   type NewCounter2 = struct{
                          Counter c;
                          int num_reset = 0;
                       }
   signature
      void reset(NewCounter2 x);
      int get(NewCounter2 x);
      void inc(NewCounter2 x);
      int howmany_resets(NewCounter2 x);
   operations
      void reset(NewCounter2 x){
         reset(x.c);
         x.num_reset = x.num_reset+1;
      }
      int get(NewCounter2 x){
         return get(x.c);
      }
      void inc(NewCounter2 x){
         inc(x.c);
```

---

[1] This is a negative effect not only on the writing of the program, but also in the size of the code produced because there are *two copies* of each operation!

```
        }
    int howmany_resets(NewCounter2 x){
        return x.num_reset;
    }
}
```

The solution is clearly better than the previous one. The operations that do not have to be modified are only called from inside a NewCounter (with its usual name overloading), so that the last problem mentioned above is solved. There remains the task of performing the calls explicitly even for the operations (such as get and inc) that have not been modified: it would be preferable to have an automatic mechanism with which to *inherit* the implementations of these two operations from Counter.

There remain problems, though, of how to handle in a uniform fashion the values of Counter and of NewCounter2. Let us assume, in fact, that are dealing with a series of counters, some simple, some enriched, and that we want to reset them all to their initial value. To fix ideas, we can imagine an array of counters; we want to reset each element of this array to its initial value. A first problem arises immediately when we try to work out what the type of this array is. If we declare it as:

```
Counter V[100];
```

we cannot store NewCounter2s there because the two types are distinct. The same thing happens when the array is declared as being of type NewCounter2. To solve the problem, we need a concept of compatibility between the 2 types. Let us remember that among the various forms of compatibility we discussed in Sect. 8.7, we find the following:

> T is compatible with S when all the operations over values of type S are also possible over values of type T.

We have exactly a case of this kind: all the operations on a Counter are possible also on a NewCounter2 (on which we can apply an additional operation). It is, therefore, sensible to require that a hypothetical language should relax the rigidity of ADTs, admitting this form of compatibility. Let us therefore assume that New-Counter2 is compatible with Counter and is therefore permitted to have a vector declared as Counter V[100] in which are stored simple and extended counters. We now come to the main point, which is to reset the initial value of each one of these counters. The obvious idea is:

```
for (int i=1; i<100; i=i+1)
    reset(V[i]);
```

which does not pose type problems. Overloading is solved, interpreting the body as a call to the reset operation on Counter. All goes well with the type checker, but what can be said about the state of NewCounter2 stored in the array? We will expect that their num_reset fields have been incremented by one, but this is not the case because the reset operation defined in NewCounter2 has not been executed, only the one defined in Counter. Compatibility has solved the problem of uniformly manipulating the values of the two types but in a certain sense has destroyed encapsulation, allowing the application of an operation to a value of type `NewCounter2` which is not correct with reference to the ADT. A moment's reflection shows how the problem derives from the static solution to the overloading of `reset`. If we could decide dynamically which `reset` to apply, depending upon the "effective" type of the argument (that is on the type of the element stored in the array before the coercion connected with compatibility is applied), this problem would also be solved.

10.1.1 A First Review

Abstract data types guarantee the encapsulation and hiding of information but they are rigid when used in a design with a degree of complexity. From what has just been said, it is not unreasonable to foresee constructs such as:

- They permit the *encapsulation* and hiding of information.
- They are equipped with a mechanism which, under certain conditions, supports the *inheritance* of the implementation of certain operations from other, analogous constructs.
- They are framed in a notion of *compatibility* defined in terms of the operations admissible for a certain construct.
- They allow the *dynamic selection* of operations as a function of the "effective type" of the arguments to which they are applied.

These four requirements are satisfied by the object-oriented paradigm. Rather, we can take them as essential characteristics of this paradigm which separates an object-oriented language from one which is not. We will discuss them in detail after introducing some basic concepts and once the terminology has been fixed.

10.2 Fundamental Concepts

In this section, we will establish the fundamental concepts which organise the object-oriented paradigm. We will begin by introducing some terminology and macroscopic linguistic concepts (object, class, method, overriding, etc.), so that we can return to the four aspects listed in Sect. 10.1.1. with the aim of discussing them in more detail. We will take them in the following order:

1. Encapsulation and abstraction.
2. Subtypes, that is a compatibility relation based on the functionality of an object.
3. Inheritance, that is the possibility of reusing the implementation of a method previously defined in another object or for another class.
4. Dynamic method selection.

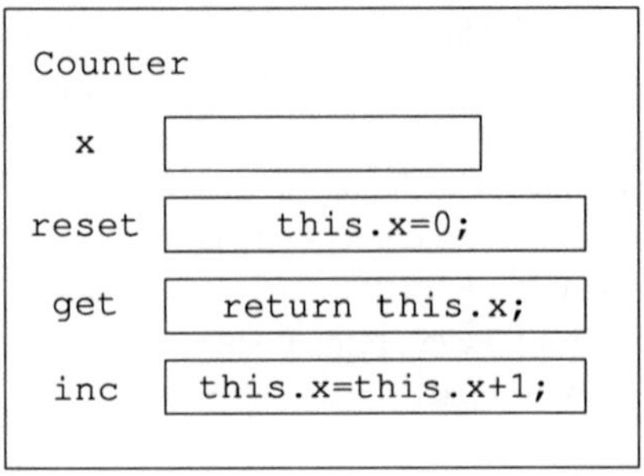

Fig. 10.1 An object for a
counter

```
Counter

  x    [                    ]

reset  [      this.x=0;      ]

 get   [    return this.x;    ]

 inc   [  this.x=this.x+1;   ]
```

These are distinct mechanisms, each exhibited on its own by other paradigms. As
will be seen, it is their interaction that makes the object-oriented paradigm so attrac-
tive to software design, even of large systems.

10.2.1 Objects

The principal construct of object-oriented languages is (clearly) that of object.
A capsule containing both data and the operations that manipulate it and which
provides an interface for the outside world through which the object is accessible.
The methodological idea which objects share with ADT is that data should "remain
together" with the operations that manipulate it. There is, then, a big conceptual difference between them and ADTs (which is translated into a considerably different
notation). Although, in the definition of an ADT, data and operations are together,
when we declare a variable of an abstract type, that variable represents only the data
which can be manipulated using the operations. In our counters example, we can
declare a counter as `Counter c` and then increment it: `inc(c)`. *Each* object, on
the other hand, is a container which (at least conceptually) encapsulates both data
and operations. A counter object, defined using the same model as the definition that
we have given for `Counter` could be represented as in Fig. 10.1.

The figure suggests that we may imagine an object as a record. Some fields correspond to (modifiable) data, for example the `c` field; other fields correspond to the
operations that are allowed to manipulate the data (that is `reset`, `get` and `inc`).

The operations are called *methods* (or functional fields or *member functions*) and
can access the data items held in the object, which are called *instance variables* (or
data members or fields). The execution of an operation is performed by sending the
object a *message* which consists of the name of the method to execute, possibly
together with parameters.[2] To represent such invocations, we use the Java and C++
notation which reinforces the analogy with records:

`object.method(parameters)`

---

[2]This is mostly Smalltalk terminology. C++ expresses the same thing by saying: calling the member function of an object.

Below, we will often read the above notation as the "invocation of the method method (with parameters *parameters*) on the object object" rather than "sending the message method(*parameters*) to the object object" as would be formally more precise.

An aspect that is not always clear is that the object receiving the message is, at the same time, also a(n implicit) parameter to the invoked method. To increment a counter object, o, which has the structure of Fig. 10.1, we will write o.inc() ("we ask the object, o, to apply the message inc to itself"). Also, the data members are accessible using the same mechanism (if they are not hidden by capsule, obviously). If an object, o, has an instance variable, v, with o.v we request o for the value of v. While the notation remains uniform, we note that accessing data is a mechanism that is distinct from that of invoking a method. Invoking a method involves (or can involve) the *dynamic selection* of the method that is to be executed, while access to a data item is static, although there are exceptions to this.

The level of opacity of the capsule is defined when the object is itself created. Data can be more or less directly accessible from the outside (for example, data could be directly inaccessible, with the object, instead, providing "observers"— recall the box on page 269), some operations can be visible everywhere, others visible to some objects, while, finally, others are completely private, that is available only inside the object itself.

Together with objects, the languages of this paradigm also make available *organisational mechanisms* for objects. These mechanisms permit the grouping of objects with the same structure (or with similar structure). Although it is conceptually permitted that *every* object truly contains its own data and methods, this would result in enormous waste. In a single program, many objects would be used which are differentiated between themselves only by the value of their data and not by their structure or by their methods (for example, many counters, all analogous to the one in Fig. 10.1). Without an organisational principle, which makes explicit the similarity of all these objects, the program would loose expository clarity and would be harder to document. Furthermore, from the implementation viewpoint, it is clear that it would be appropriate for the code of each method to be stored only once, instead of being copied inside each object with similar structure. To solve these problems, every object-oriented language is based on some organisational principles. Among these principles, the one that is by far the best known is that of *classes*, although there is a whole family of object-oriented languages that lack classes (which we will briefly describe in the box on page 286).

10.2.2 Classes

A class is a model for a set of objects. It establishes what its data will be (type together with their visibility) and fixes name, signature, visibility and implementation for each of its methods. In a language with classes, every object belongs to (at least) one class. For example, an object such as that in Fig. 10.1 could be an instance of the following class:

```
class Counter{
   private int x;
   public void reset(){
      x = 0;
   }
   public int get(){
      return x;
   }
   public void inc(){
      x = x+1;
   }
}
```

It can be seen that the class contains the implementation of three methods which are declared `public` (visible to all), while the instance variable x is `private` (inaccessible from outside the object itself but accessible in the implementation of the methods of this class).

Objects are dynamically created by *instantiation* of their class. A specific object is allocated whose structure is determined by its class. This operation differs in fundamental ways from language to language and depends on the linguistic status of classes. In Simula, a class is a procedure which returns a pointer to an activation record containing local variables and function definitions (therefore, the objects that are instances of a class are closures). In Smalltalk, a class is linguistically an object which acts as a schema for the definition of the implementation of a set of objects. In C++ and Java classes correspond to a type and all objects that instantiate a class A are values of type A. Taking this viewpoint in Java, with its reference-based model for variables, we can create a counter object:

```
Counter c = new Counter();
```

The name c, of type `Counter`, is bound to a new object which is an instance of `Counter`. We can create a new object, distinct from the previous one but with the same structure, and bind it to another name:

```
Counter d = new Counter();
```

To the right of the assignment symbol, we can see two distinct operations: the creation of the objects (allocation of the necessary storage, `new` constructor) and initialisation (invocation of the class' *constructor*, represented by the name of the class and parentheses—we will return to this shortly[3]).

We can certainly assume that the code for methods is stored one time only in its class and that when an object needs to execute a specific method, this code would be looked up in the class of which it is an instance. For this to happen, the method code must correctly access the instance variables which are different for every object

---

[3] In C++, unlike Java, it is also possible to create an object without invoking its constructor; C++ in fact allows the creation of objects on the stack (see page 286).

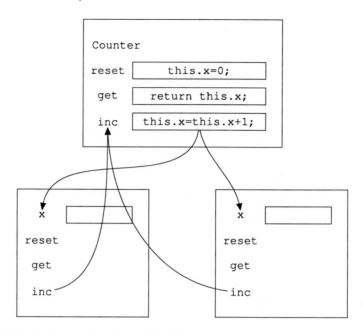

Fig. 10.2 The implementation of methods is inside classes

and are, therefore, not all stored together in the class but inside the instance (as is shown graphically in Fig. 10.2). In the figure, the methods of class `Counter` refer to its instance variables using the name `this`. We have already seen that when an object receives a message requesting the execution of a method, the object itself is an implicit method parameter. When a reference is made to an instance variable in the body of a method, there is an implicit reference to the object currently executing the method. From the linguistic viewpoint, the current object is usually denoted by a unique name, usually `self` or `this`. For example, the definition of the `inc` method could be written as follows. Here, the implicit reference to the current object is made explicit:

```
public void inc(){
    this.x = this.x+1;
}
```

In the case of a call to a method via `this`, the link between the method and the code to which it is referring is dynamically determined. This is an important aspect of this paradigm and we will discuss it in more detail in Sect. 10.2.6.

Some languages allow some variables and methods to be associated with classes (and not to their instances). They are called *class* or *static* variables and methods. Static variables are stored together in the class and static methods cannot, obviously, refer to `this` in their body because that they have no current object.

Languages based on Delegation

There also exist object-oriented languages that lack classes. In these languages, which are based on delegation (or on *prototypes*), the organising principle (see the end of Sect. 10.2.1) is not the class, but delegation; that is, the principle that one object can ask another object (its parent) to execute a method for it. Among these languages, the progenitor is Self which was developed at Xerox PARC and Stanford towards the end of the 1980s. Other languages based upon delegation are Dylan, a language for programming the Apple Newton PDA and on Javascript, which was designed to be distributed in one of the early versions of Netscape.

The fields of an object can contain values (simple data or other objects) or methods (that is, code), or references to other objects (the parent of the object). An object is created from nothing, or more often, by copying (or cloning) another object (which is called its *prototype*). Prototypes play the methodological role of classes. They provide the model for the structuring and functioning for other objects but are not special objects. Linguistically, they are ordinary objects, which, however, are used not for computation, but as a model. When a prototype is cloned, the copy maintains a reference to the prototype as its parent.

When an object receives a message but has no field of that name, it passes the message to its parent, and the process repeats. When the message reaches an object that understands it, the code associated with the method is executed. The language ensures that the reference to `self` is correctly resolved as a reference to the object that originally received the message. In general, data in the object is considered equal to methods. Access to a data item corresponds to sending a message, which the same object responds by returning the value of the field.

The delegation mechanism (and the unification of code and data) makes inheritance more powerful. It is possible and natural to create objects which share portions of data (in a language based on classes, this is possible only using static data associated with classes; however, such a template is too "static" to be profitably used). Moreover, an object can change the reference to its parent dynamically and thereby change its own behaviour.

Objects in the heap and on the stack   Every object-oriented language allows the dynamic creation of objects. Where objects are created depends on the language. The most common solution is to allocate objects in the heap and access them using references (which will be real pointers in languages that permit them, but will be variables if the language supports a reference model). Some languages allow explicit allocation and deallocation of objects in the heap (C++ is one); others, probably the majority, opt instead for a garbage collector.

The option of creating objects on the stack like ordinary variables is not very common. C++ is one such language. When a declaration of a variable of class type is elaborated, the creation and initialisation of an object of that type is performed.

The object is assigned as a value to the variable.[4] The two operations contributing to the creation of an object (allocation and initialisation) occur implicitly in cases where the constructor is not explicitly called. Some languages, finally, allow objects to be created on the stack and left uninitialised.

In our pseudo-language, we assume that object creation occurs explicitly on the heap and has a reference-variable model.

10.2.3 Encapsulation

Encapsulation and information hiding represent two of the cardinal points of data abstraction. From the linguistic viewpoint, there is not much to add to what we have already said. Every language allows the definition of objects by hiding some part of them (either data or methods). In every class there are, therefore, at least two *views*: private and public parts. In the private view, everything is visible: it is the level of access possible inside the class itself (by its methods). In the public view, however, only explicitly exported information is visible. We say that the public information is the interface to a class, by analogy with ADTs.[5]

At this level no great difference appear between object-oriented programming languages and the forms of data abstraction that we have already discussed. The encapsulation possible with objects, however, is much more flexible and, more importantly, extensible than is possible with ADTs. But this will become clear only at the end of our examination of the concepts.

10.2.4 Subtypes

A class can be made to correspond, in a natural fashion, with the set of objects which are instances of that class. This set of objects is the type associated with that class. In typed languages, this relation is explicit. A class definition also introduces the definition of a type whose values are the instances of that class. In typeless languages (like Smalltalk), the correspondence is only conventional and implicit.

Among the types thus obtained, a compatibility relation is defined (Sect. 8.7) in terms of the operations possible on values of the type. The type associated with the class T is a subtype of S when every message understood (that is which can be received without generating an error) from objects of S is also understood by the objects of T. If an object is represented as a record containing data and functions,[6]

---

[4]Things are clearly different when a variable of type pointer-to-a-class type is declared. In this case, no object is created (without an explicit request to do so).

[5]In different languages, the term "interface" means different things. Do not confuse, in particular, our use of the term "interface" with what is meant by it in Java (where it is a particular language construct, a sort of class in which the only components are names and method signatures but do not contain their implementations).

[6]That is, as a closure.

the subtype relation corresponds to the fact that T is a record type containing all fields of S, as well, possibly, other fields. More precisely, taking account of the fact that some fields of the two types could be private, we might say that T is a subtype of S when the interface of S is a subset of the interface of T (note the inversion: a subtype is obtained when we have a bigger interface).

Some languages (like C++ and Java) use a name-based equivalence for types (see Sect. 8.6) which does not properly extend to a completely structural compatibility relation. In such languages, it is not, therefore, the only structural property between interfaces that defines the subtype relation, but it must be explicitly introduced by the programmer. This is the role of the definition of subclasses, or derived classes, which in our pseudo-language will be denoted using the neutral extending construct:[7]

```
class NamedCounter extending Counter{
    private String name;
    public void set_name(String n){
        name = n;
    }
    public String get_name(){
        return name;
    }
}
```

The class NamedCounter is a subclass of Counter (which, in its turn is a superclass of NamedCounter),[8] that is the NamedCounter type is a subtype of Counter. Instances of NamedCounter contain all the fields of Counter (even its private fields, but they are inaccessible in the subclass), in addition to having new fields introduced by the definition. In this way, structural compatibility can be guaranteed (a subclass is explicitly derived from its superclass) but this is explicitly stated in the program.

Redefinition of a method   In the simple example of NamedCounter, subclasses are limited to extending the interface of the superclass. A fundamental characteristic of the subclass mechanism is ability of a subclass to modify the definition (the implementation) of a method present in its superclass. This mechanism is called *method overriding*.[9] Our extended counters from Sect. 10.1 can be defined as a subclass of Counter as:

```
class NewCounter extending Counter{
    private int num_reset = 0;
    public void reset(){
```

---

[7]In place of extending, in C++, we write ": public", while in Java extends or even implements is used, depending upon whether a class or an interface is being extended.

[8]In C++, Counter is the *base* class and NamedCOunter is the *derived* class.

[9]Method overriding is a mechanism which interacts in a very subtle way with other aspects of the object-oriented paradigm, in particular with the dynamic selection of methods; for the time being, we will note only this possibility, returning to this question in due course.

```
      x = 0;
      num_reset = num_reset + 1;
   }
   public int howmany_resets(){
      return num_reset;
   }
}
```

Class `NewCounter` simultaneously extends the interface of `Counter` with new fields and redefines the `reset` method. A `reset` method sent to an instance of `NewCounter` will cause the invocation of the new implementation.

Shadowing   In addition to modifying the implementation of a method, a subclass can also redefine an instance variable (or field) defined in a superclass. This mechanism is called *shadowing*. For implementation reasons (to be seen below), shadowing is significantly different from overriding. For the present, we merely note that, in a subclass, an instance variable can be redefined with the same name and same type as that in the superclass. We could, for example, modify our extended counters using the following subclass of `NewCounter` where, for some (strange) reason, the initial value of `num_reset` is initialised to 2 and is incremented by 2 each time:

```
class EvenNewCounter extending NewCounter{
   private int num_reset = 2;
   public void reset(){
      x = 0;
      num_reset = num_reset + 2;
   }
   public int howmany_resets(){
      return num_reset;
   }
}
```

Using the usual notion of visibility in block-structured languages, each reference to `num_reset` inside `EvenNewCounter` refers to the local variable (initialised to 2) and not to the one declared in `NewCounter`. A `reset` message sent to an instance of `EvenNewCounter` will cause the invocation of the new implementation for `reset` which will use the new `num_reset` field. However, as we will see below, there is a big difference, both at the semantic as well as at the implementation levels, between overriding and shadowing.

Abstract classes   For simplicity of exposition, we have introduced the type associated with a class as the set of its instances. Many languages, however, permit the definition of classes that cannot have instances because the class lacks the implementation of some method. In such classes, there is only the name and the type (that is, the signature) of one or more methods—their implementation is omitted. Classes of this type are called *abstract* classes. Abstract classes serve to provide interfaces and can be given implementations in subclasses that redefines (in this case,

Subtypes in Smalltalk?

Among the essential characteristics of the object-oriented paradigm, we have included subtypes. On the other hand, there are object-oriented languages which do not have types (at least do not have types over which we can perform any significant checking). Smalltalk is one of these languages. How can we have subtypes in a language without types?

When we gave the definition of subtype, we were careful to include the case of Smalltalk as well of other untyped languages. Recall that T is a subtype of S when the interface of S is a subset of the interface of T. That is, when we may freely use an object of class T (that is without generating errors) in place of one of class S. This operational definition, which is expressed in terms of the substitution of objects, makes perfect sense even in an untyped context, once we associate the set of its instances (its "type") with the class T.

On the other hand, when in the language there is no linguistic notion of subtype, it is only in the reflection of the designers that the presence of such a relationship becomes clear. In particular, in Smalltalk the definition of a subclass does not generate a subtype because Smalltalk allows subclasses to remove methods from their superclass.

define for the first time) the method lacking an implementation.[10] Abstract classes also correspond to types and the mechanism that provides implementations for their methods also generates subtypes.

The subtype relation   In general, languages ban cycles in the subtype relation between classes, that is, we cannot have both A subtype B and B subtype A, unless A and B coincide. The subtype relation is, therefore, a partial order. In many languages, this relation has a maximal element: the type of which all other types defined by classes are subtypes. We will denote such a type with the name Object. Messages that an instance of Object accepts are fairly limited (it is an object of maximum generality). We find in general a method for cloning which returns a copy of the object, an equality method and a few others. Moreover, some of these methods could be abstract in Object and therefore require redefinition before they can be used.

It can be seen that it is not guaranteed that, given a type A, there exists a *unique* type B which is the *immediate supertype* of A. In the following example:

```
abstract class A{
   public int f();
}

abstract class B{
```

---

[10] A method for which there is only a signature is, in Java, said to be an *abstract* method; in C++, it is a *pure virtual* member function.

```
   public int g();
}

class C extending A,B{
   private x = 0;
   public int f(){
      return x;
   }
   public int g(){
      return x+1;
   }
}
```

The type C is a subtype of A as well as of B and there is no other type included between C and the other two. The subtype hierarchy is not a tree in general, but just an acyclic oriented graph (see Fig. 10.3).

Constructors   We have already seen that an object is a complex structure which includes data and code all wrapped up together. The creation of an object is therefore also an operation of a certain complexity which consists of two distinct actions: first the allocation of necessary memory (in the heap or on the stack) and the proper initialisation of the object's data. This last action is performed by the *constructor* of the class. That is, by code associated with the class and which the language guarantees will execute at exactly the same time the instance is created. The constructor mechanism is of some complexity because the data in an object consists not only of that explicitly declared in the class whose instance is being created, but also the data declared in its superclasses. In addition, more than one constructor is often permitted for a class. We have, therefore, a series of questions about constructors which can be summarised as the following:

- *Constructor selection*. When the language permits it, there is more than one constructor for a class, so how is the choice made as to which one to use when creating a specific object? In some languages (for example C++ and Java), the name of the constructor is the same as the name of the class. Multiple constructors all have the same name and must be distinguished either by their type or the number of the arguments or both (they are therefore overloaded, with static resolution). Since C++ permits the implicit creation of objects on the stack, there are spe-

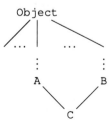

Fig. 10.3 The subtype relation is not a tree

cific mechanisms for selecting the appropriate constructor to use in each case.[11]
Other languages allow the programmer to choose constructor names freely (but
the constructors remain syntactically distinct from ordinary methods) and require
that every creation operation (our new) is always associated with a constructor.

- *Constructor chaining.* How and when is the part of object that belongs to the
  superclass initialised? Some languages limit themselves to executing the constructor of the class whose instance they are constructing. If the programmer in-
  tends calling superclass constructors, it must be done explicitly. Other languages
  (among them C++ and Java) guarantee, on the other hand, that when an object is
  initialised, the constructor for its super class will be invoked (*constructor chaining*) before any other operations are performed by the constructor specific to the
  subclass. Once more, there are many issues which each language has to resolve.
  Among these, the two most important are determining which superclass constructor to invoke and how to determine its arguments.

10.2.5 Inheritance

We have seen that a subclass can redefine the methods of its superclass. But what
happens when the subclass does not redefine them? In such cases, the subclass inherits methods from the superclass, in the sense that the implementation of the method
in the superclass is made available to the subclass. For example, NewCounter inherits from Counter the data item x and methods inc and get (but not reset
which is redefined).

More generally (including in our definition, phenomena also present in class-less
object-oriented languages), we can characterise inheritance as a mechanism which
permits the definition of new objects based on the reuse of pre-existing ones.

Inheritance permits code reuse in an extendable context. By modifying the implementation of a method, a class automatically makes the modification available to
all its subclasses, with no intervention required on the part of the programmer.

Is important to understand the difference between the relation of inheritance and
that of subtype. The concept of subtype has to do with the possibility of using an
object in another context. It is a relation between the interfaces of two classes. The
concept of inheritance has to do with the possibility of reusing the code which manipulates an object. It is a relation between the implementations of two classes.
We are dealing with two mechanisms which are completely independent, even if
they are often linguistically associated in several object-oriented languages. Both
C++ and Java have constructs which can simultaneously introduce both relations
between the two classes, but this does not mean that the concepts are the same. In
the literature, we sometimes see the distinction between *implementation inheritance*
(inheritance) and *interface inheritance* (our subtype relation).

Inheritance and visibility   We have already seen that there are two views of each
class: the private and the public, with the latter shared between all the clients of

---

[11] The case of a constructor which takes a single object as the argument (a copy constructor in C++
jargon) is especially tricky and the source of many programming errors.

the class. A subclass is a particular client of the superclass. It uses the methods of the superclass to extend the functionality of the superclass, but sometimes it has to access some non-public data. Many languages therefore introduce a third view of a class: one for subclasses. Taking the term from C++, we can refer to it as the *protected* view of a class.[12]

If the subclass has access to some details of the super class' implementation, the subclass depends in a much tighter way on the superclass. Every modification of the superclass will require a modification of the subclass. From the pragmatic view-point, this is reasonable only if the two classes are "close" to each other, for example belonging to the same package. The stronger the pairing of the two classes, the more the resulting system becomes difficult to modify and maintain. However, making protected and public interfaces coincide can be too restrictive. We may think of a class hierarchy providing data structures that gradually become more specialised. Being able to access the representation of the data structures, the subclass will be able to implement its own operations in a more efficient way.

Single and multiple inheritance   In some languages, a class can inherit from a single immediate superclass. The inheritance hierarchy is therefore a tree and we say that the language has single (or simple) inheritance. Other languages, on the other hand, allow a class to inherit methods from more than one immediate superclass; the inheritance hierarchy in such a case is an acyclic oriented graph and the language has multiple inheritance.

There are only a few languages which support multiple inheritance (among which are C++ and Eiffel), because it presents problems that do not have an elegant solution at either the conceptual or implementation level. The fundamental problems relate to name clashes. We have a name clash when a class C simultaneously inherits from A and B, which both provide implementation for methods with the same signature. The following is a simple example:

```
class A{
    int x;
    int f(){
        return x;
    }
}
class B{
    int y;
    int f(){
        return y;
    }
}
class C extending A,B{
    int h(){
        return f();
    }
}
```

---

[12]Java also has a `protected` visibility modifier, which is, though, more liberal than that in C++; it grants visibility to an entire package and not just to classes.

Inheritance and Subtypes in Java

The subtype relation is introduced in Java using either the `extends` clause (to define subclasses) or the `implements` clause when a class is declared a subtype of one or more interfaces (for Java, an interface is a kind of incomplete abstract class in which only names and method signatures are included—they do not include implementations). The inheritance relation is introduced with the `extends` clause whenever the subclass does not redefine a method and therefore uses an implementation from the superclass. It should be noted there is never inheritance *from* an interface because the interface has nothing to be inherited. The language constrains every class to having a single immediate superclass (that is a single superclass can be named in an `extends`), but allows that a single class (or interface) implements more than one interface:

```
interface A{
    int f();
}
interface B{
    int g();
}
class C{
    int x;
    int h(){
        return x+2;
    }
}
class D extends C implements A,B{
    int f(){
        return x;
    }
    int g(){
        return x+1;
    }
}
```

Java therefore has single inheritance. The inheritance hierarchy is a tree organised by `extends` clauses. In addition, the inheritance relation is, in Java, always a subhierarchy of the subtype hierarchy.

The situation of the example, when at the same time we have inheritance from superclass and implementation of some abstract interface, is often called *mix-in* inheritance (because the names of the abstract methods in the interface are mixed in with the inherited implementations). As usual, current terminology is often imprecise and confuses subtypes with inheritance. In many manuals (and even in the official definition of Java ...), it is said that Java has single inheritance for classes, but multiple inheritance for interfaces. According to our terminology there is no true inheritance where interfaces are involved.

Inheritance and Subtypes in C++

The C++ mechanisms that allow for the definition of the inheritance relation, and those responsible for subtyping, are not independent. The definition of derived classes (the C++ term for subclass) introduces the inheritance relation. It also introduces a subtype relation when the derived class declares its base class (that is the superclass) as `public`; when the base class is not public, the derived class inherits from the base class but there is not subtype relation.

```
class A{
public:
    void f(){...}
    ...
}
class B : public A{
public:
    void g(){...}
    ...
}
class C : A{
public:
    void h(){...}
    ...
}
```

Both classes B and C inherit from A but only B is a subtype of A.

Since the subtype relation follows that of subclass, with the tools seen so far, we could not introduce an *interface subtype*, that is, a class derived from a base class which provides no implementations but just fixes an interface. It is to this end that C++ introduces the concept of *abstract* base class, in which some methods need not have an implementation. In such cases, as with Java interfaces, we can have subtypes without inheritance.

Which of the two methods named f is inherited in C? We can solve this problem in three different ways, none of which is totally satisfactory:

1. Forbid name clashes syntactically.
2. Require that any conflict should be resolved by the programmer's appropriately qualifying every reference to a name that is in conflict. For example, the body of h in class C, should be written as B::f() or as A::f(), which is the solution adopted by C++.
3. Decide upon a convention for solving the conflict, for example favouring the first-class named in the `extending` clause.

From the pragmatic point of view, it is possible to give examples of situations in which any of these solutions is unnatural and counterintuitive. As far as explicit solution is concerned, it can be seen that the conflict could observed not in C but in one of its subclasses (if f is not called inside C). The designer must therefore know the class hierarchy with some precision. However it might be, in cases like this, it is methodologically better to redefine f in C. For example:

```
class C extending A,B{
    int f(){
        return A::f();
    }
    int h(){
        return this.f();
    }
}
```

such that in the subclasses of C, there are no name clashes.

The most interesting problems of multiple inheritance are present in the so-called diamond problem. This case arises when a class inherits from two superclasses, each of which inherits from the same, single superclass. A simple situation of this kind is the following (the diamond-shaped inheritance hierarchy is shown graphically in Fig. 10.4).

```
class Top{
    int w;
    int f(){
        return w;
    }
}
class A extending Top{
    int x;
    int g(){
        return w+x;
    }
}
class B extending Top{
    int y;
    int f(){
        return w+y;
    }
    int k(){
        return y;
    }
}
class Bottom extending A,B{
    int z;
    int h(){
        return z;
    }
}
```

In this case, as well, we have the usual problem of name conflict but it is crucially the implementation question which is more relevant. That is, devise a technique allowing the correct *and efficient* selection of the code for f when this method is invoked on an instance of class Bottom. We will deal with this in Sect. 10.3.4.

Fig. 10.4 The Diamond problem for multiple inheritance

In conclusion, multiple inheritance is a highly flexible tool for the combination of abstractions corresponding to distinct functionalities. Some of the situations in which it works are in reality better expressed using subtype relations ("inheriting" from abstract classes). There are no simple, unequivocal, and elegant solutions to the problems that multiple inheritance poses. The cost benefit balance between single and multiple inheritance is equivocal.

10.2.6 Dynamic Method Lookup

Dynamic method lookup (or dispatch) is the heart of the object-oriented paradigm. In this, the characteristics that have already been discussed combine to form a new synthesis. In particular, dynamic method lookup allows compatibility of subtypes and abstraction to coexist. This is, in particular, something that was seen to be problematic for abstract data types (page 281).

Conceptually, the mechanism is very simple. We have already seen that a method defined for one object can be redefined (overridden) in objects that belong to subtypes of the original object. Therefore when a method, m, is invoked on an object, o, there can be many versions of m possible for o. The selection of which implementation for m is to be used in an invocation

```
o.m(parameters);
```

is a function of the type of the object receiving the message. Note that what is relevant is the type of the *object* which receives the message, not the type of the reference (or name) to that object (which is instead static information).

Let us give an example in our pseudo-language with classes. Figure 10.5 repeats the counters discussed in Sects. 10.2.2 and 10.2.4. In the context of these class declarations, we now execute the following fragment:

```
NewCounter n = new NewCounter();
Counter c;
c = n;
c.reset();
```

Fig. 10.5 Two classes for
counters

```
class Counter{
    private int x;
    public void reset(){
        x = 0;
    }
    public int get(){
        return x;
    }
    public void inc(){
        x = x+1;
    }
}
class NewCounter extending Counter{
    private int num_reset = 0;
    public void reset(){
        x = 0;
        num_reset = num_reset + 1;
    }
    public int howmany_resets(){
        return num_reset;
    }
}
```

The (static) type of the name c is Counter but it refers (dynamically) to an instance of NewCounter. So it will be the reset method of NewCounter that is invoked.

The canonical example is the one which (negatively) concluded Sect. 10.1. Both Counter and NewCounter are stored in a data structure whose type is their supertype:

```
Counter V[100];
```

Now we apply the reset method to each:

```
for (int i=1; i<100; i=i+1)
    V[i].reset();
```

Dynamic lookup assures us that the correct method will be invoked on any counter. In general, a compiler will be unable to decide what will be the type of the object whose method will be invoked, hence the dynamicity of this mechanism.

The reader should have noted a certain analogy between overloading and dynamic method lookup. In both cases, the problem is the same: that of resolving an ambiguous situation in which a single name can have more than one meaning. Under overloading, though, the ambiguity is resolved statically, based on the type of the *names* involved. In method lookup, on the other hand, the solution of the problem is at runtime and makes use of the dynamic type of the object and not of its name. It is not, however, a mistake to think of method lookup as a runtime overloading operation in which the object receiving the message is considered the first (implicit) argument of the method whose name has to be resolved.[13]

Is important to observe explicitly that dynamic method lookup is at work even when a method in an object invokes a method in the same object, as happens in the next fragment:

```
class A{
    int a = 0;
    void f(){g();}
    void g(){a=1;}
}
class B extending A{
    int b = 0;
    void g(){b=2;}
}
```

Let us now assume that we have an object b which is an instance of B and we want to invoke on b the method f inherited by b from A. Now, f calls g: which of the two implementations of g will be executed? Recall that the object which receives the message is also an important parameter to the method. The call of g in the body of f can be written more explicitly as this.g(), where, recall, this is a reference to the current object. The current object is b and therefore the method which will be invoked is that of class B. It can be seen that, in this way, a call to a method such as this.g() in the body of f can refer to (implementations of) methods that are not yet written and which will be available only later through the class hierarchy. This mechanism, through which the name this becomes bound dynamically to the current object, is called *late binding* of self (or of this).

Let us explicitly note that, unlike overriding, shadowing is a completely static mechanism. Consider, for example, the code:

```
class A{
    int a = 1;
    int f(){return -a;}
}
class B extending A{
    int a = 2;
    int f(){return a;}
}

B obj_b = new B();
print(obj_b.f());
print(obj_b.a);
```

---

[13]The reader will not be surprised if, once more, object-oriented programming jargon contributes to the confusion. It is not uncommon to hear (and to see written) that dynamic method lookup permits polymorphism. In our terminology there is no polymorphism because we are not in the presence of a single, uniform piece of code. It is possible to talk of polymorphism in object-oriented programming but this has to do with subtypes. We will deal with this in Sect. 10.4.1.

Dynamic Dispatch in C++

In languages like Java or Smalltalk, each method invocation happens using dynamic dispatch. C++ has, as design goals, efficiency of execution and compatibility with C, meaning by this that the use of a C construct in a C++ program must be efficient as in C.

In C++, we have, therefore, static method dispatch (analogous to function call), as well as a form of dynamic dispatch which is performed using *virtual functions*. When a method (that is a member function in C++ terminology) is defined, it is possible to specify whether it is a virtual function or not. Only the overriding of virtual functions is permitted. Dynamic dispatch is performed on virtual member functions.

Let us note, incidentally, that it is not forbidden to define, in some class, a function of the same name and signature as a non-virtual function defined in the superclass. In such a case, we do not have redefinition, but overloading, and this can be resolved statically by the compiler using the type of the *name* used to refer to that object. In the example that follows we declare a class A and a subclass B:

```
class A{
public:
    void f(){printf("A");}
    virtual void g(){printf("A");}
}
class B : public A{
public:
    void f(){printf("B");}
    virtual void g(){printf("B");}
}
```

If, now, we have a pointer a of type A*, which points to an instance of B, invocation of the function a->f() prints A, while invocation of the virtual function a->g() prints B.

```
A obj_a = obj_b;
print(obj_a.f());
print(obj_a.a);
```

where `print` denotes a method which outputs the integer value passed as an argument. The first two invocations of `print` produce the value 2 twice, as should be obvious. The third call will also print the value 2, given that, as already seen above, the method f has been redefined in class B. In fact the object created (with new B()) is an instance of B, and hence every access to it, even those through a variable of type A (as in the case of obj_a), uses the redefined method (which is obviously using the redefined fields in class B). The last occurrence of print, instead, produces the value 1. In this case, in fact, given that we are not dealing with the invocation of a method but accessing a field, it is the type of the current reference

Multimethod languages

In the languages we have considered so far, a method invocation has the form:

```
o.m(parameters);
```

Dynamic method lookup uses the run-time type of the object receiving the method, while uses the static types of the parameters. In some other languages (for example, CLOS), this asymmetry is removed. Methods are no longer associated with classes but are global names. Each method name is overloaded by a number of implementations (which in this case are called *multimethods*) and the object on which the method is invoked is passed to every multimethod. When invoking a multimethod, the code that must be executed is chosen dynamically on the basis of the (dynamic) type of both the receiver and all the arguments.

In these languages, we speak of *multiple dispatch* rather than single dispatch in languages where there exists a privileged receiver.

In languages with multiple dispatch, the analogy between (multiple) dynamic dispatch and "dynamic overloading" is more evident; multiple dispatch consists in the (runtime) resolution of an overloading on the basis of dynamic type information.

---

which determines which field is to be considered. Given that obj_a is of type A, when we write $obj\_a.a$, the field in question is the one in class A (initialised to one).

This distinction between overriding and shadowing, is explained at the implementation level using the fact that the instance object of class B also contains all the fields of the superclasses of B, as we will make clear in the next section.

10.3 Implementation Aspects

Every language has its own implementation model which is optimised to the specific features that the language provides. We can, however, indicate some common lines which indicate the main problems and their solutions.

Objects   An instance object of class A can be used as the value of any superclass of A. particular, it is possible to access not just the instance variables (data fields) explicitly defined in A, but also those defined in its superclasses. An object can be represented as if it were a record, with as many fields as there are variables in the class of which it is an instance, *in addition* to all those appearing in its superclasses. In a case of shadowing, or rather when a name of an instance variable of the class is used with the same type in a subclass, the object contains additional fields, each one corresponding to a different declaration (often, the name used in the superclass

```
class A{
    int a;
    void f(){...}
    void g(){...}
}
class B extending A{
    int b;
    void f(){...} // redefined
    void h(){...}
}
B o = new B();
```

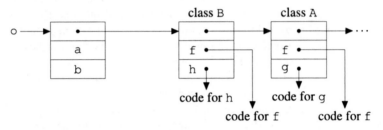

Fig. 10.6 A simple implementation of inheritance

is not accessible in the subclass, if not using particular qualifications, for example `super`). The representation also contains a pointer to the descriptor of the class of which it is an instance.

In the case of a language with a static type system, this representation allows the simple implementation of subtype compatibility (in the case of single inheritance). For each instance variable, the offset from the start of the record is statically recorded. If access to an instance object of a class is performed using a (static) reference having as type one of the superclasses of that object, static type checking ensures that access can be made only to a field defined in the superclass, which is allocated in the initial part of the record.

Classes and inheritance The representation of classes is the key to the object orientation abstract machine. The simplest and most intuitive implementation is the one which represents the class hierarchy using a linked list. Each element represents a class and contains (pointers to) the implementation of the methods that are either defined or redefined in that class. The elements are linked using a pointer which points from the subclass to the immediate superclass. When a method m of an object o which is an instance of a class C is invoked, the pointer stored in o is used to access the descriptor of C and determine whether C contains an implementation of m. If it does not, the pointer is set to the superclass and the procedure is repeated (see Fig. 10.6). This approach is used in Smalltalk, although it is inefficient because every method invocation requires a linear scan of the class hierarchy; the advantage of the technique is its simplicity. We will shortly discuss more efficient implementations after we have seen how to access instance variables from within a method invocation.

Late binding of self A method is executed in a way similar to a function. An activation record for the method's local variables, parameters and all the other information is pushed onto the stack. Unlike a function, though, a method must also access the instance variables of the object on which it is called; the identity of the object is not known at compile time. However, the structure of such an object is known (it depends on the class) and, therefore, the offset of every instance variable in an object's representation is statically known (subject to conditions depending upon the language). A pointer to the object which received the method is also passed as a parameter when a method is invoked. During execution of the body of the method, this pointer is the method's `this`. When the method is invoked on the same object that invokes it, `this` still is passed as a parameter. During the execution of the method, every access to an instance variable uses the offset from this pointer (instead of having an offset from a pointer into the activation records, as is the case for local variables of functions). From a logical point of view, we can assume that the `this` pointer is passed through the activation record typically with all other parameters, but this would cause a doubly-indirect access for every instance variable (one to access the pointer using the activation record pointer and one to access the variable using this). More efficiently, the abstract machine will maintain the current value of `this` in a register.

10.3.1 Single Inheritance

Under the hypothesis that the language have a static type system, the implementation using linked lists can be replaced by another, more efficient one, in which method selection requires constant time (rather than time linear in the depth of the class hierarchy).

If types are static, the set of methods that any object can invoke is known at compile time. The list of these methods is kept in the class descriptor. The list contains not just the methods that are explicitly defined or redefined in the class but also all the methods inherited from its superclasses.[14] Following C++'s terminology, we will use the term *vtable* (*virtual function table*) to refer to this data structure. Each class definition has its own vtable and all instances of the same class share the same vtable. When a subclass, B, of the class A is defined, B's vtable is generated by copying the one for A, replacing all the methods redefined in B and adding the new methods that B defines at the bottom (this is shown in Fig. 10.7).

The fundamental property of this data structure is, that, if B is a subclass of A, B's vtable contains a copy of A's vtable as its initial part; redefined methods are appropriately modified. In this way, the method invocation costs only two indirect accesses, the offset of every method in the vtable being statically known. It can be

---

[14]We are assuming that dynamic lookup applies to all methods. In cases like C++, where only virtual methods can be redefined, the descriptor contains only the latter, while ordinary method calls are treated like normal function calls.

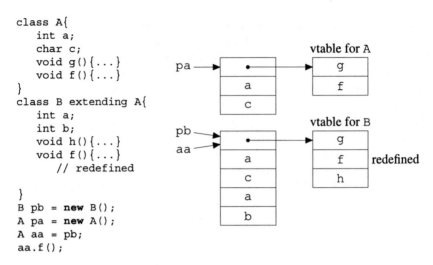

```
class A{
    int a;
    char c;
    void g(){...}
    void f(){...}
}
class B extending A{
    int a;
    int b;
    void h(){...}
    void f(){...}
        // redefined

}
B pb = new B();
A pa = new A();
A aa = pb;
aa.f();
```

Fig. 10.7 Implementation of simple inheritance

seen that this implementation obviously takes into account the fact that it is possible to access an object with a reference that belongs statically to one of its superclasses. In the example in Fig. 10.7, when method f is invoked, the compiler computes an offset that remains the same whether f is invoked on an object of class A or on an object of class B. Different implementations of f defined in the two classes are located at the same offset into the vtables of A and B.

On the whole, if we have a static reference pa of class A to some object of one of its subclasses, we can compile a call to method f (which, we assume to be the nth in A's vtable) as follows (we have assumed that the address of a method occupies w bytes):

```
R1 := pa                    // access the object
R2 := *(R1)                 // vtable
R3 := *(R2 + (n − 1) × w)   // indirect to f
call *(R3)                  // call f
```

Ignoring support for multiple inheritance, this implementation scheme is almost the same as used in C++.

Downcasting   If a class' vtable also contains the name of the class itself, the implementation we have discussed allows downward casts in the class hierarchy. This is called *downcasting* and is a fairly frequently used mechanism. It permits the specialisation of the type of object by running in the opposite direction to the subtype hierarchy. A canonical example of the use of this mechanism is found in some library methods which are defined to be as general as possible. The class Object might use the following signature to define a method for copying objects:

```
Object clone(){...}
```

The semantics is that `clone` returns an exact copy of the object which invoked it (same class, same values in its fields, etc.). If we have an object o of class A, an invocation of `o.clone()` will return an instance of A, but the static type as determined by the compiler for this expression is `Object`. In order to be able meaningfully to use this new copy, we have to "force" it to type A, which we can indicate with a cast:

```
A a = (A) o.clone();
```

By this, we mean that the abstract machine checks that the dynamic type of the object really is A (in the opposite case, we would have a runtime type error).[15]

10.3.2 The Problem of Fragile Base Class

In the case of simple inheritance, the implementation of the mechanism described above is reasonably efficient, given that all the important information, except the `this` pointer is statically determined. This staticity, though, can be shown to be the source of problems in a context known as the *fragile base class problem*.

An object-oriented system is organised in terms of a very large number of classes using an elaborate inheritance hierarchy. Often some of these general classes are provided by libraries. Modifications to a class located very high in the hierarchy, can be felt in its subclasses. Some superclasses can, therefore, behave in a "fragile" manner because an apparently innocuous modification to the superclass can cause the malfunctioning of subclasses. It is not possible to identify fragility by analysing only the superclass. It is necessary to consider the entire inheritance hierarchy, something which is often impossible because whoever wrote the superclass generally does not have access to all subclasses. The problem can arise for a number of reasons. Here, we will only distinguish two main cases:

- The problem is architectural. Some subclass exploit aspects of the superclass' implementation which have been modified in the new version. This is an extremely important problem for software engineering. It can be limited by reducing the inheritance relation in favour of the subtype relation.
- The problem is implementational. The malfunctioning of the subclass depends *only* on how the abstract machine (and the compiler) has represented inheritance. This case is sometimes referred to as the problem of *fragile binary interface*.

In this text, the first case is not our main interest; the second is. A typical case shows up in the context of separate compilation where a method is added to a superclass, even if the new method interacts with nothing else. Starting from the following:

---

[15]This is Java notation. C++ allows the same notation to be used but, for compatibility with C, it accepts the expression at compile time without introducing dynamic checks. A cast with dynamic checks would be written `dynamic_cast<A*>(o)` in C++.

```
class Upper{
    int x;
    int f(){..}
}
class Lower extending Upper{
    int y;
    int g(){return y + f();}
}
```

the super class is modified as:

```
class Upper{
    int x;
    int h(){return x;}
    int f(){..}
}
```

If inheritance is implemented as described in Sect. 10.3.2, the subclass `Lower` (which is already compiled and linked to `Super`) ceases to function correctly because the offset used to access to method `f` has been changed, since it is determined statically. To solve this problem it is necessary to recompile all the subclasses of the modified classes, a solution which is not always easy to perform.

To obviate this question, it is necessary to compute dynamically the offset of methods in the vtable (and also the offset of instance variables in the representation of objects), in some reasonably efficient manner. The next section describes one possible solution.

10.3.3 Dynamic Method Dispatch in the JVM

In this section we present a simple description of the technique used by the Java virtual machine (JVM), the abstract machine which interprets the intermediate (byte-code) language generated by the standard Java compiler. For reasons of space, we cannot go into the details of the JVM's architecture; we note that it is a stack-based machine (it does not have user-accessible registers and all operation operands are passed on a stack contained in the activation record of the function that is currently being executed). The JVM has modules for checking operation security. We limit ourselves to discussing the broad outlines of the implementation of inheritance and method dispatching.

In Java, the compilation of each class produces a file which the abstract machine loads dynamically when the currently executing program refers to the class. This file containing a table (the *constant pool*) for symbols used in the class itself. The constant pool contains entries for instance variables, public and private methods, methods and fields of other classes used in the body of methods, names of other classes mentioned in the body of the class etc. With each instance variable and method name is recorded information such as the class where the names are

defined and their type. Every time that the source code uses the name, the intermediate code of the JVM looks up the index of that name in the constant pool (to save
space—it does not look up the name itself). When, during execution, reference is
made to a name for the first time (using its index), it is *resolved* using the information in the constant pool, the necessary classes (for example the one in which the
names are introduced) are loaded, visibility checks are performed (for example the
invoked method must really exist in the class referring to it, is not a private, etc.);
type checks are also performed. At this point, the abstract machines saves a pointer
to this information so that the next time the same name is used, it is not necessary
to perform resolution a second time.

The representation of methods in a class descriptor can be thought of as being
analogous to that in the vtable.[16] The table for a subclass starts with a copy of the
one for its superclass, where redefined methods have their new definitions instead
of the old ones. Offsets, however, are not statically calculated. When a method is
to be executed, four main cases can be distinguished (which correspond for distinct
bytecode instructions):

1. The method is static. This is for a method associated with a class and not an
   instance. No reference (explicit or implicit) can be made to this.
2. The method must be dispatched dynamically (a "virtual" method).
3. The method must be dispatched dynamically and is invoked using this (a "special" method).
4. The method comes from an interface (that is from a completely abstract class
   which provides no implementation—an "interface" method).

Ignoring the last case for the moment, the 3 other cases can be distinguished primarily by the parameters passed to the method. In the first case, only the parameters
named in the call are passed. In the second case, a reference is passed to the object
on which the method is called. In case 3, a reference to this is passed. Let us
therefore assume that we can invoke method m on object o as:

```
o.m(parameter)
```

Using the reference to o, the abstract machine accesses the constant pool of its
class and extracts the *name* of m. At this point, it looks up this name in the class'
vtable and determines its offset. The offset is saved in case of a future use of the
same method on the same object.

However the same method could also be invoked on other objects, possibly belonging to subclasses of the one which o belongs to (e.g., a for loop in whose body
a call to m is repeated on all the objects in an array). To avoid calculating the offset
each time (which would be the same independent of the effective class of which the

---

[16]In reality, the specification of the JVM does not prescribe any particular representation and limits
itself to requiring that the search for the method to be executed is semantically equivalent to the
dynamic search for the method name in the list of subclasses described above. The most common
implementation, however, is of a table that is very similar to the vtable.

method m is called on is an instance), the JVM interpreter uses a "code rewrite" technique. It substitutes for the standard lookup instruction generated by the compiler an optimised form which takes as its argument the offset of the method in the vtable. In order to fix ideas (and simplifying a great deal), when translating the invocation of a virtual method m, the compiler might generate the byte code instruction:

```
invokevirtual index
```

where index is the index of the name m in the constant pool. During execution of this instruction, the JVM interpreter calculates the offset d of m in its vtable and *replaces* the instruction above with the following:

```
invokevirtual_quick d np
```

Here, np is the number of the parameters that m expects (and which will be found on the stack that is part of its activation record). Every time that the flow of control returns to this instruction, m is invoked without overhead.

There remains the case of the invocation of an interface method (that is, case 4 above). In this case, the offset might not be the same in 2 invocations of the same method on objects in different classes. Consider the following situation (in which we use Java syntax rather than pseudocode):

```java
interface Interface{
    void foo();
}
public class A implements Interface{
    int x;
    void foo(){...}
}
public class B implements Interface{
    int y;
    int fie(){...}
    int foo(){...}
}
```

Both A and B implement Interface and therefore are its subtypes. The offset of *foo* is different in the two classes, though. Consider our usual loop:

```java
Interface V[10];
...
for (int i = 0; i<10; i=i+1)
    V[i].foo();
```

At runtime, we do not know whether the objects contained in V will be instances of A, B or some other class which implements Interface. The compiler could have generated the JVM instruction for the body of loop:

```
invokeinterface index, 0
```

(the 0 serves to fill a byte that will be used in the "quick" version). It would not be correct directly to replace this instruction by a "quick" version which returns only the offset because changing the object could also change the class of which it is an instance. What we can do is to save the offset but we cannot destroy the original name of the method; we thus rewrite the instruction as:

```
invokeinterface_quick nome_di_foo, d
```

Here `name_of_foo` is suitable information with which to reconstruct the name and the signature of `foo`; d is the offset determined beforehand. When this instruction is executed again, the interpreter accesses the vtable using the offset d and checks that there is a method with the requested name and signature. In the positive case, it is invoked; in the negative case, it searches for the method by name in the vtable, as it would were this the first time it had been seen, and determines a new offset d', then writes this value in the code in place of d.

10.3.4 Multiple Inheritance

The implementation of multiple inheritance poses interesting problems and imposes a non-negligible overhead. The problems are of 2 orders: on the one hand, there is the problem of identifying how it is possible to adapt the vtable technique to handle method calls; on the other (and the problem is more interesting and also has an impact on the language) there is the need to determine what to do with the data present in the superclasses. This will lead to 2 different interpretations of multiple inheritance, which we can refer to as replicated and shared inheritance. We will take these problems successively.

Vtable Structure   We will consider the example in Fig. 10.8. It is clear that is not possible to organise the representation of an instance of C, nor a vtable for C in such a way that the initial part coincides with the corresponding structure in both A and B.

In order to represent an instance of C, we may begin with the fields of A and add then the fields of B. Finally, we need to list the fields specific to C (Fig. 10.9). We know that, using the subtype relation, we can access an instance of C using a static reference to any of the three types A, B and C. There are 2 distinct cases corresponding to the 2 different views of an instance of C. If it is an access with a static reference of type C or of type A, the technique described for simple inheritance works perfectly (except that the static offsets of the real instance variables in C must take into account the fact that the static variables belonging to B are in the middle).

When, on the other hand, an instance of C is seen as an object of B, it is necessary to take into account the fact that the variables of B are not at the start of the record but at a distance, d, from its start that is statically determined. When, therefore, we access an instance of C through a reference with static type B, it is necessary to add the constant, d, to the reference.

Fig. 10.8 An example of
multiple inheritance

```
class A{
    int x;
    int f(){
        return x;
    }
}
class B{
    int y;
    int g(){
        return y;
    }
    int h(){
        return 2*y;
    }
}
class C extending A,B{
    int z;
    int g(){
        return x + y + z;
    }
    int k(){
        return z;
    }
}
```

Similar problems arise for the structure of the vtable. A vtable for C is divided into two distinct parts: the first contains the methods of A (possibly as redefinitions) and the methods really belonging to C. A second part comprises the methods of B, possibly with their redefinitions. In the representation of an instance object of C, there are two pointers to the vtable. Corresponding to the "view as A and C", it will have pointers to the vtable with methods from A and C. Corresponding to the "view as B", it will have pointers to the vtable with the methods of B (note that this is a vtable for class C; the class B has *another* vtable, which is used for its own instances. In general, every superclass of a class under multiple inheritance has its own special part in the vtables of its subclasses). Invocation of a method belonging to C, or which was redefined or inherited from A, follows the same rules as simple inheritance. To invoke a method inherited (or redefined) from B, the compiler must take into account that the pointer to the vtable for this method does not reside at the beginning of the object but is displaced by d positions. In the example in the figure, to call the method h of an instance of C seen as an object of type B (of which we have therefore a static name, pb): add d to the reference pb; using an indirect access, obtain the address of the start of the second vtable (that for B), then using the appropriate static offset invoke method h. This call needs one additional operation (the first add) in addition to that required for simple inheritance.

We have, however, neglected the binding for this. Which current-object reference should we pass to the methods of C? If we are dealing with methods in the first vtable (to which access is performed using a this which points to the start of the object, that is with the "A and B view"), it is necessary to pass the current value of this. This would be wrong for methods in the second vtable (to which

Fig. 10.9 Representation of objects and vtables for multiple inheritance

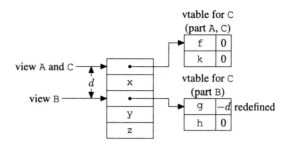

access is performed using the pointer to `this` plus the offset d), however. We must distinguish two cases:

- The method is inherited from B (the case of h in the figure). In such a case, it is necessary to pass the view of the object through which we have found vtable.
- The method is redefined in C (the case with g). In this case, the method might refer to instance variables of A, and so it is necessary to pass it a view of the superclass.

The situation is awkward because dynamic method lookup requires that this correction of the value of `this` is done at runtime. The simplest solution is to store this correction in the vtable, together with the name of the method. When the method is invoked, this correction will be added to the current value of `this`. In our example, the corrections are shown in Fig. 10.9 next to the name of the associated method. The correction is added to the view of the object through which the vtable was found.

Overall, if we have a reference, pa, to a view of class C of some object, we can compile a call to method h (which we can assume to be the nth in the vtable of B) as follows (the address of a method and the correction each occupy w bytes):

```
R1  := pa                            // view A
R1  := R1 + d                        // view B
R2  := *(R1)                         // vtable for B
R3  := *(R2 + (n − 1) × 2 × w)       // address of h
R2  := *(R2 + (n − 1) × 2 × w + w)   // correction
this := R1 + R2
call *(R3)                           // call h
```

We have three instructions and an indirect access in addition to the sequence for calling a method using single inheritance.

Replicated multiple inheritance The preceding subsection has dealt with the case in which a class inherits from 2 superclasses. These superclasses, however, can themselves inherit from a common superclass, producing a diamond, as we discussed in Sect. 10.2.5:

```
class Top{
    int w;
    int f(){
        return w;
    }
}
class A extending Top{
    int x;
    int g(){
        return w+x;
    }
}
class B extending Top{
    int y;
    int f(){
        return w+y;
    }
    int k(){
        return y;
    }
}
class Bottom extending A,B{
    int z;
    int h(){
        return z;
    }
}
```

The instances and the vtable for A have a initial part that is a copy of the structure corresponding to Top. The same is the case for instances and the replicated vtable for B. Under replicated multiple inheritance, Bottom is constructed using to the approach we have already discussed, and therefore consists of two copies of the instance variables and methods of Top, as shown in Fig. 10.10.

The implementation does not pose other problems in addition to those already discussed. Name conflicts must be resolved explicitly (in particular it will not be possible to invoke the method f of Top on an object of class Bottom, nor assign an instance of Bottom to a static reference of type Top, because we would not know which of the two copies of Top to choose).

Shared multiple inheritance Replicated multiple inheritance is not always the conceptual solution which a software engineer has in mind when designing a diamond situation. When the class at the bottom of the diagram contains a single copy of the class at the top, we speak of replicated multiple inheritance. In such a case both A and B possess their own copy of Top, but Bottom has only one copy of it.

C++ allows shared inheritance using *virtual* base classes. When a class is defined as virtual, all of its subclasses always contain of a single copy of it, even if there is more than one inheritance path, as there is in the case of the diamond. With this mechanism, a class is declared virtual or nonvirtual once and for all. If we have a non-virtual class and, later, we discover that we require inheritance with sharing,

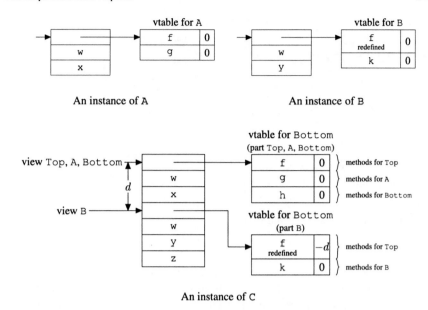

Fig. 10.10 Implementation of replicated multiple inheritance

there is nothing else to do but to rewrite the class and recompile the entire system. Worse, a class is virtual for all its subclasses, even if in some cases we wish that it were virtual for some and nonvirtual (that is replicated) for others. In such cases, it is necessary to define two copies of the class, one virtual and the other non virtual.

With inheritance with sharing there is usually a name-conflict problem. The problem is solved in arbitrary ways by different languages. In C++, for example, in the case of a virtual base class method that is redefined in a subclass, it is required that there is always a redefinition that dominates all the others in the sense that it appears in a class that is a subclass of all the other classes where this method is defined. In our example, for method f, the dominant redefinition is the one in class B. It is therefore the one inherited by Bottom. If both of the classes A and B redefine f, the definitions of these classes would be illegal in C++ because there would not be a dominant redefinition. Other languages allow inheriting classes to choose along which path the method is to be inherited; alternatively, they permit a complete qualification of names so as explicitly to choose the desired method. As usual, when dealing with multiple inheritance, there is no elegant solution that is clearly better than any other.

We now come to the implementation of the vtable for shared multiple inheritance. In Fig. 10.11, the implementation used in C++ is depicted schematically. C++ is a language in which a virtual class is shared by all of its subclasses. Since Bottom contains a single copy of Top, it is no longer possible to represent sub- and super-class in a contiguous way. To each class in the diamond there corresponds a specific view of the object. Corresponding to each view, there is both a pointer to the corresponding vtable, and a pointer to the shared part of the object. Access to instance

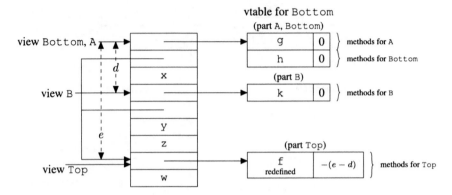

Fig. 10.11 Implementation of multiple inheritance with sharing

variables and methods of Bottom, A and B is the same as in the case of multiple inheritance without sharing. To access instance variables, or to invoke a method of Top, a preliminary indirect access instead is required (let us assume that f is the nth method of the vtable for Top and every address is w bytes wide):

```
R1  := pa                           // view Bottom
R1  := *(R1 + w)                    // view Top
R2  := *(R1)                        // vtable for Top
R3  := *(R2 + (n − 1) × 2 × w)      // address of f
R2  := *(R2 + (n − 1) × 2 × w + w)  // correction
this := R1 + R2
call *(R3)                          // call h
```

The value necessary to correct the value of this is the difference between the view of the class in which the method is declared and the view of the class in which it is redefined.

Languages which allow more elaborate situations (for example, a single super-class is replicated in some classes and shared in others) require more sophisticated techniques that we cannot explain in this book.

10.4 Polymorphism and Generics

Having studied the characteristic aspects of the object-oriented paradigm and its associated implementations, in this section we will discuss the concept of subtype, in particular the relations between polymorphism and generics. We will begin the discussion in a general fashion; later, we will go into detail on generics in Java (which supports them in a very flexible manner).

10.4.1 Subtype Polymorphism

We introduced the concept of polymorphism in Sect. 8.8, where we also distinguished between two radically different forms of it: overloading (or *ad hoc* polymorphism) and universal polymorphism (where a single value has an infinite number of different types obtained by instantiating a general type scheme). We have also seen the concept of subtype polymorphism: a value exhibits subtype polymorphism when it has an infinite number of different types which are obtained by instantiating a general type scheme, substituting for some parameter the subtypes of an assigned type.

When a language has a structural notion of compatibility between types, as a relationship of some kind between classes, it is clear that there is a form of polymorphism, even though it is not as completely general as universal parametric polymorphism. For the subtype relation, each instance of a class A has, as type, all the superclasses of A. This property is particularly interesting in the case of methods. Let us consider a method (for simplicity we will restrict the discussion to a method with a single argument):

```
B foo(A x){...}
```

By virtue of subtype compatibility, `foo` can receive as an argument a value of *any subclass of* A. The code for `foo` does not need to be adapted to specific subclasses. The structure of classes (and the associated implementations) ensure that an operation that can be performed on values of type A can also be performed on values of its subclasses. The reader will certainly recognize polymorphism here. We are dealing with subtype polymorphism because it is not completely general but is *limited to subtypes of* A.

Using the symbol "<:" (introduced in Sect. 8.8) to denote the subtype relation, we can read C<:D as "C sub D" (C is a subtype of D). We also use the concept of universal quantification introduced in the box on page 239. With these notations, we can write the type of method `foo` as:

```
∀T<:A.T->B
```

which expresses the fact that this method can be applied to a value of any subclass whatsoever of A. This is a form of implicit subtype polymorphism because instantiation occurs automatically when the method is applied to a value of the subclass.

In reality, the notation that we are using is much more expressive than the pseudolanguage that we have used so far. Let us consider a very simple method that returns its argument, of class A:

```
A Ide(A x){return x;}
```

From the semantic viewpoint, we can say that `Ide` has the type:

```
∀T<:A.T->T
```

Fig. 10.12 Stack class based
on Object

```
class Elem{
    Object info;
    Elem prox;
}
class Stack{
    private Elem top = null; // empty stack
    boolean isEmpty(){
        return top==null;
    }
    void push (Object o){
        Elem ne = new Elem();
        ne.info = o;
        ne.prox = top;
        top = ne;
    }
    Object pop() {
        Object tmp = top.info;
        top = top.prox;
        return tmp;
    }
}
```

because it returns unaltered the object passed as its argument. However, assuming that C<:A and that c is an instance of C, the following assignment would be rejected by a *static* type checker:

```
C cc = Ide(c);
```

notwithstanding the fact that it is perfectly sensible from a semantic viewpoint. The point is that common languages have a type system that is incapable of recognizing that ∀T<:A.T->T is a correct typing for Ide (as the ML typing system would do, see box on page 243), nor do they have a linguistic mechanism with which the programmer can express that the result type of a method *depends on the argument type*. However, this argument guarantees that the dynamic correction of a downcast:

```
C cc = (C) Ide(c);
```

will never cause runtime type errors.

The notation that we have used for types, in summary, allows us to express relationships between the type of the argument and the result type which are not possible in our pseudo-language (nor in the fragment of C++ or Java that we have analysed so far).

Before looking at a way in which the language can be extended, we give another, more meaningful, example of this limited form of polymorphism which it is possible through the tools we have developed so far. We want to implement a stack of elements represented as a linked list of elements. We do not immediately wish to fix the type of the objects that will appear in the list, so we declare them to be of type Object. Figure 10.12 shows one possible definition for a Stack class which contains generic elements. What interests us is that the `pop` method returns an Ob-ject (and can do nothing else, given that we have not made any assumptions about the type of the stack's elements). Now we can use our stack, but we must exercise some care. Let `C` be any class:

```
C c;
Stack s = new Stack();
s.push(new C());
c = s.pop();              // type error
```

The last line is incorrect because we are seeking to assign an `Object` to a vari-able of type `C`. It is it is necessary to force the assignment with a (dynamically checked) cast:

```
c = (C) s.pop();          // dynamic check
```

After these examples, we may recall what we said in Sect. 8.2.1: languages usu-ally impose restrictions on the types which are stricter than those which are seman-tically reasonable, so that they can guarantee efficient static checking. The next sec-tion, however, will discuss language extensions which allow more powerful *explicit* subtype polymorphism.

10.4.2 Generics in Java

In Sect. 8.7, we discussed the concept of the C++ *template*. A program fragment where some types are indicated by *parameters*, which can then be appropriately in-stantiated by "concrete" types. This leads to an interesting form of polymorphism. Java introduces a similar concept (but with very different potential and implementa-tion), giving it the name *generic*. This Java construct will be presented in this section with the objective of discussing its relationship with subtyping.

In Java, type definitions can be generic (that is, classes and interfaces can be generic), as well as methods. The syntax used is similar to that in C++ and uses angle brackets to denote parameters. Figure 10.13 shows the generic version of Fig. 10.12. The type `<A>` is the *formal type parameter* of the generic declaration and will have to be a instantiated later. A specific version of `Stack` is obtained by specifying which types must be substituted for `A`. For example stacks of strings or integers (`Integer` is a class which allows us to see an integer as an object and is different from the type `int`, which is formed of ordinary integers):

```
Stack<String> ss = new Stack<String>();
Stack<Integer> si = new Stack<Integer>();
```

```
class Elem<A>{
   A info;
   Elem<A> prox;
}
class Stack<A>{
   private Elem<A> top = null; // empty stack
   boolean isEmpty(){
      return top==null;
   }
   void push (A o){
      Elem<A> ne = new Elem<A>();
      ne.info = o;
      ne.prox = top;
      top = ne;
   }
   A pop() {
      A tmp = top.info;
      top = top.prox;
      return tmp;
   }
}
```

Fig. 10.13 Classes for a generic stack

Fig. 10.14 Generic pairs

```
class Pair<A,B>{
   private A a;
   private B b;
   Pair(A x, B y){    // constructor
      a=x; b=y;
      }
   A First(){
      return a;
      }
   B Second(){
      return b;
      }
}
```

The types which are supplied as the actual parameters must be class or array types.[17] The dynamic cast which had to be added in the non-generic version is now no longer necessary:

```
Stack<String> ss = new Stack<String>();
ss.push(new String("pippo"));
String s = ss.pop();
```

Figure 10.14 shows another simple example, this time of pairs of elements of any two types. A pair can obviously be instantiated by specific types:

---

[17]They must be reference types for implementation reasons that we have indicated on page 242.

```
Integer i = new Integer(3);
String v = new String ("pippo");
Pair<Integer,String> c = new Pair<Integer,String>(3,v);
String w = c.Second();
```

Methods too can be generic. Let us assume, for example, that we wanted to define
a method for constructing diagonal pairs (that is with two identical components).
A first attempt might be one using the subtype polymorphism already present in the
language, so we define:

```
Pair<Object,Object> diagonal(Object x){
    return new Pair<Object,Object>(x,x);
}
```

However, in a way similar to the pop method above, if we apply diagonal to
a string, the result is just a pair of Objects and not Strings:

```
Pair<Object,Object> co = diagonal(v);
Pair<String,String> cs = diagonal(v); // compilation error
```

It is necessary to parameterise the definition of diagonal, in particular the type
of its result, as a function of the type of the argument:

```
<T> Pair<T,T> diagonal(T x){
    return new Pair<T,T>(x,x);
    }
```

The first pair of angle brackets introduces a type variable, the (formal) parameter to
be used in the definition of the method. The reader will have recognized that <T>
is a universal quantifier written using a different notation. The definition states that
diagonal has type:

$\forall$ T.T->Coppia<T,T>.

Our diagonal can also be used without explicit instantiation:

```
Pair<Integer,Integer> ci = diagonal(new Integer(4));
Pair<String,String> cs = diagonal(new String("pippo"));
```

The compiler performs a genuine type inference (Sect. 8.8), in general more complex than the elementary one required in the example. In our case, it determines that
in the first call T must be replaced by Integer, while in the second, by String.

A very important aspect of the type parameters (either in the type or method
definition) is that they can have *bounds*. That is, they can specify that only a subtype
of some classes is permitted. Let us illustrate this feature using an example.

Assume we have available an interface for geometric shapes which can be drawn.
Then we have different specific classes which implements it:

```
interface Shape{
    void draw();
}
class Circle implements Shape{
    . . .
    public void draw(){....}
}
class Rhombus implements Shape{
    . . .
    public void draw(){....}
}
```

Let us now make use of a standard Java library (java.util). We have a list of shapes, that is objects of type List<Shape> and want to invoke the design method on each element of the list. The first idea will be to write[18]

```
void drawAll(List<Shape> forms){
    for(Shape f : forms)
        f.draw();
}
```

The definition is correct, but the method can be applied only to arguments which are of type List<Shape> (and not, for example, to List<Rhombus>). The reason is that the type List<Rhombus> is *not* a subtype of List<Shape>, for reasons that we will discuss shortly in Sect. 10.4.4.[19]

To obviate the problem, we can make the definition of the drawAll method parametric. Clearly, we cannot allow as arguments an arbitrary list because it must have to be composed of elements on which to call the draw method. The language allows us to specify this fact in the following way:

```
<T extends Shape> void drawAll(List<T> forms){
    for(Shape f : forms)
        f.draw();
    }
```

In this case, the formal type parameter is not an arbitrary type, but a type which extends Shape (here "extends" is used as a synonym of "is a subtype of"; by this, Shape extends itself). Using our notation of universal quantification, the type of drawAll becomes:

$\forall$ T<:Shape.List<T> -> **void**

---

[18] The body the method is an example of a *for-each* (see Sect. 6.3.3), an iterative construct which applies the body to all elements of the collection (list, array, etc.). In this case, for every f, in forms, it calls the method draw.

[19] For the moment, the reader must content themselves by knowing that, if A<:B and Def-Para<T> is any parametric type definition (like List<T>), DefPara<A> and DefPara<B> are unrelated in the subtype hierarchy.

Now `drawAll` can be called on a list whose elements belong to any subtype of Shape (Shape is obviously a subtype of itself):

```
List<Rhombus> lr = ...;
List<Shape> lf = ...;
drawAll(lr);
drawAll(lf);
```

The bound mechanism for type variables is fairly sophisticated and flexible. In particular, a type variable can appear in its own bound. We restrict ourselves to a single example of this case, and we refer the reader to the bibliography for a deeper discussion.[20]

The elements of a class are comparable if the class implements the Comparable interface. We want to define a method which, given a list of elements of generic type as its argument, returns the maximum element of this list. What is the signature we can give to this max method? A first attempt is:

```
public static <T extends Comparable<T>>
    T max(List<T> list)
```

This expresses the fact that the elements of the list must be comparable with elements of the same type. We now try to use max. We have a type Foo which allows us to compare objects:

```
class Foo implements Comparable<Object>{...}
List<Foo> cf = ....;
```

We now invoke max(cf): each element in cf (is a Foo and therefore) is comparable with any object, in particular with every Foo. But the compiler signals an error, because Foo does not implement Comparable<Foo>. In reality it is sufficient that Foo is comparable with one of its own supertypes:

```
public static <T extends Comparable<? super T>>
    T max(List<T> list)
```

Now, under the same conditions as before, Max(cf) is correct because Foo implements Comparable<Object>.

10.4.3 Implementation of Generics in Java

Unlike templates in C++, which are resolved at link time using code duplication and specialisation, Java generics always exist in a single copy. In this way, the idea

---

[20]The possibility that a type variable appears in its own bound is known in the literature as *F-bounded* polymorphism and is used in particular for typing *binary* methods, that is methods which have a parameter of the same type as the object which receives the method.

Wildcard

The `drawAll` method could be written in a more compact and elegant way using *wildcards*. The "?" character (which is read "unknown") stands for any type and can be used in generic definitions. For example, a value of type `List<?>` is a list of elements whose type is unknown. It might be thought that writing `List<?>` is the same thing as writing `List<Object>` but this is not the case because `List<Object>` is not a supertype, for example, of `List<Integer>`, while `List<?>` is really the supertype of all types `List<A>` for all A.

Using wildcards, the method `drawAll` could be written:

```
void drawAll(List<? extends Shape> forms){
   for(Shape f : forms)
      f.draw();
   }
```

In general, every wildcard can be always replaced by an explicit parameter. From the pragmatic viewpoint, for code clarity, a wildcard will be used where the parameter would be used only once (as in the case of `drawAll`), while an explicit parameter should be used when the type variable is used more than once (as in the case of `diagonal`, where the variable is used in the method's *result* type).

If two wildcards appear in the same construct, they must be considered distinct variables.

in parametric polymorphism that there exists a single value (a single class, a single method, etc.) which belongs to many different types (and, in the case of methods, works uniformly on different types) is respected by the implementation.

Generics are implemented by the compiler using an *erasure* mechanism. A program which contains generics is first subjected to type checking. When this static semantic checking has determined that everything is correct, the original program is transformed into a similar one in which all generics have been removed. All the information between angle brackets is eliminated (for example, every `List<Integer>` becomes `List`). All the other uses of type variables are replaced by the upper limit of the same variable (in general, this means `Object`). In the end, if, after these transformations, the cancelled program is incorrect with respect to types, appropriate (dynamic) casts are inserted. With this procedure, the use of generics does not worsen the code (in the majority of cases), either in terms of size or execution time. Perhaps more important are the other two consequences of this implementation:

- The underlying abstract machine (the JVM) requires no modification. The addition of generics does not imply modifications that need to be implemented on different architectures, but is localised to the compiler.
- It is possible to mix generic and non-generic code in a relatively simple way and, above all, in a way that is safe. Possible holes in the static type system that might

be locally produced by the simultaneous use of generic and non-generic code will be detected at runtime by the effect of the dynamic casts inserted by the compiler during the erasure process.

10.4.4 Generics, Arrays and Subtype Hierarchy

We have already observed that in Java, a generic type definition DefPara<T> does *not* preserve the subtype hierarchy. For any 2 types A and B, with A<:B, Def-Para<A> and DefPara<B> are not related in the subtype hierarchy. We want now to clarify some of the reasons for this choice and we will consider the contrasting behaviour that Java exhibits for arrays: if A<:B, A[] *is* a subtype of B[]! After all, arrays are a primitive form of generic construct (the unique construct "array" is specialised to arrays of specific type). Why do the 2 mechanisms behave in such different ways?

We begin by discussing why generic definitions do not preserve subtypes. Let us consider the following fragment which uses the generic definitions from Fig. 10.13:

```
Stack<Integer> si = new Stack<Integer>();
Stack<Object> so = si;                        // Incorrect in  Java
```

Let us assume, contrary to the facts, that generic definitions preserve types, that is that Stack<Integer> <: Stack<Object>. The second line of the fragment is now legal. We have two different references (and of different types) to a single stack (integers). Let us continue our code:

```
so.push(new String("pluto"));
Integer i = si.pop();                         // danger!
```

Under these hypotheses, both lines are type correct. Since so is a stack of Object, we can store any object at all in it, for example a string. On the other hand, since si is a stack of integers, by randomly selecting an element, an integer is obtained. But this amounts to a clear violation of type security. Since the source of the problem is that Stack<Integer> <: Stack<Object>, it is just this relation that must be abandoned. The type Stack<Object> is therefore not the common supertype of all specific stacks Stack<A>. On the other hand, the pragmatics suggests that such a supertype must exist in the language, because otherwise too many programming examples would be difficult, if not impossible, to write. It is for this reason that the wildcard ("?") was introduced. Stack<?> *is* the supertype of every specific stack.

The intuitive idea that A <: B implies that DefPara<A> <: DefPara<B> is erroneous because it does not take into account the fact that collections can change in time. Once a Stack<Integer> has become a Stack<Object>, it is no longer possible to check statically that its modifications are consistent with its original structure.

Co- and Contravariant Functions

Let D be a set on which a pre-order, written as $\leq$ (recall the box on page 231), is defined. A function $f : D \to D$ is *covariant* when f respects the pre-order, that is $x \leq y$ implies that $f(x) \leq f(y)$. A function is *contravariant*, whenever the pre-order is reversed, that is $x \leq y$ implies $f(x) \geq f(y)$.

If the relation is a partial order, the most common terminology in mathematics is that of a monotone increasing function (for covariant) and anti-monotone, or monotone decreasing (for contravariant). In the context of types and subtypes, the covariant-contravariant terminology is always used (it is taken from category theory).

Now we come to the problem of arrays. If we substitute arrays for stacks in our fragment of a few paragraphs ago, we obtain, *mutatis mutandis*:

```
Integer[] ai = new Integer[10];
Object[] ao = ai;              // correct: Integer[] <: Object[]
ao[0] = new String("pluto");   // correct; error at runtime
```

The fragment is statically correct, because arrays in Java preserve subtypes (technically, it is said that they are a *covariant* construct), but the compiler, in order to guarantee type security, is forced to insert dynamic type checks in cases like the last line which, in the example, will cause a runtime error because we are trying to store a string in a variable of type `Integer`.

Why then add covariant arrays to the language if they impose dynamic checks which, however, remain counterintuitive in the light of the non-covariance of generics? The point is that covariant arrays allow some limited form of polymorphism. Let us consider, for example, the problem of exchanging the first 2 elements of an arbitrary array. A possible solution is:

```
public swap(Object[] vect){
   if (vect.length > 1){
           Object temp = vect[0];
           vect[0] = vect[1];
           vect[1] = temp;
   }
}
```

The method `swap` can be called on an arbitrary arrays because of its covariance.

Covariant arrays were present in Java since the earliest days of the project, well before designers considered the problem of generics. In retrospect however, in the light of the introduction of generics, covariant arrays must be considered one of the less successful aspects of the Java project.

10.4.5 Covariant and Contravariant Overriding

Let us conclude the study of the subtype relation by discussing the types permitted
in the redefinition of methods. Java and C++ require that, when we have redefinition,
the arguments to the redefined method must be the same as those in the one being
redefined. Let us take up again our pseudo-language and let C be a fixed type. Given
a class such as:

```
class F{
    C fie (A p) {...}
}
```

a subclass of F can redefine (overwrite) `fie` only with a method which takes as its
argument an A. If the types are different, as for example in:

```
class G extending F{
    C fie (B p) {...}
}
```

we do not have redefinition, but only the definition of 2 overloaded methods.

The same does not happen to the *result* type of the method. Both C++ and Java[21]
allow the type of the result of the method redefined in subclass to be a subtype of the
corresponding type in the superclass. Let us assume that D is a subtype of C ($D <: C$):

```
class E extending F{
    D fie (A p) {...}
}
```

In E (which is a subtype of F: $E <: F$) the method `fie` is redefined with respect
to F. The reader will have no difficulty convincing themselves on their own that
this extension is semantically legitimate and not the cause of type errors. We can
however help in this argument with some general considerations.

Supertypes and Views In a language with subtype polymorphism, a type of an
object can be interpreted as a particular *view* of the object, or, in a more colourful
way, as a disguise for the object. Figure 10.15 represents this idea graphically in the
case of two types $G <: F$ (F is a class of objects which contains the methods c_1
and c_2; the objects of G respond to all the methods of F, plus c_3 and c_4).

If we apply this idea (which is informal, but which completely respects subtype semantics) to the redefinition of the method, we obtain the situation shown in
Fig. 10.16, where our method `fie`, which is defined in F with the signature `fie:`
`A -> C`, is redefined in a subclass with signature `fie: A -> D`. The figure immediately reveals the observation that this is correct with respect to types exactly
when $D <: C$. In fact, the redefined `fie` produces a value of type D. If $D <: C$, this
value is also a value of C and therefore the types are respected.

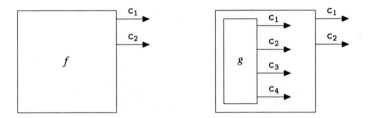

Fig. 10.15 An instance f of F and an instance g of G disguised as F

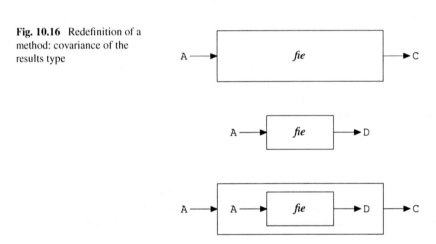

Fig. 10.16 Redefinition of a method: covariance of the results type

We can summarise the discussion with a general principle: with respect to the result type of a method, overriding is semantically correct (and permitted in many languages) when it is covariant. The result of the method that has been redefined in a subclass, is a subtype of the result of the original method.

This reasoning, however, can be easily applied also to argument types of methods. The scheme in Fig. 10.16 can, in fact, be generalised to that in Fig. 10.17, where method `fie` is redefined with the signature `fie: H->D`. Which relation must be valid between H and A so that the situation is semantically correct? The figure gives an immediate answer: it must be A<:H. With the respect to the argument type of a method, overloading is semantically correct when it is contravariant. The argument of the redefined method in the subclass, is a supertype of the argument of the original method.

From the semantic viewpoint therefore, the type of the methods S->T is a subtype of S'-> T' (S->T<:S'->T') whenever S<:S' and T'<:T: the type of the methods is covariant in the type of result and contravariant in the type of the arguments.

---

[21] Up to version 4, Java requires also that result types of a redefined method must coincide with the result type of the original method.

Fig. 10.17 Redefinition of a
method: contravariance of
argument type

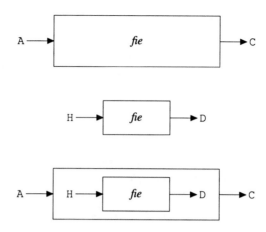

Although semantically correct, contravariant overriding (of method arguments)
is counterintuitive in some situations. The most important cases are those of *binary
methods*, that is, methods with a parameter of the same type as the object which receives the method. The typical case is that of an equivalence or comparison method.
Assuming we have a class such as the following:

```
class Point{
    ...
    boolean eq(Point p){...}
}
```

and we wish now to specialise it into the subclass:

```
class ColoredPoint extending Point{
    ...
    boolean eq(ColoredPoint p){...}
}
```

According to the contravariance rule, the `ColoredPoint` class is *not* a subclass
of `Point` because the argument of `eq` would be a subtype (and not a supertype) of
the type of the argument to `eq` in `Point`.

For these (and others) reasons, contravariant overriding is little used (one of the
few languages which use it is Emerald), while many of the most common languages
(with C++ and Java being the most common) require type identity for the argument.

There are however languages that would sacrifice static type security and only
use the rule of covariant overriding for method argument types (which is semantically incorrect). Among these are some fairly well-known language, such as Eiffel
and the language O_2 (one of the most common object-oriented database systems).
The reason is assumed greater naturalness, especially for binary methods. Extended
experimentation with O_2, amongst others, show that the semantic incorrectness of
type checking never causes problems in practice (that is in situations that are not
constructed *ad hoc* to violate the type system).

10.5 Chapter Summary

The chapter has been a general but deep, examination of the object-oriented paradigm, introduced as a way of obtaining abstractions in the most flexible and extensible way.

We have characterised the object-oriented paradigm when in the presence of:

- *Encapsulation* of data.
- A compatibility relation between types which we call *subtype*.
- A way to reuse code, which we refer to as *inheritance* and which can be divided into single and multiple inheritance.
- Techniques for the *dynamic dispatch* of methods.

These four concepts were viewed principally in the context of languages based on *classes* (even if we briefly looked at languages based on delegation). We then discussed the implementation of single and multiple inheritance and dynamic method selection.

The chapter was concluded with a study of some aspects relevant to the type systems in object oriented languages:

- Subtype polymorphism.
- Another form of parametric polymorphism which is possible when the language admits generics (which we studied in Java).
- The problem of overriding of co- and contravariant methods.

The object-oriented paradigm, in addition to represent a specific class of languages, is also a general development method for system software codified by semi-formal rules based on the organisation of concepts using objects and classes. Obviously the 2 aspects, the linguistic and the methodological, are not completely separate, given that the object-oriented development methodology finds its natural application in the use of object-oriented languages. However, within software engineering, methodological aspects are usually treated in an autonomous fashion without referring to any specific language. In this book, therefore, we did not go into the methodological aspects of object-oriented programming (we refer the reader to software engineering texts—see also the bibliographical notes below).

10.6 Bibliographical Notes

The first object-oriented language was Simula 67 [2, 9] which we cited in the previous chapter. It is Smalltalk (which explicitly depends on Simula), however, which had the greatest influence on succeeding languages and introduced the anthropomorphic metaphor of messages sent to objects [5].

On C++ the canonical reference is [13]. The Java language definition can be found in [6] and the most revealing text by its principal author [1]. An introduction to the Java Virtual Machine (and therefore to how the various mechanisms are implemented in Java) can be found in [8]; for the official specification of the JVM see [7].

Our description of the implementation of multiple inheritance is based on that of C++ [12]. The introduction of generics into Java is the result of much research work into subtype polymorphism. An introduction to generics as they appear in Java is to be found in [3], which we have closely followed in our presentation.

For the Self project, see the original article [14]; the retrospective [11] is a good source of information about the criteria for an innovative programming language project. For the diatribe on covariant and contravariant overriding, see [4].

Finally as far as object-oriented development methodologies are concerned, consult any general text on software engineering, for example, the classic [10].

10.7 Exercises

1. Consider the classes in Fig. 10.8 and the final definition:

```
class E{
    int v;
    void n(){...}
    }
class D extending E,C{
    int w;
    int g(){return x + y + v;} // redefinition with respect to C
    void m(){...}
}
```

Draw the representation for an instance object of D, as well as the structure of the vtable for such a class, indicating for each method the appropriate value required to correct the value of this.

2. Given the definitions in our pseudo-language:

```
abstract class A {
    int val = 1;
    int foo (int x);
}
abstract class B extending A {
    int val = 2;
}
class C extending B {
    int n = 0;
    int foo (int x){ return x+val+n; }
}
class D extending C {
    int n;
    D(int v){n=v;}
    int foo (int x){return x+val+n;}
}
```

Consider now the following program fragment

```
int u, v, w, z;
A a;
B b;
C c;
D d = new D(3);
a = d;
b = d;
c = d;
u = a.foo(1);
v = b.foo(1);
w = c.foo(1);
z = d.foo(1);
```

Give the values of u, v, w and z at the end of execution.

3. Given the following Java definitions:

```
interface A {
    int val=1;
    int foo (int x);
}
interface B {
    int z=1;
    int fie (int y);
}
class C implements A, B {
    int val = 2;
    int z =2;
    int n = 0;
    public  int foo (int x){ return x+val+n;}
    public int fie (int y){ return z+val+n;}
}
class D extends C {
    int val=3;
    int z=3;
    int n=3;
    public int foo (int x){return x+val+n;}
    public int fie (int y){ return z+val+n;}
}
```

Consider now the following program fragment:

```
int u, v, w, z;
A a;
B b;
D d = new D();
a = d;
b = d;
System.out.println(u = a.foo(1));
System.out.println(v = b.fie(1));
System.out.println(w = d.foo(1));
System.out.println(z = d.fie(1));
```

Give the values of u, v, w and z at the end of execution.
4. Is the following fragment of Java correct? In the positive case, the method fie is redefined (overridden)? What does it print?

```
class A {
    int x = 4;
    int fie (A p) {return p.x;}
}

class B extends A{
    int y = 6;
    int fie (B p) {return p.x+p.y;}
}


public class binmeth {
    public static void main (String [] args) {
        B b = new B();
        A a = new A();
        int zz = a.fie(a)+ b.fie(a) ;
        System.out.print(zz);
    }
}
```

References

1. K. Arnold, J. Gosling, and D. Holmes. *The Java Programming Language*, 4th edition. Addison-Wesley Longman, Boston, 2005.
2. G. Birtwistle, O. Dahl, B. Myhrtag, and K. Nygaard. *Simula Begin*. Auerbach Press, Philadelphia, 1973. ISBN: 0-262-12112-3.
3. G. Bracha. Generics in the Java programming language. Technical report, Sun Microsystems, 2004. Disposable on-line at java.sun.com/j2se/1.5/pdf/generics-tutorial.pdf.
4. G. Castagna. Covariance and contravariance: Conflict without a cause. *ACM Trans. Prog. Lang. Syst.*, 17(3):431–447, 1995. citeseer.ist.psu.edu/castagna94covariance.html.
5. A. Goldberg and D. Robson. *Smalltalk-80: The Language and Its Implementation*. Addison-Wesley Longman, Boston, 1983. ISBN: 0-201-11371-6.
6. J. Gosling, B. Joy, G. Steele, and G. Bracha. *The Java Language Specification, 3/E*. Addison Wesley, Reading, 2005. Disposable on-line a http://java.sun.com/docs/books/jls/index.html.
7. T. Lindholm and F. Yellin. *The Java Virtual Machine Specification*, 2nd edition. Sun and Addison-Wesley, Reading, 1999.
8. J. Meyer and T. Downing. *Java Virtual Machine*. O'Reilly, Sebastopol, 1997.
9. K. Nygaard and O.-J. Dahl. The development of the SIMULA languages. In *HOPL-1: The First ACM SIGPLAN Conference on History of Programming Languages*, pages 245–272. ACM Press, New York, 1978. doi:10.1145/800025.808391.
10. R. Pressman. *Software Engineering: A Practitioner's Approach*, 7th edition. McGraw Hill, New York, 2009.
11. R. B. Smith and D. Ungar. Programming as an experience: The inspiration for Self. In *ECOOP '95: Proc. of the 9th European Conf. on Object-Oriented Programming*, pages 303–330. Springer, Berlin, 1995. ISBN: 3-540-60160-0.

12. B. Stroustrup. Multiple inheritance for C++. In *Proc. of the Spring 1987 European Unix Users Group Conference*, Helsinki, 1987. citeseer.ist.psu.edu/stroustrup99multiple.html.

13. B. Stroustrup. *The C++ Programming Language*. Addison-Wesley Longman, Boston, 1997.

14. D. Ungar and R. B. Smith. Self: The power of simplicity. In *OOPSLA '87: Conf. Proc. on Object-Oriented Programming Systems, Languages and Applications*, pages 227–242. ACM Press, New York, 1987. ISBN: 0-89791-247-0. doi:10.1145/38765.38828.

Chapter 11
The Functional Paradigm

In this chapter, we present the main properties of functional programming. In functional programming, computation proceeds by rewriting functions and not by modifying the state. The fundamental characteristic of the languages in this paradigm, at least in their "pure" form, is precisely that of not possessing the concept of memory (and therefore side effect). Once an environment is fixed, an expression always denotes the same value.

We will discuss the pure paradigm in the first sections, explaining the fundamental aspects. Functional programming languages, however, merge these "pure" ingredients in a context that adds many other mechanisms; we will review them in Sect. 11.3.

We will touch on the SECD machine, an abstract machine for higher-order functional languages which constitutes the prototype of many real implementations.

We will, at this point, be in a position to discuss the reasons why the functional programming paradigm is interesting with respect to ordinary imperative languages.

The chapter concludes with a more theoretical section which provides a succinct introduction to the λ-calculus, a formal system for computability which inspires all functional languages and which has, since the time of ALGOL and LISP, been a constant model for the design of programming languages.

11.1 Computations without State

Though developed and abstract, all conventional languages base their computational model on the transformation of the *state*. The heart of this model is the concept of *modifiable variable*, that is, a container with a name to which, during the computation, can be assigned different values, while the same association is always maintained in the environment. Correspondingly, the principal construct in conventional languages is *assignment*, which modifies the value contained in a variable (but does not modify the association between the name of the variable and the location to which it corresponds; it modifies the r-value but not the l-value, which is fixed once and for all when the variable is declared).

M. Gabbrielli, S. Martini, *Programming Languages: Principles and Paradigms,*
Undergraduate Topics in Computer Science,
DOI 10.1007/978-1-84882-914-5_11, © Springer-Verlag London Limited 2010

Conventional languages differ in the their level of abstraction, their types, in the constructs which allow the manipulation of variables, but they all share the same computational model. This is an abstract view of the underlying, conventional physical machine. Computation proceeds by modifying values stored in locations. This is an extremely important model. It is called the *von Neumann Machine*, named after the Hungarian-American mathematician who, in the 1940s, saw that the Turing Machine (see box on page 61) could be engineered into a physical prototype, thereby originating the modern computer.

This is not, however, the only possible model upon which to base a programming language. It is possible to compute without using modifiable variables, that is without referring to the concept of state. The computation proceeds not by modifying the state but by *rewriting* expressions, that is by changes that take place only in the environment and do not involve the concept of memory. If there are no modifiable variables, there is no longer a need for assignment, that is the principal command in conventional languages. The entire computation will be expressed in terms of the sophisticated modification of the environment in which the possibility of manipulating (higher-order, see Sect. 7.2) functions plays a fundamental role.

Without assignment, iteration also looses its real sense. A loop can only repeatedly modify the state until the values of certain variables satisfy a guard. The reader already knows (see Chap. 6) that iterative and recursive constructs are two mechanisms permitting infinitely long (and possibly divergent) computations. In the stateless computational model, iteration disappears, recursion remains and becomes the fundamental construct for sequence control.

Higher-order functions and recursion are the basic ingredients of this stateless computational model. The programming languages which presuppose this model are called *functional languages* and the paradigm that results from this is called the *functional programming paradigm*.

This is a paradigm as old as the imperative one. Since the 1930s, beside the Turing Machine, there has existed the λ-calculus, an abstract model for characterising computable functions that is based on exactly the concept we have been briefly explaining. LISP was the first programming language explicitly inspired by the λ-calculus and many others have followed in the intervening years (Scheme, ML, in all its different dialects, Miranda, Haskell, to name only the most common). Among these, only Miranda and Haskell are "purely functional"; the others also have imperative components (often to assist programmers accustomed to conventional languages) but the structure of these languages assign a subordinate role to them.

In this chapter, we undertake an introduction to the pure functional paradigm; it is not a superficial one and we will discuss different general aspects of the paradigm. To make the treatment more concrete, it is desirable to refer to a specific language rather than to use a neutral pseudocode. ML has been chosen for this because, through its coherence and elegance of design, it is the most suited of them all to didactic presentation. It is not our aim to introduce the language (for which, the reader should refer to the bibliography), but only to use the syntax in an instrumental fashion to discuss some general questions that apply also to other functional languages.

11.1.1 Expressions and Functions

In the usual mathematical practice, there is some ambiguity about when we are defining a function and when we are applying it to a value. It is not uncommon to encounter expressions of the kind:

Let $f(x) = x^2$ be the function that associates with x its square. If now we have $x = 2$, it follows that $f(x) = 4$.

The syntactic expression $f(x)$ is used to denote two things that are quite different: the first time, it serves to introduce the *name*, f, of a specific function; the second time, it serves to denote the result of *applying* the function f to a specified value. In mathematical practice, this ambiguity is completely innocuous because the context helps us to distinguish which of the two uses is intended. The same does not hold for an artificial language (such as a programming language) which describes functions. Here, it is appropriate to distinguish the two cases.

When a mathematician asserts that they are defining the function, $f(x)$, in reality, they are defining the function f with one *formal* parameter, x, which serves to indicate the transformation that f applies to its argument. To distinguish linguistically between the name and the "body" of the function, following ML syntax, we can write:

```
val f = fn x => x*x;
```

The reserved word `val` introduces a declaration. The declaration is used to extend the environment with a new association between a name and a value. In our case, the name f is bound to the transformation of x into $x * x$. In all functional languages, functions are *expressible* values; that is, they can be the result of the evaluation of a complex expression. In our case, the expression on the right of the $=$ and introduced by `fn` is an expression that denotes a function.

For the application of a function to an argument, we retain the traditional notation, writing `f(2)` or `(f 2)`, or `f 2`, for the expression that results from the application of a function f to the argument 2. We can also use `val` to introduce new names, as in:

```
val four = f 2;
```

The introduction of specific syntax for an expression which denotes a function has an important consequence. It is possible to write (and possibly apply) a function without having necessarily to assign it a name. For example, the expression

```
(fn y => y+1) (6);
```

has the value 7 which results from the application of the (anonymous) function `fn y => y+1` to the argument 6. To make the notation less imposing, we assume (as does ML) that application can be denoted by simple juxtaposition (that is without parentheses) and that is associates to the left (prefix notation). If g is the name of a function,

```
g a1 a2 ... ak
```

will mean:

```
(...((g a1) a2)... ak).
```

Nothing prevents one functional expression from appearing inside another, as in

```
val add = fn x => (fn y => y+x);
```

The value add is a function which, given an argument, x, returns an anonymous function which, given an argument y, returns x+y. We can use add in many different ways:

```
val three = add 1 2;
val addtwo = add 2;
val five = addtwo 3;
```

Note that, in particular, addtwo is a function which is obtained as the result of the evaluation of another expression.

The notation which uses val and fn is important but is a little verbose. ML also allows the use of a more compact notation which resembles the usual way of defining functions in a programming language. The first function, f, which we defined (the one which computes the square of its argument) could also be defined as follows:

```
fun f x = x*x;
```

In general, a definition of the form:

```
fun F x1 x2 ... xn = body;
```

is only syntactic sugar (that is, in programming language jargon, only a nicer abbreviation) for:

```
val F = fn x1 => (fn x2 => ... (fn xn => body)...);
```

As a last example of functions which manipulate functions, this time in the form of a formal parameter, consider the definition:

```
fun comp f g x = f(g(x));
```

This returns the function composed of its first two arguments (which are, in their turn, functions).

Finally, every functional program permits the definition of recursive functions. Assuming that we have available a *conditional expression* (which in ML is written with the familiar if then else syntax), we can define the usual factorial as:

```
fun fatt n = if n=0 then 1 else n*fatt(n-1);
```

11.1.2 Computation as Reduction

If we exclude arithmetic functions (which we can assume predefined with the usual semantics) and the conditional expression, at the conceptual level, we can describe the procedure used to transform a complex expression into its value (*evaluation*) as the process of *rewriting*. We call this process *reduction*. In a complex expression, a subexpression of the form "function applied to an argument" is textually replaced by the body of the function in which the formal parameter is replaced, in its turn, by the actual parameter.[1] We can compute a simple expression using this computational model (we use → to indicate a reduction step).

```
fact 3 → (fn n => if n=0 then 1 else n*fact(n-1)) 3
       → if 3=0 then 1 else 3*fact(3-1)
       → 3*fact(3-1)
       → 3*fact(2)
       → 3*((fn n => if n=0 then 1 else n*fact(n-1)) 2)
       → 3*(if 2=0 then 1 else 2*fact(2-1))
       → 3*(2*fact(2-1))
       → 3*(2*fact(1))
       → 3*(2*((fn n => if n=0 then 1 else n*fact(n-1)) 1))
       → 3*(2*(if 1=0 then 1 else 1*fact(1-1))
       → 3*(2*(1*fact(0))
       → 3*(2*(1*((fn n => if n=0 then 1 else n*fact(n-1)) 1)))
       → 3*(2*(1*(if 0=0 then 1 else n*fact(n-1))))
       → 3*(2*(1*1))
       → 6
```

Note how, with the exception of arithmetic calculations and the use of the conditional expression, all of the rest of the computation proceeds by symbolic manipulation of strings: no variables, no update of stacked variables. Figure 11.1 contains another example of pure symbolic manipulation. (It is a complicated way to write the identity function!) (While studying the figure, recall that fun is just an abbreviation for val ... fn.)

Finally, the reader will have no have difficulty in convincing themselves that, given the definition

```
fun r x = r(r(x));
```

each computation which involves an evaluation of *r* resolves into an infinite rewriting. We say, in such a case, that the computation *diverges* and that the result is undefined.

---

[1] The reader will certainly have recognised in this description the "copy rule" we already discussed in the context of the by-name parameter passing. For the time being, we will be vague about the exact semantics to assign to this process—all of Sect. 11.2 will be devoted to it.

```
fun K x y = x;
fun S p q r = p r (q r);
val a = ...;

S K K a → (fn p => (fn q => (fn r => p r (q r)))) K K a
        → (fn q => (fn r => K r (q r))) K a
        → (fn r => K r (K r)) a
        → K a (K a)
        → (fn x => (fn y => x)) a (K a)
        → (fn y => a) (K a)
        → a
```

Fig. 11.1 Some definitions and a computation using rewriting

11.1.3 The Fundamental Ingredients

In these first subsections, we have introduced all the fundamental ingredients of the pure functional paradigm. We can make this precise and summarise the main concepts in the following way.

From the syntactic viewpoint, a language such as the one under consideration has no commands (there being no state to modify using side effects) but only expressions. Apart from possible values and primitive operators for data (such as integer, boolean, characters, etc.) and the conditional expression, the two principal constructs for defining expressions are:

- *Abstraction* which, given any expression, exp and an identifier, x, allows the construction of an expression fn x => exp denoting the function that transforms the formal parameter x into exp (the expression exp is "abstracted" from the specific value bound to x).
- The *application* of an expression, f_exp, to another expression, a_exp, which we write f_exp a_exp, which denotes the application of the function (denoted by) f_exp to the argument (denoted by) a_exp.

There are no constraints on the possibilities of passing functions as arguments to other functions, or to returning functions as the results of other (higher-order) functions. As a consequence, there is perfect *homogeneity* between programs and data.

From the semantic viewpoint, a program consists of a series of value definitions, each of which inserts a new association into the environment and can require the evaluation of arbitrarily complex expressions. The presence of higher-order functions and the possibility of defining recursive functions makes this definition mechanism flexible and powerful.

To a first approximation, the semantics of computation (*evaluation*) refers to no linguistic aspects other than the ones introduced so far. It can be defined using simple symbolic rewriting of strings (*reduction*), which repeatedly uses two main operations to simplify expressions until they reach a simple form which immediately denotes a value. The first of these operations is the simple search through the environment. When an identifier is determined as being bound in an environment, replace the identifier by its definition. For example, in Fig. 11.1, we used this operation for the first and the fifth reduction. In what follows this step will not be explicitly considered again. We will consider a name as a simple abbreviation for the value associated with it.

The second operation, which is more interesting, deals with a functional expression applied to an argument and uses a version of the copy rule (which in this context is called the β-rule).

Definition 11.1

Redex A *redex* (which stands for a *red*ucible *ex*pression) is an application of the form ((fn x => body) arg).

Reductum The *reductum* of a redex ((fn x => body) arg) is the expression which is obtained by replacing in body each (free) occurrence of the formal parameter, x, by a copy of arg (avoiding variable capture[2], see p. 175).

β**-rule** An expression, exp, in which a redex appears as a subexpression is reduced (or rewrites, simplifies) to exp1 (notation: exp $\rightarrow$ exp1), where exp1 is obtained from exp by replacing the redex by its reductum.

From an implementation viewpoint, finally, every abstract machine for functional languages adopts extensive garbage-collection mechanisms because, in the case in which functions are returned as values by other functions, we know that the local environment must be preserved for an unlimited period of time (see Sect. 7.2.2).

If these are the cardinal notions of a functional language, on a more attentive reading, these few lines raise more problems than they solve. We undertake a deeper analysis of these semantic concepts in the next section.

11.2 Evaluation

In the brief semantic description with which we concluded the last section, we did not provide details about two fundamental aspects:

- What is the termination condition for reduction (that is what does "a simple form which immediately denotes a value" mean?)
- What precise semantics must be given to the β-rule, not just concerning possible variable capture (which we already described in the context of parameter passing) but more importantly, the order to follow during rewriting should more than one redex be present in the same expression.

---

[2]In the context of functional programming, identifiers bound to values are often referred to as "variables". The reader is by now experienced enough to allow us to continue with this traditional use without being confused by the absence of modifiable variables in pure functional programming languages.

11.2.1 Values

A *value* is an expression which cannot be further rewritten. In a functional language, there are values of two kinds: values of primitive type and functions. There is little to say about values of simple types. If the language provides some primitive types (integers, booleans, characters, etc.) is clear that a set of primitive values is associated with each type thus defined and that these values do not admit evaluation (for example, constants of type integer, boolean, characters, etc.). In the example of the previous subsection, we terminated the evaluation of fact when we reached primitive values of integer type: 3, 2, 1.

Functional values are more interesting. Let us consider the following definition:

```
val G = fn x => ((fn y => y+1) 2);
```

We have said that a definition entails the evaluation of the expression on the right of the equality and the binding of the value thus derived to the name on the left of the =. But, in this case, it is not immediately clear what the value to be associated with G is. Do we have:

```
fn x => 3
```

in which we have rewritten the body of G by evaluating the redex it contains, or do we have

```
fn x => ((fn y => y+1) 2)
```

in which there has been no evaluation in the body of G? The first case appears to be the one that more respects the informal semantics that we gave at the end of the last subsection. The second, on the other hand, is closer to the usual definition of function in a conventional language, in which the body of a function is only evaluated when it is called.

Although at first sight, this can appear strange, it is the second of the above that is adopted for all functional languages in common use. Evaluation does not occur "under" an abstraction. Every expression of the form

```
fn x => exp
```

represents a value, so redexes possibly contained in exp are *never* rewritten until the expression is applied to some argument.

11.2.2 Capture-Free Substitution

To implement capture-free substitution, we saw in Chap. 7 that closures can be used. This is, in effect, the mechanism also used by abstract machines for functional

Fig. 11.2 An expression
with more than one redex

```
fun K x y = x;
fun r z = r(r(z));
fun D u = if u=0 then 1 else u;
fun succ v = v+1;

val v = K (D (succ 0)) (r 2);
```

languages (see Sect. 11.4). For the elementary description we are giving at present, though, a syntactic convention suffices. In every expression, there are never two formal parameters with the same name and the names of the possible variables that are not formal parameters are all distinct from those of the formal parameters.

Using this convention, there will never be variable capture in the simple examples that we consider.[3]

11.2.3 Evaluation Strategies

In Chap. 6, while discussing expressions, we saw how every language must fix a specific strategy (that is a fixed order) for the evaluation of expressions. The presence of higher-order functions in functional languages makes this question even more fundamental. To clarify the problem, consider the definitions in Fig. 11.2. Which value is associated with v and how is it determined?

The β-rule on its own is not of much use because, in the right-hand part of the definition of v, there are 4 redexes (after the expansion of the names with the values associated with them by the definitions):

```
K (D (succ 0))
D (succ 0)
succ 0
r 2
```

Which of them is reduced first? Every commonly used language uses a leftmost strategy which reduces the redexes starting with the one at the leftmost end. But even having stipulated this, it is not clear which is the leftmost redex of

```
K (D (succ 0))
D (succ 0)
succ 0
```

because these three redexes are superimposed on each other. Having fixed a leftmost evaluation order, we then find that we have three different strategies.

---

[3]In the more general case, if we do not want to bring into play the concept of closure, for the correct description of computation using rewriting, it is necessary precisely to define the concepts of bound and free variable and substitution, all concepts which we treat formally in Sect. 11.6.

Evaluation by value   In evaluation by value (which is also called applicative-order evaluation or *eager* evaluation, or *innermost* evaluation), a redex is evaluated only if the expression which constitutes its argument part is already a value.

More precisely, leftmost evaluation in applicative order works as follows.

1. Scan the expression to be evaluated from the left, choosing the first application encountered. Let it be (f_exp a_exp).
2. First evaluate (recursively applying this method) f_exp until it has been reduced to a value (of functional type) of the form (fn x => ...).
3. Then evaluate the argument part, a_exp, of the application, so that it is reduced to a value, val.
4. Finally, reduce the redex ((fn x => ...) val) and goto to (1).

Considering Fig. 11.2, case (1) first chooses the application K (D (succ 0)). Now some elementary applications of (1), (2) and (3) will serve to show that K, D and succ are already values (recall that we are implying that a name is an abbreviation for the expression associated with it). The first redex to be reduced is then succ 0 (that is, ((fn v => v + 1) 0)) which will be completely evaluated and yields 1. Then the redex (D 1) (that is ((fn u => if u =0 then 1 else u) 1)) is reduced to give the value 1. Then (K 1) is evaluated to produce the value (fun y ==> 1). At this point in the evaluation, the expression has become

(**fun** y => 1) (r 2)

Since the functional part of this application is already a value, the strategy prescribes that the argument (r 2) is evaluated. The evaluation leads to rewriting to r (r 2), then to r (r (r 2)) and so on in a divergent computation.

No value is therefore associated with v because the computation diverges.

Evaluation by name   In the evaluation by name strategy (which is also called *normal order* or *outermost*), a redex is evaluated before its argument part.

More precisely, leftmost evaluation in normal order proceeds as follows.

1. Scan the expression to be evaluated from the left, choosing the first application encountered. Let it be (f_exp a_exp).
2. First evaluate f_exp (recursively applying this method) until it has been reduced to a value (of functional type) of the form (fn x => ...).
3. Reduce the redex ((fn x => ..) a_exp) using the β-rule and goto (1).

Considering Fig. 11.2, the first redex to be reduced is therefore:

K (D (succ 0))

It is rewritten to:

fn y => D (succ 0)

which is a functional value. The expression now is of the form:

```
(fn y => D (succ 0)) (r 2)
```

for which the strategy prescribes reducing the outermost redex, so we obtain:

```
D (succ 0)
```

Now reducing this expression, we obtain:

```
if (succ 0)=0 then 1 else (succ 0)
```

and then:

```
if 1=0 then 1 else (succ 0)
```

and finally

```
succ 0
```

from which we obtain the final value, 1, which is then associated with v.

Lazy evaluation In evaluation by name, a single redex might have to be evaluated more than once because of some duplication that has occurred during rewriting. In the example that we are discussing, the redex (succ 0) is duplicated because of the function D and is reduced twice[4] in the conditional expression that forms the body of D. This is the price that must be paid for postponing the evaluation of an argument until after the application of a function (and it is really this that allows evaluation by name to obtain a value where evaluation by value would diverge). But it is very expensive in terms of efficiency (when the duplicated redex requires a significant amount of computation).

To obviate this problem and maintain the advantages of evaluation by name, the lazy strategy proceeds like that by name but the first time that a "copy" of a redex is encountered, its value is saved and will be used should any other copies of the same redex be encountered.

The by-name and lazy strategies are examples of the *call by need* strategies in which a redex is reduced only if it is required by the computation.

11.2.4 Comparison of the Strategies

In the last subsection, the by-name strategy produces a value when the by-value strategy diverges. It is sensible to ask the question as to whether it can be the case that the two strategies produce *distinct* values for the same expression.

---

[4]The purist does not speak of copies of redexes but will rather say that the redex (succ 0) has given way to two *residuals*, each of which has been reduced independently of the other.

An answer to this question is given by the following theorem which expresses one of the most important characteristics of the *pure* functional paradigm. We say that an expression in the language is *closed* if all of its variables are bound by some fn. Let us recall, then, from Sect. 11.2.1, that by *primitive value*, we mean a value of a primitive type (integer, boolean, character, etc.), excluding, therefore, functional values.

Theorem 11.2 *Let* exp *be a closed expression. If* exp *reduces to a primitive value,* val, *using any of the three strategies of Sect.* 11.2.3, *then* exp *reduces to* val *following the by-name strategy. If* exp *diverges using the by-name strategy, then it also diverges under the other two strategies.*

Let us note that the theorem excludes the case in which a (closed) expression can yield a primitive value, val, in one strategy and yield *another* primitive value, val2, using another strategy.[5] Two strategies can therefore differ only by the fact that one determines a value while the other diverges, as we saw in our example. We cannot go into the details of how the theorem can be proved but it is important to stress that the following basic property is fundamental to its validity:

> Once any strategy has been fixed in a given environment, the evaluation of all occurrences of a single expression always yields the same value

This property, which is immediately falsified when there are side effects, is taken by many authors as the *criterion* for a pure functional language: a language is purely functional if it satisfies this condition. This is a very important property which makes it possible to *reason* about a functional program and to which we will return in Sect. 11.5. Let us again note, before going on, that it is just by virtue of this property that lazy evaluation is correct. The value obtained by the evaluation of an expression does not change when another copy of the same expression is encountered (clearly, in the meanwhile, the environment has not been changed).

In the light of the preceding theorem, it can be asked what interest there is in the by-value strategy, given that by-name is the most general of all possible strategies. Moreover, reasons of efficiency would seem to suggest that we only adopt call-by-need strategies, given that it is not clear why useless redexes should be reduced, with the consequent waste of computing time. The point is that the efficiency case is not so simple. To implement a call-by-need strategy is, in general, more expensive that a simple call-by-value strategy. The by-value strategy has efficient implementations

---

[5]The theorem is no longer valid if the hypothesis that the value is *primitive* is removed. Having assumed that evaluation is not performed under abstraction, in fact, the two strategies can yield (functional) values that are distinct. By way of an example, define I = fn x => x and P = fn x => (fn y => y x). The term P (I I) reduces to fn y => y (I I) under the by-name strategy, while, using the by-value strategy, it reduces to fn y => y I. This difference is not very important in programming languages (where we mainly want to compute values of primitive type). In Sect. 11.6, we will define an abstract calculus in which reduction also occurs in the presence of abstractions. This calculus satisfies the *confluence* property (stronger and more general than Theorem 11.2), which we will discuss on page 361.

on conventional architectures, even if, sometimes, it performs unnecessary work (every time that an argument that is not required in the body of the function is evaluated, as happens with the second argument of the function K in Fig. 11.2). This last case, moreover, can be treated in an efficient manner with abstract evaluation strategies that attempt to identify useless arguments.

Among the functional languages that we have cited at the beginning of this chapter, LISP, Scheme and ML use a by-value strategy (also because they include major imperative aspects), while Miranda and Haskell (which are pure functional languages) use lazy evaluation.

11.3 Programming in a Functional Language

The mechanisms we described in the last section are sufficient to express programs for every computable function (they constitute, indeed, a Turing-complete language). This is the nucleus of every functional language, which, however, is too austere for us to be able to use as a real programming language. Every functional language, therefore, embed this nucleus in a wider context which provides mechanisms of different kinds, each aiming to make programming simpler and more expressive.

11.3.1 Local Environment

The mechanism of global definitions in the environment that we have used this far has too little structure for a modern language. As in conventional languages, it is appropriate to provide explicit mechanisms to introduce definitions with limited scope, as for example:

```
let x = exp in exp1 end
```

This introduces the binding of x to the value of exp in a scope which includes only exp1.

To tell the truth, the presence of functional expressions already introduces nested scopes and associated environments which are composed of the formal parameters of the function bound to the actual parameters. From the point of view of evaluation, we can indeed consider the construct

```
let x = exp in exp1 end
```

as syntactic sugar for

```
(fn x => exp1) exp.
```

The use of local scopes is too important, however, and justifies the introduction of special syntax for them.

11.3.2 Interactiveness

Every functional language has an interactive environment. The language is used
by entering expressions which the abstract machine evaluate and whose value it
returns. Definitions are particular expressions which modify the global environment
(and may return a value).

This model immediately suggests interpreter based implementations, even if
there are efficient implementations that use compilation to generate compiled code
the first time a definition is stored in the environment.

11.3.3 Types

As in conventional languages, the type system is an aspect of primary importance in
functional languages, as well. Every functional language we have cited provides the
usual primitive types (integers, booleans, characters) with operations on their values.
With the exception of Scheme, which is a language with dynamic type checking, all
the others have elaborate static type systems. These type systems allows the definition of new types such as pairs, lists, "records" (that is tuples of labelled values).
For example, in ML, we can define a function add_p which takes as arguments a
pair of integers and returns their sum:

```
fun add_p (n1,n2) = n1+n2;
```

Note the fundamental difference between add_p and add which we defined on
page 336. add_p requires a pair of integers and it would make no sense to provide
just one value for n1 and none for n2. Instead, add it is a function which inputs
one number and returns a function that takes another number and returns the sum of
both.[6]

An important part of the type system in functional languages is that dedicated to
the types of functions, given that functions are denotable and expressible values (and
often also storable, if the language includes imperative aspects). In typed functional
languages, this also means that some functional expressions are illegal because they
cannot be typed. For example, the following higher-order function is illegal in a
typed language:

```
fun F f n = if n=0 then f(1) else f("pippo");
```

The reason for this is that the formal parameter, f, must simultaneously have types
int -> 'a and string -> 'a (where 'a denotes a type variable, that is a
generic type that is not yet instantiated).

---

[6]The passage from a function requiring, as argument, a pair (or, more generally, a tuple) to a unary
higher-order function, is called the *curryfication* of a function. The operation is named after Haskell
Curry, one of the founding fathers of the theory of the λ-calculus.

Another illegal expression (because it violates typing) is self application:

```
fun Delta x = x x;
```

The expression, (x x), is illegal because there is no way to assign a unique and consistent type to x. Given that it occurs on the left as an application, it must have a type of the form ′a -> ′b. Since, then, it also appears as the argument to a function (on the right of the application), it must have the type that the function requires: therefore, x must be of the type ′a. Putting the two constraints together, we have it that x must, at the same time, be of type ′a and of type ′a -> ′b and there is no way to "unify" these two expressions.

In languages without a strong typing system, such as Scheme, the function Delta is, instead, legal. In Scheme, we can also apply Delta to itself. The expression (obviously written in Scheme syntax)

```
(Delta Delta)
```

constitutes a simple example of a divergent program. The lack of a static type check makes it possible in Scheme to write expressions such as:

```
(4 3)
```

Here, the aim is to apply the integer 4 to the integer 3. Since the left-hand part of this application is not a function, the abstract machine will generate an error at execution time.

In the case of ML, the most interesting aspect of its type system is its support for polymorphism (see Sect. 8.8 and, in particular, the box on page 243).

11.3.4 Pattern Matching

One of the most annoying aspects of recursive functional programming is handling terminal cases by means of explicit "if" expressions. Let us take, for example, the (inefficient) function which returns the nth term of the Fibonacci series:

```
fun Fibo n = if n=0 then 1
              else if n=1 then 1
                  else Fibo(n-1)+Fibo(n-2);
```

The mechanism of *pattern matching* present in some languages such as ML and Haskell, allows us to give a definition (which is equivalent to the above) as follows:

```
fun Fibo 0 = 1
  | Fibo 1 = 1
  | Fibo n = Fibo(n-1)+Fibo(n-2);
```

The "|" character is read "or". Each branch of the definition corresponds to a different case of the function. The most interesting part of this definition is the formal parameters. They are no longer constrained to be identifiers but can be *patterns*, that is, expressions formed from variables (the last is an example), constants (in the other cases) and other constructs that depend on the language's type system (we will see an example using lists below). A pattern is a kind of schema, a model against which to match the actual parameter. When the function is applied to an actual parameter, it is compared with the patterns (using the order in which they appear in the program) and the body corresponding to the first pattern which matches with the actual parameter is chosen.

The pattern-matching mechanism is particularly flexible when structured types are used, for example lists. In ML syntax, a list is denoted by square brackets with the elements separated by commas. For example

```
["one", "two", "three"]
```

is a list of three strings. The operator, : : denotes "cons" (that is the operator that adds an element to the head of a list):

```
"zero"::["one", "two", "three"]
```

is an expression whose value is the list:

```
["zero", "one", "two", "three"].
```

Finally, nil is the empty list. Thus

```
"four"::nil
```

has value ["four"]. Using pattern matching, we can define a function which computes the length of a generic list such as:

```
fun length nil = 0
 |   length e::rest = 1 + length(rest);
```

Note that the names used in the pattern are used as formal parameters to indicate parts of the actual parameter. It should be clear the advantage in terms of conciseness and clarity with respect to the usual definition:

```
fun length list = if list = nil then 0
                     else 1 + length(tl list);
```

This definition, moreover, requires the introduction of a *selection* function (which we have written tl) to obtain the list that is obtained by removing the head element. The selection operation is, on the other hand, implicit in pattern matching.

An important constraint is that a variable cannot appear twice in the same pattern. For example, consider the following "definition" of a function which, applied to a list, returns true if and only if the first two elements of the list are equal:

```
fun Eq nil = false
  | Eq [e] = false
  | Eq x::x::rest = true
  | Eq x::y::rest = false;
```

This definition is syntactically illegal because the third pattern contains the variable x twice, where it is used to test the equality of the first two elements. The pattern-matching mechanism is one way to check that the *form* of an actual parameter agrees with a pattern, not that the values it contains bear certain relationships. Otherwise stated, pattern matching is *not* unification, a much more general mechanism (and more complex to implement) and which we will discuss in the context of the logic programming paradigm (Chap. 12).[7]

11.3.5 Infinite Objects

In the presence of by-name or lazy strategies, it is possible to define and manipulate *streams*, that is, data structures that are (potentially) infinite. In this section, we will give a small example of how this can be done. We cannot give the example in ML because it uses a by-value strategy. The example is possible, though, in Haskell. So as not to load the reader with different syntax, we will write the terms with the same concrete syntax as ML but with the stipulation that evaluation must be understood as lazy.

First, we have to clarify the concept of value for data structures such as lists. In a language that uses eager evaluation, a value of type T list is a list whose elements are *values* of type T. In a lazy language, this is not a good notion of value because it might require the evaluation of useless redexes, contrary to the call-by-need philosophy. To see the reason, define the functions:

```
fun hd x::rest = x;
fun tl x::rest = rest;
```

The functions return, respectively, the first element (that is, the head) and the rest (that is, the tail) of a non-empty list (in the case of the empty list, the abstract machine will generate an error when doing pattern matching).

Let us now consider the expression

```
hd [2, ((fn n=>n+1) 2)].
```

---

[7]The implementation of pattern matching is nothing other than the "obvious" translation into a sequence of ifs. In the case of Eq, the third pattern would require checking the equality of two elements *of arbitrary type*. If we have values for which the language does not define equality (as happens, for example, for functional values), it would not be possible to implement an equality test.

To calculate its value (that is, 2), it is not necessary to reduce the redex that comprises the second element of the list because it will never be used in the body of the hd function. For these reasons, in a by-need context, a value of type list is any expression of the form:

```
exp1 :: exp2
```

where exp1 and exp2 can also contain redexes.

It is then possible to define a list by recursion, as for example:

```
val infinity2 = 2 :: infinity2;
```

The expression infinity2 corresponds to a potentially infinite list whose elements are all 2 (using eager evaluation, such a list would be divergent).

This value is perfectly manipulable under lazy evaluation. For example,

```
hd infinity2
```

is an expression whose evaluation terminates with the value 2. Another expression with value 2 is

```
hd (tl (tl (tl infinity2))).
```

As a last example of a stream, the following function constructs an infinite list of natural numbers starting with its argument, n:

```
fun numbersFrom n = n :: numbersFrom(n+1);
```

We can define a higher-order function that applies its functional argument to all the elements of a list, as in:

```
fun map f nil = nil
  | map f e::rest = f(e)::rest;
```

We can now produce the infinite list of all the squares starting from n*n:

```
fun squaresFrom n = map (fn y => y*y) (numbersFrom n);
```

11.3.6 Imperative Aspects

Many functional languages also include imperative mechanisms which introduce a notion of state that can be modified by side effects.

In ML, there are real modifiable variables (called "reference cells") with their own types. For every type T in the language (including functional types, therefore), the type T ref is defined and its values are modifiable variables that can contain values of type T. A modifiable variable of type T, initialised to the value v (of

Side effects in LISP

LISP, the first functional language, is based on a data structure called a *dotted pair* (or cons cell, see the box on page 121). Dotted pairs are composed of two parts: the *car* (for *contents of the address register*) and *cdr* (for *contents of the decrement register*). An expression of the form:

```
(cons a b)
```

allocates a dotted pair and initialises it so that its `car` points to the value of a and its `cdr` points to the value of b. The two components of a dotted pair can be selected using the functions `car` and `cdr`. So,

```
(cdr (cons a b))
```

has the value b. These are characteristics that belong to the pure part of LISP.

LISP has, in addition, imperative mechanisms. For example, there are functions such as (rplaca x a) and (rplacd x a) which, respectively, *assign to the car* and *assign to the cdr* of the dotted pair x the value of a:

```
(cdr (rplacd (cons 'a 'b) 'c))
```

This has the value ' c. Other side-effecting functions are `set` and `setq`.

type T) is created by:

```
ref v
```

The usual constructs that associate names and values can also be used on values of type T ref. For example:

val I = ref 4;

This creates a reference cell of type int ref, which is initialised to 4 and has the name I. This is what, in imperative languages, we call "the modifiable variable (with name) I." Obviously, I is the name of the reference cell and not of the value it contains (it is an l-value). To obtain its r-value, it is necessary to dereference it explicitly using the ! operator:

val n = !I + 1;

The expression !I is of type int. In general, if V is an expression of type T ref, !V is of type T. The line above associates the name n with the value 5. At risk of being pedantic, let us observe that n is not a modifiable variable, it is an ordinary name bound to a value in the environment.

Reference cells can be modified using assignments:

```
I := !I + 1;
```

Note the difference with the definition of the value n given above. Here, we are modifying (using a side effect) the r-value of a reference cell that already exists. The type of an imperative construct of this kind is unit (recall Sect. 8.3.7).

The presence of modifiable variables clearly introduces the possibility of aliasing. Let us indeed consider the following definitions:

```
val I = ref 4;
val J = I;
```

The second line associates the value of the name I (that is the reference cell—the l-value) with the name J. We here have a classic situation of aliasing: I and J are different names for the same l-value. After execution of the fragment

```
I := 5;
val z = !J;
```

the name z is associated with the value 5.

The language definition does not specify how to implement an assignment between modifiable variables. From the examples given so far using integers, one could imagine a traditional implementation with the r-value being copied from the source to the destination of the assignment. However, values with quite different memory sizes can be stored in reference cells. Let us consider, for example, modifiable variables that contain lists and strings:

```
val S = ref "pear";
val L = ref ["one", "two", "three"];
```

The name S is of type string ref, while L is of type (string list) ref. The two modifiable variables associated with the names S and L can contain, respectively, *any* string and *any* list. For example, we can perform two assignments:

```
S := "this_is_a_string_much_longer_than_previously";
L := "zero" :: "four" :: "five" :: !L;
```

The new values of L and S require more memory than their previous values did. It is not possible to implement these assignments using a simple (and traditional) value copy. The abstract machine will, in this case, copy references (or pointers) to these values. All of this is, though, completely invisible to the language user. The implementation handles the two space requirements by allocating the necessary memory for each case and then modifies the references.

As well as modifiable variables, ML also provides imperative control constructs, such as sequential composition (;) and loops.

It is appropriate to note that, in the presence of these imperative features, both Theorem 11.2 and the property that we cited immediately after it *do not apply*. This is particularly relevant in the case of a lazy evaluation strategy which would become incorrect in the presence of side effects. It is for this reason that languages such as Miranda and Haskell, which use lazy evaluation, do not admit side effects of any kind (they are purely functional languages).

11.4 Implementation: The SECD Machine

The technology for implementing functional programming languages is today sophisticated and cannot be adequately described in this book. The techniques for passing functions as parameters we described in Chap. 7 constitute the heart of these implementations. In order to give more details on how to handle higher-order functions, we will limit ourselves to summarising the SECD machine, a prototype proposed in 1964 by Peter Landin for evaluation *by value*. Many other abstract machines have developed out of the SECD machine.

We will describe the SECD machine in an abstract manner, using a very simple, purely functional language that uses only abstraction and application. The primitive elements of the language are the names of constants and variables and some primitive functions (for example, we could have constants 0, 1, true, etc. and primitive functions succ and pred). The important part of the machine is not concerned with these aspects of the language but with the presence of higher-order functions. Let us assume, for simplicity, that we are only dealing with unary functions. Let us assume that *Var* is a non-terminal from which can be derived a denumerable number of names (of variables) and that *Const* and *Fun* are, respectively, the non-terminals from which are derived the appropriate constants and primitive functions. We can state the grammar of our example language as:

$$exp ::= Const \mid Var \mid Fun \mid (exp \quad exp) \mid (\text{fn} \quad Var \quad => \quad exp).$$

The SECD machine has four main components:

- A Stack to store the partial results which will be used during the computation.
- An Environment, that is a list of associations between names and values. We have already noted that "there is no evaluation under an abstraction". The value of an abstraction is a *closure*, that is a pair formed of the abstraction and the environment in which the free variables in its body are to be evaluated. To simplify the concept, let us assume that a closure is a *triple* composed of an environment, an expression (which will always be derived from the body of an abstraction) and from a variable (representing the variable that was bound in the abstraction). We will therefore write a closure as $cl(E, exp, x)$, which will represent the value in the environment, E, of the abstraction (fn $x => exp$).
- A Control, represented by a stack of expressions to be evaluated. Among the expressions is also the special operator, @, which is read "app" and which indicates

that an application should be executed (because the two expressions that comprise an application have already been evaluated and are stored in the next two positions on the stack).

- A storage area called the **Dump**, that is a stack in which previous states of the machine have been saved when the computation was suspended to evaluate internal redexes.

We write $[a_1, \ldots, a_n]$ to denote the stack composed of the elements $a_1, \ldots, a_n$ with a_1 at its top. [] is the empty stack. If P is a stack, $top(P)$ denotes the topmost element, while $tl(P)$ denotes P with the top element removed.

A state of the machine is composed of a quadruple, (S, E, C, D). A dump is always composed of a structure of the form:

$$(S_1, E_1, C_1, (S_2, E_2, C_2, (S_3, E_3, C_3, []))).$$

This state of the dump has been obtained by first saving the state

$$(S_3, E_3, C_3, [])$$

then the state

$$(S_2, E_2, C_2, (S_3, E_3, C_3, []))$$

which includes the previous dump, and so on.

To evaluate an expression, *exp*, the machine starts its operation in the state $([], [], [exp], [])$ and terminates when both the control, C, and the dump, D, are empty.

The operation of the SECD is described by a transition function which allows it to pass from one state to a succeeding one using the following rules. The machine selects the rule according to the expression on the control list (imagine that control is described using abstract syntax). Let us assume, therefore, that the machine finds itself in the generic state, (S, E, C, D), then:

1. A constant, c (e.g., 1, 0, *true*), is on top of the control list, that is, there is an expression that does not need to be evaluated. In this case, the new state of the machine is $(c :: S, E, tl(C), D)$ in which the (immediate) value of the expression is pushed onto the stack and the expression just evaluated is removed from the stack.
2. There is a variable, x, on the top of the control list. In this case, the value is the one which the environment associates with x. Therefore, the new state of the machine is $(E(x) :: S, E, tl(C), D)$.
3. On the top of the control list, there is an application of the form $(exp_f \ exp_a)$. In this case, since the SECD implements eager evaluation, it is necessary to follow the evaluation procedure we described in Sect. 11.2.3. The new state is therefore $(S, E, exp_f :: exp_a :: @ :: tl(C), D)$ which expresses the fact that the next expression to be evaluated is the functional part of the application (which will have as its value a closure, as we will see), followed by the argument part of the application, followed, finally, be the special expression, @, which will force the real application of the function to its argument.

4. On the top of control list, there is an abstraction, (fn x => exp). We know that we are already in the presence of a value which must however be "closed" with the current environment. The new state of the machine is therefore $(cl(E, exp, x) :: S, E, tl(C), D)$.

5. The special value @ is on the top of the control list. We then know, by construction, that on the stack there are two values that represent, respectively, an argument (on the top of the stack) and a function to apply (the second element). There are two subcases which depend on the function to be applied:

   - The function is a *primitive function*, f, such as *succ*. The function must be directly applied to its argument and the new state of the machine is $(f(top(S)) :: tl(tl(S)), E, tl(C), D)$.
   - The function on the top is a closure of the form $cl(E_1, exp, x)$. This is one of the central points of the SECD machine; it brings the dump into play. It is necessary to use the copy rule. The computation passes to exp in the environment of the closure, E_1, (and not in the current environment, E) modified by the binding of the formal parameter. But the computation performed up to now must not be forgotten. It is frozen on the dump. The new state of the machine is therefore $([], E_1[x \leftarrow top(S)], [exp], (tl(tl(S)), E, tl(C), D))$.

6. The control list is empty. This can happen when the computation has terminated (in which case, the dump is also empty). It can also happen when a computation started by the previous rule (the one for applying a closure to a value) is finished. In this second case (that is, non-empty dump of the form (S_1, E_1, C_1, D_1)), it is necessary to resume the computation saved on the dump, restoring, at the same time, the value just computed (which is on the top of the stack). The new state of the machine is $(top(S) :: S_1, E_1, C_1, D_1)$.

Figure 11.3 shows how the SECD machine computes the value of the expression $(F\ 3)$, where:

$$F = \text{fn } x => (sqrt\ ((\text{fn } y => (succ\ x))\ x)).$$

The computation is shown as a table in which every row represents a transition of the machine. The rule being used for the transition is indicated in the rightmost column.

11.5 The Functional Paradigm: An Assessment

Having reached the end of our presentation on the functional paradigm, it is appropriate to ask ourselves wherein resides the interest in it and functional languages. Such a question, in reality, must be asked on at least two different planes:

- That of practical programming.
- That of programming language design.

We will try to give an answer on these two levels but it is appropriate to divert our attentions for an instant to clarify the context in which we can talk correctly about "practical programming."

S	E	C	D	r
[]	[]	$[(F\ 3)]$	[]	
[]	[]	$[F, 3, @]$	[]	3
$[ch_1]$	[]	$[3, @]$	[]	4

where $ch_1 = cl([], (sqrt\ ((\texttt{fn}\ y\ \texttt{=>}\ (succ\ x))\ x)), x)$

S	E	C	D	r
$[3, ch_1]$	[]	$[@]$	[]	1
[]	$[x \leftarrow 3]$	$[(sqrt\ ((\texttt{fn}\ y\ \texttt{=>}\ (succ\ x))\ x)))]$	d_1	5

where $d_1 = ([], [], [], [])4$

S	E	C	D	r
[]	$[x \leftarrow 3]$	$[sqrt, ((\texttt{fn}\ y\ \texttt{=>}\ (succ\ x))\ x), @]$	d_1	3
$[sqrt]$	$[x \leftarrow 3]$	$[((\texttt{fn}\ y\ \texttt{=>}\ (succ\ x))\ x), @]$	d_1	1
$[sqrt]$	$[x \leftarrow 3]$	$[(\texttt{fn}\ y\ \texttt{=>}\ (succ\ x)), x, @, @]$	d_1	1
$[ch_2, sqrt]$	$[x \leftarrow 3]$	$[x, @, @]$	d_1	4

where $ch_2 = cl([x \leftarrow 3], (succ\ x), y)$

S	E	C	D	r
$[3, ch_2, sqrt]$	$[x \leftarrow 3]$	$[@, @]$	d_1	2
[]	$[x \leftarrow 3, y \leftarrow 3]$	$[(succ\ x)]$	d_2	5

where $d_2 = ([sqrt], [x \leftarrow 3], [@], d_1)$

S	E	C	D	r
[]	$[x \leftarrow 3, y \leftarrow 3]$	$[succ, x, @]$	d_2	3
$[succ]$	$[x \leftarrow 3, y \leftarrow 3]$	$[x, @]$	d_2	1
$[3, succ]$	$[x \leftarrow 3, y \leftarrow 3]$	$[@]$	d_2	2
$[4]$	$[x \leftarrow 3, y \leftarrow 3]$	$[]$	d_2	5
$[4, sqrt]$	$[x \leftarrow 3]$	$[@]$	d_1	6
$[2]$	$[x \leftarrow 3]$	$[]$	d_1	5
$[2]$	[]	$[]$	[]	6

Fig. 11.3 A computation using the SECD machine

Program Correctness   The computing beginner often holds that the design and writing of an efficient program are the most important operations on which their occupation is based. Software Engineering, however, has largely shown, both in theory, as in ample experimental studies, that the most critical factors in a software project are its correctness, readability, maintainability and its dependability. In economic terms, these factors account for more than fifty percent of the total cost; in social terms, software maintenance (which depends in a critical way on its readability) can involve hundreds of different people over a period of tens of years. In ethical terms, the life, or health, of many hundreds of people can depend on the reliability and correctness of a software system.

In particular, the time is still far away when we will be able to produce software with correctness guarantees comparable to those with which a civil engineer releases their own products (bridges, columns, structures). The civil engineer, indeed, has at his disposal a whole corpus of applied mathematics with which to "calculate" the structures. If a bridge must take a certain load, be subjected to certain winds, can be exposed to seismic events of given magnitude, etc., it must have given dimensions, must be built using materials with certain characteristics, etc. These characteristics are not determined by the designer's taste but are calculated using appropriate mathematical techniques. The information-system designer is far from having at their disposition a mathematics even remotely on a par with those available to the building designer.

One of the reasons for the delay in being able to produce such a level of correctness guarantee is that to reason about programs with side effects is particularly difficult and expensive in terms of computation time. On the contrary, there are standard techniques, based on appropriate variants of induction, that allow reasoning about side-effect free programs.

Here, then, is a first reason for the study of pure functional languages. If reliability, readability, correctness are more important than efficiency, there is no doubt that functional programming generates more readable software, whose correctness is easier to establish and, therefore, is more reliable.

Program schemata   Higher-order functions, which are commonly used in the functional paradigm, have important pragmatic advantages. A typical way of using higher-order is that of exploiting it to define *general programming schemata* from which specific programs can be obtained by instantiation. Let us consider, for example, a simple program that adds the elements of a list of integers. We can write this in ML as:

```
fun addl nil = 0
  | addl n::rest = n + addl(rest);
```

If we now want the product of a list, we can write:

```
fun prodl nil = 1
  | prodl n::rest = n * prodl(rest);
```

It is clear that these two programs are instances of a single program schema, which is generally called *fold*:

```
fun fold f i nil = i
  | fold f i n::rest = f(n, fold f i rest);
```

Here, f is the binary operation to be applied to successive elements of the list (+ or *), i is the value to use in the terminal case (the neutral element of the operation) and the third parameter is the list over which to perform the iteration.

If we ignore the fact that + and * are infix operators rather than prefix, we can immediately see that we can define our two functions using *fold*:

```
val suml = fold + 0;
val prodl  = fold * 1;
```

Here, the fact that the function is higher-order is used both to pass to *fold* the function to iterate over the list, and to make fold + 0 returns a function which requires an argument of list type.

The extensive use of program schemata increases the modularity of code and allows correctness proofs to be factored.

Assessment   The arguments we have adduced in favour of functional languages do not just come from academic environments. Probably the most passionate defence of the functional paradigm is that in John Backus' 1977 Turing Award acceptance lecture (the award was bestowed for his work on FORTRAN).

Anticipating the times, in some sense, Backus put the concepts of correctness and readability at the centre of the process of software production, relegating efficiency to second place. He also identified *pure* functional programming as the tool with which to proceed in the direction he advocated. Today, we have machines that are much more efficient than those of 1977 but we have not made the necessary progress in the area of software correctness techniques.

No-one has however really experimented with large-scale purely functional programs in such a way that a real comparison with imperative programs can be made. Significant experiments have been conducted at IBM using the FP language defined by Backus, and in academic research centres using the language Haskell. All the other functional languages in use have conspicuous imperative aspects which, although used in ways and places very different from those of ordinary imperative languages, dissipate the advantages of functional languages in terms of correctness proofs (but not in terms of readability and schema reuse). In conclusion, we must say that, from the practical point of programming (understood in the light of the entire software production process), the superiority of one paradigm over the other has yet to be shown.

It is on the second level, that of programming language design, that the studies and experience with functional languages has had a significant impact. Many individual concepts and experiments in functional programming have later migrated to other paradigms. Among these concepts, the best known to the reader is that of type system. The concepts of generics, polymorphism, type safety, all originated in functional languages (because is it simpler to study and to implement them in an environment without side-effects).

11.6 Fundamentals: The λ-calculus

At the start of the chapter, we saw that the functional paradigm is inspired by a foundation for computability theory, different to that based on Turing machines (but equivalent to that as far as expressive power is concerned). In this section, we present the important points of this formal system, which is called the λ-calculus.

The syntax of the λ-calculus is extremely austere and can be given in one line using the following grammar, where X is a non-terminal which represents a generic variable, M is the initial symbol, the dot and the two parentheses are terminal symbols:

$$M ::= X \mid (MM) \mid (\lambda X.M).$$

In addition, let us assume that we also have a denumerable set of terminal symbols for variables which, for ease of notation, we will in general write using the last lower-case letters of the alphabet: x, y, z, etc.

The reader will recognise in these clauses both application and abstraction (written using λ instead of fn) which we introduced informally in Sect. 11.1.3. We call λ-terms (or, simply, terms) the strings of terminals which are derived from this grammar.

Syntactic conventions, free and bound variables   The "official" books on the λ-calculus introduce many additional conventions to simplify the notation. For example, application associates to the left, or:

$$M_1 M_2 \cdots M_n \quad \text{stand for } (\cdots (M_1 M_2) \cdots M_n).$$

The scope of a λ extends as far as possible to the right (that is, $\lambda x.xy$ stands for $(\lambda x.(xy))$ and not for $((\lambda x.x).y)$). We will seek to use these conventions as little as possible by using parentheses where necessary. We will also speak of *subterms*, with the obvious meaning (for example, (xy) is a subterm of $(\lambda x.(xy))$ but λx is not).

The abstraction operator *binds* the variable upon which is acts,[8] in the double sense that, semantically, consistent renaming of the bound variable does not modify the semantics of an expression and, syntactically, possible substitutions have no effect on bound variables. We formalise these aspects in the following definitions. First, we define, for an arbitrary expression, M, the set of its *free variables*, which we denote by $Fv(M)$, and of its bound variables $Bv(M)$:

$$
\begin{aligned}
Fv(x) &= \{x\} & Bv(x) &= \emptyset, \\
Fv(MN) &= Fv(M) \cup Fv(N) & Bv(MN) &= Bv(M) \cup Bv(N), \\
Fv(\lambda x.M) &= Fv(M) - \{x\} & Bv(\lambda x.M) &= Bv(M) \cup \{x\}.
\end{aligned}
$$

Substitution   We can formally define the concept of substitution without variable capture which constitutes the core of the copy rule. We define, therefore, the notation, $M[N/x]$ which we read as the substitution of N for the free occurrences of x in M:

$$
\begin{aligned}
x[N/x] &= N, \\
y[N/x] &= y & &\text{when } x \neq y, \\
(M_1 M_2)[N/x] &= (M_1[N/x]M_2[N/x]), \\
(\lambda y.M)[N/x] &= (\lambda y.M[N/x]) & &\text{when } x \neq y \text{ e } y \notin Fv(N), \\
(\lambda y.M)[N/x] &= (\lambda y.M) & &\text{when } x = y.
\end{aligned}
$$

The definition is simple. Practically, to substitute N in place of x in M, we "push" the substitution down towards the leaves of the syntax tree, that is to the variables, and check if the leaf is labelled with x or with some other variable. But the definition is subtle, since it avoids capture of the variables in N by some λ. This is the reason why the last clause requires that $y \notin Fv(N)$. What happens if, on the other hand, y *is present in N*? We can rename the variable bound by λ. As we said above, indeed,

---

[8]Remember what was said in Sect. 7.1 about formal parameters to procedures.

it is not the name of the variable that counts when a λ is applied, but only the way in which it is used. In other words, we will consider as equivalent two terms that differ only by the names of their bound variables. For example, $\lambda x.x$ and $\lambda y.y$, or $\lambda x.\lambda y.x$ and $\lambda v.\lambda w.v$.

Alpha equivalence   The intuitive idea that two expressions are equivalent when they differ only in the names of their free variables is formalised in the concept of α-equivalence:

$$\lambda x.M \equiv_\alpha \lambda y.M[y/x] \quad y \text{ fresh}$$

where by "y fresh", we mean that y is a new variable not present in M.

Two terms that differ by just the replacement of some subterm of one term by an α-equivalent subterm will be considered identical.

Computation: β reduction   Computation proceeds by rewriting according to the prescriptions of β-reduction:

$$(\lambda x.M)N \rightarrow_\beta M[N/x].$$

More generally, we will say that M β-reduces to N (and we write $M \rightarrow N$) when N is the result of the application of one step of β-reduction to some subterm of M. A subterm of the form $(\lambda x.M)N$ is a *redex* whose *reductum* is $M[N/x]$. Note that the concept of β-reduction is not deterministic. Whenever there exists more than one redex in the same term, it is not prescribed which one will be chosen.

β-reduction is a relation that is not symmetric. In general, if $M \rightarrow N$, it is not the case that $N \rightarrow M'$. It is useful to introduce a symmetric relation which we call β-equivalence, defined as the reflexive and transitive closure of β-reduction and denoted by $=_\beta$. Intuitively, $M =_\beta N$ means that M and N are connected through a sequence of β-reductions (not necessarily all in the same direction).

Normal forms   When a λ-term that does not contain a redex, β-reduction terminates; such terms are called *normal forms*. For example, $\lambda x.\lambda y.x$ is a normal form, while the term $\lambda x.(\lambda y.y)x)$ is not a normal form because it contains the redex $(\lambda y.y)x$. We have, then:

$$\lambda x.(\lambda y.y)x \rightarrow \lambda x.x$$

and $\lambda x.x$ is now a normal form.

Some terms have reductions that terminate (in a normal form). There are however also terms which reduce an infinite number of times without ever producing a normal form, as for example:

$$(\lambda x.xx)(\lambda x.xx) \rightarrow (xx)[(\lambda x.xx)/x]$$
$$= (\lambda x.xx)(\lambda x.xx)$$
$$\rightarrow (\lambda x.xx)(\lambda x.xx)$$
$$\rightarrow \dots.$$

Fig. 11.4 The confluence
property for λ-terms

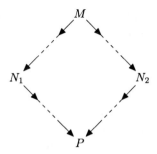

Confluence   A fundamental property of the λ-calculus is that its inherent non-determinism has no dangerous effects. In any way we might choose the redex to reduce inside a term, the final result (the normal form) of a sequence of reductions is always the same. Stated in a more formal manner, we have the following property, called *confluence* and graphically represented in Fig. 11.4.

> If M reduces to N_1 in a number of reduction steps, and M also reduces to N_2 in a number of reduction steps, then there exists a term, P, such that both N_1 and N_2 both reduce to P in a number of steps.

An important consequence of this property is that if a term can be reduced to a normal form, this normal form is unique and independent of the path followed to reach it.

Fixpoint operators   We have seen how the λ-calculus formalises many concepts that we have seen in this chapter.[9] We have not however introduced any mechanisms for the definition of recursive functions. The λ-calculus has no notion of external or global environment in which to assign names to terms, as happens when defining a recursive function, for which naming seems to be a fundamental concept.

The point (surprising at first sight) is that the concepts of abstraction and local environment (which is derived from the possibility of nested λ's) are *on their own sufficient* for the definition of recursion or, more precisely, fixed points.

Let us consider the following very simple recursive definition, which, for simplicity, we write in a λ-calculus extended with integers and conditional expressions:[10]

$$Z = \lambda n. \text{ if } n = 0 \text{ then } 0 \text{ else } 1 + Z(n-1). \tag{11.1}$$

---

[9]We should rather say: formalises many of the concepts that we have seen in this *book*. The λ-calculus was a fundamental inspiration to the design of programming languages starting with AL-GOL and LISP. Concepts such as scope, local environment, call by name, to mention only the most important, have been "imported" into programming languages on the basis of analogous concepts in the λ-calculus.

[10]We use this extension only to simplify the presentation. In the λ-calculus, it is possible to *codify* numbers and conditions using only variables, abstractions and applications.

Our experience with programming languages suggests, perhaps, that we should read this relation as a *definition*:

$$Z \stackrel{def}{=} \lambda n. \text{ if } n = 0 \text{ then } 0 \text{ else } 1 + Z(n - 1).$$

But this is not the only reading possible (in particular, it is not possible in the λ-calculus, which has no concept of global environment to allow us to use the name of a term inside an expression). A mathematician would probably read it as an *equation* with unknown Z (recall the discussion on inductive definitions in Sect. 6.5). For this very simple equation, it is clear that one solution (rather, in this case, the unique solution) is the identity function:

$$Id(n) = n. \tag{11.2}$$

What we are looking for is a general method which allows us to pass from an equation such as (11.1) to an *algorithm*, that is to a λ-term, which is a solution to this equation when the equality symbol is interpreted as β-equivalence:

$$Z =_\beta \lambda n. \text{ if } n = 0 \text{ then } 0 \text{ else } 1 + Z(n - 1). \tag{11.3}$$

Note that this is to ask more than simply provide an arbitrary function such as (11.2). It requires a term which *in the calculus* satisfies (11.3).[11]

Let us consider, first, the function that is obtained from (11.3) by λ-abstracting on the unknown function:

$$F \stackrel{def}{=} \lambda f.\lambda n. \text{ if } n = 0 \text{ then } 0 \text{ else } 1 + f(n - 1).$$

Hence our problem is to find a suitable term g such that:

$$g =_\beta F(g).$$

A term, g, which satisfies an equation of this type is called a *fixed point* of F. Therefore our problem of finding a solution to (11.3) can be reformulated as a problem of finding the fixed point of some function.

We want now to show that the λ-calculus provides a general method "automatically" to solve these equations. Let us, indeed, consider the following term, which for convenience (and following tradition), we name Y:

$$Y \stackrel{def}{=} \lambda f.(\lambda x.f(xx))(\lambda x.f(xx)).$$

This is a term which can be reduced an infinite number of times without reaching normal form. But it can be put to good use. Let us indeed try to apply it to an

----

[11] The term $\lambda n.n$ is an algorithm for the only function which satisfies (11.1), but it is *not* a solution of (11.3), which expresses a determinate behaviour through reduction.

arbitrary term, M:

$$Y M =_\beta (\lambda x.M(xx))(\lambda x.M(xx))$$
$$=_\beta M((\lambda x.M(xx))(\lambda x.M(xx)))$$
$$=_\beta M(Y M).$$

In the last step, we have used the fact that was established in the first line, that

$$Y M =_\beta (\lambda x.M(xx))(\lambda x.M(xx))$$

and we have then substituted equals for equals. $Y M$ is therefore a fixed point of M: Y is a term in the calculus which can compute the fixed point of an arbitrary term.[12] We say that Y is a *fixpoint operator*. It is then quite clear that Y provides solutions to any recursive equation. In particular, it gives us a solution to (11.3):

$$Id \stackrel{def}{=} Y F.$$

The term Id thus defined has a reduction behaviour which satisfies the relation with which we started. It is instructive to try to apply this function to a specific argument to see how the mechanism of fixed points is really capable of computing a recursive function. For example:

$$Id\ 2 \stackrel{def}{=} (Y F)\ 2$$
$$\rightarrow F(Y F)\ 2$$
$$\rightarrow \text{if } 2 = 0 \text{ then } 0 \text{ else } 1 + ((Y F)(2 - 1))$$
$$\rightarrow 1 + ((Y F)\ 1)$$
$$\rightarrow 1 + (F\ (Y F)\ 1)$$
$$\rightarrow 1 + ((\text{if } 1 = 0 \text{ then } 0 \text{ else } 1 + ((Y F)(1 - 1))))$$
$$\rightarrow 1 + (1 + ((Y F)\ 0))$$
$$\rightarrow 1 + (1 + (\text{if } 0 = 0 \text{ then } 0 \text{ else } 1 + ((Y F)\ (0 - 1))))$$
$$\rightarrow 1 + (1 + 0)$$
$$\rightarrow 2.$$

At each "recursive call", $Y F$ provides a new copy of the body of the function which is used on the next call.

What we have just seen is also true for the definition of recursive values which are not functions. The stream that we defined in Sect. 11.3.5 as:

---

[12]This shows also that, in the λ-calculus, every term has always at least one fixed point, that computed by Y.

```
val infinity2 = 2 :: infinity2;
```

is nothing more than a fixed point:

$$\texttt{infinity2} \stackrel{def}{=} Y(\lambda l. \, 2 :: l).$$

Observe that Y is a fixpoint operator with respect to β-equality.[13] If, instead of β-reduction, we use a different strategy, for example, the analogue of reduction by value which we defined for functional languages, Y is no longer able to compute fixed points. For reduction by value, another operator must be used, for example:

$$H \stackrel{def}{=} \lambda g. ((\lambda f. ff)(\lambda f. (g(\lambda x. ffx)))).$$

For reasons of efficiency, implementations of functional programming languages do not use fixpoint operators to implement recursion. However, fixpoint operators play a role that is very important to the theory of these languages.

Expressiveness of the λ-calculus   This very simple formal system, constructed only from the concepts of application and abstraction, is not as rudimentary as it seems, if it can express arbitrary recursions. Indeed, it is possible to show that the λ-calculus is a Turing-complete formalism. In the first place, it is possible to encode the natural numbers as λ-terms (a λ-term, $\underline{n}$ is associated with the number n) and, then, show that to every computable function, f, there corresponds a λ-term M_f which computes f: if $f(n) = m$, then $M_f \underline{n} \to \underline{m}$.

11.7 Chapter Summary

In this chapter, we have presented the functional programming paradigm. In its *pure* form, this is a computational model which does not contain the concept of modifiable variable. Computation proceeds by the rewriting of terms that denote functions. The main concepts that we have discussed are:

- *Abstraction*. A mechanism for passing from one expression denoting a value to one denoting a function.
- *Application* A mechanism dual to abstraction, by which a function is applied to an argument.
- *Computation by rewriting* or *reduction*, in which an expression is repeatedly simplified until a form that can not be further reduced is encountered.
- *Redex*. The syntactic structure which is simplified during reduction and is formed from the application of an abstraction to an expression.
- The centrality of *higher order* in this mode of computation.

---

[13]Clearly it is not unique. For another operator slightly more complex than Y but which satisfies a stronger relation, see Exercise 7.

- The concept of *value* which corresponds to those syntactic forms not otherwise reducible and where reduction therefore terminates.
- The different *evaluation strategies*: by value (or eager), by name, lazy.
- Some mechanisms that the most common functional languages add to the fundamental nucleus. Among these, recall: an interactive environment, a rich system of types, pattern matching, imperative aspects such as variables and assignments.
- The *SECD machine*, a prototype abstract machine for higher-order functional languages using the by-value strategy.
- A comparison of the functional and imperative paradigms, centred on the notion of program correctness.
- The λ-calculus, a simple and powerful formal system that constitutes the formal nucleus of all functional languages.

11.8 Bibliographical Note

Reading the original article by John McCarthy on LISP is still didactically important [7]. An elementary introduction to programming using ML is to be found in [11], while [4] is a more advanced text (which uses the Caml dialect); [9] is the official definition of the language and it is useful to read it together with the commentary [8].

The implementation of functional languages, with particular regard to lazy evaluation is dealt with in [10]. The SECD machine was introduced in the pioneering work of Peter Landin [6].

John Backus' lecture for the Turing Award [1] should be essential reading (at least for its first part) for every student of programming languages.

The lambda calculus was introduced in the 1930s by Alonzo Church. An original reference is [3]. The modern reference text is [2], even if [5] is a clearer and more accessible introduction.

11.9 Exercises

1. Consider the following definitions in ML:

```
fun K x y = x;
fun I x = x;
fun Omega x = Omega x;
```

State what the result of evaluating the following expression will be.

```
K (I 3) (Omega 1).
```

What would be the result if ML adopted a lazy strategy?

2. Write a function map which applies its first parameter (which will be a function) to all the elements of a list passed as its second argument.
3. Describe formally the operation of the SECD machine, by giving a definition using the structural operational semantics that we introduced in Sect. 2.5.
4. In λ-calculus, we define the code of a natural number, n, as:

$$\underline{n} \stackrel{def}{=} \lambda f.\lambda x. f^n x \stackrel{def}{=} \lambda f.\lambda x. f(f \cdots (fx) \cdots),$$

where, in the body, there are n occurrences of f. Give the definition of a term, *prod* such that:

$$prod\ \underline{n}\ \underline{m} \rightarrow \underline{n * m}.$$

5. Apply the technique of calculating fixed points to solve the following equation for the unknown *fact*:

$$fact =_\beta \lambda n. \text{ if } n = 0 \text{ then } 1 \text{ else } n * fact(n - 1)$$

and describe the reduction which computes the value of its solution applied to argument 2.
6. Apply the technique of calculating fixed points to solve the following equation for the unknown h:

$$h =_\beta \lambda x. \text{ if } x > 100 \text{ then } x - 10 \text{ else } h(h(x + 11)).$$

Call the solution *Ninetyone*, then calculate *Ninetyone(99)*.
7. Consider the λ-terms:

$$A = \lambda x.\lambda y.y(xxy),$$

$$\Theta = AA.$$

Show that Θ is a fixed-point operator for which the relation:

$$\Theta M \rightarrow \cdots \rightarrow M(\Theta M).$$

is true. This relation is stronger than that satisfied by Y, for which only $YM =_\beta M(YM)$ is true. The term, Θ, is called the Turing fixpoint operator.

References

1. J. Backus. Can programming be liberated from the von Neumann style? A functional style and its algebra of programs. *Commun. ACM*, 21(8):613–641, 1978. doi:10.1145/359576.359579.
2. H. Barendregt. *The Lambda Calculus: Its Syntax and Semantics*. Elsevier, Amsterdam, 1984.
3. A. Church. *The Calculi of Lambda Conversion*. Princeton Univ. Press, Princeton, 1941.
4. G. Cousineau and M. Mauny. *The Functional Approach to Programming*. Cambridge Univ. Press, Cambridge, 1998.

5. R. Hindley and P. Seldin. *Introduction to Combinators and Lambda-Calculus*. Cambridge Univ. Press, Cambridge, 1986.
6. P. J. Landin. The mechanical evaluation of expressions. *The Computer Journal*, 6(4):308–320, 1964. citeseer.ist.psu.edu/cardelli85understanding.html.
7. J. McCarthy. Recursive functions of symbolic expressions and their computation by machine, part I. *Commun. ACM*, 3(4):184–195, 1960. doi:10.1145/367177.367199.
8. R. Milner and M. Tofte. *Commentary on Standard ML*. MIT Press, Cambridge, 1991.
9. R. Milner, M. Tofte, R. Harper, and D. MacQueen. *The Definition of Standard ML—Revised*. MIT Press, Cambridge, 1997.
10. S. Peyton-Jones. *The Implementation of Functional Programming Languages*. Prentice Hall, New York, 1987. Online at http://research.microsoft.com/Users/simonpj/papers/slpj-book-1987/index.htm.
11. J. D. Ullman. *Elements of ML Programming*. Prentice-Hall, Upper Saddle River, 1994.

Chapter 12
The Logic Programming Paradigm

In this chapter we analyse the other paradigm which, together with functional programming, supports declarative programming. The logic programming paradigm includes both theoretical and fully implemented languages, of which the best known is surely PROLOG. Even if there are big differences of a pragmatic and, for some, of a theoretical nature between these languages, they all share the idea of interpreting computation as logical deduction.

In this chapter, we will therefore examine these concepts while trying to limit the theoretical part. We also adopt the approach that has characterised the rest of the text while examining this paradigm. We do not mean therefore to teach programming in PROLOG, even if we present various examples of real programs, but we do intend to provide enough basis for understanding and, in a short time, mastering this and other logic programming languages.

12.1 Deduction as Computation

A well-known slogan due to R. Kowalski, exactly captures the concepts that underpin the activity of programming: Algorithm = Logic + Control. According to this "equation", the specification of an algorithm, and therefore its formulation in programming languages, can be separated into three parts. On the one side, the logic of the solution is specified. That is, the "what" must be done is defined. On the other, those aspects related to control are specified, and therefore the "how" of finding the desired solution is clarified. The programmer who uses a traditional imperative language must take account of both these components using the mechanisms which we have variously analysed in the chapters that precede this one. Logic programming, on the other hand, was originally defined with the idea of cleanly separating these two aspects. The programmer is only required, at least in principle, to provide a logical specification. Everything related to control is relegated to the abstract machine. Using a computational mechanism based on a particular deduction rule (resolution), the interpreter searches through the space of possible solutions for the one specified

M. Gabbrielli, S. Martini, *Programming Languages: Principles and Paradigms,*
Undergraduate Topics in Computer Science,
DOI 10.1007/978-1-84882-914-5_12, © Springer-Verlag London Limited 2010

by the "logic", defining in this way the sequence of operations necessary to reach the final result.

The basis for this view of computation as logical deduction can be traced back to the work of K. Gödel and J. Herbrand in the 1930s. In particular, Herbrand anticipated, even in an incompletely formal way, some ideas on the process of unification, which, as we will see, forms the basic computational mechanism of logic programming languages.

It was not until the 1960s that a formal definition (due to A. Robinson) of this process appeared and only ten years later (in the early 1970s) it was realised that formal automatic deduction of a particular kind could be interpreted as a computational mechanism. The first programming languages in the logic programming paradigm were created, among which PROLOG (the name is an acronym for PROgramming in LOGic, for more information on the story of this language, see Sect. 13.4).

Today there are many implemented versions of PROLOG and there exist various other languages in this paradigm (as far as applications are concerned, those including constraints are of particular interest). All of these languages (and PROLOG was the first) allow the use of constructs permitting the specification of control for reasons of efficiency. Since these constructs do not have a direct logical interpretation, they make the semantics of the language more complicated, and cause the loss of part of the purely declarative nature of the logic paradigm. This notwithstanding, we are still dealing with logic programming languages, even including these "impure" aspects, which require the programmer to do little more than formulate (or declare) the specification of the problem to be solved. In some cases, the resulting programs are really surprising in their brevity, simplicity and clarity, as we will see in the next section.

Terminological Note Logic programming, which constitutes the theoretical formalism, is distinguished from PROLOG, a language which has different implementations and for which a standard has recently been defined. The concepts we introduce below, if not otherwise stated, are valid for both formalisms. The important differences will be explicitly pointed out. The programming examples which we include (usually in `this font`) are all PROLOG code which could be run on some implementation of the language. The theoretical concepts, on the other hand, even when they are valid for PROLOG, use mathematical concepts and are rendered in *italic characters*. Moreover, we will follow the PROLOG convention that we always write variables as strings of characters beginning with an upper-case letter. Finally note that, as mentioned before, there exist several other languages, different from PROLOG, in the logic programming paradigm. We call these logic programming languages, or logic languages, for short.

12.1.1 An Example

We try to substantiate what we said in the last section with an example which will
be fairly informal, at least for now, given that we have introduced neither the syntax
nor the semantics of logic languages.

Let us therefore consider the following problem. It is desired to arrange three 1s,
three 2s, ..., three 9s in a list (which therefore will consist of 27 numbers) such that,
for each $i \in [1, 9]$, there are exactly i numbers between two successive occurrences
(in the list) numbered i. Therefore, for example, $1, 2, 1, 8, 2, 4, 6, 2$ could be a part
of the final solution, while $1, 2, 1, 8, 2, 4, 2, 6$ might not be one (because there is
only a single number between the last two occurrences of 2). The reader is invited
to try to write a program that solves this problem using their preferred imperative
programming language. This is not a difficult exercise but does requires some care,
because even if the "what" must be done is clear, the "how" of the desired solution is
not immediately clear. For example, in a very naive (and completely inefficient) way,
it might be thought that all possible permutations of a list of 27 numbers containing
three 1s, three 2s, three 3s, ..., three 9s, could be generated and then checked to see
if one of them satisfies the required propriety. This solution, too, probably one of
the simplest, however, requires the specification in detail of the aspects of control
necessary to generate the permutations of a list.

Reasoning in a declarative fashion, on the other hand, we can proceed as follows. First, we need a list which we will call Ls. This list will have to contain 27
elements, something that we can specify using a unary predicate (that is, a relation
symbol)[1] list_of_27. If we write list_of_27(Ls), we mean, therefore, to
say that Ls must be a list of 27 elements. In other words, list_of_27 defines
a relation formed of all possible lists of 27 elements. To achieve this aim, we can
define list_of_27 as follows:

```
list_of_27(Ls):-
Ls = [_,_,_,_,_,_,_,_,_,_,_,_,_,_,_,_,_,_,_,_,_,_,_,_,_,_,_].
```

where the part to the left of the : - symbol denotes what is being defined, while
the part to the right of : - indicates the definition. The = denotes an equality concept whose definition is left to intuition, for the present (it is different, however,
from assignment). Anticipating the PROLOG notation for lists, here we write [X1,
X2, ...,Xn] to denote the list that contains the n variables X1, X2, ..., Xn (see
Sect. 12.4.5 for more details about lists).

In order to satisfy our specification, the list, Ls, in addition to being composed of
27 elements, will have to contain a sublist[2] in which the number 1 appears followed
by any other number, by another occurrence of the number 1, then another number
and finally a last occurrence of the number 1. Such a sublist can be specified as

---

[1] Recall that unary means that it has a single argument while n-ary means that there are n arguments.

[2] Recall that Li is a sublist of Ls if Ls is obtained by concatenating a (possibly empty) list with
Li and with another list (itself also possibly empty).

```
[1,X,1,Y,1]
```

where X and Y are variables. More efficiently, we can write:

```
[1,_,1,_,1]
```

where _ is the *anonymous* variable, that is a variable whose name is of no interest and which is distinct from all other variables present, including all other anonymous variables. Assuming that we have available a binary predicate sublist(X,Y) whose meaning is that the first argument (X) is a sublist of the second (Y),[3] our requirement therefore can be expressed by writing:

```
sublist([1,_,1,_,1], Ls)
```

Moving on to number 2 and reasoning in a similar fashion, we obtain that the list Ls must also contain the sublist:

```
[2,_,_,2,_,_2]
```

and therefore the following must also be true:

```
sublist([2,_,_,2,_,_,2], Ls)
```

We can repeat this reasoning as far as number 9, hence the sol program that we want to produce can be described as follows:

```
sol(Ls) :-                                                              1
  list_of_27(Ls),
  sublist([9,_,_,_,_,_,_,_,_,9,_,_,_,_,_,_,_,_,_,9], Ls),              3
  sublist([8,_,_,_,_,_,_,_,8,_,_,_,_,_,_,_,_,8], Ls),
  sublist([7,_,_,_,_,_,_,7,_,_,_,_,_,_,_,7], Ls),                       5
  sublist([6,_,_,_,_,_,6,_,_,_,_,_,6], Ls),
  sublist([5,_,_,_,_,5,_,_,_,_,5], Ls),                                 7
  sublist([4,_,_,_,4,_,_,_,4], Ls),
  sublist([3,_,_,_,3,_,_,_,3], Ls),                                     9
  sublist([2,_,_,2,_,_,2], Ls),
  sublist([1,_,1,_,1], Ls).                                             11

list_of_27(Ls):-                                                        13
Ls = [_,_,_,_,_,_,_,_,_,_,_,_,_,_,_,_,_,_,_,_,_,_,_,_,_,_,_].
```

where, as before, the part to the right of the :- symbol is the definition of what lies to its left. What we have written above says that to find a solution to our problem (sol(Ls) in line 1), all the properties described in lines 2–11 must be satisfied. The commas that separate the various predicates are to be interpreted as "and", that is as conjunctions in the logical sense. What we have provided therefore is nothing

---

[3]The definition of sublist is given in Sect. 12.4.5.

more than a specification that, in substance, formally repeats the formulation of the problem and which, as we will see below, can be interpreted in purely logical terms.

This declarative reading, for all of its elegance and compactness, would not be of great of use as the solution to our problem if it were not accompanied by a procedural interpretation and must therefore be translated into a conventional programming language. The important characteristics of the paradigm that we are considering is precisely that the (logical) specifications we write are to all intents and purposes executable programs. The code described above in lines 1–14 (plus the definition of sublist in Sect. 12.4.5) is indeed a genuine PROLOG program that can be evaluated by an interpreter to obtain the desired solution.

In other words, our specification can also be read in a procedural fashion, as follows. Line (1) contains the declaration of a procedure called sol; it has a single formal parameter, Ls. The body of this procedure is defined by lines (2) to (11), where we find the following ten procedure calls. On line (2), procedure list_of_27 is called with actual parameter Ls which is defined as we have seen above and which therefore instantiates[4] its actual parameter into a list of 27 anonymous variables. Therefore, on line (3), we have the call:

```
sublist([9,_,_,_,_,_,_,_,_,_,9,_,_,_,_,_,_,_,_,_,9], Ls)
```

We assume that this call arranges matters so that the list which appears as the first parameter is a sublist of the list which is bound to the second parameter (Ls), possibly by instantiating the variable Ls. Similarly for the other calls until line (11). Parameter passing occurs in a way similar to call by name and, in PROLOG, the order in which the different procedure calls appear in the text specifies the order of evaluation (in the case of pure logic programs, on the other hand, no order is specified).

Given the preceding definition of procedure sol, the call sol(Ls) returns Ls instantiated with a solution to the problem, such as for example the following:

```
1,9,1,2,1,8,2,4,6,2,7,9,4,5,8,6,3,4,7,5,3,9,6,8,3,5,7.
```

Successive calls to the same procedure will allow us also to obtain the other solutions to the problem.

With this procedural interpretation, one has therefore a true programming language which allows us to express, in a compact and relatively simple fashion, programs that solve even very complex problems. For this power, the language pays the penalty of efficiency. In the preceding program, despite its apparent simplicity, the computation performed by the language's abstract machine is very complex, given that the interpreter must try the various combinations of possible sublists until it finds the one that satisfies all the conditions. In these search processes, a *backtracking* mechanism is used. When the computation arrives at a point at which it cannot

---

[4]Even if the terminology is intuitively clear: by instantiation of a variable is meant substituting for it a syntactic object. We will give a precise definition in Sect. 12.3.

proceed, the computation that has been performed is undone so that a decision point can be reached, if it exists, at which an alternative is chosen that is different form the previous one (if this alternative does not exist, the computation terminates in failure). It is not difficult to see that, in general, this search process can have exponential complexity.

12.2 Syntax

Logic programs are sets of logic formulæ of a particular form. We begin therefore with some basic notions for defining the syntax.

The logic of interest here is first-order logic; it is also called *predicate calculus*. The terminology refers to the fact that symbols are used to express (or, in a more old-fashioned terminology, to "predicate") properties of elements of a fixed domain of discourse, $\mathscr{D}$. More expressive logics (second, third, etc., order) also permit predicates whose arguments are more complicated objects such as sets and functions over $\mathscr{D}$ (second order), sets of functions (third order), etc., in addition to elements of $\mathscr{D}$.

12.2.1 The Language of First-Order Logic

If we are to speak of predicate calculus (and therefore of logic programs), we have to define the language. *The language of first-order logic* consists of three components:

1. An *alphabet*.
2. *Terms* defined over this alphabet.
3. *Well-formed formulæ* defined over this alphabet.

Let us look at the various components of this definition in the order in which they appear above.

Alphabet   The alphabet is usually a set[5] of symbols. In this case, we consider the set to be partitioned into two disjoint subsets: the set of *logical symbols* (common to all first-order languages) and the set of *non-logical* (or *extra-logical*) *symbols* (which are specific to a domain of interest). For example, all first-order languages will use a (logical) symbol to denote conjunction. If we are considering orderings on a set, we will probably also have the < symbol as one of the non-logical symbols.

The set of *logical symbols* contains the following elements:

- The logical connectives $\wedge$ (conjunction), $\vee$ (disjunction), $\neg$ (negation), $\rightarrow$ (implication) and $\leftrightarrow$ (logical equivalence).
- The propositional constants *true* and *false*.

---

[5] All the sets we consider below are finite or denumerable.

- The quantifiers ∃ (exists) and ∀ (forall).
- Some punctuation symbols such as brackets "(" and ")" and comma ",".
- An (denumerably) infinite set V of *variables*, written $X, Y, Z, \ldots$

The *non-logical* (or *extra-logical*) symbols are defined by a *signature with predicates* (Σ, Π). This is a pair in which the first element, Σ is the *function signature*, that is a set of function symbols, each considered with its own arity.[6] The second element of the pair, Π, is the *predicate signature*, a set of predicate symbols together with their arities. Functions of arity 0 are said to be *constants* and are denoted by the letters $a, b, c, \ldots$. Function symbols of positive arity are, as usual, denoted by $f, g, h, \ldots$, while predicate symbols are denoted by $p, q, r, \ldots$. Let us assume that the sets Σ and Π have an empty intersection and are also disjoint from the other sets of symbols listed above. The difference between function and predicate symbols is that the former must be interpreted as functions, while the latter must be interpreted as relations. This distinction will become clearer when we discuss formulæ.

Terms The concept of term, which is fundamental to mathematical logic and Computer Science, is used implicitly in many contexts. For example, an arithmetic expression is a term obtained by applying (arithmetic) operators to operands. Other types of construct, too, such as strings, binary trees, lists, and so on, can be conveniently seen as terms which are obtained using appropriate constructors.

In the simplest case, a term is obtained by applying a function symbol to as many variables and constants as required by its arity. For example, if a and b are constants, X and Y are both variables and f and g have arity 2, then $f(a, b)$ and $g(a, X)$ are terms. Nothing prevents the use of terms as the arguments to a function, provided that the arity is always respected. We can, for example, write $g(f(a, b), Y)$ or $g(f(a, f(X, Y)), X)$ and so on.

In the most general possible case, we can define terms as follows.

Definition 12.1 (Terms) The terms over a signature Σ (and over the set, V, of variables) are defined inductively[7] as follows:

- A variable (in V) is a term.
- If f (in Σ) is a function symbol of arity n and $t_1, \ldots, t_n$ are terms, then $f(t_1, \ldots, t_n)$ is a term.

As a particular case of the second point, a constant is a term. According to the letter of the definition, a term which corresponds to a constant must be written with parentheses: $a(), b(), \ldots$. Let us establish, for ease of reading, that in the case of function symbols of arity 0, parentheses are omitted. Terms without variables are said to be *ground* terms. Terms are usually denoted by the letters $s, t, u, \ldots$. Note that predicates do not appear in terms; they appear in formulæ (to express the properties of terms).

---

[6] Recall that, as stated above, the arity denotes the number of arguments of a function or relation.

[7] See the box on page 153 for inductive definitions.

Formulæ The *well-formed formulæ* (or *formulæ* for short) of the language allow us to express the properties of terms which, from the semantic viewpoint, are properties of some particular domain of interest. For example, if we have the predicate $>$, interpreting it in the usual fashion, writing $> (3, 2)$, we want to express the fact that the term "3" corresponds to a value with is greater than that associated with the term "2." Predicates can then be used to construct complex expressions using logical symbols. For example, the formula $> (X, Y) \land > (Y, Z) \rightarrow > (X, Z)$ expresses the transitivity of $>$; it asserts that if $> (X, Y)$ is true and $> (Y, Z)$ is also true then, it is the case that $> (X, Z)$.

Wanting to define formulæ precisely, we have first atomic formulæ (or atoms), constructed by the application of a predicate to the number of terms required by its arity. For example, if p has arity 2, using two the terms introduced above, we can write $p(f(a, b), f(a, X))$. Using logical connectives and quantification, we can construct complex formulæ from atomic ones. As usual, we have an inductive definition (or, equivalently, a free grammar—see Exercise 1).

Definition 12.2 (Formulæ) The (well-formed) formulæ over the signature with terms (Σ, Π) are defined as follows:

1. If $t_1, \ldots, t_n$ are terms over the signature Σ and $p \in \Pi$ is a predicate symbol of arity n, then $p(t_1, \ldots, p_n)$ is a formula.
2. *true* and *false* are formulæ.
3. If F and G are formulæ, then $\neg F$, $(F \land G)$, $(F \lor G)$, $(F \rightarrow G)$ and $(F \leftrightarrow G)$ are formulæ.
4. If F is a formula and X is a variable, then $\forall X.F$ and $\exists X.F$ are formulæ.

12.2.2 Logic Programs

A formula of first-order logic can have a highly complex structure which often determines the effort required to find a proof. In automatic theorem proving, and also in logic programming, particular classes of formulæ, called *clauses*, have been identified which lend themselves to more efficient manipulation, in particular using a special inference rule called *resolution*. A restricted version of the concept of clause, called *definite clauses*, as well as restricted forms of resolution (*SLD resolution*—see page 392) are of interest to us. Using them, the procedure for seeking a proof is not only particularly simple but also allows the explicit calculation of the values of the variables necessary for the proof. These values can be considered as the result of the computation, giving way to an interesting model of computation based on logical deduction. We will see this model in more detail below, for now we will concentrate on syntactic aspects.

Definition 12.3 (Logic Program) Let $H, A_1, \ldots, A_n$ be atomic formulæ. A definite clause (for us simply a "clause") is a formula of the form:

$$H : -A_1, \ldots, A_n.$$

If $n = 0$, the clause is said to be a *unit*, or a fact, and the symbol $:-$ is omitted (but not the final full stop). A logic program is a set of clauses, while a pure PRO-LOG program is a sequence of clauses. A query (or goal) is a sequence of atoms $A_1, \ldots, A_n$.

Let us clarify some points about this definition. First, the symbol $:-$ which we did not include in our alphabet, is simply a symbol denoting (reversed) implication ($\leftarrow$) and is the same as often encountered in real logic languages.[8]

The commas in a clause or in a query, from the logical viewpoint, should be interpreted as logical conjunction. The notation "$H : -A_1, \ldots, A_n$." is therefore an abbreviation for "$H \leftarrow A_1 \wedge \cdots \wedge A_n$." Note that the full stop is part of the notation and is important because it tells a potential interpreter or compiler that the clause it is working on has terminated.

The part on the left of $:-$ is called the *head* of the clause, while that on the right is called the *body*. A fact is therefore a clause with an empty body. A program is a set of clauses in the case of the theoretical formalism. In the case of PROLOG, on the other hand, a program is considered as a sequence because, as we will see, the order of clauses is relevant. Here, we used the simplified terminology found in many recent texts (for example, [1]). For more precise terminology, see the next box. The set of clauses containing the predicate symbol p in their head is said to be the *definition* of p. Variables occurring in the body of a clause and not in the head are said to be *local* variables.

12.3 Theory of Unification

The fundamental computational mechanism in logic programming is the solution of equations between terms using the unification procedure. In this procedure, substitutions are computed so that variables and terms can be bound (or instantiated). The composition of the different substitutions obtained in the course of a computation provides the result of the calculation. Before seeing the computational model for logic programming in detail, we must analyse unification in a little detail, a task we undertake in this section.

12.3.1 The Logic Variable

Before going into detail on the process of unification, it is important to clarify that the concept of variable we are considering is different from that seen in Sect. 6.2.1. Here, we consider the so-called *logic variable* which, analogously to the variables

---

[8]: $-$ is used for pragmatic reasons. When logic languages were being introduced, it was much easier to type $:-$ rather than a left arrow.

Clauses

The reader familiar with first-order logic will have recognised the notion of clause given in Definition 12.3 as being a particular case of the one used in logic. A clause, in the general sense, is indeed a formula of the form:

$$\forall X_1, \ldots, X_m (L_1 \vee L_2 \vee \cdots \vee L_n)$$

where $L_1 \ldots L_n$ are *literals* (atoms or negated atoms) and $X_1, \ldots, X_n$ are all the variables that occur in $L_1 \ldots L_n$. For greater clarity, we separate the negated atoms from the others and therefore we will see a clause as a formula of the form:

$$\forall X_1, \ldots, X_m (A_1 \vee A_2 \vee \cdots \vee A_m, \neg B_1 \vee \neg B_2 \vee \cdots \vee \neg B_k).$$

Using a known logical equivalence which allows implications to be written as disjunction, we can express this formula in the following special form (which is equivalent to the previous one);

$$A_1, \ldots A_m \leftarrow B_1, \ldots, B_k. \tag{12.1}$$

A *program clause*, also called a *definite clauses*, is a clause that has only one unnegated atom. In the form shown in (12.3), a definite clause always has $m = 1$, which is exactly the notion introduced in Definition 12.3. A fact is therefore a definite clause containing no negated atoms. Finally, a *negative clause*, also called a *query* or *goal*, is a clause of the form (12.3) in which $m = 0$.

---

which we have already spoken of, is an unknown which can assume values from a predetermined set. In our case, this set is that of definite terms over the given alphabet. This fact, together with the use to which logic variables are put in logic programming, gives rise to three important differences between this concept and the modifiable variables in imperative languages:

1. The logic variable can be bound only once, in the sense that if a variable is bound to a term, this binding cannot be destroyed (but the term might be modified, as will be explained below). For example, if we bind the variable X to the constant a in a logic program, the binding cannot later be replaced by another which binds X to the constant b. Clearly, this is possible in imperative languages using assignment. The fact that the binding of a variable cannot be eliminated does not mean, however, that it is impossible to modify the value of the variable. This apparent contradiction merits more consideration; this is done in the next point.
2. The value of a logic variable can be partially defined (or can be undefined), to be specified later. This is because a term that is bound to a variable can contain, in its turn, other logic variables. For example, if the variable X is bound to the term $f(Y, Z)$, successive bindings of the variables Y and Z will also modify the value of the variable X: if Y is bound to a and Z is bound to $g(W)$, the value of X

will become the term $f(a, g(W))$. The process could continue by modifying the value of W. This mechanism for specifying the value of a variable by successive approximations, so to speak, is typical of logic languages and is somewhat different from the corresponding one encountered in imperative languages, where a value assigned to a value cannot be partially defined.

3. A third important difference concerns the bidirectional nature of bindings for logic variables. If X is bound to the term $f(Y)$ and later we are able to bind X to the term $f(a)$, the effect so produced is that of binding the variable Y to the constant a. This does not contradict the first point, given that the binding of X to the term $f(Y)$ is not destroyed, but the value of $f(Y)$ is specified through the binding of Y. Therefore, we can not only modify the value of a variable by modifying the term to which it is bound, but we can also modify this term by providing another binding for that variable. Clearly, this second binding must be consistent with the first, that is if X is bound to the term $f(Y)$, we cannot try to bind X to a term of the form $g(Z)$.

The last point is fundamental. This is the point that allows us to use a single logic program in quite different ways, as will be seen below. Essentially, we are talking about a property that derives from the unification mechanism, which we will discuss shortly. First, however, we must introduce the concept of substitution.

12.3.2 Substitution

The connection between variables and terms is made in terms of the concept of substitution, which, as its name tells us, allows the "substitution" of a variable by a term. A substitution, usually denoted by the greek letters $\vartheta, \sigma, \rho, \ldots$, can be defined as follows.

Definition 12.4 (Substitution) A substitution is a function from variables to terms such that the number of variables which are not mapped to themselves is finite. We denote a substitution ϑ by the notation:

$$\vartheta = \{X_1/t_1, \ldots, X_n/t_n\}$$

where $X_1, \ldots, X_n$ are different variables, $t_1, \ldots, t_n$ are terms and where we assume that t_i is different from X_i, for $i = 1, \ldots, n$.

In the preceding definition, a pair X_i/t_i is said to be a *binding*. In the case in which all the $t_1, \ldots, t_n$ are ground terms, then ϑ is said to be a *ground substitution*. We write ϵ for the empty substitution. For ϑ represented as in Definition 12.4, we define the domain, codomain and variables of a substitution as follows:

$Domain(\vartheta) = \{X_1, \ldots, X_n\},$

$Codomain(\vartheta) = \{Y \mid Y \text{ a variable in } t_i, \text{ for some } t_i, 1 \le i \le n\}.$

A substitution can be applied to a term, or, more generally, to any syntactic expression, to modify the value of the variables present in the domain of the substitution. More precisely, if we consider an expression, E (which could be a term, a literal, a conjunction of atoms, etc), the result of the application of $\vartheta = \{X_1/t_1, \ldots, X_n/t_n\}$ to E, denoted by $E\vartheta$,[9] is obtained by simultaneously replacing every occurrence of X_i in E by the corresponding t_i, for all $1 \leq i \leq n$. Therefore, for example, if we apply the substitution $\vartheta = \{X/a, Y/f(W)\}$ to the term $g(X, W, Y)$, we obtain the term $g(X, W, Y)\vartheta$, that is $g(a, W, f(W))$. Note that the application is simultaneous. For example, if we apply the substitution $\sigma = \{Y/f(X), X/a\}$ to the term $g(X, Y)$, we obtain $g(a, f(X))$ (and not $g(a, f(a))$).

The *composition*, $\vartheta\sigma$, of two substitutions $\vartheta = \{X_1/t_1, \ldots, X_n/t_n\}$ and $\sigma = \{Y_1/s_1, \ldots, Y_m/s_m\}$ is defined as the substitution obtained by removing from the set

$$\{X_1/t_1\sigma, \ldots, X_n/t_n\sigma, Y_1/s_1, \ldots, Y_m/s_m\}$$

the pairs $X_i/t_i\sigma$ such that X_i is equal to $t_i\sigma$ and the pairs Y_i/s_i such that $Y_i \in \{X_1, \ldots, X_n\}$. Composition is associative and it is not difficult to see that, for any expression, E, it is the case that $E(\vartheta\sigma) = (E\vartheta)\sigma$. The effect of the application of a composition is the same as it is obtained by successively applying the two substitutions that we want to compose.

For example, composing

$$\vartheta_1 = \{X/f(Y), W/a, Z/X\} \quad \text{and} \quad \vartheta_2 = \{Y/b, W/b, X/Z\}$$

we obtain the substitution

$$\vartheta = \vartheta_1\vartheta_2 = \{X/f(b), W/a, Y/b\}.$$

If we apply the latter to the term $g(X, Y, W)$, we obtain the term $g(f(b), b, a)$. The same term is obtained first by applying ϑ_1 to $g(X, Y, W)$, then applying ϑ_2 to the result. Note that, in the result ϑ of the composition, the Y in ϑ_1 is instantiated to b because of the binding occurring in ϑ_2. The X occurring in Z/X is instantiated to Z using the binding X/Z in ϑ_2, after which the binding Z/Z is eliminated from the resulting substitution (because it is the identity). The bindings W/b and X/Z present in ϑ_2 finally disappear from ϑ because both W and Z appear in the domain (or, on the left of a binding) in ϑ_1.

A particular type of substitution is formed from those which simply rename their variables. For example, the substitution $\{X/W, W/X\}$ does nothing more than change the names of the variables X and W. Substitutions like this are called renamings and can be defined as follows.

---

[9]Note that there exist two opposing versions, both for the notation used for denoting substitutions and for that one used for application of a substitution. The notation for substituting of a term N in place of a variable X used on page 359 is N/X using the conventions adopted in functional programming. Here, on the other hand, such a binding is written X/N (i.e., backwards). In general, we will use the notation most commonly used in logic programming.

Definition 12.5 (Renaming) A substitution ρ is a renaming if its inverse substitution ρ^{-1} exists and is such that $\rho\rho^{-1} = \rho^{-1}\rho = \epsilon$.

Note that the substitution $\{X/Y, W/Y\}$ is not a renaming. Indeed, it not only changes the names of the two variables, but also makes the two variables equal that were previously distinct.

Finally, it will be useful to define a preorder, $\leq$, over substitutions, where $\vartheta \leq \sigma$ is read as: ϑ is more general than σ. Let us therefore define $\vartheta \leq \sigma$ if (and only if) there exists a substitution γ such that $\vartheta\gamma = \sigma$. Analogously, given two expressions, t and t', we define $t \leq t'$ (t is more general t') if and only if there exists a ϑ such that $t\vartheta = t'$. The relation $\leq$ is a preorder and the equivalence induced by it[10] is called the *variance*; t and t' are therefore variants if t is an instance of t' and, conversely, t' is an instance of t. It is not difficult to see that this definition is equivalent to saying that t and t' are variants if there exists a renaming ρ such that t is syntactically identical to $t'\rho$. These definitions can be extended to any expression in an obvious fashion. Finally, if ϑ is a substitution that has as domain the set of variables V, and W is a subset of V, the *restriction* of ϑ to the variables in W is the substitution obtained by considering only the bindings for variables in W, that is the substitution defined as follows:

$$\{Y/t \mid Y \in W \text{ and } Y/t \in \vartheta\}.$$

A comparison with the imperative paradigm can help in better understanding the concepts under consideration. As we saw in Sect. 2.5, in the imperative paradigm, the semantics can be expressed by referring to a concept of state that associates every variable with a value.[11] An expression containing variables is evaluated with respect to a state to obtain a value that is completely defined.

In the logic paradigm, the association of values with variables is implemented through substitutions. The application of a substitution to a term (or to a more complex expression) can be seen as the evaluation of the terms, an evaluation that returns another term, and therefore, in general, a partially defined value.

12.3.3 Most General Unifier

The basic computation mechanism for the logic paradigm is the evaluation of equations of the form $s = t$,[12] where s and t are terms and "$=$" is a predicate symbol

---

[10]Given a preorder, $\leq$, the equivalence relation *induced* by $\leq$ is defined as $t = t'$ if and only if $t \leq t'$ and $t' \leq t$.

[11]Wishing to be precise, as we have seen in the box on page 135, in real languages, this association is implemented using two functions, environment and memory. This however does not alter the import of what we are saying.

[12]We draw attention to the notation that, as usual, overloads the "$=$" symbol. By writing $\vartheta = \{X_1/t_1, \ldots, X_n/t_n\}$, we mean that ϑ is the substitution $\{X_1/t_1, \ldots, X_n/t_n\}$, while writing $s = t$, we mean an equation.

interpreted as syntactic equality over the set of all ground terms; this set is called the *Herbrand Universe*.[13] We will attempt better to clarify this equality.

If we write $X = a$ in a logic program, we mean that the variable X must be bound to the constant a. The substitution $\{X/a\}$ therefore constitutes a solution to this equation since, by applying the substitution to the equation, we obtain $a = a$ which is an equation that is clearly satisfied. The syntactic analogy with assignment in imperative languages should not be allowed to deceive, for it deals with a completely different concept. Indeed, unlike in an imperative language, here we can also write $a = X$ instead of $X = a$ and the meaning does not change (the equality that we are considering is symmetric, as are all equality relations). Also the analogy with the equality of arithmetic expressions can be, in some ways, misleading, as illustrated by the following example.

Let us assume that we have a binary function symbol $+$ which, intuitively, expresses the sum of two natural numbers, and consider the equation $3 = 2 + 1$, where, for simplicity, we use infix notation for $+$ and we represent in the usual fashion the natural numbers. Given that the equation $3 = 2 + 1$ does not contain variables, it can be either true (or, solved) or false (that is, insoluble). Contrary to what arithmetic intuition would suggest to us, in a (pure) logic program this equation cannot be solved. This is because, as we have said, the symbol $=$ is interpreted as syntactic equality over the set of ground terms (the Herbrand universe). It is clear that, from the syntactic viewpoint, the constant 3 is different from the term $2 + 1$ and since they are treated as ground terms (that is completely instantiated terms) there is no way that they can be made syntactically equal. Analogously, the equation $f(X) = g(Y)$ has no solutions (it is not solvable) because however the variables X and Y are instantiated, we cannot make the two different function symbols, f and g, equal. Note that the equation, $f(X) = f(g(X))$, also has no solutions, because the variable X in the left-hand term must be instantiated with $g(X)$ and therefore the possible solution must contain the substitution $\{X/g(X)\}$. The application of this substitution to the term on the right would instantiate X, producing the term $f(g(g(X)))$, so the X in the right-hand term would have to be instantiated to $g(g(X))$ rather than to $g(X)$ and so on, without ever reaching a solution.[14] In general, therefore, the equation $X = t$ cannot be solved if t contains the variable X (and is different from X).

If, on the other hand, we consider the equation $f(X) = f(g(Y))$, it is solvable; one solution is the substitution $\vartheta = \{X/g(Y)\}$ because if this is applied to the two terms in the equation, it makes them syntactically equal. Indeed, $f(X)\vartheta$ is identical to $f(g(Y))$ which is identical to $f(g(Y))\vartheta$. In more formal terms, we can say that the substitution ϑ *unifies* the two terms of the equation and it is therefore called a *unifier*. Note that we have said "a solution" because there are many (an infinite number) of substitutions that are unifiers of X and $g(Y)$. It is sufficient to instantiate Y in the definition of ϑ. So, for example, the substitution $\{X/g(a), Y/a\}$ is also an

---

[13]The symbol "$=$" is usually written in infix notation for increased readability. Different logic languages can have different syntactic readings for it and use different equality symbols, each with a different meaning. Here, we refer to "pure" logic programming.

[14]Note that by admitting infinite terms, we can find a solution, however.

unifier, as are $\{X/g(f(Z)), Y/f(Z)\}$, $\{X/g(f(a)), Y/f(a)\}$, and so on. All these substitutions are, however, *less general* than ϑ according to the preorder that we defined above. Each of them, that is, can be obtained by composing ϑ with some other, appropriate, substitution. For example, $\{X/g(a), Y/a\}$ is equal to $\vartheta\{Y/a\}$ (we denote the composition of substitutions with juxtaposition as already seen). In this sense, we say that ϑ is the most general unifier (or m. g. u.) of X and $g(Y)$.

Before moving to general definitions, note one last important detail: the process of solving an equation, and thus a unification, can create bidirectional bindings, that is the direction in which the associations must be realised is not specified. For example, a solution of the equation $f(X, a) = f(b, Y)$ is given by the substitution $\{X/b, Y/a\}$, where a variable on the left and one on the right of the $=$ symbol are bound. Instead, in the equation, $f(X, a) = f(Y, a)$, to find a solution, we can choose whether to bind the variable on the left (using $\{X/Y\}$) or the one on the right (using $\{Y/X\}$) or even both (using $\{X/Z, Y/Z\}$).

This aspect, to which we will return, is important because it allows the implementation of bidirectional parameter-passing mechanisms and, a unique characteristic of the logic paradigm, to use the same program in different ways, turning input arguments into outputs and vice versa, without modifying the program at all.

We now have the formal definition.

Definition 12.6 (M. g. u.) Given a set of equations $E = \{s_1 = t_1, \ldots, s_n = t_n\}$, where $s_1, \ldots, s_n$ and $t_1, \ldots, t_n$ are terms, the substitution, ϑ, is a unifier for E if the sequence $(s_1, \ldots, s_n)\vartheta$ and $(t_1, \ldots, t_n)\vartheta$ are syntactically identical. A unifier of E is said to be the *most general unifier* (m. g. u.) if it is more general than any other unifier of E; that is, for every other unifier, σ, of E, σ is equal to $\vartheta\tau$ for some substitution, τ.

The preceding concept of unifier can be extended to other syntactic objects in an obvious fashion. In particular, we say that ϑ is a unifier of two atoms $p(s_1, \ldots, s_n)$ and $p(t_1, \ldots, t_n)$ if ϑ is a unifier of $\{s_1 = t_1, \ldots, s_n = t_n\}$.

12.3.4 A Unification Algorithm

An important result, due to Robinson in 1965, shows that the problem of determining whether a set of equations of terms can be unified is decidable. The proof is constructive, in the sense that it provides a *unification algorithm* which, for every set of equations, produces their m. g. u. if the set is unifiable and returns a failure in the opposite case.[15]

---

[15]Robinson's original algorithm considers the unification of just two terms but this, obviously, is not reductive given that the unification of $\{s_1 = t_1, \ldots, s_n = t_n\}$ can be seen as the unification of $f(s_1, \ldots, s_n)$ and $f(t_1, \ldots, t_n)$.

It can also be proved that a m. g. u. is unique up to renaming. The unification algorithm which we will now see is not Robinson's original but is Martelli and Montanari's from 1982 and it makes use of ideas present in Herbrand's thesis of 1930.

Martelli and Montanari's unification algorithm   Given a set of equations

$$E = \{s_1 = t_1, \ldots, s_n = t_n\},$$

the algorithm produces either failure or a set of equations of the following, so called, solved form:

$$\{X_1 = r_1, \ldots, X_m = r_m\},$$

where $X_1, \ldots, X_m$ are distinct variables which not appearing in the terms $r_1, \ldots, r_m$. The set of equations is equivalent to the starting set, E, and from it we can obtain a m. g. u. for E simply interpreting every equality as a binding. Therefore, the m. g. u. that we seek is the substitution:

$$\{X_1/r_1, \ldots, X_m/r_m\}.$$

The algorithm is non-deterministic in the sense that when there are more possible actions, one is chosen in an arbitrary fashion, with no priority between the various actions.[16] The algorithm is given by the following steps.

1. Nondeterministically select one equation from the set E.
2. According to the type of equation chosen, execute, if possible, one of the specific operations as follows (where on the left of the ":" we indicate the type of equation and, on the right, we have the associated action):
   a. $f(l_1, \ldots, l_k) = f(m_1, \ldots, m_k)$: eliminate this equation from the set E and add to E the equations $l_1 = m_1, \ldots, l_k = m_k$.
   b. $f(l_1, \ldots, l_k) = g(m_1, \ldots, m_k)$: it f is different from g, terminate with failure.
   c. $X = X$: eliminate this equation from the set E.
   d. $X = t$: if t does not contain the variable X and this variable appears in another equation in the set E, apply the substitution $\{X/t\}$ to all the other equations in the set E.
   e. $X = t$: if t contains the variable X, terminate with failure.
   f. $t = X$: if t is not a variable, eliminate this equation from the set E and add to E the equation $X = t$.
3. If none of the preceding operations is possible, terminate with success (E contains the solved form). If, on the other hand, an operation different from termination with failure has been executed, go to (1).

This, as can be seen, is a very simple algorithm. We will discuss it in detail, nonetheless.

---

[16]We will return to the non-determinism briefly when we discuss the operational semantics of logic programs.

The first case is one in which the two terms agree on the function symbol. In this case, in order to unify the two terms, it is necessary to unify the arguments, so we replace the original equation with the equations obtained by equating the arguments in each position. Note that this case also includes equivalence between constants of the form $a = a$ (where a is a function symbol of arity 0) which are eliminated without adding anything.

The second case produces a failure given that, when f and g are different, the two terms cannot be unified (as we have already seen).

The equation $X = X$ is eliminated using the identity substitution which therefore produces no change in the other equations.

The fourth case is the most interesting. An equation $X = t$ is already in solved form (because, by assumption, t does not contain X). In other words, the substitution $\{X/t\}$ is the m. g. u. of this equation. For the effect of such an m. g. u. to be combined with those produced by other equations, we must apply the substitution $\{X/t\}$ to all the other equations in the set E.

On the other hand, in the case in which t contains the variable X, as we have already seen, the equation has no solution and therefore the algorithm terminates with failure. It is important to note that this check, called the *occurs check*, is removed from many implementations of PROLOG for reasons of efficiency. Therefore, many PROLOG implementations use an incorrect unification algorithm!

The last case, finally, serves only to obtain a result form in which the variables appear on the left and the terms on the right of the $=$ symbol.

It is easy to convince oneself that the algorithm terminates, given that the depth of the input terms is finite. It is, moreover, possible to prove that the algorithm produces an m. g. u. which is obtained by the interpretation as substitutions of the final result form of the equations.

By a careful consideration of the algorithm, it can be seen that the computation of the most general unifier occurs in an incremental fashion by solving ever simpler equations until a result form is encountered. It is also possible to express this process in terms of substitution compositions as happens in the operational model of logic languages. We will exemplify this point with an example which also constitutes an example of the application of the unification algorithm that we have just seen. To simplify, we will always choose the leftmost equation (the final result, anyway, does not depend upon such an assumption; any other selection rule would lead to the same result up to renaming).

Let us consider the set of equations:

$$E = \{f(X, b) = f(g(Y), W), h(X, Y) = h(Z, W)\}.$$

Choosing the first equation on the left, using the operation described in (a), the set E is transformed into:

$$E_1 = \{X = g(Y), b = W, h(X, Y) = h(Z, W)\}.$$

Using operation (d), we therefore obtain:

$$E_2 = \{X = g(Y), \ b = W, \ h(g(Y), Y) = h(Z, W)\}.$$

Using (f) and then (d) again on the second equation, we finally obtain:

$$E_3 = \{X = g(Y),\ W = b,\ h(g(Y), Y) = h(Z, b)\}.$$

This already contains the result of the first equation in the set E. In fact, the substitution:

$$\vartheta_1 = \{X/g(Y), W/b\}$$

is an m. g. u. for $f(X, b) = f(g(Y), W)$.

Continuing with the second equation from the original set, suitably instantiated by the substitutions already computed, using operation (a), we obtain:

$$E_4 = \{X = g(Y),\ W = b,\ g(Y) = Z,\ Y = b\};$$

then, by (f), we obtain:

$$E_5 = \{X = g(Y),\ W = b,\ Z = g(Y),\ Y = b\}.$$

Finally, using (d) applied to the last equation, we have:

$$E_4 = \{X = g(b),\ W = b,\ Z = g(b),\ Y = b\},$$

which constitutes the result form for the set E and therefore also provides the m. g. u. of the initial set in the form of the substitution

$$\vartheta = \{X/g(b), W/b, Z/g(b), Y/b\}.$$

There are two important observations to be made. First, note how the value of some variables can be partially specified first, and then later refined. For example, ϑ_1 (m. g. u. of the first equation in E) tells us that X has $g(Y)$ as its value and only by solving the second equation do we see that Y has b as its value. Therefore it can be seen that $g(b)$ is the value of X (as, indeed, it results in the final m. g. u.).

Moreover, we can see that if we consider $\{h(g(X), Y) = h(Z, W)\}\vartheta_1$ (the second equation in E instantiated using the m. g. u. of the first), we obtain the equation

$$h(g(Y), Y) = h(Z, b)$$

for which the substitution

$$\vartheta_2 = \{Z = g(b), Y = b\}$$

is a m. g. u. Using the definition of composition of substitutions, it is easy to check that $\vartheta = \vartheta_1 \vartheta_2$. The m. g. u. of the set E can therefore be obtained by composing the first equation's m. g. u. with that of the second (to which the first m. g. u. has already been applied). This, as we have already said, is what, indeed, normally happens in implementations of logic languages, where, instead of accumulating all the equations and then solve them, an m. g. u. is computed on each step of the computation and is composed with the ones that were previously obtained.

12.4 The Computational Model

The logic paradigm, implementing the idea of "computation as deduction", uses a computational model that is substantially different from all the others that we have seen so far. Wishing to synthesise, we can identify the following main differences from the other paradigms:

1. The only possible values, at least in the pure model, are terms over a given signature.
2. Programs can have a declarative reading which is entirely logical, or a procedural reading of an operational kind.
3. Computation works by instantiating the variables appearing in terms (and therefore in goals) to other terms using the unification mechanism.
4. Control, which is entirely handled by the abstract machine (except for some possible annotations in PROLOG) is based on the process of automatic backtracking.

Below, we will try therefore to illustrate the computational model for the logic paradigm by analysing these four points. We will explicitly discuss the differences between logic programming and PROLOG.

12.4.1 The Herbrand Universe

In logic programming, terms are a fundamental element. The set of all possible terms over a given signature is called the *Herbrand Universe* and is the domain over which computation in logic programs is performed. It has some characteristics that must be understood.

- The alphabet over which programs are defined is not fixed but can vary as far as non-logical symbols are concerned.
- As a (partial) consequence of the previous point, unlike what happens in imperative languages, no predefined meaning is assigned to the (non-logical) symbols of the alphabet. For example, a program can use the + symbol to denote addition, while another program can use the same symbol to denote string concatenation. The exceptions are the (binary) equality predicate and some other predefined ("built-in") symbols in PROLOG.[17]
- As a final consequence, no type system is present in logic languages (at least in the classic formalism). The only type that is present is that of terms with which we can represent arithmetic, list, expressions, etc.

From the theoretical stance, the fact that there are no types and that computation occurs in the Herbrand Universe is not limiting, rather it permits the highly elegant and, all considered, simple expression of the formal semantics of logic programs. For example, with only two function symbols, 0 (constant zero) and *s* (successor,

---

[17] As well as predefined predicates in constraint languages, a topic we will not consider.

of arity 1), we can express the natural numbers using the terms 0, $s(0)$, $s(s(0))$, $s(s(s(0)))$, etc. With a little effort, we can express the normal arithmetic operations in terms of this two-symbol representation.

From the practical view point, on the other hand, the lack of types is a serious problem. In fact, in PROLOG, as in other, more recent, logic languages, some primitive types have been introduced (for example, integers and associated arithmetic operations). The languages of this paradigm are therefore always somewhat lacking as far as types are concerned.

12.4.2 Declarative and Procedural Interpretation

As we have just hinted, a clause, and therefore a logic program, can have two different interpretations: one *declarative* and one *procedural*.

From the *declarative* viewpoint, a clause $H : -A_1, \ldots, A_n$ is a formula which, basically, expresses the fact that if A_1 and A_2 and ... and A_n are true, then H is also true. A query (or goal) is also a formula for which we want to prove, provided that it is appropriately instantiated, that it is a logical consequence of the program, and is, therefore, true in all interpretations in which the program is true.[18] This interpretation can be developed using the methods of logic (in particular, some elementary concepts of model theory) in such a way as to give a meaning to a program in purely declarative terms without referring at all to a computational process. For this interpretation, while interesting, we refer the reader to the specialist literature cited at the end of the chapter.

The *procedural* interpretation, on the other hand, allows us to read a clause such as:

$$H : -A_1, \ldots, A_n$$

as follows. To prove H, it is necessary first to prove $A_1, \ldots, A_n$, or rather to compute H, it is necessary first to compute $A_1, \ldots, A_n$. From this, we can view a predicate as the name of a procedure, whose defining clauses constitute its body. In this interpretation, we can read an atom in the body of a clause, or in a goal, as a procedure call. A logic program is therefore a set of declarations and a goal is no more than the equivalent of "main" in an imperative program, given that it contains all the calls to the procedures that we want to evaluate. The comma in the body of clauses and in goals, in PROLOG (but not in other pure logic programming languages), can be read as the analogue of ";" in imperative languages.

Precise correspondence theorems allow us to reconcile the declarative and procedural views, proving that the two approaches are equivalent.

From a formal viewpoint, the procedural interpretation is supported by so-called SLD resolution, a logical inference rule which we will discuss in the box on

---

[18]Here we will content ourselves with an intuitive idea of this concept. The interested reader can consult any text on logic for more information.

page 392. It is also possible to describe the procedural interpretation in a more informal manner, using only the analogy with procedure calls and parameter passing which we have just outlined. This is the approach we will use below.

12.4.3 Procedure Calls

Let us consider for now a simplified definition of clause in which we assume that, in the head, all the arguments of the predicate are distinct variables. An arbitrary clause of this type therefore has the form:

$$p(X_1, \ldots, X_n) : -A_1, \ldots, A_m$$

and, as we have anticipated, it can be seen as the declaration of the procedure p with n formal parameters, $X_1, \ldots, X_n$. An atom $q(t_1, \ldots, t_n)$ can be seen as a call to the procedure q with n actual parameters, $t_1, \ldots, t_n$. In the definition of p, therefore, the body is formed from the calls to m procedures which constitute the atoms $A_1, \ldots, A_m$.

In accordance with this view, and analogously to what happens in imperative languages, the evaluation of the call $p(t_1, \ldots, t_n)$ causes the evaluation of the body of the procedure after parameter passing has been performed. Parameter passing uses a technique similar to call by name, replacing the formal parameter X_i with the corresponding actual parameter t_i. Moreover, given that the variables appearing in the body of the procedure are to be considered as logical variables, they can be considered to be distinct from all other variables. In block-structured languages, this happens implicitly given that the body of the procedure is considered as a block with its own local environment. Here, on the other hand, the concept of block is absent, so, in order to avoid conflicts between variable names, we assume that, before using a clause, all the variables appearing in it are systematically renamed (so that they do not conflict with any others).

Using more precise terms, we can say that the evaluation of the call $p(t_1, \ldots, t_n)$, with the definition of p seen above, causes the evaluation of the m calls:

$$(A_1, \ldots, A_m)\vartheta$$

present in the body of p, appropriately instantiated by the substitution

$$\vartheta = \{X_1/t_1, \ldots, X_n/t_n\}$$

which performs parameter passing. In the case in which the body of the clause is empty (or that $m = 0$), the procedure call terminates immediately. Otherwise, the computation proceeds with the evaluation of the new calls. Using logic programming terminology, this can be expressed by saying that the evaluation of the goal $p(t_1, \ldots, t_n)$ produces the new goal:

$$(A_1, \ldots, A_m)\{X_1/t_1, \ldots, X_n/t_n\}$$

which, in its turn, will have to be evaluated. When all the calls generated by this process have been evaluated (provided there has been no failure), the computation terminates with success and the final result is composed of the substitution that associates the values computed in the course of the computation with the variables present in the initial call ($X_1, \ldots, X_n$, in our case). This substitution is said to be the *answer computed* by the initial goal in the given program. We will see a more precise definition of this concept below. For now, we will see a simple example. Let us consider the procedure list_of_2 defined below and identical to the procedure list_of_27 of Sect. 12.1.1, except for the lesser number of anonymous variables:

```
list_of_2(Ls):- Ls = [_,_].
```
                                                                                                              |

The evaluation of the call list_of_2(LXs) causes the evaluation of the body of the clause, but instantiated by the substitution $\{Ls/LXs\}$, that is:

```
LXs = [_,_]
```

This is a particular call because = is a predefined call which, as we saw in the previous section, is interpreted as syntactic equality over the Herbrand Universe and, operationally, corresponds to the unification operation. The previous call therefore reduces to the attempt (performed by the language interpreter) to solve the equation using unification. In our case, clearly, this attempt succeeds and produces the m. g. u. $\{LXs/[\_, \_]\}$ which is the result of the computation. The previous substitution is therefore the answer computed by the goal list_of_2 in the logic program defined by the single line (1) above.

Evaluation of a non-atomic goal   The view presented in the previous subsection must be generalised and made more precise to clarify the logic-programming computational model. Below, in order to conform with current terminology, we will talk of atomic goals and goals rather than procedure calls and sequences of calls. The analogy with the conventional paradigm remains valid, though.

In the case in which a non-atomic goal must be evaluated, the computational mechanism is analogous to the one seen above, except that now we must choose one of the possible calls using some *selection rule*. While in the case of pure logic programming no such rule is specified, PROLOG adopts the rule that the leftmost atom is always chosen. It is however possible to prove that whatever rule is adopted, the results that are computed are always the same (see also Exercises 13 and 14 at the end of the chapter).

Assuming, for simplicity, that we adopt the PROLOG rule, we can describe the progress of the evaluation process. Let

$$B_1, \ldots, B_k$$

with $k \geq 1$, be the goal to be evaluated. We distinguish the following cases according to the form of the selected atom, B_1:

1. If B_1 is an equation of the form $s = t$, try to compute a m. g. u. (using the unification algorithm). There are two possibilities:

   a. If the m. g. u. exists and is the substitution σ, then the result of the evaluation is the goal:

$$(B_2, \ldots, B_k)\sigma$$

   obtained from the previous one by eliminating the chosen atom and applying the m. g. u. thus computed. If $k = 1$ (and therefore $(B_2, \ldots, B_k)\sigma$ is empty), the computation terminates in success.

   b. If the m. g. u. does not exist (or the equation has no solutions), then we have failure.

2. If, on the other hand, B_1 has the form $p(t_1, \ldots, t_n)$, we have the following two cases:

   a. If, in the program, there exists a clause of the form:

$$p(X_1, , \ldots, X_n) : -A_1, \ldots, A_m$$

   (which we consider renamed to avoid variable capture), then the result of evaluation is a new goal:

$$(A_1, \ldots, A_m)\vartheta, B_2, \ldots, B_k$$

   where $\vartheta = \{X_1/t_1, \ldots, X_n/t_n\}$. If $k = 1$ (then we have an atomic goal) and $m = 0$ (the body of the clause is empty), then the computation terminates with success.

   b. If, in the program, there exists no clause defining the predicate p, we have failure.

To be able exactly to define the results of the computation (the answers computed), we need to clarify some aspects of control, which we will do in Sect. 12.4.4.

Heads with arbitrary terms So far, we have assumed that the heads of clauses contain just distinct variables. We have made this choice to preserve the similarity with procedures in traditional languages. However, real logic programs also use arbitrary terms as arguments to predicates in heads, as we have seen in the example in Sect. 12.1.1. The box on page 392 provides the evaluation rule for such a general case. Note, however, that our assumption is in no way limiting (apart, perhaps, from textual convenience). Indeed, as seems clear from what was said in the box and from the preceding treatment, a clause of the form:

$$p(t_1, \ldots, t_n) : -A_1, \ldots, A_m$$

can be seen as an abbreviation of the clause:

$$p(X_1, \ldots, X_n) : -X_1 = t_1, \ldots, X_n = t_n, A_1, \ldots, A_m.$$

In the following examples, we will often use the notation with arbitrary terms in heads.

SLD Resolution

Definite clauses allow a natural procedural reading based on *resolution*, an inference rule which is complete for sets of clauses and which was introduced by Robinson and used in automated deduction. In logic programming, we have *SLD resolution*, that is linear resolution guided by a clause selection rule (SLD is an acronym for Selection rule-driven Linear resolution for Definite clauses).

This rule can be described as follows. Let G be the goal $B_1, \ldots, B_k$ and let C be the (definite) clause $H : -A_1, \ldots, A_n$. We say that G' is *derived* from G and C using ϑ or, equivalently, G' is a *resolvent* of G and C if (and only if) the following conditions are met:

1. B_m, with $1 \leq m \leq k$, is a *selected* atom from those in G.
2. ϑ is the m. g. u. of B_m and H.
3. G' is the goal $(B_1, \ldots, B_{m-1}, A_1, \ldots, A_n, B_{m+1}, \ldots B_k)\vartheta$.

Note that, unlike Sect. 12.4.3, here it is necessary also to apply ϑ to the other atoms occurring in the goal G because the heads of the clauses contain arbitrary terms and therefore ϑ could instantiate variables that are also in the goal.

Given a goal, G, and a logic program, P, an *SLD derivation* of $P \cup G$ consists of a (possibly infinite) sequence of goals $G_0, G_1, G_2, \ldots$, of a sequence $C_1, C_2, \ldots$ of clauses in P which have been renamed in such a way as to avoid variable capture and a sequence $\vartheta_1, \vartheta_2, \ldots$, of m. g. u. s such that G_0 is G and, for $i \geq 1$, every G_i, is derived from G_{i-1} and C_i using ϑ_i. An *SLD refutation* of $P \cup G$ is a finite SLD derivation of $P \cup G$ which has the empty clause as the last resolvent of the derivation. If $\vartheta_1, \vartheta_2, \ldots$ are the m. g. u. s used in the refutation of $P \cup G$, we say that the substitution $\vartheta_1 \vartheta_2 \cdots \vartheta_n$ restricted to the variables occurring in G is the *answer substitution computed* by $P \cup G$ (or for the goal G in the program P).

Classic results, due to K. L. Clark, show that this rule is sound and complete with respect to the traditional first-order logical interpretation.

Indeed, it can be proved that if ϑ is the *answer substitution computed* by the goal G in program P, then $G\vartheta$ is a logical consequence of P (soundness). Moreover, if $G\vartheta$ is a logical consequence of P, then no matter which selection rule is used, there exists a SLD refutation of $P \cup G$ with computed answer σ such that $G\sigma$ is more general than $G\vartheta$ (strong completeness).

12.4.4 Control: Non-determinism

In the evaluation of a goal, we have two degrees of freedom: the selection of the atom to evaluate and the choice of the clause to apply.

For the first, we have said that we can fix a selection rule, without influencing the final results of the computation that terminate in success.

For the selection of clauses, on the other hand, the matter is more delicate. Given that a predicate can be defined by more than one clauses, and we have to use only one of them at a time, we could think about fixing some rule for choosing clauses, analogous to the one used to choose atoms. The following reveals however a problem. Let us consider the following program, which we call Pa:

```
p(X):- p(X).                                                                    1
p(X):- X=a.                                                                     2
```

and let us assume that we choose clauses from top to bottom, following the textual order of the program. It is easy to see that by adopting this rule, the evaluation of p(Y) never terminates and therefore we do not have an answer computed by the program. Indeed, using clause (1) and the substitution $\{X/Y\}$, the initial goal, after one computation step, becomes the goal p(Y), which is again the starting goal. According to the clause-selection rule, we must choose clause (1) and apply it to this (new) goal, and so on. It is however clear that using clause (2) we would immediately obtain a computation which terminates, producing the substitution $\{Y/a\}$ as result. Note that to fix another order, for example, from bottom to top, would not in general solve this problem.

In the light of this example, let us carefully reconsider the evaluation rule for a goal seen in the previous subsection and, in particular, let us fix on point 2(a), where we wrote "if there exists a clause" without specifying how this can be chosen. By doing this, we have therefore introduced into the computation model a form of non-determinism: in the case in which there is more than one clause for the same predicate, we can choose one in a non-deterministic fashion, without adopting any particular rule. This form of non-determinism is called "*don't know*" non-determinism because we do not know which the "right" clause will be that allows the termination of the computation with success. The theoretical model of logic programming keeps this non-determinism when it considers all possible choices of clause and therefore all possible results of the various computations that are produced as a consequence of this choice. The result of the evaluation of a goal G in the program P is therefore a set of computed answers, where each of these answers is the substitution obtained by the composition of all the m. g. u. s which are encountered in a specific computation (with specific choices of clauses), restricted to the variables present in G. For a more precise definition of this idea, as well as of the whole process of evaluating a goal, see the box on page 392.

Turning to our previous example, the only answer computed for the goal p(Y) in program Pa is the substitution $\{Y/a\}$ while, for the same program, the goal p(b) has no computed answer given that all its computations either terminate with failure (when the second clause is used) or do not terminate (when the first clause is used).

Backtracking in PROLOG   When moving from the theoretical model to an implemented language, such as PROLOG, non-determinism must, at some level, be transformed into determinism, given that the physical computing machine is deterministic. This can obviously be done in various ways, and in principle does not cause loss of solutions. For example, we could think of starting k parallel computations when there are k possible clauses for a predicate[19] and therefore consider the results of all the possible computations.

In PROLOG, however, for reasons of simplicity and implementation efficiency, the strategy we first saw is employed: clauses are used according to the textual order in which they occur in the program (top-to-bottom). We saw in the previous example that this strategy is *incomplete*, given that it does allow us to find all possible computed answers. This limit, however, is adjustable by the programmer who, knowing this property of PROLOG, can order the clauses in the program in the most convenient way (typically putting first those relating to terminal cases and then the inductive steps). Note, though, that this trick, at least in principle, eliminates some of the declarative nature of the language, because the programmer has specified an aspect of control.

In addition to infinite computations, there is a second, more important aspect to be considered by adopting the deterministic model of PROLOG and deals with the handing of failures. Let us first see an example. Let us consider the program Pb:

```
p(X):- X=f(a).                                            1
p(X):- X=g(a).                                            2
```

Let us consider the evaluation of the goal p(g(Y)). By the PROLOG strategy, clause (1) is chosen, which, using the substitution $\{X/g(Y)\}$, produces the new goal g(Y) = f(a). This fails, given that the two terms in the equation cannot be unified. Moreover, given that there is still one clause to use, it would not be acceptable to terminate the computation by returning a failure. "Backtracking" then occurs, returning to the choice of the clause for p(g(Y)) and therefore continues the computation by trying clause (2). In this way, the computation achieves success with the computed answer $\{Y/a\}$.

In general, therefore, when arriving at a failure, the PROLOG abstract machine "backtracks" to a previous choice point at which there are other choices; that is, where there are other clauses to test. In this backtracking process, the bindings that might have been computed in the previous computation must be undone. Once a choice point has been reached, a new clause is tried and the computation continues in the way we have seen. If the previous choice point contains no possibilities for computations, an older choice point is sought and, if there are no more, the computation terminates in failure. Note that all of this is handled directly by the PROLOG abstract machine and is completely invisible to the programmer (except the use of particular constructs such as the cut which we will introduce in Sect. 12.5.1).

It is also easy to see how this procedure, which uses a search corresponding to a depth-first search through a tree representing the possible computations, can be computationally demanding. The solution to the problem seen in Sect. 12.1.1, for example, requires extensive backtracking and is fairly wasteful in computation time.

Let us now see another example. Consider the program Pc:

---

[19]Clearly, on a machine with one processor, the k parallel computations must be appropriately "scheduled" so they can be executed in a sequential manner, analogous to what happens with processes in a multitasking operating system.

```
p(X):- X=f(Y), q(X).                                                          1
p(X):- X=g(Y), q(X).                                                          2
q(X):- X=g(a).                                                                3
q(X):- X=g(b).                                                                4
```

Let us analyse the goal p(Z). Using clause (1), we obtain the goal Z=f(Y),q(Z). The evaluation of the equation produces the m. g. u. $\{Z/f(Y)\}$ and we obtain the goal q(f(Y)). Using clause (3), we obtain the goal f(Y) = g(a), which fails. At this point we must turn to the last choice point, that is to the point where the choice of clause for the predicate q occurred. In this case, there are no bindings to undo, and therefore we try clause (4), obtaining therefore the goal f(Y)=g(b) which also fails. We return again to the choice point for q and we see that there are no other possible clauses and therefore we return to the previous choice point (the one for predicate p). Doing this, we have to undo the binding $\{Z/f(Y)\}$ calculated by clause (1) and therefore we return to the initial situation, where variable Z is not instantiated. Using clause (2), we obtain the goal Z=g(Y),q(Z) and therefore by the evaluation of the equation, we obtain the m.g.u. $\{Y/a\}$ and the new goal q(g(Y)). At this point, using clause (3), we obtain the goal g(Y)=g(a) which succeeds and produces the m. g. u. $\{Y/a\}$. Given that there remain no more goals to evaluate, the computation terminates with success. The result of the computation is produced by composing the computed m. g. u. s $\{Z/g(Y)\}\{Y/a\}$ and restricting the substitution $\{Z/g(a), Y(a)\}$ obtained by this composition to the single variable present in the initial goal. Therefore, the computed answer obtained is $\{Z/g(a)\}$. Note that there is another computed answer, $\{Z/g(b)\}$, which we can obtain using clause (4) rather than (3). In PROLOG implementations, answers subsequent to the first can be obtained using the ";" command. Finally, the reader can easily check that the goal p(g(c)) in program Pc terminates with failure, a result that is obtained after having proved all four of the possible clause combinations.

12.4.5 Some Examples

In this subsection, we will focus on the PROLOG language, and we will make use of its syntax. The notation [h|t] is used to denote the list which has h as its head and t as its tail. Let us remember that the head is the first element in the list, while the tail is what remains of the list when the head has been removed. The empty list is written [], while [a,b,c] is an abbreviation for [a | [b | [c |[]]]] (the list composed of elements a, b and c). Note that in PROLOG, as in pure logic programming language, there exists no list type, for which the binary function symbol [|] can be used for terms that are not lists. For example, we can also write [a | f(a)] which is not a list (because f(a) is not a list).

As the first example, let us consider the following program member which checks whether an element belongs to a given list:

```
member(X, [X | Xs]).
member(X, [Y | Xs]) :- member(X, Xs).
```

The declarative reading of the program is immediate: Clause (1) consists of the terminal case in which the element that we are looking for (the first argument of the member predicate) is the head of the list (the second argument to the member predicate). Clause (2) instead provides the inductive case and tells us that X is an element of the list [Y|Xs] if it is an element of the list Xs.

Formulated in this way, the member program is similar to the one that we could write in any language that supports recursion. However, let us note that, unlike in the imperative and functional paradigms, this program can be used in two different ways.

The more conventional mode is the one in which it is used as a test. In a PROLOG system, once the previous program has been input, we have:

```
?- member(hewey, [dewey, hewey, louie]).
Yes
```

where ?- is the abstract machine's prompt, to which we have added the goal whose evaluation we require. The next line contains the interpreter's answer. In this case, we have a simple "boolean" answer which expresses the existence of a successful computation of our goal. Moreover, as we know, we can also use the program to compute. For example, we can ask for the evaluation of:

```
?- member(X, [dewey, hewey, louie]).
X = dewey
```

The abstract machine returns $\{X/dewey\}$ as the computed answer. We can also obtain more answers using the ";" command. When there are no more answer, the system replies "no".

Finally, even if it is used in a rather unnatural fashion, we can use the first argument to instantiate the list that appears as the second argument. For example:

```
?- member(dewey, [X, hewey, louie]).
X = dewey
```

This possibility of using the same arguments as inputs or as outputs according to the way in which they are instantiated is unique to the logic paradigm and is due to the presence of unification in the computational model.

We can clarify this point further by considering the following append program which allows us to concatenate lists:

```
append([], Ys, Ys).                                          1
append([X|Xs], Ys, [X|Zs]) :- append (Xs, Ys, Zs).          2
```

In this case, too, the declarative reading is immediate. If the first list is empty, the results is the second list (clause(1)). Otherwise, (inductively), if Zs is the result of the concatenation of Xs and Ys, the result of the concatenation of [X|Xs] and Ys is obtained by adding X to the head of the list Zs, as indicated by [X|Zs].

The normal use of the this program is that illustrated by the following goal:

```
?- append([dewey, hewey], [louie, donald], Zs).
Zs = [dewey, hewey, louie, donald]
```

Moreover, we can use `append` also to know how to subdivide a list into sublists, something that is not possible in a functional or imperative program:

```
?- append(Xs, Ys, [dewey, hewey]).
Xs = []
Ys = [dewey, hewey];
Xs = [dewey]
Ys = [hewey];
Xs = [dewey, hewey]
Ys = [];
no
```

Here, as before, the ";" command causes the computation of new solutions.

As a third example, we give the definition of the `sublist` predicate (we used this in Sect. 12.1.1). If `Xs` is a sublist of `Ys`, then there exist another two (possibly empty) lists `As` and `Bs` such that `Ys` is the concatenation of `As`, `Xs` and `Bs`. We note that this means that `Xs` is the suffix of a prefix of `Ys`. Hence using `append`, we can define `sublist` as follows:

```
sublist(Xs, Ys) :- append(As, XsBs, Ys), append(Xs, Bs, XsBs).
```

This program, combined with the `append` program and the `sequence` program of Sect. 12.1.1 allow us to solve the problem stated in Sect. 12.1.1. Note the conciseness and simplicity of the resulting program. Clearly other definitions of `sublist` are possible (see Exercise 8).

As a last example, let us consider a program that solves the classical problem of the Towers of Hanoi. We have a tower (in Computer Science terms, we would say a stack) composed of n perforated discs (of different diameters), arranged on a pole in order of decreasing diameter and we have 2 free poles. The problem consists of moving the tower to another pole, recreating the initial order of the discs. The following rules apply. The disks can be moved only from one pole to another. Only one disc at a time can be moved from one pole to another and the top disc must be taken from a pole. A disc cannot be put onto a smaller disc.

According to legend, this problem was assigned by the Divinity to the monks of a monastery near to Hanoi. There were three poles and 64 discs of gold. The solution to the problem would have signalled the end of the world. Given that the optimal solution requires time exponential in the number of discs, even if the legend comes true, we can still remain calm for a while: 2^{64} is a large enough number.

The following program solves the problem for an arbitrary number of disc, N, and three poles called A, B and C. It uses the coding of the natural numbers in terms of 0 and successor that we saw above.

```
hanoi(s(0), A, B, C [move(A,B)]).
```

```
hanoi(s(N), A, B, C, Moves):-
  hanoi(N, A, C, B, Moves1),
  hanoi(N, C, B, A, Moves2),
  append(Moves1, [move(A,B)|Moves2], Moves).
```

The call hanoi(n, A, B, C, Move), where n is a (term which represents a) natural number, solves the problem of moving the tower of discs from A to B using C as an auxiliary pole. The solution is contained in the Move variable which, when the computation terminates, is instantiated with the list containing move which contribute to the solution. Every move is represented by a term of the form move(X, Y) to indicate the move of the top disc of pole X to pole Y.

This amazingly simple program amply shows the power of logic programming and also recursive reasoning. As usual, we give its logical interpretation. The first clause is clear: if we have just one disc, all we have to do is to move it from A from B. The reading of the second clause also is quite intuitive. If Moves1 is the list of moves that solves the problem of moving a tower of N discs from A to C using B as an auxiliary pole and Moves2 is the list of moves needed to move the tower of N disc from C to B using A as an auxiliary pole, to solve our problem in the case of N+1 (or s(N)) discs, clearly we would have to do the following: first, execute all the moves in Moves1, then move from A to B (with the move move(A,B)) the N+1st disc in A which, being the largest, must be the last (at the bottom) in B as well. Finally, execute all the moves in Moves2. This is exactly what is done by the append predicate which therefore will use the variable Moves to provide the solutions to this problem.

12.5 Extensions

Until now, we have seen pure logic programming and some, highly partial, aspects of PROLOG. In this last section, we will briefly outline each of the numerous extensions to the pure formalism, each of which would require an entire chapter to do it justice. In the bibliographical notes we have included some references for those wishing to learn more.

12.5.1 Prolog

PROLOG is a language that is much richer than it might appear from what has been said so far. Let us recall that, as already seen, this language differs from logic programming in its adoption of precise rules for selecting the next atom to be rewritten (left to right) and for selecting the next clause to use (top to bottom, according to the program text).

In addition to these, there are other important differences with the theoretical formalism. We will list some of these without pretending to be exhaustive.

Arithmetic   A real language cannot allow itself the luxury of using a completely symbolic arithmetic in which natural numbers are represented as successors of zero and there are no predefined operators.

In PROLOG, there exist therefore integers and reals (as floating point) as predefined data structures and various operators for manipulating them. These include:

- The usual arithmetic operators $+$, $-$, $*$ and $//$ (integer division).
- Arithmetic comparison operators such as $<$, $<= >=$, $=:=$ (equal), $= \backslash =$ (different).
- An evaluation operator called is.

Unlike other symbols (function and predicate) used in PROLOG, these symbols use infix notation for ease of use. There are however numerous delicate aspects that require a deep knowledge to avoid simple errors which the programmer used to imperative languages can easily cause.

First, comparison operators always require that their operands are ground arithmetic expressions (they cannot contain variables). Thus, while we have:[20]

```
?- 3*2 =:= 1+5
Yes
? 4 > 5+2
no
```

if we use terms that are not arithmetic expressions or which contain variables, error will be signalled, as in:

```
?- 3 > a
error in arithmetic expression: a is not a number
?- X =:= 3+5
instantiation fault.
```

The last example is particularly disturbing. What we want to say is that the evaluation of the arithmetic expression 3+5 produces the value 8 which will therefore be bound to the variable X. This cannot be done using $=:=$, as seen above, nor can it be done using equality between terms as considered in the previous paragraph. If we write X = 3+5, indeed, the effect is that of binding X to the term 3+5 (rather than the value 8). To avoid this problem, the expression evaluation operator is is introduced. This operator allows us to obtain the effect we desire; s is t indeed *unifies* s with the *value* of the ground arithmetic expression t (if t is not a ground arithmetic expression, we have an error). The following are some examples of the use of is:

```
?- X is 3+5;
X = 8
?- 8 is 3 + 5
```

---

[20] As said above, the line with ?- returns the query that we want to evaluate and the following one is the PROLOG interpreter's reply.

```
Yes
?- 6 is 3 * 3
no
?- X is Y* 2
error in arithmetic expression: Y*2 is not a number
```

The use of is, necessary to be able to evaluate an expression, makes the use of arithmetic in PROLOG rather complicated. For example, given the following program:

```
evaluate(0,0).
evaluate(s(X), Val+1) :- evaluate(X, Val)
```

The goal evaluate(s(s(s(0))), X) does not compute the value 3 for X, as perhaps would have been expected but the term 0+1+1+1 (see Exercise 9 at the end of this chapter, too).

Cut   PROLOG provides various constructs for interaction with the abstract PROLOG machine's interpreter so that the normal flow of control can be modified. Among these, one of the more important (and most discussed) is *cut*. This is an argument-free predicate, written as an exclamation mark, which allows the programmer to eliminate some of the possible alternatives produced during evaluation, with the aim of increasing execution efficiency. It is used when we are sure that, when a condition is satisfied, the other clauses in the program are no longer useful. For example, the following program computes the minimum of two values, if a comparison condition is true, the other is necessarily false, so we can use ! to express the fact that once the first clause has been used, there is no need to consider the second.

```
minimum(X, Y, X) :- X < Y, !.
minimum(X, Y, Y) :- X > Y.
```

Alternatively, if we are interested only in testing whether a value appears at least once in a list, we can use the following modification to the member program:

```
member(X, [X | Xs]) :- !.
member(X, [Y | Xs]) :- member(X, Xs).
```

In general, the meaning of cut is the following. If we have n clauses to define the predicate p

```
p(S1) :- A1.
...
p(Sk) :- B, !, C.
...
p(Sn) :- An.
```

if, during the evaluation of the goal p(t), we find the kth clause in the list being used, we have the following cases:

1. If an evaluation of B^{21} fails, then we proceed by trying the $k+1$st clause.
2. If, instead, the evaluation of B succeeded, then ! is evaluated. It succeeds (it always does) and the evaluation proceeds with C. In the case of backtracking, however, all the alternative ways of computing B are eliminated, as well as are eliminated all the alternatives provided by the clauses from the kth to the nth to compute p(t).

There is no need to say that cut, in addition to not being easy to use, eliminates a good part of the declarativeness of a program.

Disjunction   If we want to express the disjunction of two goals, G1 and G2, that is the fact that it is sufficient that at least one of the two succeeds, we can use two clauses of the form:

```
p(X)  :- G1.
p(X)  :- G2.
```

with the goal p(X). The same effect can be obtained writing G1;G2, where we have used the predefined predicate ";", which represents disjunction.

If-then-else   The traditional construct from imperative languages:

If B **then** C1 **else** C2

is provided in PROLOG as a built-in with syntax B -> C1;C2. The if then else can be implemented using the cut as follows:

```
if_then_else(B, C1, C2)  :- B, !, C1.
if_then_else(B, C1, C2)  :- C2.
```

In effect, this is the internal definition of the B -> C1;C2 construct.

Negation   Thus far, we have seen that in the body of a clause, only "positive" atomic formulæ can be used; in other words, they cannot be negated.[22] Often, however, it can also be useful to use negated atomic formulæ. For example, let us consider the following program, flights:

```
direct_flight(bologna, paris).
direct_flight(bologna, amsterdam).                              2
direct_flight(paris, bombay).
direct_flight(amsterdam, moscow).                               4
flight(X, Y):- direct_flight(X, Y).
flight(X, Y):- direct_flight(X, Z), flight(Z, Y).              6
```

---

[21] Here, B, just like Ai and C, is considered as an arbitrary goal and not necessarily an atomic one.

[22] Here, we refer, clearly, to the $H : -A_1, \ldots, A_n$ notation. If, instead, we consider a clause as a disjunction of literals, the atoms in the body are negated, given that the preceding representation is equivalent to $\neg A_1 \vee \cdots \vee \neg A_n \vee H$.

Here, we have a series of facts defining the `direct_flight` predicate, which denotes the existence of a connection without stopover between two destinations. Then, we have the `flight` predicate which defines a flight, possibly with intermediate stops, between two locations. This will be a direct flight (clause 5) or rather a direct flight for a stopover different from the one that is the destination, followed by a flight from this stopover to the destination (clause 6). With this program, we can check the existence of a flight, or we can ask which destinations can be reached from a given airport:

```
?- flight(bologna, bombay)
Yes
?- direct_flight(bologna, moscow)
no
?- flight(bologna, X)
X = paris
```

However, we fail to express the fact that there exists only non-direct flights because we do not know how to express the fact that there *does not* exist a direct flight. To do this, we require negation. If we write:

```
indirect_flight(X, Y) :- flight(X, Y), not direct_flight(X, Y).
```

we mean to say that there exists an indirect flight between X and Y if there exists a flight (between X and Y) and there exist no direct flight. With this definition, we have:

```
?- indirect_flight(bologna, bombay)
Yes
?- indirect_flight(bologna, paris)
no
```

These results can be explained as follows. The PROLOG interpreter evaluates a goal such as not G by trying to evaluate the un-negated goal G. If the evaluation of this goal terminates (possibly after backtracking) with failure, then the goal not G succeeds. If, on the other hand, the goal G has a computation that terminates with success, then that of not G fails. Finally, if the evaluation of G does not terminate, then not G fails to terminate. This type of negation is called "negation as failure",[23] in that, exactly, it interprets the negation of a goal in terms of failure of the un-negated goal. Note that, because of infinite computations,[24] this type of negation differs from the negation in classical logic, given that the lack of success of G is not equivalent to the success of the negated version not G. For example, neither the goal p nor the goal not p succeed in the program p :- p.

---

[23] To be more precise, negation as failure, as defined in the theoretical model of logic programming, has a behaviour that is slightly different from that described because of the incompleteness of the PROLOG interpreter.

[24] And also non-ground goals, which we will not consider here.

12.5.2 *Logic Programming and Databases*

The `flight` program above indirectly indicates a possible application of logic programming in the context of databases.

A set of unit clauses, such as those defining the `direct_flight` predicate, is indeed, to all effects, the explicit (or extensional) definition of the relation denoted by this predicate. In this sense, this set of unit clauses can be seen as the analogue of a relation in the relational database model. To express a query, while in the relational model we would use relational algebra with the usual operations of selection, projection, join, etc., or more conveniently, a data manipulation language such as SQL, in the logic paradigm we can use the usual computational mechanisms that we have already seen. For example, to know if there exists a direct flight that arrives at Paris, we can use the query `direct_flight(X,paris)`. The predicates defined by the non-unit clauses such as `flight`, define relations in an implicit (or intensional) manner. They, indeed, allow us to compute new relations which are not explicitly stored, through the mechanism of inference as we have seen. Using database terminology, we will say that these predicates define "views" (or virtual relations).

Note, moreover, how in the `flights` program, function symbols are not used. Indeed, if we want only to manipulate relations, as is the case in relational algebra, function symbols are not needed.

These considerations were crystallised in the definition of *Datalog*, a logic language for databases. In its simplest form, it is a simplified version of logic programming in which:

1. There are no function symbols.
2. Extensional and intensional predicates are distinguished, as are comparison predicates.
3. Extensional predicates cannot occur in the head of clauses with a non-empty body.
4. If a variable occurs in the head, it must occur in the body of a clause.
5. A comparison predicate can occur only in the body of a clause. The variables occurring in such a predicate must occur also in another atom in the body of the same clause.

The last two conditions deal with the specific evaluation rule which Datalog uses[25] and will here will be ignored. The distinction between extensional and intensional predicates corresponds to the intuitive idea that has already been discussed. Extensional predicates, as condition (3) implies, can be defined only by facts.

The `flights` program can therefore be considered as a Datalog program, to all intents and purposes.

The reader who knows SQL or relational algebra will have no difficulty in understanding how the presence of recursion increases the expressive power of Datalog beyond that of these other formalisms. The same program, `flights`, provides us

---

[25]Datalog adopts a kind of bottom-up evaluation mechanism for goals. This differs from the top-down one we saw for logic programming. The results obtained are, however, the same.

with an example in this sense: the query `flight(bologna, X)` allows us to find all the destinations that can be reached from Bologna with an arbitrary number of intermediate stops. This query is not expressible in relational algebra or in SQL (at least, in its initial version) since the number of joins that we must create depends on the number of intermediate stops and, in general, not knowing how many of them there are (we are making no assumptions about how relations are structured), we cannot define such a number *a priori*.

12.5.3 Logic Programming with Constraints

To conclude, we will briefly discuss logic programming with constraints, or CLP (*Constraint Logic Programming*), an extension of logic programming which adds sophisticated constraint-satisfaction mechanisms to the mechanisms we have already seen. The resulting paradigm is certainly interesting for practical application and is today used in different application areas.

A constraint is nothing more than a particular first-order logic formula (normally we use a conjunction of atomic formulæ) which uses only predefined predicates. An example of constraint has already been given: if we write in a logic programming: `X=t`, `Y= f(a)`, we have used constraints, where the predicate symbol, =, as we know, is interpreted as syntactic equality over the Herbrand Universe,[26] while the comma indicates logical conjunction.

The idea of constraint logic programming is that of replacing the Herbrand Universe with another computational domain which usually is symbolic, but can also be arithmetic in some cases. Such a domain is suitable for the specification of the application area of interest. Constraints, rather than relations between ground terms, define relations over the values in the new domain under consideration. Correspondingly, the basic computational mechanism will no longer be the solution of equations between terms (using unification) but will be composed of a constraint-solving mechanism, that is an appropriate algorithm for determining solutions to the constraints to be solved. For example, we could consider the real numbers as the domain of computation, conjunctions of linear equations as constraints and use the Gauss-Jordan method as the constraint solver.

The principal advantage of this approach is clear. We can integrate into the logic paradigm (in a semantically clean fashion) very powerful computational mechanisms that were developed in other contexts (such as linear programming, operation research, etc.). Particularly interesting domains for the practical application of constraints are, as mentioned, the reals[27] and, above all, finite domains in which variables can take a finite number of values. In this last case, we also speak of *Constraint*

---

[26]Recall that this is the set of ground terms.

[27]Clearly, as always, when dealing with computers, what is represented is, in effect, a subset of the reals.

Satisfaction Problem (CSP). There exist many specific algorithms for the solution of this type of problems.

To obtain an idea of the possibilities of constraint logic programming, consider the problem of defining the amount of the instalments of a loan. The variables involved in this problem are the following: F is the requested financing, or the initial sum loaned, NumR is the number of the instalment, Int is the amount of interest, Rate is the amount of a single instalment and, finally, Deb is the remaining debt. The relation between these variables is intuitively the following. In the case in which there is no amount paid back (or that NumR = 0), clearly the debt is equal to the initial financing:

```
Deb = Fin.
```

In the case of the payment of a single instalment, we have the following relation:

```
Deb = Fin + Fin*Int - Rate
```

Here, the remaining debt is the initial sum to which we have added the interest accrued and have subtracted the amount repaid in an instalment. In the case of two instalments, matters are more complicated because interest is calculated on the remaining debt and not on the initial sum. The remaining debt, then, becomes the new financing. Using the NuFin1 and NuFin2 variables to indicate this new value of financing, we then have therefore the relation:

```
NuFin1 = Fin + Fin*Int - Rate
NuFin2 = NuFin1 + Fin*Int - Rate
Deb = NuFin2
```

In the general case, we can reason recursively. We have therefore the following constraint program, which we will call loan:

```
loan(Fin, NumR, Int, Rate, Deb):-
  NumR = 0,
  Deb = Fin.

loan(Fin, NumR, Int, Rate, Deb):-
  NumR >= 1,
  NuFin = Fin+Fin*Int-Rate,
  NuNumR = NumR-1,
  loan(NuFin, NuNumR, Int, Rate, Deb).
```

Understanding this program, given what we have already said, should not be too difficult.

Such a program can be used, just like logic programs, in many ways. For example, if we take out a loan of 1000 Euros and having paid 10 instalments of 150 Euros each at 10% interest, we can use it to find out what the remaining debt is, The query to solve this problem is:

```
loan(1000, 10, 10/100, 150, Deb)
```

This is evaluated and produces the result `Deb = 203.13`.

We can also use the same program in an inverse fashion. That is, rather finding out what the requested funding was, knowing that we have paid the same 10 instalments at 150 Euros each, again at 10% interest, but with residual debt of 0. The goal in this case is:

```
loan(Fin, 10, 10/100, 150, 0)
```

This yields the result `Fin = 921.685`.

Finally, we can also leave more than one variable in the goal, for example to determine the relation that holds between financing, instalment and debt, knowing that we pay 10 instalments at 10% interest. We can therefore formulate the query:

```
loan(Fin, 10, 10/100, Rate, Deb)
```

With appropriate assumptions on the constraint solver[28] we obtain the result:

```
Fin = 0.3855 * Deb + 6.1446 * Rata.
```

That is, and this is unique to the various paradigms that we have seen so far, it allows us to obtain a relation on the numerical domains as a result.

12.6 Advantages and Disadvantages of the Logic Paradigm

The few examples given in this chapter must however be sufficient to show that logic languages require a programming style that is significantly different from that of traditional languages and they also have a different expressive power. Clearly, given that every language (or almost) which have been named in this text is a Turing-complete formalism, it is not true that PROLOG or CLP or any other logic language allows the "computation of more things" than a common imperative language. The expressive power to which we refer is of a pragmatic kind, as we will make clearer in this section.

First, it is worth repeating that logic languages, in a way analogous to functional languages, allow us express solutions even to very complex problems in a "purely declarative" way, and therefore in an extremely simple and compact way. In our specific case, these aspects are further reinforced by three unique properties of the

---

[28]The `loan` program is written using the syntax of CLP(R). The adaptation to other CLP systems, even if they are defined over the reals, can require fairly substantial modifications even if the basic idea is always the same. In particular, the possibility of obtaining the results just discussed depends a great deal on the power of the constraint solver adopted by the CLP language. The results given here are derived from [9].

logic paradigm: (i) the ability to use a program in more than one way by transforming input arguments into outputs and viceversa; (ii) the possibility of obtaining a complex relationship between variables as a result, which implicitly expresses an infinite number of solutions (given by all the values of the variables that satisfy the relation); (iii) the possibility of reading a program directly as a logical formula.

The first characteristic derives from the fact that the basic computational mechanism, unification, is intrinsically bi-directional. This does not happen either with assignment in imperative languages, or with pattern matching in functional languages because both of these mechanisms presuppose a direction in variable bindings. This flexibility clearly allows us to use every program to its best, avoiding the duplication of code for modifications that are often only of a syntactic nature.

The second property of the logic paradigm is clear in the case of constraint logic languages, as we saw in the last program of the last section. This aspect is particularly important to all application areas in which a single solution, understood as a set of specific values of interesting variables, either cannot be obtained (because the data do not contain enough information), or is not interesting, or is particularly difficult to obtain computationally.

The third aspect, finally, at least in principle, makes it easier to verify the correctness of logic programs than imperative ones, where a logical reading of programs is possible but requires much more expressive (and complicated) tools. As already emphasised in Sect. 11.5, this aspect is essential to be able to obtain formal correctness-verifying tools that are easily usable on programs of significant size.

These three aspects, which we can summarise in the principle of "computation as deduction", allow us to express in a very natural fashion forms of reasoning that are typical of the problems that we encounter in artificial intelligence and knowledge representation (for example, in the context of the Semantic Web). The fact (in those languages that have been implemented) that control is handled entirely by the abstract machine through backtracking, allows us, for example, extremely easily to express problems that involve aspects of search in a space of solutions.

Logic languages can also profitably be used as tools for the rapid prototyping of systems. Using PROLOG, it is possible to describe in a very short period and in a compact way, even very complex systems, with the advantage, as far as specification languages are concerned, that it can be executed.

The use of sophisticated constraint solvers and also optimisers (for example, based on the Simplex algorithm) makes constraint logic programs competitive with respect to other formalisms in many commercial applications where solutions to combinatorial problems, solutions to optimisations and more generally solutions to problems expressible as relations over appropriate domains are required. Examples in this sense, include scheduling problems and electrical circuit diagnosis; commercial mathematics and financial planning; civil engineering and others (for other examples, the reader should consult the text cited in the Bibliographical Notes at the end of this chapter).

Thus far, advantages. Beside them, however, we can record various negative aspects of logic languages, at least in the classical versions that currently exist.

First, as already noted in this chapter, the control mechanism based on backtracking is of limited efficiency. Various devices can be used to improve this aspect, be it at the level of constructs that can be used in programs, or at the implementation level. For example, abstract machines specific to logic languages such as the WAM (Warren Abstract Machine) have been defined and have been variously optimised. However, the efficiency of a PROLOG program remains fairly limited.

The absence of types or modules is a second bad point, even if in this sense some more recent languages have proposed partial solutions (for example, the logic language, Mercury). From what was said in Chap. 8, it should be clear that the lack of an adequate type system makes program correctness checking relatively difficult, despite the possibility of declarative reading.

Also, the arithmetic constructs and, in general, built-ins in PROLOG certainly do not facilitate the correctness of programs. This is because their use is not easy due to various semantic subtleties. This is particularly evident in the control constructs, which frequently force us to choose between a clear program that is not very efficient and an efficient program that is, however, relatively hard to understand.

Finally, and for many reasons (not just a limited commercial interest), unfortunately logic languages almost always have a programming environment that is rather deficient, where there are few of the characteristics available, for example, in the sophisticated environments for object-oriented programming.

12.7 Chapter Summary

In this chapter, we have presented the primary characteristics of the logic programming paradigm, a relatively recent paradigm (which has developed since the mid-1970s), which implements the old aspiration of seeing computation as a process that is entirely governed by logical laws. With only one chapter available to us, we have had to limit ourselves to introductory aspects, however what has been presented has enough formal precision to illustrate the computational model for logic programming languages. In particular, we have seen:

- Some syntactic concepts in first-order logic which are necessary for the definition of clauses and therefore logic programs.
- The process of unification which comprises the basic computational mechanism. This required a few concepts relating to terms and substitutions. We have also seen a specific algorithm for unification.
- How computation in a logic language works using a rule of deduction called SLD Resolution. In the text, we have chosen an approach that was inspired by a procedural reading of the clauses that demonstrate the similarity with "normal" procedures in imperative languages. Two boxes more formally introduced the concepts.

After some examples, we saw some important extensions to the pure formalism, in particular:

- Some specific characteristics of the PROLOG language. We did not cover meta-programming, higher-order programming or constructs that manipulate the program at runtime, all of which are very important.

- The idea of the use of logic languages in connection with databases.
- Constraint logic languages (but only through a single example).

For more information on those aspects of PROLOG that we have omitted or for a better introduction to Datalog or to constraint-logic languages, the reader is recommended to the literature listed below.

12.8 Bibliographical Notes

Herbrand's ideas on unification are in his doctoral dissertation from 1930 [6]. The definition of the resolution rule and the first formalisation of the unification algorithm are in A. Robinson's work [11]. The unification algorithm that we have presented was introduced in [10]. Major details of theory of unification can be obtained from various articles and texts, among which is [5].

The "historic" paper by R. Kowalski which introduced SLD Resolution and therefore the theory of logic programming is [7]. K.L. Clark's results on correctness and completion are in [3].

There are many texts both on the theory of logic programming and on programming in PROLOG. Among the former, there is the text by Lloyd [8] and the more recent and detailed treatment by K. Apt [1]. For programming in PROLOG and for numerous (non-trivial) examples of programming, we advise the reader to consult the classic text by L. Sterling and E. Shapiro [12], from which we have taken the program that solves the problem of the Towers of Hanoi; there is also the book by H. Coelho and J.C. Cotta [4], from which we have taken the program in the example presented in Sect. 12.1.1.

Finally, as for Datalog and, more generally, the use of logic programs with databases, [2] can be consulted, while [9] provides a good introduction to languages with constraints.

12.9 Exercises

1. State a context-free grammar which defines propositional formulæ (that is those obtained by considering only predicates of arity 0 and without quantifiers).
2. Assume that we have to represent the natural numbers using 0 for zero and s(n) for the successor of n. State what is the answer computer by the following logic program for a generic goal p(s,t,X), where s and t are terms that represent natural numbers:

```
p(0, X, X).
p(s(Y), X, s(Z)):- p(Y, X, Z).
```

3. State what are the answers computed by the following logic program for the goal p(X):

```
p(0).
p(s(X)):- q(X).
q(s(X):- p(X).
```

4. Given the following logic program:

```
member(X, [X| Xs]).
member(X, [Y| Xs]):- member(X, Xs).
```

State what is the result of evaluating the goal:

```
member(f(X), [1, f(2), 3] ).
```

5. Given the following PROLOG program (recall that X and Y are variables, while a and b are constants):

```
p(b):- p(b).
p(X):- r(b).
p(a):- p(a).
r(Y).
```

State whether the goal p(a) terminates or not; justify your answer.
6. Consider the following logic program:

```
p(X):- q(a), r(Y).
q(b).
q(X):- p(X).
r(b).
```

State whether the goal p(b) terminates or not; justify your answer.
7. Assuming that the natural numbers are represented using 0 for zero and s(n) for the successor of n and using a primitive write(x) that writes the term t, write a logic program that prints all the natural numbers.
8. Define the sublist predicate in a direct fashion without using append.
9. Write in PROLOG a program that computes the length (understood as the number of elements) of a list and returns this value in numeric form. (Hint: consider an inductive definition of length and use the is operator to increment the value in the inductive case.)
10. List the principle differences between a logic program and a PROLOG program.
11. If in a logic program, the order of the atoms in the body of a clause is changed, is the semantics of the program altered? Justify your answer.
12. If in PROLOG, the clause-selection rule were changed (for example, always selecting the lowest instead of the highest) would it change the semantics of the language? Justify your answer.
13. Give an example of a logic program, P, and of a goal, G, such that the evaluation of G in P produces a different effect when two different selection rules are used. (Suggestion: given that we have seen that for computed answers, there is no difference in the use of different selection rules, consider what happens to computations that do not terminate and that fail.)

14. Informally describe a selection rule that allows us to obtain the least possible number of computations that do not terminate. (Suggestion: computations that do not terminate, by changing the selection rule, would become finite failures. Consider a rule that guarantees that all atoms in the goal are evaluated.)

References

1. K. Apt. *From Logic Programming to Prolog*. Prentice Hall, New York, 1997.
2. S. Ceri, G. Gottlob, and L. Tanca. *Logic Programming and Databases*. Springer, Berlin, 1989.
3. K. L. Clark. Predicate logic as a computational formalism. Technical Report Res. Rep. DOC 79/59, Imperial College, Dpt. of Computing, London, 1979.
4. H. C. Coelho and J. C. Cotta. *Prolog by Example*. Springer, Berlin, 1988.
5. E. Eder. Properties of substitutions and unifications. *Journal of Symbolic Computation*, 1:31–46, 1985.
6. J. Herbrand. *Logical Writings*. Reidel, Dordrecht, 1971. Edited by W.D. Goldfarb.
7. R. A. Kowalski. Predicate logic as a programming language. *Information Processing*, 74:569–574, 1974.
8. J. W. Lloyd. *Foundations of Logic Programming*, 2nd edition. Springer, Berlin, 1987.
9. K. Marriott and P. Stuckey. *Programming with Constraints*. MIT Press, Cambridge, 1998.
10. A. Martelli and U. Montanari. An efficient unification algorithm. *ACM Transactions on Programming Languages and Systems*, 4:258–282, 1982.
11. J. A. Robinson. A machine-oriented logic based on the resolution principle. *Journal of the ACM*, 12(1):23–41, 1965.
12. L. Sterling and E. Shapiro. *The Art of Prolog*. MIT Press, Cambridge, 1986.

Chapter 13
A Short Historical Perspective

Even if the first computers in the modern sense, and therefore the first programming languages, appeared only at the end of the 1940s, since then many hundreds (if not thousands) of languages have been defined. In the previous chapters of this book we have sought to identify the most important design and implementation characteristics that are common to large classes of contemporary languages.

In this last chapter, we seek to understand what were the reasons that lead, in the last sixty years, to the affirmation of these characteristics and, therefore, to the success of some languages and the disappearance of many others.

13.1 Beginnings

The first electronic computers appeared in the second half of the 1940s, a relatively recent time when considered from the perspective of the history of science, a remote one when the rate of development of information technology is considered. To realize distance that separates us from the early history of computing, one should think that the first computers were elephantine machines (length greater than 10 metres, weight greater than 4 tons), so expensive that they could only be tackled by government institutes or by large agencies and they had processing rates less than that of an old programmable pocket calculator.

There is even now something of a debate about what must be considered the first computer because this primacy depends on upon what is exactly meant by this term. In computing circles, there is a certain agreement that a computer in the modern sense must have the following properties: (i) it is electronic and digital; (ii) is able to perform the four elementary arithmetic operations (iii) it is programmable; (iv) it allows the storage of programs and data. If we consider this definition, probably the first computer that was operational, with an adequate memory, was the EDSAC designed and developed at the University of Cambridge by Maurice Wilkes' group. It went live in 1949 and it should be remembered that the EDSAC was influenced by famous work by J. Mauchly and J.P. Eckert of the Moore School at the University of Pennsylvania, who used some of J. von Neumann's ideas; their device was described

M. Gabbrielli, S. Martini, *Programming Languages: Principles and Paradigms,*   413
Undergraduate Topics in Computer Science,
DOI 10.1007/978-1-84882-914-5_13, © Springer-Verlag London Limited 2010

as a computer and was called EDVAC. The EDVAC had properties similar to those enumerated above. However it was not constructed until 1951.

If instead we admit a more general definition of computer, then we can also consider as the pretender to the title of first computer, ASCC/MARK I and ENIAC (1946) which, however it may be, remain fundamental precursors. These machines were able to execute sequences of arithmetic operations in a controlled fashion using a real program, even if it was not stored and was expressed using very rough formalisms, using physical representations in some cases.

ASCC/MARK I (IBM Automatic Sequence Controlled Calculator or Harvard Mark I) was constructed in 1944 by IBM with the cooperation of Harvard University with H. Aiken as principal investigator. This machine, used by the U.S. Navy for military tasks, was very rudimentary to our modern eyes. Indeed, it succeeded only in carrying out the work of a few tens of people and required the use of punched tapes and other external physical media to obtain its instructions and to transmit data to the computation devices. Think, for example that a (decimal) constant of 23 figures was specified manually using 23 switches, each of which could occupy 10 positions corresponding to the 10 decimal figures!

ENIAC, on the other hand, was constructed in 1946 by J. Mauchly and J.P. Eckert at the Moore School of the University of Pennsylvania and initially J. von Neumann also worked on the design. ENIAC also did not have program storage and was programmed using physical devices, for example using electrical cables internal to the machine to connect the different physical parts of the computer according to input parameters. Furthermore, many consider this machine as the first real computer because, unlike ASCC/MARK I, ENIAC was many orders of magnitude faster than humans at computing and was immediately recognised as a tool for fundamental progress. Already in 1947, L.P. Tabor of the Moore School foresaw that the speed of ENIAC and computers would allow "the solution of mathematical problems until now never considered because of the enormous amount of computation required." ENIAC was used effectively for the complicated calculation of ballistic trajectories.

The limitations of these first machines were clearly due to their novelty. All of the hardware technology (the electronic devices used in modern computers) was still to be invented, as was Computer Science itself (it was just at its beginning). The importance of the programming task and the development of linguistic tools to support it were not yet recognised. In the first applications (which were often military), the programming activity was seen as a phase additional to that of the proper calculation. Even with the more general applications, such as those to which EDSAC and other machines of this time were put, matters were not much better. To program, one used a low-level machine language which described, using binary code, the operations and calculation mechanisms of the machine itself. This was *machine language*, composed of elementary instructions (for example, instructions for adding, loading a value into a register, and so on) that could be immediately executed by the processor. The process of coding was completely manual, there being not even the concept of a symbolic assembly code. Machine languages are also called *first-generation* languages (or 1GL).

Without reaching the limit cases of "physical" coding constants in MARK I, it is clear that the use of such languages made the writing of programs more difficult and the correction of such programs, once they had reached a certain size, was impossible. It was soon realised that to exploit the full use of the power of the computer, it was necessary to develop adequate formalisms that were far from machine "languages" and closer to the user's natural language.

A first step in this direction was the introduction of *assembly languages*. These languages can be seen as symbolic representations of the machine language and, indeed, there is a one-to-one correspondence between a large number of machine language instructions and assembly language codes. Programs written in assembly language are translated into programs written in machine language by a program called an *assembler*. Every model of computer has its own assembly language, so the portability of these programs is nearly impossible. Assembly languages are also called second-generation languages (or 2GL).

The true jump in quality was achieved in the 1950s with the introduction of *high-level languages*, also called third-generation languages (or 3GL). These were designed as abstract languages which would ignore the physical characteristics of the computer and were instead suited to express algorithms in a way that was relatively easy for the human user. Among the first attempts in this sense were some formalisms that permitted the use of symbolic notation to indicate arithmetic expressions. The expressions thus encoded could then be translated automatically into instructions executable by the machine. From these attempts, as the name itself suggests, the FORTRAN (FORmula TRANslation) language was born in 1957. FORTRAN can, as we will see below, be considered in all respects to be the first true high-level language.

From 1957 until today, many hundreds of programming languages have been implemented and it is thought that there have been more than 100 in widespread use. In addition to fashion, commercial (certainly the most important) and chance circumstances, in the development of high-level languages it is possible to recognise some guiding lines and some developmental principles. In the remainder of this chapter, we will therefore seek to delimit these principles in such a way as to provide a way of orienting oneself when entering the modern "Babel" of programming languages. We do not pretend to be exhaustive because a complete guide would require another book.

13.2 Factors in the Development of Languages

High-level languages have always been designed with the aim of assisting the task of programming computers. However, from the 1950s to the present, the importance and the cost of the various components involved in the implementation of programs has changed and therefore priorities when designing a language have completely changed.

In the 1950s, the hardware was certainly the most expensive and important resource (consider that Thomas Watson, president of IBM, asserted in 1943 that there would be a world-wide market for 5 computers!). The first high-level languages were therefore designed with the aim of obtaining efficient programs which would use the potentiality of the hardware to the maximum. This attitude in the first languages is reflected by the presence of many constructs that were inspired directly by the structure of the physical machine. For example, the "three-way jump" present in FORTRAN directly derives from the corresponding instruction on the IBM 704. The fact then that programming was very difficult and required very long times was considered as a problem of secondary importance, which could be solved by means of large amounts of human resources which were certainly less expensive than the hardware.

Today, the situation is the direct opposite. Hardware is relatively cheap and efficient and the preponderant costs of information-system development are linked to the tasks performed by computing specialists. Furthermore, given the increasingly critical application of computer systems (one thinks of applications in avionics or nuclear power), there are considerations of correctness and security that were minimal if not wholly absent 50 years ago. Modern languages are therefore designed taking into account first the improvement of various software project activities, while the preoccupation with efficient use of the physical machine has dropped to second place, except in some particular cases.

Clearly, we have not passed from the 1950s to the present with a single solution: the development of programming languages has followed a long, continuous process governed by a number of factors. Here, we can only see some of the most important:

Hardware The type and performance of available hardware devices clearly influenced the languages that used it. We will see this point better in the next sections, where we indicate, in various historical contexts, the influence of physical machines on the languages of their time.

Applications Applications of computers, initially solely of a numeric type, rapidly extended to many different fields, including some that required the processing of non-numeric information. New application fields can require languages with specific properties. For example, in Artificial Intelligence and knowledge processing languages are needed that allow the manipulation of symbolic formalisms rather than the solution of mathematical problems. As another example, computer games are usually implemented using particular programming languages.

New Methodologies The development of new programming methodologies, particularly programming in the large, has influenced the development of new languages. A significant example in this sense is object-oriented programming.

Implementation The implementation of language constructs is significant for the development of successive languages because it allows to understand the validity of a construct to be taken into consideration as well as its practical use.

Theory Finally, the role of theoretical studies should not be forgotten. They play an important role in selecting some typologies of structure and in particular in identifying new technical tools to improve the programming activity. One can think of, for example, what we have seen on the elimination of the `goto` and the introduction of refined type systems.

These factors, as well as others, are discovered during the lifecycle of a programming language, which, for the most part, is relatively brief. Some languages are an exception and, either because of the quality of the original design or, more commonly, because of commercial motives, live for more than a decade. We will see some below.

13.3 1950s and 60s

As we saw at the start of this chapter, the first computers, during the period from the end of the 1940s to the start of the 1950s, can be considered as interesting precursors from an historical viewpoint, but which are still very far from the modern computer, in terms both of the languages they used as in the applications implemented on them.

Towards the end of the 1950s and in the 1960s, mainframes, the first true general-purpose computers that could be used for many different applications, came to the fore. These machines were, however, available only at a few major processing centres because of their enormous size and cost (they filled a room and cost millions of Euros, in modern terms). They were usable only by specialised people. The IBM 360 is a famous mainframe example which has held on for many years in the largest data centres.

The processing methods used by mainframes were called *batch* processing. In this kind of system, programs were executed in a strictly sequential manner. The entire computational resource of the computer was assigned to a program which took a "batch" of data as input and produced, as output, another batch of data. When a program terminated, the next program would execute. Data and program were initially represented on punched cards which were read by suitable equipment. The data structures mainly used for data input and output were files. Such systems did not engage in much interaction with users. For example, when there was an error during a run, the program had to be capable of re-establishing the correct state itself, given that no external interactive intervention was possible.

The first high-level languages were developed for this type of processing system. They were languages that offer few opportunities for interaction with the machine and which were suited to writing monolithic programs to be executed from start to finish without external interaction.

FORTRAN   As has already been said, the first real high-level imperative language can be considered to be FORTRAN, developed by John Backus' group in 1957 and designed for applications of a numerical-scientific type. At a time in which programming was only done in assembly language and in which the biggest preoccupation was with the efficiency of programs, high-level language design could not ignore the performance of compiled code. Also the design of FORTRAN put performance first and therefore the characteristics of a specific physical reference machine (the IBM 704) was considered in the design. However, unlike previous languages, FORTRAN was already a high-level language in the modern sense in its first version. In fact, this first version contained many constructs that were more or less independent of a specific machine. In particular, it should be emphasised that FORTRAN was the first programming language to allow the direct use of a symbolic arithmetic expression.

A simple expression such as a * 2 + b that today we can use in (almost) any high-level language, could not be used in a language prior to FORTRAN. After a number of modifications and new versions (in particular, those in 1966, 1977 and 1990), FORTRAN has survived until today and is still used for some numerical applications. It is, though, a dated language whose survival is mainly linked to practical matters such as the vast library of functions for scientific and engineering calculations. A FORTRAN program consists of a main routine and a series of subprograms that can be separately compiled. It is not possible to define nested environments (it is possible only in FORTRAN90 to define nested subprograms) and there are two kinds of environment: the local and the global. This, as we know, greatly simplifies the handling of names, as well as the environment. Memory, either for subprograms or for main, is statically allocated and there is no dynamic memory management (FORTRAN90 is again an exception by providing dynamic memory). The sequence control commands in the first version referred directly to assembly language and therefore goto was used a great deal. In successive versions more structured commands (for example, if then else) were introduced. Parameter passing is by reference or rather by value-result. Types are present in a highly limited way, including only numeric (integer, real in single and double precision, complex), boolean, array, string and file.

ALGOL   ALGOL means, more than a language, a family of imperative languages introduced at the end of the 1950s. These languages, even if they have not become true commercial successes, were predominant in the academic world in the 1960s and 70s and had a formidable impact on the design of all successive programming languages. Many of the concepts and constructs that are found in modern languages were introduced, or experimented with, for the first time in the languages of the ALGOL family.

The progenitor was ALGOL58, designed in 1956 by a committee lead by Peter Naur. The committee was the fusion of two previous groups, one European and one American, each tasked with the definition of a new language. The name ALGOL is an acronym for ALGOrithmic Language and clearly indicates the finality of the language. Unlike FORTRAN, indeed, ALGOL was designed as a universal language, suited to expressing algorithms in general, rather than for use in specific types of application. There were various revisions to the language, all originating from the collective work of an international committee (which had a turbulent life, particularly towards the end). In 1960, ALGOL60 was defined. This is the version that is perhaps the most important (it had a minor revision in 1962). Beginning in 1966, dissenting from the majority of the committee, C.A.R. Hoare and N. Wirth started the basic design of ALGOLW, later implemented in 1968 by Wirth and which constitutes the progenitor of Pascal. The majority of the committee, instead, continued their own work which led to the definition of ALGOL68.

ALGOL58 and, in particular, ALGOL60 greatly increased the machine-independence of the language, making the notation used for programming closer to mathematical notation and avoiding almost every reference to specific architectures, even at the cost of some additional design complications. For example, the input and output operations, rather than being coded by suitable instructions in the language, must be implemented by appropriate procedures that are defined specifically for the devices that are being used at a particular installation.

ALGOL60 made at least three fundamental contributions to modern languages. The first consists of the introduction of parameter passing by name, a mechanism, as we have seen, that is complicated to implement (and for this reason later abandoned), but which has been of great importance for defining mechanisms that are used in current languages for passing functions.

Another important innovation in ALGOL60 was the introduction of blocks and therefore the ability of hierarchically structuring the environment.

At the syntactic level, though, thanks to the contribution of John Backus, AL-GOL60 was the first language to use Chomsky's generative grammars to express the syntax of the language (in particular context-free grammars were used in the form that we now know as Backus Naur Form or BNF). This novelty opened the way to a whole new area of research that has been of extreme importance to the theory and practice of compilers.

Among the other contributions of the languages in the ALGOL family to modern languages, let us further note: recursion and dynamic memory management (but for these features see also what we say below about LISP); type systems with the ability to permit new user-defined types; finally, many structured commands for sequence control in the form that we use today, (if then else, for and while from ALGOL60 or case from ALGOL68).

LISP   LISP (LISt Processor) was designed in 1960 by a group led by John Mc-Carthy at MIT (Massachusetts Institute of Technology) and was one of the first languages designed especially for non-numeric applications. As we have already seen in the box on page 121, it is a language designed to manipulate symbolic expressions (called s-expressions) which are basically lists and which are typically used in Artificial Intelligence. Among LISP applications were the first attempts to implement programs for the automatic translation of texts.

Even if this is a non-standard language, developed and implemented over the course of 30 years in many different versions and not much used commercially, it is a very important language, in which various techniques have been developed that are of interest to languages. In the academic world LISP still enjoys a following (the Scheme language, currently used in many courses was born from a variant of LISP). The first implementations of LISP were very inefficient, so much so that architectures specially designed for LISP (so-called LISP machines) were constructed. Later, the use of various tricks, and in particular the improvement of garbage-collection techniques allowed efficient implementations even on traditional architectures.

LISP is a functional language which, as has been said, manipulates special data structures. Every program consists of a sequence of expressions to be evaluated. Some of these expressions can be function definitions that are to be used in other expressions. Typically, the language is implemented using an interpreter and programs are evaluated in an interactive environment. Among the contributions of LISP, we

can note: the introduction of higher-order programming, i.e. the possibility of constructing functions that accept as parameters and/or produce as the result of evaluation other functions, as well as dynamic management of memory using a heap and a
garbage collector. Other specific properties of LISP have remained confined almost
exclusively to this language, such as, for example, the use of the dynamic scope rule
implemented using A-lists.

COBOL   Like LISP, also this language was designed in the 60s and its name is
also an acronym: COBOL stands for COmmon Business Oriented Language. The
similarities between this language and LISP end there, however. COBOL was designed with the aim of producing a language that was specific to commercial applications and whose syntax was as close as possible to the English language. After
various revisions of the initial language, which was designed by a team lead by
Grace Hopper at the US Department of Defense, the language became a standard in
1968 and, even if in revised and modified versions, is still in use today.

COBOL programs are composed of 4 "divisions". In the "procedure division",
the code for the algorithmic aspects of the program are written. In the "data division", the descriptions of the data are written. The "environment division" contains
the specification of the environment external to the program provided by the physical machine on which the language is implemented. Finally, there is the "identification division" which contains information used to identify the program (name,
author, etc.). This organisation has the aim of separating, even if in a very crude
fashion, data from the programs that use it, and separating machine-independent
and dependent aspects. These are highly rudimentary mechanisms that have been
superceded by linguistic devices that we have seen in modern languages (types, abstract data types, objects, modules, intermediate code, etc.). Furthermore, this program structure, together with a syntax that is close to natural language, also makes
simple programs quite long. Memory management is entirely static.

Simula   Simula, another descendent of ALGOL60, is a textbook case of a technology that was too advanced for its time. Developed from 1962 at the Norwegian
Computing Centre by K. Nygaard and O.J. Dahl, Simula is an extension of ALGOL.
It was designed for discrete-event simulation applications, that is for the implementation of programs that simulate load and queue situations so that fundamental parameters can be measured (average waiting time, length of queue, etc.). In its most
important version, Simula67, the language introduced for the first time the concepts of class, object, subtype and dynamic method dispatch. This is without doubt
the first object-oriented language and it had a considerable influence on its successors (Smalltalk and C++) even if the concept of "object" was a biological metaphor
which would only arrive with Smalltalk and its volcanic creator, Alan Kay.

From the linguistic viewpoint, Simula67 makes small modifications to the constructs that were present in ALGOL60 (the most import of which is the default mode
for passing parameters which is changed from name to value-result) but adds various
mechanisms, among which call-by-reference, pointers, coroutines (a mechanism for
defining concurrent procedures that is fairly close to the modern concept of thread),

classes and objects. A class in Simula is a procedure which, when it terminates, leaves its activation record on the stack and returns a pointer to it. An activation record of this kind, which contains the variables declared local to the procedure (today we would say: instance variables) and (pointers to) local functions (methods), is an object. Subtypes, dynamic dispatch and inheritance are already present in Simula67, while later versions introduced abstraction mechanisms.

Simula has always had an big impact even outside the academic world. In 2003, applications written in this language were still being cited.

13.4 The 1970s

Thanks to the advent of the microprocessor, the 1970s saw the rise of the minicomputer, computers of smaller size and power comparable to that of the older mainframes.

From the software viewpoint, batch processing gave way to a more interactive approach in which the user, using a terminal, could interact directly with the execution of the program. The characteristics of the languages developed in the mainframe era were not really suited to interactive systems. For example, it became necessary to be able to express operations for input and output (that were more sophisticated than simply reading and writing files) using a program and therefore through the constructs of the language. In interactive systems there are constraints on the response time and therefore new languages included appropriate linguistic constructs of a temporal nature (for example, timeout mechanisms). In general, "traditional" high-level languages from the 1970s allow more direct interaction with the machine that was impossible with the languages of the preceding generation.

Above, we said "traditional", meaning by this the imperative languages inspired by the classical computational model based on the modification of values stored in memory locations. The 1970s however saw the birth of two new programming paradigms: object-oriented programming and declarative programming. The second can be more accurately divided into functional and logical approaches. We will see below the more important languages of these years in the different paradigms.

C   Among the new languages of the 1970s, the most important is probably C, a language designed by Dennis Ritchie and Ken Thompson at AT&T Bell Laboratories. Initially designed as a systems programming language for the Unix operating system, C soon became a general purpose language, even if systems programming remains one of its more important application areas. By way of an anecdote, let us note that the name derives from the fact that the language in 1972 was the successor to a language called B, which in its turn was a reduced version of the system language BCPL.

Compared with the languages in the ALGOL family, from which it inherited a great deal, C offers more opportunities to access the low-level functionality of the machine and to program interactive systems. For example, in C it is possible to access directly the characters emitted by a terminal; it is also possible to use specific commands to process data in real time. C rapidly established itself, both for system programming and as a language for general use, thanks to these characteristics, to its compact syntax and to the possibility of translating its programs into efficient machine code.

In the chapters above, we saw numerous references to C in connection with specific constructs or specific implementation characteristics; it would be useless to repeat them all here. Let us recall just some of the important characteristics. We have seen how C includes many arithmetic and assignment operators and how the block structure of C considerably simplifies that found in languages of the ALGOL family (basically, C does not allow nested functions). This allows a much simpler handling of environments and, therefore, of the passing of functions as parameters. The explicit presence of pointers that can be directly manipulated by the program and the equivalence between them and arrays, if on one hand allows very powerful operations, on the other cause insidious errors. This fact, together with the lack of a strong type system, constitutes one of the critical points of the language. Indeed, when one wants more reliability than efficiency, one can find valid alternatives in other modern languages.

Pascal   Pascal was developed around 1970 by Niklaus Wirth as a development and simplification of ALGOLW and was the most used educational language right up to the end of the 1980s. The name is in honour of the mathematician (as well as physicist, philosopher and writer) Blaise Pascal, who, to help a father overloaded by a difficult job as part of the administration of Normandy, in 1642 designed an "arithmetic machine", the precursor of mechanical calculating machines.

One of the main reasons for the success and fame of Pascal is that it was the first language which, prefiguring Java and its bytecodes by nearly 20 years, introduced the concept of intermediate code as an instrument for program portability. A Pascal program was translated by the Pascal compiler (which was also written in Pascal) into P-code. P-code was a language for an intermediate machine with a stack architecture which was then implemented in an interpretative way on the host machine. In this way, to port Pascal to a different machine, it was only necessary to rewrite the P-code interpreter. Pascal was also implemented in a compilative way that did not use an intermediate machine thus allowing greater efficiency.

We have included many references to Pascal in this book and we do not mean to summarise them in their entirety. Instead, we merely record some of the more important properties in an attempt to compare them with C.

Pascal is a block-structured language in which it is possible to define functions and blocks that can be nested with arbitrary complexity. This fact, if on the one hand increases the structuring of code, complicates the handling of the environment and the mechanisms for passing functions as parameters, as has already been observed. Pascal (like C), uses the static scope rule and includes dynamic memory management both using a stack (for activation records) and a heap (for explicitly allocated memory). The Pascal type system is fairly extensive and supports abstraction mechanisms by allowing the user to define new types using the `type` primitive. The types are for the most part checked statically by the compiler, even if some checks are executed at runtime. In Pascal, it is also possible to handle pointers explicitly, even if not all the operations (particularly the dangerous ones) provided by C are available. For example, in Pascal, arrays and pointers are two different types. Perhaps, in the search for a reliable type system, concerning arrays Pascal is too restrictive; indeed, in Pascal, two array declarations that have different dimensions and contain objects of the same type define two different types, a property which make general design of array-manipulating procedures difficult. Another limit of the language, at least in its original version, is the lack of separately compilable modules, although this has been solved in many subsequent implementations which allow the definition of external procedures.

Smalltalk   A strong limitation of Pascal, like all "conventional" programming languages from the 1970s was in the lack of mechanisms to support the concept of encapsulation and information hiding in a truly efficient manner. Indeed, even if in Pascal it is possible to define new data types, there is no way to limit access to values to a pre-determined set of operations in such a way as to guarantee abstraction over the data.

Smalltalk presents a novel way to integrate in a programming language mechanisms for encapsulation and information hiding using the concepts of class and object (previously introduced by Simula) and precise visibility rules for classes (methods are public, instance variables are private). Developed during the 1970s by Alan Kay at Xerox PARC (Palo Alto Research Center),[1] Smalltalk is a unique language, some of whose characteristics we saw in Chap. 10 and whose description would require much more space than available here. It is also important for us to note that, unlike some object-oriented languages that were introduced later (for example, C++), Smalltalk was designed from the start to include as primitive the concept of object rather than grafting it on to an existing language. This means that all the mechanisms used in its implementation (procedure call, memory management, etc.) were developed using this concept. Moreover, Smalltalk was designed not only to be a language but also a sort of "total system" which included language, programming environment and also a special dedicated machine for increased efficiency of program execution. Indeed, given that the language's type system is entirely dynamic, the implementation of an efficient method lookup mechanism was quite difficult. Very soon, however, implementations of Smalltalk were also proposed for conventional machines with satisfactory results. A standard has never been defined for Smalltalk and various, quite different, versions of the language exist today.

Declarative languages   In Chap. 6, we saw, at least on the formal level, the difference between imperative and declarative programming. From the intuitive viewpoint, the slogan of declarative programming, so to speak, is that the activity of

---

[1] In those years, Xerox PARC was a research centre of mythical proportions. In addition to Smalltalk, the following were all PARC innovations: Ethernet; laser-printer technology (later developed by Adobe, a PARC spin-off); PostScript; the first personal computer (the Alto) for "office automation", equipped with a graphical user interface using the desktop metaphor; the remote procedure call.

programming should concentrate on what is to be done, leaving the language interpreter to concentrate on how to reach the desired result. In imperative programming, on the other hand, the programmer must specify both the what and the how. Obviously this is an ideal vision. Leaving the interpreter to decide everything about how the computation is to be undertaken (that is, substantially, memory management and sequence control) without the programmer providing any indication in this sense imposes a great penalty on program efficiency. In reality, therefore, to the "pure" version of declarative languages, which conform to this vision, we need to add "impure" versions which add constructs of an imperative nature to improve the efficiency of programs and also to permit the use of commands (for example, assignments) with which many traditional programmers are acquainted.

Declarative languages can be divided into functional and logic-programming languages. We will look at the two most important representatives of the two classes, both of which were introduced in the 1970s.

ML   ML was born as Meta Language (hence its name) for a semi-automatic system for proving properties of programs and was developed by Robin Milner's group at Edinburgh, starting the middle of the 1970s. Very soon it became a true programming language that could be used, in particular, for the manipulation of symbolic information.

In ML, as in LISP, a program consists of a set of function definitions. Various imperative constructs were added to the purely functional part of ML, in particular assignment (which is limited to so-called "reference cells" which can be regarded as modifiable variables which use the reference model).

The most important contribution of ML concerned types. The language was indeed provided with a safe type system that is static and extends the type system of Pascal in various ways. First, the concept of type safety that we have already encountered has a rigorous and very precise definition that excludes (in a provable way) the possibility of unsignalled runtime errors that derive from type violations. The ML type checker statically determines the type of every expression in a program and there is no way to change this type. If the type checker determines that an expression has an integer type, then we can be sure that every evaluation of this expression that succeeds will yield an integer.

Moreover, the ML type system supports a type inference mechanism. The programmer can leave some information about types unspecified and the system, using a form of logical inference, deduces the type of the identifiers from the way in which they are used. Even if similar mechanisms were previously studied in the context of the λ-calculus, ML was the first language to be equipped with a type-inference mechanism.

Finally, ML support parametric polymorphism. That is, it supports the use of type variables that can then be consistently instantiated by concrete types.

PROLOG   PROLOG was defined in the 1970s as well. This was the first logic-programming language and is still available today in various versions and implementations.

If, as we have said, some ideas on logic programming can be traced back to the work of Kurt Gödel and Jacques Herbrand, the first solid theoretical bases were published by A. Robinson who, in the 1960s, made an essential contribution to the theory of automatic deduction. Robinson indeed provided a formal definition of the unification algorithm and defined *resolution*, a deduction mechanism that uses unification and allows the proof of theorems in first-order logic.

Given its simplicity, resolution is perfect for implementing automatic theorem provers (for first-order logic), but it does not provide a computational mechanism such as that normally provided by a programming language. The proof of a theorem, of itself, does not produce an observable result what could be seen as the result of a computation. To obtain this computational vision of the activity of proof, 10 years had to pass and a restricted version of resolution had to be developed. This version is SLD resolution, proposed by Robert Kowalski in 1974. SLD resolution unlike previous mechanisms for automated theorem proving, allows to prove a formula by explicitly computing the values of the variables that make the formula itself true and which, therefore, at the end of the proof, constitute the result of the computation. If Kowalski defined the theoretical model, we must record that in reality the PROLOG language was developed by Pierre Roussel and Alain Comerauer who, in 1970, were working on a formalism for manipulating natural language based on automatic theorem-proving mechanisms. These experiments led to the first implementation of PROLOG in 1972 and then, after various interactions with Robert Kowalski, to the 1973 version which is mostly the same as current versions. The ISO PROLOG standard was defined in the 1990s.

13.5 The 1980s

The 1980s were dominated by the development of the personal computer or PC. The first commercial PC can be considered to be the Apple II, produced by Apple in 1978. Even if today, with the massive increase in the use of computing devices in everyday life, the PC seems an indispensable tool, it should be noted that when they first appeared, most people remained sceptical about their potential. It is sufficient to observe that even in 1977, Ken Olson, the president of Digital Equipment Corp. (a major producer of minicomputers at that time), stated that he did not see any reason for anyone to want to have a computer in their home! This initial confusion evaporated when, in 1981, IBM launched its first PC and Lotus created the first electronic spreadsheet. This application made people immediately see the possibilities in this new technology which then went into general use in 1984. In that year, Apple released onto the market the Macintosh, a computer that had the first operating system with a graphical interface based on windows, icons and a mouse, a system that was similar to the windowing interface that we use today. Later (in the 1990s), Microsoft also introduced its own windows system.

The PC has completely changed the role of programming languages. The development of systems for personal use which provides easy-to-user graphical interfaces, has brought the need to develop easily interactive graphical systems that are needed to manage windowed interfaces. These system are produced using very large and complex programs and therefore it is essential to be able to reuse already existing code (possibly produced by others). These systems have, therefore, provided an application area that is ideal for object-oriented languages which, as we have seen, provide natural mechanisms for code reuse and for organising vast and complex systems. Indeed, the languages of the 1980s were conceived as object-oriented languages which saw significant development during this period and their first large commercial applications.

In this decade, the first embedded systems were also developed. These are systems composed of computers connected to physical devices which perform control tasks (for example, motors, parts of industrial machinery, domestic electrical goods, etc.). Embedded systems pose many problems, most of all relating to reliability and correctness of programs. For a program that controls the engines of an aircraft, an error must not, clearly, be handled in an interactive fashion by the programmer and termination of the program is not an acceptable option. Moreover, embedded systems introduce other problems as far as response time is concerned; these problems are tackled by so-called real-time programming languages.

C++   The first version of C++ was defined by Bjarne Stroustrup in 1986 at Bell Laboratories of AT&T after a number of years of work (and after the definition of various other languages) on finding out how to add classes and inheritance to the C language without prejudicing efficiency and without compromising compatibility with the existing C language. C had to remain a subset of C++ and as such had to be acceptable to the C++ compiler. To these primary objectives, the improvement of C's type system was added.

We can say that these objectives were substantially achieved. Even if there are some inconsistencies between C++ and C, the most C programs can be translated by a C++ compiler. There was significant effort expended to obtain a language in which those constructs that are not used by a program do not exert a negative influence on the efficiency of the program itself. This means, in particular, that the C subset of C++ must not feel, in any way, the presence of objects and the structures necessary to handle them. C++ does not use any form of garbage collector so that it remains compatible with C and is still as efficient.

In particular, the static type system was improved and, in C++, in particular, it is possible to use a generic form of class, called a template, which supports a form of parametric polymorphism. An important design decision was that of handling C++ objects as a generalisation of the structures (`struct`) in C. The significance of this is that objects can also be allocated in activation records on the stack and, unlike Simula and Java, they can be manipulated directly rather than via pointers. An assignment in C++ can then physically copy an object to the memory space that was occupied by another object rather than just manipulating a pointer.

The lookup mechanism for methods in C++ is simpler and more efficient than that in Smalltalk, given that in C++ information provided by the static type system can be used (this does not exist in Smalltalk).

Ada Byron Lovelace

The name of the Ada language is a tribute to Ada Byron, Countess of Lovelace (1815–1852). Daughter of the poet Byron, she was one of the first female figures in the story of automatic computing. She was a great supporter of Charles Babbage (1792–1871), a mathematician at the University of Cambridge and modern calculating machine pioneer. Babbage designed two calculating machines (the "analytic" and the "difference" engines) which were well ahead of their time and were of such technical complexity that they could not be constructed. In 1842, the Italian mathematician L. Menabrea published a memoire in French on Babbage's analytic engine. In 1843, Ada Lovelace translated this memoire into English, adding numerous notes from which came a farseeing account of a calculating machine for general use which would allow "the development and tabulation of any function ... the machine [is] the expression of every undefined function, capable of generality and complexity."

Finally, C++ also allows the use of multiple inheritance, a construct that poses various implementation problems. The standard version of C++ was approved in 1996.

Ada   Another important language defined in the 1980s is Ada. The Ada definition project was sponsored by the US Department of Defense. The Ada language was defined in a slightly unusual way, starting with a competition between a number of groups of designers, both academic and industrial, for the design of a new formalism which would satisfy the requirements of the Department of Defense. The competition was won by Jean Ichbiah in 1979 with a language based on Pascal which included many new constructs required for programming real-time and embedded systems, as well as other kinds of systems. Ichbiah's proposal included abstract data types, the concept of task, timing mechanisms and mechanisms for the concurrent execution of tasks. In particular, this last feature introduced problems that were completely new to the commercial programming languages existing at that time. The basic idea of the task is simple: if a task A calls a task B, task A continues to be executed while B executes (in the case of normal subprograms or procedures, on the other hand, the execution of A is suspended while B executes). This parallel or, better, concurrent execution of two tasks poses problems of synchronisation, communication and management that require appropriate linguistic constructs and adequate implementation mechanisms. These problems, which are extremely complex as well as important, are beyond the scope of this book where, by intention, we limit ourselves to the sequential aspects of programming languages.

The standard version of Ada was defined in 1983, even if, because of checks for conformance with the standard, the first translators appeared in 1986, perhaps a unique occurrence in programming language history.

CLP   In the 1980s, Constrain Logic Programming languages (CLP) were introduced. These are languages that allow the manipulation of relations over appropriate domains (we have alluded to them in Chap. 12). The idea of adding to logic programming classical mechanism for the solution of constraints was developed independently by three independent groups of researchers. Colmerauer and his group in Marseille was the first to define a language with constraints in 1982. This language was PROLOG II, an extension of PROLOG which allowed the use of equations and *inequalities* over terms (rational trees, to be precise). Thereafter, in the middle of the 1980s, the language was extended to PROLOG III which allowed generic constraints over strings, booleans and reals (limited to linear equations). At Monash University in Australia, the language CLP(R) was developed; it has constraints over reals. Jaffar and Lasez defined the theoretical aspects of the CLP paradigm. In particular, it was shown how all the various logic languages with constraints could be seen as specific instances of this paradigm and how the paradigm inherits all the main results from logic programming. Finally, Dincbas, van Hentenryck and others at ECRC in Monaco defined CHIP, an extension of PROLOG which allowed various types of constraint, in particular constraints over finite domains.

13.6 1990s

During the 1990s, as we know, we saw the rise of the Internet and the World Wide Web, two tools that have profoundly changed many aspects of computing and therefore of programming languages, as well. The possibility of connecting millions of computing devices in a network, to share data and programs that reside on machines that are separated by thousands of kilometres, to transmit meaningful data and access saved information using channels shared by thousands of users, has introduced innumerable problems of efficiency, reliability, correctness and security that involve the entire spectrum of levels present in an computer system: from the level of communications protocol to the languages used for the final applications. From the programming language viewpoint, the most relevant aspect of these years was surely the definition of the Java language, which we have already seen in Chap. 10. In the same decade, HTML (HyperText Markup Language) was defined by Tim Berners-Lee in 1989, which is used for the definition of Web pages. Both HTML and its development XML, a language for the representation of semi-structured data, though important, are not discussed in this book because they are not programming languages in the strict sense.

Java   The object-oriented language Java was developed by a group (the *Green team*) led by Jim Gosling at SUN. The initial project, started in 1990, had the aim of defining a language, based on a new implementation of C++, to be used in small computing devices with relatively limited power, connected to a network and to be used linked to a television which was to provide the input/output peripheral. These devices were to implement a kind of browser to be used for navigation through the network, but without using all the technology necessary for this task. Indeed, the initial language, which was first available in a functioning version in 1992, was pretty much ignored. In 1993, however, the release of Mosaic, the first Internet browser, immediately caught the Green team's attention; they saw that the language they were working on had great potential in the world of the Web. Indeed, the reduced communications bandwidth of home computers and the large number of requests to the servers that held especially popular Web pages made the use of the first browsers punitive. These problems could be solved, at least partially, by sending little programs (the famed *applet*) across the network so that they execute on the user's client machine when it requests a particular service. In this way, the load on the server from which the service is required is reduced. The language to be used to implement such applets would, additionally, have to satisfy the following requirements:

Portability Clearly, when a program is sent to a remote machine, normally the architecture of this machine is not known. It is necessary, therefore, that on every machine that can act as a client, there must be an implementation of a version of the language in which the applet is written, something that is not easy if the language is particularly large or complicated.

Security Executing programs received remotely from the network requires precise guarantees about the security and reliability of these programs.

Java was therefore designed by taking into account these two basic requirements, in the context of the object-oriented paradigm.

The first problem was solved by definition of the *Java Virtual Machine* (JVM) and its associated bytecode. A Java program is translated (compiled) into an intermediate language, called *bytecode*, whose abstract machine is precisely the JVM. This machine, which is simpler to implement than the entire Java machine, is implemented in an interpretative mode on many different physical machines. The Java program, which is translated to bytecodes, can therefore be sent over the network to be locally executed on the user's machine. The real applicability of this approach was shown in 1994 when Sun developed the HotJava browser containing the JVM. It was in 1995 that Java started its rapid expansion when the JVM was incorporated in the Netscape browser (which, in its turn, was the reincarnation of Mosaic).

The security problem, on the other hand, was confronted by various techniques. First, a type system guaranteeing type safety was used. The execution of a Java program can not cause a runtime type error that has not been detected (at least within the limits of the sequential subset of the language). Type safety is obtained by type checking at three levels: the Java compiler, like those for other typed languages, does not permit the translation of programs that violate the Java type system; the bytecodes that result from compilation are also checked by a type checker before execution and, finally, at runtime, the bytecode interpreter performs some type checks which, by their nature, cannot be made statically (for example, array bounds checks).

Another important design choice in Java, which is also related to improving the reliability and simplicity of the language, is the avoidance of the explicit handling of pointers and the presence of a garbage collector to recover memory that is not in use. Thus, even if all Java objects are accessible using (an abstract version of) pointers and memory is dynamically allocated, there is no "pointer" type. The programmer can manipulate references to objects only indirectly by using assignment and parameter passing where objects are involved. Let us recall, while we are on the subject, that in Java, values of the basic types of integer, boolean and string are not objects and that, while variables of these basic types use the value model, variables representing objects use the reference model. Parameter passing is always by value (where objects are passed, the value passed is a reference to the object, given that variables in this case use the reference model). Java uses static scope.

In addition to dynamic method dispatch, which is typical of object-oriented languages, Java also allows the dynamic loading of classes. If, during execution, a program invokes a method on a class that is not present and which, for example, resides in a physically remote location on the network, the class can be dynamically loaded into the Java virtual machine. This incremental approach allows programs to start executing even though some of their components are still missing, something which has been of practical use for browsers.

Finally, even if in this book we have not considered concurrency, we must record that Java allows the concurrent execution of processes using threads. The synchronisation and communication primitives necessary for the execution of concurrent processes are an important part of Java's design and contribute the portability of the language because they make no reference to the system operations on a specific machine.

All these security and reliability features in Java have a cost in terms of efficiency The existence of runtime type checks, the bytecode interpreter, the garbage collector and other aspects significantly influence the execution time of programs. However, this inefficiency is not particularly important for the application domain typical of Java programs. In particular, it is certain that the time spent waiting by a browser for use of the network makes the execution times of Java applets negligible.

13.7 Chapter Summary

In this concluding chapter, we have sought to put the most important programming languages defined up to the present into historical perspective. We have sought to understand the reasons for various design decisions, the reasons for the success of some languages and for the failure of others.

Clearly, an adequate treatment of these questions would require a new book which would not be easy to write because, even if it is not difficult to locate the documentation for different languages (even for extinct ones), determining the influences between one proposal and another is often extremely complicated.

Concerning the possible future (sequential) languages, Chaps. 10–12 contain indications about paradigms in which research effort is currently being concentrated. Probably the programming languages of the near future will develop in this context by seeking to improve on the many weak points of current languages (some cues for reflection in this sense are indicated in the text).

There are, then, other contexts from which it is possible to expect significant progress. One, perhaps the most important, is concurrent languages, whose exclusion from this book was explained in the introduction. But it is possible to expect important language developments even from sectors such as bio-informatics and quantum computing. Even if Church's Thesis seems destined to resist the stress of these new areas, it is doubtless true that mechanisms for biological or quantum computation will open paths that have so far been unexplored. Here, we are dealing with developments that will require time; probably we will have to leave to others, perhaps to one of the young readers of this text, the task of taking into account the developments that are to come.

13.8 Bibliographical Notes

The bibliography for this chapter is, as can be predicted, endless. Every single programming language has been the subject of numerous publications from manuals to more theoretical treatments. For some of the main languages currently in use, we note only [7] for C, [5, 8] for Java, [15] for C++, [9] for ML and [14] for PROLOG.

Wishing to limit ourselves to publications about programming languages in an historical context, an excellent source of information is the proceedings of the conference on the history of programming languages organised by the American Association for Computing Machinery (see for example two past editions of this, from 1978 [16] and from 1993 [1]). Almost all the languages mentioned in this chapter are the object of an introductory note in these proceedings, the note being written by the language designers themselves. Also, the Annals of the History of Computing from the IEEE contain much interesting material. An historical account of software of the 1950s and 60s is contained in [2].

There are also many books which provide an overview of various languages, for example [6] and, for older languages, [11]. Some books, whose purpose is similar to this one, are [13], [12] and the classic [10]. They also contain short descriptions of the most important languages. In addition, there are various texts which present the history of various aspects of the automatic computer, such as [17]. It can also be interesting to consult monographs about the pioneers of the modern electronic computer because, in addition to biographical aspects, they provide interesting points for reflection on the difficulties encountered by those who, basically, invented a completely new discipline. A good example in this sense is [3].

Finally, to understand the different, often contrasting, viewpoints, of the protagonists of this story of programming languages, it is certainly useful to consult the original articles which they have written. The article by Dijkstra [4] (which we have already cited) and that by Wirth [18] are two of the many that are available.

References

1. Association for Computing Machinery (ACM). *Proceedings of the Second ACM Sigplan Conference on History of Programming Languages*. ACM Press, New York, 1993.
2. P. E. Ceruzzi. *A History of Modern Computing*. MIT Press, Cambridge, 1998.

3. I. B. Cohen. *Howard Aiken: Portrait of a Computer Pioneer*. The MIT Press, Cambridge, 2000.
4. E. Dijkstra. Go to statement considered harmful. *Communications of the ACM*, 11(3):147–148, 1968.
5. J. Gosling, B. Joy, G. Steele, and G. Bracha. *The Java Language Specification, 3/E*. Addison Wesley, Reading, 2005. Disposable on-line at http://java.sun.com/docs/books/jls/index.html.
6. E. Horowitz. *Programming Languages: A Grand Tour*. Computer Science Press, New York, 1987.
7. B. W. Kernighan and D. M. Ritchie. *The C Programming Language*. Prentice Hall, New York, 1988.
8. T. Lindholm and F. Yellin. *The Java Virtual Machine Specification*, 2nd edition. Sun and Addison-Wesley, Reading, 1999.
9. R. Milner, M. Tofte, R. Harper, and D. MacQueen. *The Definition of Standard ML—Revised*. MIT Press, Cambridge, 1997.
10. T. W. Pratt and M. V. Zelkowitz. *Programming Languages: Design and Implementation*. Prentice-Hall, New York, 2001.
11. J. Sammet. *Programming Languages: History and Fundamentals*. Prentice-Hall, New York, 1969.
12. M. L. Scott. *Programming Language Pragmatics*. Morgan Kaufmann, San Mateo, 2000.
13. R. Sethi. *Programming Languages: Concepts and Constructs*. Addison-Wesley, Reading, 1996.
14. L. Sterling and E. Shapiro. *The Art of Prolog*. MIT Press, Cambridge, 1986.
15. B. Stroustrup. *The C++ Programming Language*. Addison-Wesley Longman, Boston, 1997.
16. L. Wexelblat, editor. *Proceedings of the First ACM SIGPLAN Conference on History of Programming Languages*. ACM Press, New York, 1978.
17. M. R. Williams. *A History of Computing Technology*. Prentice-Hall, New York, 1985. Revised edition: ACM Press, 1997.
18. N. Wirth. From programming language design to computer construction. *Communications of the ACM*, 28(2):159–164, 1985.

Index

M. Gabbrielli, S. Martini, *Programming Languages: Principles and Paradigms*,
Undergraduate Topics in Computer Science,
DOI 10.1007/978-1-84882-914-5, © Springer-Verlag London Limited 2010